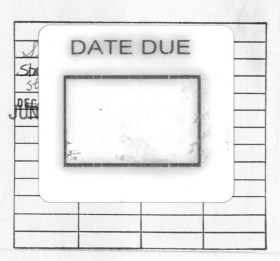

DATE DUE

# BROTHERS & SISTERS

# BROTHERS & SISTERS

## JOHN COYNE

**E. P. DUTTON**
**NEW YORK**

## PUBLISHER'S NOTE

*This novel is a work of fiction. Names, characters, places, and incidents are either the product of the author's imagination or are used fictitiously, and any resemblance to actual persons, living or dead, events, or locales is entirely coincidental.*

*Published in the United States by E. P. Dutton, a division of New American Library, 2 Park Avenue, New York, N.Y. 10016*

*Grateful acknowledgment is made for permission to reprint the following material: "To an Isle in the Water" from COLLECTED POEMS OF W. B. YEATS (New York: Macmillan, 1956): Macmillan Publishing Company, Michael B. Yeats, and Macmillan London Ltd.; an extract from CHILL OF THE EVE by James Stephen: The Society of Authors on behalf of the copyright owner, Mrs. Iris Wise.*

**Library of Congress Cataloging-in-Publication Data**

*Coyne, John.*
  *Brothers and sisters.*

  *I. Title.*
*PS3553.O96B7  1986     813'.54     85-20698*
*ISBN 0-525-24385-2*

*Published simultaneously in Canada by*
*Fitzhenry & Whiteside Ltd., Toronto*

*COBE*

*Designed by Leonard Telesca*

*10 9 8 7 6 5 4 3 2*

*First Edition*

For Judy, who makes it all happen

# · BOOK ONE ·

## ILLINOIS HOMECOMING
## 1982

# · CHAPTER 1 ·

ILLINOIS: 1982

"IS THAT YOU, EMMETT?" his mother asked, calling from the spare room off the kitchen.

"Who else would it be, Mom?"

Still in his underwear, Emmett got off the cot and crossed the kitchen to turn the gas on under the kettle. It was freezing in the room. The wood stove had gone out during the night, but he had been warm inside the sleeping bag. Now he knelt down before the old, cast-iron stove, stirred up the embers, and added wood.

"Would you be wetting the tea for me, son?" She pronounced it the Irish way—"tay."

He did not answer. Every morning it was the same request, the same exchange. It used to upset him, her forgetfulness and the repeated questions, and he would storm out of the house to do the morning chores. Now he blocked her from his mind. They were just two fish, he kept telling himself, swimming in the same pond.

"Is it snowing, Emmett?" she asked next. Her brogue was thickening by the day, and often he had difficulty understanding her.

He glanced out the window, wondering himself if it had; overnight snows were common here in southern Illinois this time of year. The windows above the sink looked across the apple orchard to the barns, which were on a slight rise a thousand yards away. The ground was bare and frozen, the trees stripped of leaves. In summer he could not see the barns from the kitchen windows; they were blocked then, by the apple blossoms and the leaves of the maple trees that lined the horseshoe drive around the farmhouse.

It was early, before seven o'clock, but enough light had broken for him to see it had not snowed. He had been hoping for snow, expecting it. He planned to go rabbit hunting after finishing the milking.

"No, Mom, it's not snowing." The question, he knew, she had already forgotten.

He heard her in the spare room, heard the metal frame creak as she got out of the single bed. Soon, he realized, she wouldn't be able to get out of bed, or wash, or dress herself.

"I heard the jew's harp last night, Michael?" she asked. She was in the doorway now, coming out of the bedroom.

"No, Mom, and I'm not Michael. I'm Emmett, remember?" he shouted. "You don't remember a goddamn thing, do you?" He couldn't stop himself, but as always he was immediately sorry.

Emmett stood and grabbed two teacups from the dirty dishes in the sink. Every morning now it was the jew's harps. Jesus Christ, she was driving him crazy with her stupid Irish superstitions. His hands were trembling. He took a deep breath to steady himself and said softly, "Come on, Mom, drink your tea." He glanced over at her.

She was crying. Standing in the bedroom doorway, one hand braced against the wooden frame to support herself, she was quietly sobbing.

"Oh, Christ, Mom, come on, I'm sorry." He softened his voice and carried the two cups to the table. "Would you like some soda bread? I made it yesterday, remember?" There were tears in his own eyes and he bit his lower lip. "Mom, your tay," he said softly, encouraging the old woman to come into the kitchen.

He took the milk out of the refrigerator and brought the pitcher to the table. The dishes from last night's supper were still on the table, and he stacked them to make space for the cups and milk. Then he got the kettle from the stove.

"Theren't not a bit of snow, now is there, Emmett?" she said, wiping the tears from her face and taking short, careful steps across the room.

Moving a chair out of the way, he helped her to the table. As he took her arm, her elbow in his fingers felt like the bones of a starving child. She no longer had an appetite. It was Maggie's leaving, he had finally decided, that hurt her the most, made her give up living.

He remembered his mother from his childhood, how strong she had been then—working on the tractor all day, keeping a herd of cattle, raising chickens and turkeys, as well as raising all of them.

"I'll have some of that soda bread, Emmett. Will you cut a slice for me like a good boy? I can't for the life of me remember where I put the knife." Her spirit seemed to pick up once she was at the kitchen table. "Emmett, these dishes . . . Where's herself? Where's that little Teasy? Would you be telling the girl to wash up the plates? Why, she eats us out of house and home and doesn't lift a finger around the place."

"It's okay, Mom. It's okay." Emmett spoke quickly before she became too excited, before she began calling up more names from the past. "I'll take care of the dishes. Drink your tea before it gets cold." He edged the cup closer to her. At times, she would simply forget to eat or drink and he would find her, after he had done the morning chores, still sitting at the table, staring confusedly at the cold tea.

He filled the cup only halfway, but her bony fingers trembled so much that she spilled tea onto herself and her housecoat. He glanced away and said nothing. Later he would make her change clothes, and perhaps, take a bath. She already smelled, and he was having trouble making her wash. She was afraid of the tub, afraid of drowning, and she wouldn't let him see her without clothes.

"Here, Mom, a slice of buttered soda bread." He handed the small piece to her.

"Oh, no, Emmett, I don't think . . . I'm not hungry, you know." She smiled up at him, looking guilty.

"You've got to eat something, for chrissake!" He raised his voice.

"It doesn't taste right," she complained, frowning, and pushed away the food.

Emmett held out the soda bread again. "Come on, Mom, one piece, for me? You like soda bread with a cup of tay, remember?" He watched her, waited to see if he was making an impression, if she might finally eat something.

He hated to look at her, Emmett realized. It upset him to see how old she had become. And it was his fault. He should make her take care of herself. She never washed or combed her hair. It stuck out from her head in clumps, like ragweed. And she dressed like a bag lady, wearing layers of sweaters and untied shoes.

It would be better in the spring, he thought. He would be able to open the house, get her outside and into the sun. She would be better in the spring, he told himself. She kept staring at the slice of buttered bread, then said, "Do you know now, who could make the best soda bread? Father O'Connor." She grinned, nodding her tiny gray head. "The man had a real talent for baking. Many's a day, mind you, when you and Maggie were tots, he'd come out after Sunday Mass and make soda bread—for himself, for the nuns. Sure, he loved to bake, that man. And it's strange, you know, for the Irish men, they aren't cooks. Your father couldn't boil water."

"Here, Mom, try a bit of this," Emmett said again. He was afraid she would start on his father, upset herself over some long-ago incident.

"There was a time once," she went on, ignoring her son, "before you were born. I was carrying Catty." She stopped to think, then corrected herself. "No, it wasn't Catty. Paddy Jack it was. Oh, he was a hard delivery, that one. It was winter. A cold day it was, in March. If it wasn't for Dermot O'Connor, dear God, I would have gone out of my mind. That man was a saint, coming out, doing the milking, feeding the animals. We had two feet of snow that March. The power went: I was living in this dark house with Michael and . . ." She had begun to cry, rambling and muttering. She would always do that, begin a story and then lose track. In a few minutes she would fall silent, worn out from talking. Emmett had learned not to listen.

He stood, leaving the buttered soda bread beside her tea, went to the cupboard, unlocked it, and took out his rifle, the small twenty-gauge Winchester. He also took out a box of shells and his cleaning oils, then locked the other guns away.

"Are you going after rabbit?" she asked, suddenly attentive.

Emmett returned to the table and stacked more dishes to give himself room. He broke open the breech to oil the chamber and glanced across at her. She was so tiny, he thought. Perhaps she would fade away a little more each day, until there was nothing left of her. He concentrated on his twenty-gauge.

"I think so, Mom. Would you like rabbit for dinner?"

"Your brother Mike hunted rabbit. Did you know that? Not Paddy; he wouldn't kill a thing, that boy. But Mike." She giggled, thinking of something. "Musha, Emmett, are you going to make tay for me, lad?"

"It's right there, Mom. It's right there in front of you." He lifted the rifle, sighted it out the windows, and slowly squeezed the trigger. It jammed. "Shit!" He turned the rifle in his hands, held it closer. The trigger wouldn't retract. He would have to take the whole casing off and fix it.

"Your brother Mike had a gun," she went on, nodding her head as she spoke. "Your father bought it for him. It cost twenty-five dollars from Sears. He went for rabbits, pheasants. That boy was a great one for killing things. You wouldn't think it now, him being a bishop and all."

"This *is* Michael's gun, Mom. It's just broken." He set the rifle down, unlocked the cupboard, and took out the smaller, lighter .410. "It's okay; I'll use Dad's." He explained to her what he was doing but knew she did not understand a word.

"Your father never hunted, not since he left the old country." She shook her head, upset again. Then she started to rock back and forth in the chair, humming softly to herself, lost in her own world. Emmett recognized the tune, the Irish lullaby she had often sung when only he and Maggie were living at home.

He could remember her and Maggie hanging wash in the backyard on a summer day. He was inside the house somewhere, deep in the dark, cool house, and their singing came to him, across the yard:

A long, green swell
Slopes soft to the sea,

> And a far-off bell
> Swings sweet to me.

He could remember only the refrain. She was teaching Maggie the lyrics, singing a verse, then letting Maggie respond:

> As the gray, chill day
> Slips away from the lea.

He had gotten up, gone through the empty house to the back bedroom, the one he'd taken from Paddy Jack, to look out through the second-floor window screen.

They were using the clothesline strung between two poplars. He was ten years old then and he sat in the quiet house, listening as his mother sang one line, his twin sister the next. His mother had a beautiful voice. It carried over the summer breeze, the flapping of the bedsheets. Maggie he could barely hear; only a word or phrase reached him in the wind's lull.

> A long, green swell
> Slopes soft to the sea . . .

He had wanted to run to them, through the house, out the back screen door, letting it bang as he crossed the sloping yard to where they stood between the poplars. He wanted to run, his arms outstretched, fly against the drying white sheets, and let his mother catch and cradle him in her arms.

But he never left the high corner window. Down below, he saw his mother sweep Maggie into her arms and swing her in wide circles on the grass. He remembered not feeling jealous of his twin. It seemed only natural that she should be down on the lawn with their mother. It seemed only natural that he should be alone, watching silently from the dark house as his mother and sister played together like girls home from school.

"I'm worried about us, Emmett," his mother said, stopping her humming.

He recognized the tone. Her mind had snapped back into order. She would be rational for a few minutes, and they could talk.

"Now look at this place. My God, we're living like pigs!" She pressed her fingers against her pale cheek and shook her head.

"It's okay, Mom. In the spring, I'll open up the house. You know, in the good weather." It had upset her, he knew, when he had closed down most of the house and moved them both into the kitchen and the spare room. It would be better in the spring, he told himself. He would take her out onto the porch, where she could get some fresh air, sit in the sun. He finished oiling the rifle, set it down on the kitchen table, then opened the box of ammunition and counted out a half-dozen shells.

"I don't see why you turned off the furnace," she complained. "It worked fine enough for me all these years."

"We don't have money for oil, Mom. I've told you. They won't give us any more oil."

"Jesus, Mary, and Joseph, what will we do?"

"We'll do fine, Mom, don't you worry, okay?" He smiled, tried to cheer her up. Sometimes it was worse when she was coherent, he decided.

"I'll have a word with your brother Michael," she said. "I'll talk to Father Mike."

"Don't go calling him!" Emmett turned on her, angry in spite of his resolution. "I'm taking care of you and this farm. I won't have him, or any of them, telling me what to do. They'd have put you away, you know, if it wasn't for me. They'd have turned you over to the nuns."

She turned away from him, trembling, and looked around the kitchen. It no longer looked like her kitchen. There were dishes, pots and pans on every counter. The floor was filthy and tracked with mud. Emmett had brought the milk cans in from the back porch, and they crowded one corner of the room. His tools, too, were scattered about: chain saws, bags of nails, hammers and saws. He dropped his things everywhere, as he had done as a child. She knew she should get up and start washing dishes, but the thought of all that work paralyzed her, and she sat still, too confused to move.

"Hey, Mom, why don't you go back to bed? It's early, okay? I'm going out hunting after I finish the chores. Maybe I can get us a rabbit. You want rabbit for dinner, Mom?" He grinned at her, then stood, picking up the .410.

Emmett did not look like any of the other children, she thought, and wondered why. He had the same dark features as the other boys, the black hair and blue eyes, but there was something strange about him. It was the war, she decided. All the atrocities he had seen, maybe committed himself, among those yellow people. He frightened her at times, the way he got angry and stormed around the house. She tried to keep quiet, so he wouldn't get mad at her.

"I'll speak to Father O'Connor," she said.

"Leave him out of this, Mom, okay? I'll take care of you. Don't I take good care of you?" he asked, challenging her to disagree. He went to his cot, picked his clothes off the floor, and began to dress. His pants smelled of cowshit.

"You should wash yourself, Emmett," she said, watching him out of the corner of her eye.

"Look who's talking."

"Mind yourself." She turned in the chair so she couldn't see him, and stared up at the clock over the back door. Perhaps she should telephone Father O'Connor, get him on the phone before he left for morning Mass. He would help. He would tell her what to do.

She couldn't remember things, she knew. Names and faces disappeared. She forgot what she was doing. Something was wrong, but she couldn't tell Emmett. He could be a cruel one, that child.

"Why hasn't Maggie written me?" she asked suddenly. "Where is Maggie, now that I need her? She went off with that sister of hers, didn't she? In Chicago, the two of them, living with men, I wouldn't be surprised."

"Hey, Mom, ease off, okay?" Emmett stopped lacing his boots and sat up. "Maggie's in Africa. Remember? Her newspaper sent her to Ethiopia last September. We got a letter just yesterday. I read it to you." He spoke patiently, not sure if any of it made sense to her.

His mother giggled, shook her gray head, saying, "Sure, she was a great one for traveling. Always talking about going places, seeing things." She fell silent, thinking of Maggie as a little girl, of sitting on the front porch in the summer evening and listening to her tell of all the places she'd visit once she was old enough to leave home. "Well, she didn't lick it off the grass," she went on, "I was the same way as a child. I couldn't wait to get away from Tourmakeady."

"They're all like that, Mom. Paddy Jack's on the golf tour. Father Mike's in Washington. Catty's in Chicago."

"Don't mention that one!" She turned sideways in the chair, to show she wouldn't listen.

"Okay, Mom. I'm sorry." He softened his voice. "But I didn't leave you, did I? I stayed right here on the farm." An edge of resentment, like a knife, cut through his gentle tone. He waited for her to say something nice to him, something to show that she appreciated what he had done. Instead, she went on with a story about Maggie.

"The nuns, you know, they loved her. She was always bringing them flowers. Lilacs. Remember the bush we had out back? She'd cut flowers in the morning, wrap them up in newspapers, and carry them off on the school bus. Sister Elizabeth was her favorite. Do you remember Sister Elizabeth, Emmett? Maggie loved that nun. She was a good child, wasn't she?" She fell silent, thinking of her youngest daughter. Oh, dear Maggie, she thought, why did you leave me alone with Emmett? You, of all my children, my little baby. There were tears again on her cheeks and she spoke up, asking, "Now why would she go off and leave me? And not even a letter home!"

"She wrote you, Mom; we got a letter."

"What letter?"

"Maggie's letter, Mom," he answered patiently. "You have it by your bed. I'll get it for you." He stood up.

"You leave my things alone." She began to weep. She cried most of the day, and she did not know why. She didn't even know she was crying until she felt the tears on her face, dripping from her chin.

"I'm going to call Father O'Connor, Emmett," she said again, sitting up in the kitchen chair. "He'll take me away from this godforsaken place. It's a poor place, this farm; in the back of beyonds, it is. I'm after the man to take me from here, and with the help of God, I won't see this land again, not in my lifetime." She nodded her head, firm in her decision.

"Mom, come on, please," Emmett said nicely.

"Don't be giving me that please and what have you, Emmett Thomas DeLacey. Not after what I've been through with this place. It's not a land for farming, or raising cows, or anything at all but rocks. I told your father as much the first time I laid eyes on it. But, no, sure if he didn't think it reminded him of Tourmakeady. I was after him from the first to leave here, to go up to Chicago where my cousins were. They would have taken us in for the time being, and I could have gotten a job working out, cleaning for the Jews."

"Hey, Mom, come on. I'm taking care of you okay. You make me feel like a piece of shit talking like that." Emmett grabbed his army jacket off the back door.

"I don't need the likes of you," she shouted, color returning to her face. "You little bastard!"

"Oh, Christ!" He jerked open the kitchen door, slammed it behind him and started walking, his head bent against the strong early morning wind. There were tears in his eyes, and he couldn't tell whether it was the cold or his own hurt feelings. She made him feel rotten, calling him names.

Emmett pulled open the door and walked into the cow barn. He grabbed the pitchfork and started to work quickly to keep himself warm. He fed the cows, then started the milking. As he finished each cow, he opened the stanchion and turned her into the yard. They wouldn't stay out long this morning, he knew, not in the freezing weather.

He carried the pails into the milk house, then started to separate the milk, working fast. He finished with the milk, then backed the pickup truck from the barn and across to the pigpen. There he unloaded the garbage he had brought home the night before from the Crossroads Tavern. The animals squeaked and ran across the frozen dirt to the food.

He wouldn't have to feed the pigs much longer, he knew. Already he had begun to sell them off for cash, to make enough money to keep him and his mother in food. By spring, he guessed, all the livestock but the cows would be sold off, and he would have to hire himself out at one of the dairy farms south of town. Either that, or tell the family the farm was a failure, and ask them for help.

He shook his head. He would never let the others know that he had failed at keeping the farm.

Emmett kept going from the pigpen back into the main barn to pour oats for the sheep, and Mekong, his gelding. Working steadily in the cold morning, it took him over an hour to finish the chores. He left the cows out until he had the barn cleaned, then opened the double doors and stood back as they fought to get inside.

He should go hunting now, he thought, while it was still early. He'd go down by the creek and flush out a cottontail. The more he thought about it, the better he liked the idea. He would finish the work later, he told himself, get in a good two hours before lunch.

He started down across the back pasture. The long winter grass was thick in the low marshland and he flushed a cottontail and fired at once, as he had been taught in the army. The rabbit never had a chance.

"The fuckin' rabbit," Emmett said out loud. "The fuckin' dead rabbit. I fixed its ass!" He began to sweat. He always felt that way right after he had killed anything. He couldn't get his breath. It's okay, he told himself. Everything was going to be okay.

Emmett laughed, and his voice surprised another cottontail. It jumped from the grass half a dozen yards ahead and sprang toward the creek, clearing it easily in one sharp leap.

Without thinking, he turned and fired. The blast knocked the cottontail off flight and it hit the ground hard, tumbling into the thick grass.

The rifle was shaking in his hands as Emmett broke open the chamber, and when he reached into the pocket of his fatigue jacket, he couldn't hold on to a shell. They kept slipping between his clumsy fingers.

"Oh, God," he whispered, terrified now. He knew he had lost control, that he had started to wet his pants. He dug deeper into his pockets, clawed at the lining, searching for a shell.

Still, he kept moving. He knew better than to get pinned down in an open field, caught in cross fire. He hit the creek running and cracked the thin winter ice. Stumbling forward, he managed to keep his rifle up, kept it dry as he ran for cover.

There were buildings ahead. He could hide. They wouldn't get him. He wouldn't let them take him alive, never again. He kept run-

ning, stumbling forward, dodging, ducking the incoming rounds, and
smashed through the kitchen door. Something moved, and the sound
of a shotgun blast filled the house.

Margaret Mary DeLacey stood at the top of Mount Entoto above
Addis Ababa, Ethiopia, and gazed over the forest of eucalyptus trees
toward the massive and extinct Mount Zuqualla volcano. She had
come to enjoy her late afternoon visits to this remote corner of the
city. Here she could see beyond Addis Ababa, into the far distance
where lakes, rivers, and more green eucalyptus woods stretched
across the Abyssinian plateau, to the very edge of the great Rift Valley
itself.

She even forgot that in this lovely and lonely spot, a few miles
above the American Embassy compound, her life was again in danger.
She had been waiting here in the hour before dusk for an Ethiopian
to step forward and whisper, *"Min aynet mekina allot?"* The question
about her car would indicate he was an informant, a man sent from
the Ethiopian People Revolutionary Party to tell her about the famine
conditions in the north of Ethiopia.

It was growing chilly on the hillside. She pulled her coat closer and
glanced again across the square. Two young men were still standing
casually by the whitewashed two-story church. They had been there
for twenty minutes, she guessed, certainly since she had parked her
VW and walked to the edge of the cliff.

Something wasn't right about them. No one hung around Entoto
Reguel that long unless they were monks, and these men weren't
priests. Her luck might have run out, she thought. Perhaps the secret
police were on to her. She had been making contact with Ethiopian
rebels, here, and at other locations around the city. For a while she
had even used the back pew of the Catholic church, meeting informants there after Saturday evening Mass.

Well, she thought, reassuring herself, she hadn't committed any
crime. Not yet. None of her articles had appeared in the paper. She
wondered what would happen then. Kenneth had already warned
her. "They'll declare you *persona non grata,* Margaret. You'll be out
of Addis within two days." He had looked worried. "And I don't want
to lose you."

"I have to do my job, Kenneth, regardless." They were on a colli-
sion course, she realized, both personally and professionally. But she
couldn't stop. It had to be done. She had a story to file. An important
story about hunger and famine in Africa, even if it was going to cause
trouble for the American ambassador.

She would miss Ethiopia, Maggie thought, gazing down at Addis
Ababa, the loose, disorganized capital spread out on the foothills of

Entoto. It appeared as if the round tukul homes of the city had been scattered like seed on the gentle slopes. Their tin roofs glittered in the fading sunset, flashed in the thick foliage, emerald green after the Small Rains. The few paved streets cut wide irregular swaths through the woods, and only the modern office buildings towered over the tall, thin eucalyptus trees. Maggie could still see, in the gathering darkness, the former palace of Haile Selassie, and across town, the new city hall at the top of Churchill Road. Farther away, beyond it all, was the Mercato, the largest outdoor market in Africa.

Catty would love Ethiopia, she thought. She should ask her to visit, and bring Wendy with her. It would be fun to have her older sister in-country, to show her around, to show off how knowledgeable she was, how grown up. Maggie smiled, amused by her own silliness.

Maggie missed her nieces and nephews. And she missed her mother, the farm, and Emmett. She missed her twin.

It was Emmett she worried most about. The others could take care of themselves, but not Emmett. He had seemed so lost and withdrawn when she had been home.

Catty would have to help out, she decided. Catty would have to go downstate to Gatesburg and heal the old wounds with their mother, then get Emmett into some sort of therapy. Maggie couldn't do it herself, not from Africa.

And what about me, she thought next. When was she going to get her life in order? That thought immediately made her anxious, and she turned from the view. The two men were still standing together near the church. And this time, she noticed their shoes.

Their thick leather army shoes. No peasant wore such shoes. Time to move. She walked slowly back to her car, not hurrying, not wanting to alert them.

Out of the corner of her eye, she saw them straighten up and stare after her. They were still holding hands, as all Ethiopian men did—a cultural trait she knew had no significance. The secret police held hands.

Maggie was within ten feet of the car when they dropped their pretense of lounging and started for her. She broke for the VW, pulling out her keys as she ran. Perhaps they weren't CID agents, but just two local thieves, or worse. She had heard about foreign women being raped and robbed in Addis. It didn't matter to thieves that she was a foreign correspondent. Oh, God, she thought, suddenly frightened for her life.

She jumped into the front seat, slammed down both door locks, and turned on the ignition. The car lunged forward. She was still not used to standard shift and had forgotten to step on the clutch. The sudden jerk of the VW startled the men and they fell back, giving her a moment longer to get away. Then they were at her again, shouting in Amharic, banging their fists against the front windows, grabbing at the door handles.

Maggie popped the clutch. The VW jumped ahead in the soft, muddy parking lot. She spun the wheel, throwing one of the men off the car. The second one still clung to the doorknob, was sprawled halfway over the roof. With one hand on the wheel, and speeding down the steep rocky mountain road, Maggie lowered her side window and, reaching out, grabbed his testicles. He yelled in pain, let go of the door handle, and slid off the car. She floored the accelerator and raced to the bottom of Entoto and the safety of her compound.

Her compound was below the American Embassy on a muddy side street near the lions' cages of the city's zoo. She pulled her VW into the yard and made sure her guard locked the gates before she went inside the stone house. She did not turn on the kitchen lights. She felt safer in the dark, freer and more secure. She liked to roam at night from room to room, wearing underwear or nothing at all. And now, crossing the living room, she found herself smiling at the pleasure of being safely home and alone. Privacy was something she needed. That, more than anything else she suspected, explained why, at twenty-eight, she was still unmarried.

Kelemwork, her maid, had laid a fire in the bedroom fireplace and Maggie knelt to light the kindling. The wood was scraps of lumber from building sites and thin eucalyptus branches that smoked and smelled like antiseptic. She thought of her mother's medicine cabinet, of skinned knees, hurt while playing in the farmyard, and of coming crying home for help.

When the fire caught, blazing up hot and intense, Maggie went into the bathroom and turned on the hot water in the tub. She unzipped her dress and stepped out of it. Reaching back with both hands, she unhooked her bra. Then, slipping her fingers under the waist of her panties, she pulled them off and stuffed the black underwear into the hamper.

Enjoying the feel of the thick rug between her toes, she crossed the bedroom to her dresser, where she pinned her hair up on top of her head. She took off her jewelry next, the single blue stone ring Paddy Jack had given her after he won the Open, and her earrings—two small rubies Jack McGraff had given her that night in his Georgetown home when he asked her to marry him.

Walking naked through the dark house, she put a stack of Brahms on the stereo. Whoever had lived in this house before her had installed speakers in several rooms. She turned them all off except for her bedroom and then went back to the bathroom and the running tub.

This evening she only stayed a few minutes in the warm water, then toweled herself dry and sprayed her body with cologne before beginning in earnest to comb out her dark hair.

Her hair was her most exquisite feature and Maggie took special care of it, combing it out several times a day. She built her whole look around her hair. It was thick and black and always curly, even in the dry season of Ethiopia.

Her eyes, however, disappointed Maggie. They did not have her mother's dark blue color. Hers were a rich brown, the color of thick chocolate.

Yet she knew her face commanded attention. She had a good complexion, good bone structure. And she realized, with satisfaction, that as she approached thirty, her face was beginning to develop a look of mystery. As if she had secrets of her own.

Her body was small breasted and slender; she could count her ribs. She thought of Sister Saint Stephen at her high school, Our Lady of Wisdom, how she would lecture all the girls about never looking at their naked bodies. Dress in the dark, the old nun had told them, for seeing one's own body was an occasion of sin. Maggie smiled at herself in the bathroom mirror.

"Sister Saint Stephen, wherever you are: breasts this small are no occasion of sin," she said out loud, then flipped off the light and returned to the bedroom.

Before the maid left, she had turned down one side of the bed and laid out a silk nightgown. But instead of putting it on, Maggie set it on the chair of her vanity table. The gown glowed like a star in the soft reflection of the fire.

She slipped into the bed, spreading her dark hair out on the blanket like a fan, and stretched lovingly in the wide smoothness of the sheets until the soles of her feet settled on the hot-water bottle that Kelemwork had wrapped in a towel and placed at the foot of the bed.

Maggie did not know how long she had been sleeping when she woke, fully alert, to the sound of the back door slowly opening and closing. Sharp footsteps crossed the kitchen floor. Then there was silence as someone moved through the living room, and sound again when he reached the hard wood of the hallway outside her bedroom. She turned her head to see him standing in the doorway.

"Darling," she whispered, and her nipples rose as if he had already caressed them.

"Yes," he answered softly, but not whispering. He was incapable of that. His voice filled whatever room he was in.

She watched him undress in the firelight. He did it slowly, smoothing each piece of clothing as he set it on the sofa. He was not a careless man. Their affair, she had come to believe, was totally out of character for him.

He moved toward the bed through the shadows. His hand touched the covers and he followed the edge of the bed up toward her. She reached over and pulled back the heavy blanket, inviting him into her arms.

"Well," he said, slipping in beside her, "what happened?"

She told him, speaking in a soft, calm voice of what had happened on Mount Entoto.

"My God, Margaret, you could have been hurt," he said angrily.

"It's my job, Kenneth. What more can I do?"

"Those damn idiots at the *Washington Post* don't realize what sort of precarious position they're putting you in."

"Darling, it's my responsibility."

"And you're my responsibility!"

"I want to be more than your responsibility," she said to soften the exchange.

"You are, Margaret. You know you are." He kissed her on the forehead, pulled her closer.

She sighed, said thoughtfully, "I shouldn't have gotten us into such a fix."

"It was my idea, too."

"Yet, but . . . " She nestled closer. "I could have protected us."

"You could not have, darling. I wanted you from the first moment I saw you. You came into my office, remember? The day after you arrived in-country and you couldn't keep awake from the jetlag. You were yawning in my face." He smiled, recalling, and Maggie turned her face into his body, smelled again his scent, and the breath went out of her.

"I love you," she whispered, and kissed his chest. Unlike most of the young men she had known, he had a mat of thick hair, like a warrior's shield of fur, across his chest.

Maggie loved knowing that she had been wanted, even before she had realized it the night of the embassy Christmas party.

She had been in the dining room, standing with Jane Campbell and Carol Scott, two of the single women who worked in the consulate. They were talking about making a weekend trip to Awash Station, just the three of them in Carol's car, having lunch at the small railway station and then going to look at animals in the game park.

"John Pettit went to Awash last week," Maggie said. As she turned to scan the room for him, she saw the ambassador watching her.

He was alone, standing by the Christmas tree, and she thought how beautiful the tree looked, brilliant with lights and tinsel. She was reminded of home, of the farm, and then she saw he was still watching her, and recognized the desire in his eyes.

That night she had left the back door open and he had come to her. They had made love without speaking, as if it had already been agreed upon.

Now, it began to rain again and Kenneth stopped speaking. He would have to shout to be heard over the downpour. She pressed her cheek against his chest, but the rain was too distracting. She wondered if he would want to leave before they had a chance to make love. She knew that his wife was afraid in storms.

But then, just as suddenly, the dense downpour stopped, the high winds faded. Maggie heard the heavy wet leaves of the false banana tree brush against the closed wooden shutters of the bedroom windows.

She moved against him to focus his attention on herself. Feeling his need for her made her feel both in control and helpless to his desire.

He made love slowly, as if he had all night to be with her, as if he would be there with her in the morning. And he made love in silence, never once whispering that he loved her or calling out her name in passion.

His fingers spoke to her, moved across her body. She kept imagining waves breaking on her naked flesh, water receding between her thighs.

It was cold in the room. The fire had died away, but his body was a furnace of heat and she was clinging to his warmth when the telephone rang, startling her with its suddenness.

It rang twice, two rapid bursts. A sharp, tinny sound, like a cheap toy, and Maggie reached for the receiver just to stop the sound.

"Miss DeLacey?" The man's voice was young and American and fully awake.

Maggie held the receiver away from her ear and the voice boomed into the bedroom. "This is the Marine Guard, ma'am. Corporal Burns, from the American Embassy."

"Yes, Corporal," she said slowly. They were looking for the ambassador, she thought at once.

"I'm sorry to wake you but a cable just arrived. It's unclassified."

"Yes?" Maggie had a sudden image of the Illinois farm on a fall afternoon—a clean, cold day with a winter sun low on the horizon. She was walking home from school, cutting through the orchards, with the smell of apples and snow in the air and the sun flashing off the steep, slanting tin roofs of the barns. She could see her mother below, crossing the barnyard after feeding the animals, carrying the galvanized buckets. She was wearing old boots, Paddy Jack's heavy blue pea jacket, and her white apron was filthy with blood from killing and cleaning chickens at the barn sink.

"Yes?" she said again to encourage the young soldier, and listened silently as he read the brief cable from home. And then she thanked the marine and replaced the receiver, taking her time, doing it as carefully and slowly as possible, hoping the simple gesture might last forever. And then she lay back against the pillow and cried,

"Oh, Mommy . . . Oh, Mommy . . ."

Cathleen DeLacey Duffy could hear her family downstairs in the kitchen of their suburban Chicago home. A sudden shout or burst of laughter would be followed by silence as Joe told them to be quiet, told them their mother was still sleeping. She did not need the rest, but she took it, giving Joe his hour, and not wanting to break the children's routine. Still, the thought of them having a meal without her made Catty feel guilty.

Her own mother would never have skipped breakfast, she thought. Catty tried to remember one time during her childhood when her mother had been sick, but she couldn't, though surely she must have been, especially after their father left the family.

Still, there was very little of her childhood that Catty did remember. It all seemed to have just drifted by her. Or maybe, as her shrink had suggested, she had simply suppressed those memories in her subconscious.

What she did remember was working around the house, doing dishes, helping with the meals, cleaning. Her childhood was spent rushing to finish one job so she could start another, with her mother always after her, pushing her to get the work done. It seemed to Catty that she never had any time to play as a child, but every day went from schoolwork to farm chores.

She hadn't done that with her children. She hadn't taken away their childhood with long days of work. She didn't want her children to look back with hatred on their childhood. Or their mother.

The bedroom door opened, surprising her, shaking her from her memories as her daughter Clare swept in, whispering excitedly.

"Wendy isn't in her room!"

The breath went out of Catty, but she managed to say, "It's almost ten o'clock; she's up and gone out."

Clare slowly shook her head, pleased with her information. At thirteen, Clare was big for her age, heavy, with long arms and legs. "She didn't sleep here, Mommy. I know! She's been out all night"—she dropped her voice to an emphatic whisper—"with Jeff Golden!"

"She's not with Jeff," Catty said quickly. "I forgot; she called last night and said she was spending the night with Donna. They were all going to Donna's after the basketball game. And, Clare, don't say anything to your father. He'll only get upset. I forgot to tell him, and you know how he is about you kids being out overnight. Don't go spoiling it for yourself."

And then, to get Clare out of the bedroom, she hurried on, "Please go get Timmy and Sara dressed." She closed the door behind Clare and leaned back against it, as if to steady herself. Oh, Wendy, why? Catty asked herself, near tears. Why couldn't you just wait?

Catty pulled herself together, stripped off her nightgown, and began to dress. If she got downstairs in time, she might get Joe and the kids out of the house before Wendy came home.

From the back of the closet door, she picked off her jeans and slipped them on, zipped them up. The jeans were loose at the waist, and Catty paused to glance at herself in the closet-door mirror. She had lost weight recently and was pleased with herself and at how well she looked. She patted her flat stomach, as if its tautness was a mark of achievement. Not bad, she thought, after four kids. She looked as if she were still in her twenties.

The telephone rang.

That would be Wendy, Catty guessed, calling to see if the coast was clear.

Clare was shouting, saying she would get the phone. From behind the bedroom door, Catty could hear her daughter running downstairs. It was like having a linebacker in the family.

The phone rang a second time, then was caught in the middle of the third ring, and Catty stood motionless, holding her breath.

"Daddy . . . ?" Clare's voice shattered the silent house.

Catty sighed. It was okay. She was safe awhile longer. She pulled on her jogging sweat shirt and brushed her black hair. It was dirty, and she pulled it back into a thick braid. She'd wash it later, after Joe took the kids to swim, after Wendy came home and they had a talk. She began to plan her day.

She needed to get a letter off to Maggie, airmail her sister the books she couldn't find in Ethiopia, and at two o'clock she was due at the pottery studio.

But what was important now was talking to Wendy, a long, serious mother-daughter talk. She had made a mistake, Catty realized. She hadn't taken Wendy's desire for independence seriously enough. She couldn't stop her from sleeping with Jeff Golden, Catty knew, but she could keep her from running off and marrying the boy. She could stop Wendy from making the same mistake she had.

Catty heard Joe's footsteps on the stairs and then he tried the door. "Catty?"

"Just a moment, Joe." She opened the bedroom door, explaining as she did, "I'm sorry. I was just trying to keep the kids out while I dressed. Joe . . . ?" When she saw his dark face, her heart tumbled as if it were dropping through space. "Joe, what is it?" It was worse than she'd thought; Wendy was hurt. No, she was dead. Catty's mind whirled out of control. "Please, Joe, tell me," she begged.

He shut the door, and still wordless, took her gently into his arms. Catty remembered moving her face away from his rough gray beard and thinking how old he looked as she listened to him tell her the news about her mother.

Padraic John DeLacey used his nine iron on the final fairway of Pebble Beach Golf Course and hit the ball straight at the flag. The ball rose high into the California sky and fought the ocean breeze off Carmel Bay before catching the back edge of the green and spinning toward the stick.

"Hey, Paddy Jack! That's stickin' it to 'em!" The black caddy swung Paddy's heavy tour bag onto his shoulder and pulled out the gooseneck putter. "Now get up there and ram that mother home. We're looking at a sixty-five, son. We've got it going."

The caddy slipped off the leather cover and handed the putter to Paddy, then strode off, up the fairway. Paddy couldn't keep up with him. It had been a long day, and now both his legs hurt.

He concentrated on the gallery, pulling strength from the cheers. Paddy Jack's Platoon, the golf writers called them. When he had been at the top of his game—winner of the Open, a leading contender at any PGA event—his Platoon had followed him from tournament to tournament, cheering his every shot.

He clenched his teeth and braced himself against the pain. He needed a massage and steam bath. And rest. A good night's sleep, Padraic reasoned, and he would be okay on Sunday. He would be able to play the last round and finish the tournament—maybe even win. It had been a long time since Paddy Jack had let himself even think of winning.

"Ken Venturi, now what do you think of that approach shot? It was a nine iron, we're told up here in the CBS booth. DeLacey needs only a six-foot putt for another birdie and a round of sixty-five," Pat Summerall said to his fellow announcer and the television audience.

"Well, Pat," Venturi replied. "I tell you, it's so great to see Paddy Jack back in contention for a major tournament. There were many people who thought after the accident he might never walk again, let alone play."

"For those of you who don't know," Summerall added, "Paddy Jack was hit by lightning, what? Four years ago, Ken?"

"That's right. In the second round of the PGA at Midlothian, Illinois. It was one of those freak accidents, similar to the lightning that struck down Lee Trevino and six other players at the Western Open, also outside Chicago. Those August thunderstorms around Chicago are something else, I tell you."

"It is great to see Paddy Jack in position to win," Pat Summerall continued. "He's looking at a sixty-five, as I mentioned, and a share of the lead. So stay with us. We'll be right back after these messages to bring you the exciting conclusion of this third round of the Bing Crosby National Pro-Am from Pebble Beach, California."

The gallery was on its feet, standing in the wooden bleachers and in the tight crushes behind the bunkers, all applauding Paddy Jack as he came up to the final green. He slipped off his white cap, held it up, waved back, forced a smile onto his taut face. It was Maggie who had told him to take off his cap.

"We can't see your face," she had told him, when she was still at home on the farm. "Take your cap off when they cheer so everyone on TV can see how handsome you are." Paddy smiled to himself, thinking of Maggie, remembering how she had come to stay with him while he recovered from the accident.

He reached the apron of the green and paused there to rally his strength. His legs were trembling from the climb and he used the gooseneck putter to steady himself.

Spike was behind him, whispering, "Come on, Paddy Jack, we got one putt left." The caddy glanced down and saw that DeLacey's hands were trembling. "Hey, man, don't die on me now!"

Paddy bowed his head and stared at his feet. The wingtips of his white golf shoes were blurry in his sight. The legs go first. He knew the truth of that golf cliché. That's what had destroyed all the great ones: Hogan, Snead, Palmer. Now him. He couldn't keep himself steady over the ball, couldn't get comfortable, and he could no longer putt.

Paddy glanced at his caddy and whispered back, "You aren't asking for much, are you, Spike? A little downhill six-footer to shoot lights out. Well, go out there and read me the line."

Spike dropped DeLacey's bag on the apron and together they walked onto the smooth surface of the eighteenth green. The caddy moved around the hole, squatted down, and studied the break from the far side of the cup. Paddy knelt behind the ball and, using the shaft of the club, plumbed the contour of the green. He shook his head unbelievingly and looked again. He could not focus on the hole. He blinked his eyes, squeezed them tight, and looked again at the line of the six-foot putt. The flag stick shimmered in his sight. It was not a long putt, but if he couldn't find the correct line, he'd never make it.

Spike came up behind him and leaned over his shoulder.

"The grain is working toward the water, Paddy. It'll hold up the ball. Give that baby maybe two inches to the right of the cup. We got ourselves a slick green here."

"I can't see the hole, Spike." Paddy Jack did not move.

"What're you talking about, you can't see the hole?" There was a note of panic in the big man's voice.

"I'm seeing double." Paddy Jack rubbed his eyes. "Coming up the hill, I started to get dizzy."

Spike hitched his pants and looked again at the cup, as if he were still lining up the putt. "Hey, Paddy, we got the whole course tied up. They're going to slap us with a penalty if you don't move." The caddy glanced over at Tom Watson, their playing partner. Watson was moving about impatiently, waiting for Paddy Jack to hole out.

Paddy stood up. He could not let this chance to win escape. Not after all his work. Not after all the days of therapy, and of Maggie urging him on, helping him get back into playing shape. "Okay," he whispered to his caddy. "Here's what we'll do. You set the club face for me. We'll do it like Nicklaus used to do with his kid." He took off his white cap and wiped the sleeve of his sweater across his face, sweeping away a shower of sweat.

Spike came up and positioned the putter's club face, whispering as he did, "Just tap it lightly. Let the ball take the roll. We want to get close, that's all. I'll settle for two putts." He stepped away, saying, "You're looking good, Paddy Jack."

He listened to the gallery. Listened to their reaction as the ball rolled off the putter, gaining speed as it followed the contour of the green, went downhill to the hole. He waited for the collective sigh that would tell him the ball had missed the cup.

The roar broke around him. A burst of cheers.

"Jesus H. Christ, if you ain't something else!" Spike swore, hugged him around the shoulders, then stepped quickly forward and plucked the ball from the hole.

Paddy Jack turned slowly toward the gallery that circled the eighteenth green and took off his cap again, acknowledging the acclaim. He could see the spectators clearly now, pick out faces in the soft reddish afternoon sun. Even the pain in his legs was gone. He stepped off the green and motioned to the gallery for quiet; it was Tom Watson's turn to putt.

Jim Wright was waiting for him at the edge of the gallery. Paddy Jack smiled at the PGA press officer, but the man looked grim. "Paddy," he whispered, "a call came in about an hour ago. It's important." He pressed the note into Padraic's fingers, adding, "I'm really sorry."

Paddy Jack flipped open the note. His fingers shook again as he read the message, and all he could think of was that it no longer mattered that he had just shot sixty-five and had a share of the third round lead. He wouldn't be playing on Sunday. Not after what had happened at home.

Bishop Michael James DeLacey, his arms spread wide, turned slowly toward the waiting studio camera. It had been positioned slightly below eye level, as he had instructed, so that he appeared to be staring down at the television audience, as if from a high pulpit.

"We have spoken of Ireland," he said softly, summing up his half-hour program. "We have spoken of all the sons and daughters of Erin who have gone off to other lands, spreading our faith, our love of freedom, our dreams.

"Today the fight still goes on for Irishmen, however far they travel from home. We, the sons and daughters of Erin, no matter how many generations away from that lovely, blessed land, know we owe a debt to the country that has given so much to the world.

"Jews know this! Israel is kept alive today by the faith and funds of Jews in America, South Africa, Brazil, wherever the diaspora sent the Chosen People.

"Now it is our turn to go to the aid of our own people."

He turned from the camera, moved across the stage, looking down, as if deeply in thought. He knew the second camera had pulled back to take in the whole set, the bookcases and desk, the portraits of John F. Kennedy and Pope John, the full-size statue of the Blessed Virgin. He stepped to the stage mark, then looked directly into the camera and said thoughtfully, "Ireland needs you. All you sons and daughters of the old sod. I am asking you to join me. To join our people. The children of Erin."

He paused again, slipped his hands beneath his purple cassock, and turned his shoulders slightly so that the camera caught his right profile. It was his strong side, he knew. His face, they wrote in *TV Guide*, looked like it had been chiseled from the rocks of Connemara. He liked that description, had used it in advertisements for his program, "Erin Go Bragh—Ireland Forever."

"I am asking all of you within the sound of my voice to join me in our struggle, and under the new banner of blue and white, named in honor of Our Blessed Virgin, we will once again forge an alliance with the good Roman Catholics of Northern Ireland and finally drive from the shores of Erin the imperial forces of Great Britain.

"I ask you today to write us here in Washington, D.C., and we will begin the work in Congress. We will forge this alliance not in violence, but with reason and God's grace, and end England's occupation of Ulster, of Northern Ireland."

The bishop stopped, stepped away from the camera and smiled. His face softened and he seemed shy, momentarily, as if he were afraid he might have spoken too long. In a gentler voice he went on, "I'll leave you until next week. And remember: we are all in exile from Ireland, all of us have a place in our hearts for Erin. So come join our troops, our Blue and White Battalion. Until then . . . " He paused, waited a beat, then said loudly, "Ireland Forever. Erin go bragh!"

Bishop DeLacey waited for the set director to signal him that the taping was over, then he relaxed, let his posture slip. He was always exhausted once he finished a taping. Sighing, he turned to his assistant, who was coming out from the wings.

"I had some trouble there with the prompter, Dary. Could you see about having it moved closer? I think my eyes are going on me." He smiled at the younger priest.

"Your Grace," the man said nervously, "there's been a telephone call. From Father O'Connor . . . in Gatesburg."

"Yes?" The bishop studied the other priest. "Is it mother then?" he asked quickly.

The monsignor nodded, then said softly, "God rest her soul."

Bishop DeLacey looked away, looked off at nothing. His mind was fixed only on how he could get home.

"Father O'Connor would like you to telephone him as soon as possible. He'll be at the rectory, he said. I have the number."

"Thank you, Dary. It was her heart, wasn't it?"

"It was an accident, Father O'Connor said. She was shot with your brother's hunting rifle in the kitchen of the farmhouse."

The bishop shut his eyes and staggered slightly, hearing the news. It had come to this, he thought. It had ended the way he had feared the most. With a killing in his own home.

# · CHAPTER 2 ·

EARLY ON MONDAY, MAGGIE lay listening to the heavy rain beat down on the tin roof of her bedroom, waiting for the dawn, when she could drive to the airport and catch the morning flight out of Africa.

She thought again of her mother, as she had been doing constantly since the cable came from America. She had called Catty before dawn on Saturday morning, but her sister knew only the barest of details: it was an accident; her mother had moved Emmett's rifle when it was loaded. Maggie began to cry thinking of what an awful death it was, how her mother must have suffered.

Maggie remembered how her mother had looked in September, how fragile and tiny she had become, suddenly an old woman. Her mother had always been so strong, working from daybreak to dusk, never tiring, but the strength seemed to have gone out of her almost overnight. She shouldn't have left her, Maggie realized; she shouldn't have gone off and left her alone with Emmett. The weight of her guilt felt like a stone dragging her heart into deep water.

She got out of bed and began to dress in the dark, lifting her clothes off the chair—Kenneth's chair, she called it. She had already decided what she was going to wear on the plane: her long brown skirt, cream-color knit sweater, and boots. It was her best outfit, the same she had worn that first morning at the embassy, when she had gone into her office for introductions.

She added to the outfit the small gold medallion Kenneth had brought back from his trip to Dire Dawa. "I bargained with a Somali in the Old City," he told her proudly, like a schoolboy.

Maggie finished dressing, carried her overnight bag to the front door, then went back through the house, looking to make sure that everything was in order. She kept busy, not wanting to have more time to think.

She hated leaving anywhere. It seemed that was all she ever did—left apartments, cities, countries. She was in the wrong business, she thought ruefully.

Well, she would only be gone a week, two at the most. Just time enough to fly halfway around the world and bury her mother.

She slipped on her coat and picked up her suitcase and purse, checking again, as she had already done several times, for her passport and ticket. For a foreign correspondent, she was a lousy traveler.

A car pulled into the compound and Maggie ran to it. The embassy driver hurried to open the rear door of the limousine and Kenneth leaned forward in the deep backseat to take her luggage. The car's light was on, and the soft luxury of the Cadillac's interior seemed safe and secure.

"Oh, Margaret!" Kenneth said, frowning as he helped her. "You're freezing!"

The driver slammed the door and the rear seat was dark again. Maggie sighed, leaning against Kenneth, needing to feel the strength and warmth of his body.

As daybreak came, Maggie could see down the length of King George VI Street, see the blue-gray smoke of eucalyptus cooking fires hanging over the treetops. A few cars were out, small Fiat taxis and old lorries. And a handful of people emerged from dung wall houses, coming up muddy paths to the street, the women carrying their shoes until they reached the sidewalk.

What a way to live, Maggie thought, feeling sorry for the beautiful Ethiopian women. They were dressed in Western clothes, going off in the cold dawn to work, and walking barefoot in the mud until they reached the public water pumps, where they'd wash off their feet and slip into heels.

"You'll write me from Illinois, won't you?" The ambassador turned sideways so he could see her face.

Maggie nodded but did not look at him, afraid she'd begin to cry.

"I'm going to speak with Virginia," he said calmly, as if it were a routine piece of embassy business.

Maggie knew his ways. There was never anything rash about Kenneth. He wasn't spontaneous, like other men, but she found his deliberateness reassuring. She had known too many impulsive boys in her life, including her ex-husband, Jack McGraff, who never thought of consequences.

"Yesterday, when I realized you were leaving me—and that I wouldn't be seeing you—I knew I had to do something." Impatiently, he began to drum his fingers on his thigh.

The limousine slowed. They had reached Revolution Square and were caught up in a herd of cattle being driven to market. The driver inched the car forward, tapping impatiently on the horn, and the straggly country cattle bolted at the sound.

Maggie hated pushing through a herd. She thought of the farm, of going out into the pasture late in the day to bring back the cows for evening milking, walking them slowly across the fields in the warm summer afternoons, their full udders dripping milk. Such gentle animals, she thought, feeling sorry that they were being abused by the limousine. She saw the fear in their large brown eyes.

"We have time, Tedesse," the ambassador spoke up, "let them pass."

Maggie squeezed his hand to thank him. She waited until Tedesse started the car again, picking up speed on the long straight Africa Avenue out to the airport, before saying, "Don't speak to Virginia until after I return."

"I want to get this over with, Margaret. Out in the open. I think it would be best if I told Virginia while you're out of the country."

"I don't want Virginia to think I am afraid to face her."

"You're not running off. There's been a death in your family." He snapped his words, as he always did when arguing. "She's planning to take home leave at the end of the month. I'm flying with her as far as Madrid, and Muffy's coming down from Paris. Sandy will be over from Boston. I want to have the matter settled before the children arrive."

"Kenneth, please. I want to be sure . . . first."

She could feel his body tense beside her. "I thought you were sure."

She heard the hurt in his voice and she reached to hold his hand with both of hers. "Darling, within the last twenty-four hours my whole world has gone haywire, what with Mommy's death." She pleaded with her eyes. "Please, Kenneth . . . understand. I have to go home, see this through, see my family, make some arrangements for my brother Emmett. I don't think he can live alone on the farm any longer." She turned away to blow her nose before she began to cry. She had to get hold of herself, she realized. At the airport there would be people she knew.

"I've contacted the airport manager; he's setting aside the VIP room. And there will be someone to clear you through Customs and Emigration."

"Thank you, Kenneth." He was like that, always smoothing the path, taking care of things. Jack McGraff had been that way and her brothers, too. Michael especially had run interference for her with the world.

The ticket counter was already crowded, Maggie saw. The airport could not handle the crush of people trying to get boarding passes. Everyone was out of control and panicky.

Kenneth ushered her through the swarming mass and into the quiet and peace of the VIP lounge. He was anxious and would not sit down. He stood above her, his hands in both pockets of his pin-striped suit.

The suit was new. Maggie knew most things about him that a wife would. His clothes were tailor-made in Rome, Paris, and at J. Press in New York. He was better dressed than any diplomat she had met, and much handsomer.

When she had first seen him at the embassy, standing up behind his desk to welcome her, she had thought he looked like a leading man. He was handsome in the same movie-star way, with his short hair, graying at the temples, and his finely chiseled features.

"You needn't wait, Kenneth. We can say good-bye now." She didn't want to keep him from his work, but she also wanted to be alone, to begin the long process of adjusting for America, preparing herself for the farm without her mother. She had never gone home and not had her mother there, waiting, watching for her arrival.

"Are you all right, Margaret?" Kenneth asked, sitting down beside her, awkward at not being able to take her hands in his in so public a place.

"No, I guess not. I'm just thinking about home."

"What was your mother like?" he asked, hoping it would help her to talk.

"Oh, I don't know. What child really knows a parent, anyway? Emmett and I were a surprise, born late in her life."

"Emmett is your twin?"

Maggie nodded. "He was a POW. He hasn't really been well since Vietnam. He's been living on the farm since he came home from the war. He's never really been okay. Even as a child he would become very depressed. I'm afraid Mom—and the rest of us—have been too protective. It's my fault, I should have gotten him into some treatment center."

"And you have a brother a bishop?"

"Michael's the priest. Paddy Jack, the next oldest, is a professional golfer. Then Catty, my sister, who lives near Chicago."

"It's like a Dickens novel," he had remarked the first time she had listed her brothers and sisters.

". . . Catty never got along with Mommy. I don't really know why. Something happened between them when I was a kid, but I've never been able to find out what. You know how life is when you're a child. You just sort of go along, living in this great cocoon, never worrying about anything except whether it will snow enough so you can stay home from school, or how long you can play outside after dark."

"You've always spoken fondly of your mother. That's rare today.

Sometimes, I think, it might be better if all children were raised by nannies. What about your father?"

"I never knew my father. He died on a visit back to Ireland when I was just a child. I guess that's one reason why Mom and I were very close. I hated going east to Washington for college. I wanted to go to a Catholic school near where Catty lived so I'd be close to home, but Father Mike got me a full scholarship to Georgetown, and Mommy insisted I go. I think she was afraid if I went to Chicago, I'd start seeing Catty, and Catty might come between us. Oh, I don't know."

For a moment neither one of them spoke. Maggie was beginning to realize how exhausted she actually was. She could sleep on the plane, she thought, curl up under a blanket and get some rest before they reached Rome.

"What you must do, Margaret, is take this trip one day at a time. If you think of it all, the journey, the funeral, seeing the family, all of it at once, well, it will seem overwhelming. If you can break up the trip into manageable pieces, you'll do much better."

Maggie smiled. It was so like him to see the trip home as a management problem. He tried to run his whole life that way; as if life itself were a diplomatic mission. He always wanted to bring his intelligence to a situation, to solve a problem with common sense. It was so sweet of him, she thought, but he didn't know how an Irish Catholic family got along.

"I love you," she said. Even though they were in public, she reached out and took his hand. He did not flinch.

"I know I'm being premature about this, Margaret, not even having spoken to Virginia, but you're leaving . . . and I'd like to have it settled. . . ."

Maggie slowly shook her head, teary again. "I can't say anything, Kenneth. Don't ask me. It's not because I don't love you. I do. You have to keep remembering that. I do want to marry you—or at least I believe I do—but you can't ask me here, not today, when I'm flying home. You understand, don't you, darling?"

The ambassador looked away. The bright early daylight was in his face, and Maggie saw, in spite of his tan, how weathered and deeply lined his skin was, how clearly it showed his age, the long years he had lived in the tropics.

"I don't have a lot of time, Margaret. I'm not a young man, you realize."

"And would you stay with Virginia if I don't marry you?" She was startled by her own question, startled that she had even thought of this possibility.

Kenneth looked at her. She could see in his eyes how he was trying to decide what to say. He wouldn't lie to her. He never lied. Not to her, not to anyone.

"Yes. If you decided you couldn't marry me, I would stay with Virginia."

"Why? You've told me you don't love her, that the marriage has been over for years." She could hear her voice turn cold.

"No, I'm not in love with Virginia. I don't think that either one of us was actually ever in love. We married young; we came from the right sorts of families. We had friends in common, interests." He gestured weakly. "We were busy. I had the foreign service; Virginia had the children, her charities. For both of us, marriage was not the focus of our lives. So we were . . . suitable for each other."

Maggie felt cold, as if he were stripping away her clothes.

"But then . . ." He gestured again, describing the turn of events. "I didn't think, I guess, that anyone like you existed. I never meet young women in the Foreign Service, just those bright hotshot men from Yale and Harvard. Then you came out to Africa."

She met his eyes. He looked hurt and sad, as if she had disappointed him. How he must suffer, she thought, living with this affair. It was so beneath him, all this sordidness.

She could see that the plane was boarding. A long line of passengers were being led across the tarmac to where the Ethiopian Airlines 747 was parked, surrounded by service trucks and a small detachment of armed soldiers.

"You've hurt me, Kenneth, telling me you won't leave Virginia. I know I have no rights, but in my mind your decision diminishes our relationship. I don't want to think she and I are equal in this equation." She turned away at once, unable to stand the pressure of his gaze. It was as if he were reading her heart. She looked toward the far horizon as she went on.

"I'm not sure now if it was really me that you fell in love with. Or did you just discover younger women—intelligent, resourceful, beautiful younger women?"

"Margaret, this is ridiculous!" He began to drum again on his knee.

She picked up her hand luggage and stood. An Ethiopian nodded to her from the doorway. It was time to leave.

"I'll walk you to the plane," Kenneth said.

Maggie let him have his way. At the door, the airline official handed back her passport and a boarding pass, using both his hands and bowing slightly, in the polite Ethiopian way.

Passengers were stretched across the tarmac, but Kenneth guided her toward the front entrance of the plane, avoiding the line.

"You can't leave Addis thinking as you do," he said.

"And what am I thinking, Kenneth?" She was walking as fast as she could, her high heels snapping on the tarmac. She rarely wore heels in Ethiopia and the sound reminded her of the States, of walking to work in Washington.

"That somehow I've betrayed you by saying I'd stay with Virginia. You're being childish, Margaret."

"I think it's odd, that's all. You're not risking anything, are you? You won't give up Virginia, the perfect ambassador's wife, or your well-run home, unless, of course, I agree to take up the slack."

"Goddamnit, Margaret, you're being a fool!"

He had never sworn at her before and the tone of his voice, the anger, frightened her. She tried not to listen. She kept her eyes on the giant 747 up ahead, but it seemed to be receding into the blue-gray horizon.

"All right, I won't do anything until you come back. We'll talk then, once you have this family matter settled." The rough edge was gone from his voice.

They had reached the plane, and stopped at the bottom of the ramp.

"You'll come back to me?" he asked, his voice rising with tension.

Maggie nodded. At the top of the stairs, she waved to him.

"Write," he called up to her.

She nodded and waved again. He looked so handsome standing alone on the wet tarmac, a tall, thin sliver of a man, impeccable in his pin-striped suit, blue silk tie. Even in the wind, his hair was unruffled. He was never at a loss, anywhere.

He moved back from the jet, avoiding the puddles of shallow water as he did, yet always keeping his eyes on her. She felt like his child leaving home. Then she turned into the open hatchway and boarded the 747 out of Africa.

## · *CHAPTER 3* ·

THE TRAIN, FOLLOWING THE curve of the river, went south into southern Illinois. It was a gray, bleak morning. Spiritual weather, her mother had called such days, using the West of Ireland expression, and Catty, staring out the window, wondered now what that had really meant. Was it a day for suffering, a day for repentance?

She looked across the landscape, the brown fields, the black trees, the open space. A lone house here, another there, posted like sentry boxes in the midst of flat land. She watched for the crossroads.

The train picked up speed as it moved away from the river. They were crossing a cornfield, going west, she knew, toward the country club, before looping back to the river again and Gatesburg itself.

The intersection, Skelton's Crossing, was ahead. She spotted where the road crossed the train track then went west, the same direction as the train. And there, ahead of her, was the country crossing. A traffic light, she saw, now hung over the corner. At long last, she thought, but without bitterness.

"See that crossing, Wendy?" She spoke quickly, wanting suddenly, after all the years, to share this story with her daughter.

Wendy glanced up in time to catch the stoplight, the red blinking over the empty corner. The train sped on, whistle screeching.

"When I was your age, I was in a car accident at that crossroads." She spoke offhandedly, as if she were telling a story about another person.

"Oh, yeah?" Wendy's attention perked. It always surprised her to learn something new about her parents, to realize that they had lives before she was born. She slipped off her headphones to listen.

"It was a terrible accident. A man . . . a boy really, was killed."

"Oh, God!" Wendy looked back toward the intersection again. "Were you hurt or anything? I mean, who was he? Someone you knew?"

Wendy had the DeLacey look. The Irish face, round and healthy, with thick black hair, thick eyebrows, beautiful skin. And Catty's brown eyes as well, the shape of pennies, the color of bisqued clay. From her father she had inherited a look of innocence and beguilement, *and*, Catty was beginning to discover, his willfulness.

"Yes, I knew him." She looked away from Wendy. They were passing the golf course. It was desolate and empty, useless on the cold day. The strips of fairway, ponds and greens, all the strange geometry of the landscape, stretched away from the passing train.

"He was my husband," she went on. "My first husband." Catty looked back at Wendy as the words registered, and saw the shock in the child's face, the moment of fear in her eyes.

She was sorry at once that she had told Wendy so abruptly, that she had not prepared her daughter for this secret past.

"You mean Daddy isn't . . . Daddy wasn't . . ." She stumbled with the question. It had been a year since she had last called her father Daddy.

"I met your father when I was twenty-one and living in Texas. I had graduated from college by then and moved away from home."

"Does Daddy . . . know?"

"Yes, Daddy knows. This isn't a great secret of mine."

"Well, I didn't know! I mean, we didn't know . . . Clare . . . Why didn't you tell us?"

"Wendy . . ." Her heart wrenched, seeing how upset the girl was. She reached across the seats and took her daughter's hands, felt the cold fingers.

"I told you now, sweetheart, because . . . because you are an adult, and we're going home, to my old home, and we'll be meeting a lot of people, strangers. My first marriage, and things that happened before you were born, will come up and be talked about. And I want you to know what my life was like when I was your age."

Catty crossed the double seats, wrapped her arms around Wendy. They were riding backward and Catty pressed Wendy's face against her chest, looked over her head at the receding farmland. They had passed the golf course and were making the turn beneath Lamont Hill, going into the state forest preserve.

"When I was seventeen, I fell in love with a boy named Sal Marino. He was Italian, and we were classmates at Our Lady of Wisdom. Sal was really my only boyfriend. I wasn't popular, not like you, and, well, we decided, in our infinite seventeen-year-old wisdom, to get married.

"I'm not sure we were all that much in love. I thought I was, but I was also trying to get away from home. I wanted to get away from here, from this place." She nodded toward the train window. They had cleared the preserve and were following Dry Weather Creek. Wendy sat up to watch her mother.

"Your grandmother was against it, of course, because we were so young, and also because Sal was Italian. She said Italians never went to church, that they weren't real Catholics." Catty smiled, amused that she could remember such a detail.

"She caught us one night necking outside the house. We weren't doing much of anything; I was afraid even to let him touch me, afraid I might get pregnant. But even a little necking in the front seat of his car was too much for mother. She said if he couldn't respect me, he couldn't see me anymore. And she meant it."

Catty shook her head, remembering the pathos of it all. "So we decided to run away and get married. That's what Catholic girls did in those days instead of just sleeping with their boyfriends. We ran away to a place called, of all things, French Lick, Indiana, and were married by a justice of the peace. It was just like in the movies."

Tears were streaming down Wendy's face, but Catty kept talking, determined to tell the whole story. It had been a family secret after all, she realized, a tragedy that she had kept from the children, in the same way they concealed broken household items from her.

"We spent our wedding night in a sleazebag in Clay City . . . God, why have I remembered all this?" She remembered the wetness of the night when she stepped from the car, carrying her tiny overnight bag and walking up to the motel door, lit only with a dim bulb.

"Oh, Mom, how tacky!" Wendy was caught up in the story, the sordidness of detail.

"Yes, I guess. But it was romantic, too. You have to remember, I grew up on all those Susan Hayward movies." Catty glanced away from the look of eagerness in the young girl's face. She stared out the window. Instead of the familiar cornfields, they were passing a housing development, suburban streets and cul-de-sacs, dozens of black rooftops and tiny raw backyards. Catty was confused—had the train detoured somehow?—but then she spotted Silver Pond among the rows of ranch houses. Silver Pond, surrounded by a park and a children's playground. The cows were gone; the sycamore trees, too, were gone from the muddy banks of their old swimming hole.

Home was next. Her heart dropped. Home was beyond Silver Pond, a mile away as the crows fly, her mother would have said. She had to finish the story.

"We rode back in triumph the next day, proud of outfoxing our parents, Father O'Connor, and all the nuns. Sister Saint Stephen especially. She was the principal at Wisdom and was on to us.

"Sal was speeding. There was a dance that night at school and we wanted to make an entrance, you know. To startle everyone with the news. I had a diamond—a tiny, hopeless little half carat. We were really feeling smug, especially about having been to bed together. I guess that's what I wanted to show my girlfriends. 'Look, I did it!' We were so young."

She had lowered her voice and Wendy leaned closer to hear her mother.

"There was a train coming through. The Chicago Daylight, heading south to St. Louis. It went through Gatesburg at five o'clock and reached that intersection—Skelton's Corner—at five-fourteen.

"We saw the train. Heard it. I shouted to Sal, told him not to try and beat it across the tracks. But I couldn't tell him what to do. No one could. No one could tell either of us."

"Oh, God!" Wendy exclaimed, realizing what was next.

"I heard myself screaming," Catty went on, still speaking in a soft voice. "We reached the tracks and shot across. Sal was right; we beat the train by fifty yards. A piece of cake, Sal would have said, if he had lived."

"The train didn't hit you?"

"No. But racing over the tracks, Sal lost control of the car. We skidded through Skelton's Corner. There was no traffic light then, not even a stop sign. And usually there was no traffic, not that late in the afternoon." Catty paused a moment, as if to summon up the rest of her courage. "It was a hay truck that hit us, and the truck spun about forty degrees on the wet pavement; somehow, I was thrown free and landed on a grassy bank.

"But poor Sal, my husband of twenty-one hours and six minutes, was killed outright. The truck's rearview mirror broke through the windshield. . . ."

She could clearly remember how she had landed in the field and looked back to see his head flying through the open window, loose as a Halloween pumpkin.

"Oh, God, no!" Wendy said, turning away and pressing her face against the damp pane of thick train glass. She covered her ears, not wanting to hear more.

Catty was no longer crying. She saw her home in the distance, in the shallow valley of their property, saw the clutter of the barn buildings and the white frame farmhouse encircled by maple trees. The pretty, old-fashioned farm scene, that she had grown to hate.

"Look, Wendy," Catty said, distracting her daughter. "There's the farm."

The train skirted the property line, keeping the house in sight as it curved back toward the river and town.

Wendy opened her eyes. She spotted the house on one small rise, the barns beyond it, and between them, in the dip of land, an orchard of apple trees.

"I see someone," she said.

Catty saw him. From that distance, the man was only a dark dot, someone moving slowly through the gray day.

"It must be your uncle Emmett," she said. He would be finishing the morning chores, Catty thought, going up to the house for breakfast. She could remember her father, and then her older brothers, coming back to the house for breakfast, crossing through the orchard. She'd be standing at the sink, doing the dishes, rushing to finish before the school bus arrived.

She did not know Emmett, not as an adult. She had last seen him when he passed through Chicago on his way to basic training. He had been seventeen then and leaving the farm, as she had left the farm before him.

"What did you feel? I mean, what was it like having your husband die like that . . . in front of you and everything?" Wendy asked, turning to look at her mother.

The full impact of the story was taking hold of Wendy's imagination. She had personalized it, tried to imagine herself as the wife, and Jeff Golden dead at her feet.

Catty kept her eyes on the farm, thinking of how tiny and innocuous it seemed from that distance. It resembled a toy she had been given as a child, a miniature play farm. It was a Christmas present she had never played with. There had never been a time when she had liked the farm.

"I went numb," she told her daughter. "For a long time I was sort of catatonic. They sent me away—they being your grandmother, Father O'Connor, and your uncle, Father Mike. I went to school at Mundelein College.

"For a while I thought of becoming a nun. A Trappistine. I wanted to take the vow of perpetual silence and go off and live in a mountain monastery. Nothing came of that, of course."

"Oh, Mom!" There was concern in Wendy's voice, and a new empathy. She never thought of her mother as someone romantic, someone suffering a lost love. "How could you stand it?" She moved closer to her mother as if to share in the suffering.

"Like almost everything else, you finally get over it. You heal. You meet new people. And, I guess, you decide that carrying around all that self-pity is just too damn much work." Catty looked sad again, and thoughtful.

"Did you ever come home again?"

Catty shook her head. "Not after college. They wanted me to return and teach at Blessed Sacrament, the Catholic elementary school. But I wouldn't. The day after I graduated, I cashed in my train ticket, sold off the jewelry I had, which wasn't much besides my half-carat wedding ring, and bought a bus ticket for Texas."

"You couldn't have sold your wedding ring!"

"I was twenty years old, Wendy, and I needed the money to get away. Yes, I could sell it." She smiled sadly at her daughter. Wendy needed to hear what it meant to grow up, to be on one's own and faced with no future.

"But you loved him, Mom."

The tears had returned, but this time Catty did not go to her daughter. She let the child cry, let her settle down, then went on calmly, "Yes, I loved him. Did love him. But he had been dead almost four years. And I had to start thinking about myself, what would happen to me. I had a life to live without him, darling."

She softened her voice as Wendy wiped away the tears. Her eyes were red, her cheeks blotchy. "It's twenty years since Sal's death. I'm a different person than I was at your age. People change, honey. That's why I'm cautioning you about Jeff." She could see Wendy's back stiffen. Still Catty kept talking. Being away from home, out of their family surroundings, gave Catty courage to speak her mind. "Sweetheart, you're so young."

"I'm not, Mother. Kids my age are already married. Jackie Beaven has a girlfriend who has a baby already, and—"

"Wendy, I don't care about those people. I love you. I care about you. I want you to realize how long your life is; how wrong it would be to get married so young."

"Then we won't get married! We'll just live together." Wendy slumped down in the seat defiantly.

"Your father won't let you."

"That's his problem, not mine." She turned her face to the train window.

In the reflection, Catty could see the anger in Wendy's eyes, the set jaw. She thought again how much Wendy was her father's child. They would hurt each other, if she let them.

"I don't want you to be hurt the way I was," Catty said quietly.

"Mother, everyone who gets married isn't killed on their honeymoon! Give me a break!" Wendy sat up and began to search for her purse in the pile of their luggage.

The train was slowing, switching tracks. At the end of the car, the conductor shouted out Gatesburg, the next station stop. Catty looked Wendy over quickly. The girl was a sight, her mascara streaked, her wool shirt twisted and wrinkled. Perhaps it had been foolish to force Wendy out of her jeans and cotton shirt, to make her dress up and curl her hair for the trip home. But she had wanted Wendy to look beautiful arriving in Gatesburg.

Young people, Catty was learning from watching them in airports and at train stations, never dressed when they traveled. Travel wasn't anything special to them. They expected to go places and do things.

Wendy was spoiled, Catty knew. All her children were. But she had never wanted them to feel the deprivations she had, the sense of growing up poor and isolated, and worse, of growing up under the thumb of a mother. She would not do to her children—especially Wendy—what her mother had done to her. And because of that, she had treated her children like guests in her own home.

When she had left town for good after college, both the brewery and factory had just closed. On her last train ride out of Gatesburg she had seen the unemployment lines from the window. The town was dying. People were moving to Michigan and Ohio, where there were jobs in automobile factories. Stores were closing. Sears and Montgomery Ward had left Gatesburg. But that had changed.

Now, as they crossed Illinois Avenue, Catty saw a line of cars. A traffic jam in Gatesburg, she thought, surprised at the number of people downtown on a Sunday morning.

The train reached River Street and rattled onto the trestle. Catty glanced back at the shopping street, where, as a teenager, she had hung out after school, going from Sears to Ward's, to the Sweet Shoppe for a malted milk, killing time, never wanting to go home.

"Oh, how cute," Wendy said, spotting the brightly painted storefronts and the cobblestone street. "It looks like Old Towne, doesn't it, Mom? You know, with all those boutiques."

Catty had forgotten about the street, forgotten that it was even cobblestoned. When they were growing up, they had thought of cobblestones as just old and decrepit.

Urban renewal had occurred in Gatesburg, she saw. Deep in her memory, Catty remembered reading something in the *Tribune* about how the town had gotten federal funding. She had noticed the article because Jack McGraff's name was mentioned. He had arranged the grant.

The train crossed the river and went past the abandoned brewery, a long block of dark warehouses and factory buildings.

"This was all owned by the Holtz family," Catty explained. "They were the richest family in town, and employed just about everyone who didn't farm. I went to school with Hilda Holtz. We were classmates at Wisdom." Hilda had been Sal's girl before Catty took him away. Catty hadn't thought of her in years, and she wondered what had happened to Hilda Holtz, and all the other kids from school.

"Mom, come on!" Wendy stepped into the aisle as the train arrived at the station. She led the way toward the exit door.

Wendy stepped into the cold February day and was helped down the metal stairs by the conductor, who turned next to Catty, and then their luggage. They were the only ones getting off in Gatesburg.

"Back from a big shopping spree in Chicago, ladies?" the conductor said, smiling. "Off spending the hubby's money, right?" He laughed and swung up onto the train steps.

"We don't live in this town," Wendy spoke up. "And we have our own money, not my father's."

"Got yourself a little libber there, don't you?" The conductor grinned at Catty as he replied, then stepped into the coach as the Amtrak train pulled out of the station and continued south toward St. Louis.

"Bastard!" Wendy shouted into the wind.

"Wendy!"

"Old jerks like him make me furious. Shopping . . . spending Daddy's money!"

"Your father would have said the same thing."

"That's different. That's Daddy."

Wendy kept talking, but Catty was not paying attention. She had spotted the car, saw him driving carefully, slowly into the parking lot. Of course he would meet the train, she thought.

"Be quiet!" Catty said, silencing her daughter.

He was much older, she saw at once. His hair had all gone white. He must be in his seventies, she thought, trying to place him in time.

"Who's that?" Wendy asked, following her mother's gaze.

"Wendy, I want you to promise me something. I don't want you to say anything to this man. I don't want you to tell him anything about our family, or Jeff, or anything. Absolutely nothing. Do you understand?" She spoke quickly. He had stepped from the car and was coming slowly up the steps onto the old wooden train platform.

"Why? Who is he?" Some fear had returned to Wendy's young voice.

"His name is Father Dermot O'Connor. He's the pastor here at Saint Patrick's, and a friend of your grandmother's."

"You don't like him?"

"I hate him," Catty replied, and then stepped forward, hand outstretched, and said, "Father O'Connor, so nice of you to come. But, really, you shouldn't have gone to all the trouble."

# ·CHAPTER 4·

"AND THIS IS MY oldest child, Wendy Ann." Catty turned to her daughter. "Wendy, this is Father O'Connor. Father O'Connor was a very good friend of your grandmother."

"And aren't you a lovely-looking lass. Ah, she's the spitting image of yourself, Cathleen. Hello, my dear." The old priest took both of Wendy's small hands in his, held them gently.

"Hello," Wendy whispered, smiling, looking down at the small, stoop-shouldered priest. She was embarrassed and kept glancing at her mother, not knowing what to say.

"You've got the map of Ireland all over your face, now don't you?"

"What?" Wendy began to giggle.

"I'm not sure Wendy even knows that expression, Father," Catty said. Stepping forward, she slipped her arm protectively into Wendy's.

"And you have two now, isn't that right, Cathleen?"

"Four."

"Ah, four. Well, isn't that lovely. A fine Catholic family. You're out there in Elk Grove, aren't you?" the priest went on, as they walked slowly to his car.

"Yes, Father. We've been there almost ten years, since Joe was transferred up from Texas."

"Well, let's see, that would be Saint James parish, now wouldn't it?"

"Yes it is, Father," Catty answered. It hadn't taken him long, she thought, to get around to that. He would be after Wendy next.

"And now where is it that you go to school, Wendy Ann?" he said, as if on cue.

"To the high; Elk Grove High."

"Ah, Elk Grove High . . . well, I don't think I know that one," he murmured.

Catty pressed her lips together to keep from smiling.

"Ah, but there are so many schools all popping up. An old man like myself . . . I can't keep them all straight. We had to close Wisdom, did you know that, Cathleen?" They had reached the parish car, an old Cadillac.

"Yes, Maggie told me."

"Ah, Margaret Mary! God bless that child. She'll be home now, won't she?" He looked over at Catty. They had separated at the car, as the two women moved to the passenger side.

"I spoke to her in Africa. In Ethiopia. She's on her way."

"You can telephone Africa, now, can you?" he asked, searching his overcoat pockets for the keys.

"Yes. She called."

"It's a wonder, isn't it? The missionaries did a grand job out there, didn't they?" He slid into the Cadillac and unlocked both doors. "You can't be too careful," he said, explaining as they climbed in. "We've got a lot of new people hanging out down here. Good-for-nothing colored kids, you know, all doped up."

Catty glanced quickly over her shoulder at Wendy, warning her with a look not to say anything.

"I noticed a lot of new shops on River Street," Catty said, changing the subject as the priest struggled to start the old car.

Father O'Connor snorted, shook his head. "It's the wrong kind of people, I'm afraid. All those fairies from Chicago's Old Towne are opening these places. They call them 'boutiques.' That's French, now isn't it? Well, I wouldn't be caught dead in one." The engine turned over and he moved the car slowly from the parking lot, both hands tight on the steering wheel. The Cadillac was too much for him, Catty saw; already she was tensing up, watching him manage the downtown turns.

"Gatesburg was dying when I left," Catty said, wanting to talk to keep her mind off the man's driving. "But today I actually saw a traffic jam on Illinois Avenue."

"It's those computer people. Some outfit from Chicago came here six years ago and built a brand-new building on Highway Seven. They make those, what d'ya call them, personal computers? It's called Ram . . . something or other."

"RamDisk." Wendy spoke up from the backseat.

"What's that, lass?"

"The company is called RamDisk. We have one at home."

"Ah, now, you do, do you!" He turned around again to smile at Wendy.

"Sweetheart, don't bother Father O'Connor while he's driving." Catty had grabbed hold of the door handle.

"I'm not bothering him, Mother!"

"Indeed you're not, darling. Indeed you're not. Why, this Caddy could go on its own, it's been traveling these town streets for so long. The diocese wanted to give me a new car, one of those little Jap things, but I wouldn't have it; they're not safe a'tall."

The priest ran a red light and Catty closed her eyes briefly, waiting for a crash. Perhaps everyone in Gatesburg was aware of him and kept out of his way. They had crossed the bridge and were going uphill toward the square.

"There's Carpozi's," she said suddenly, surprised to see the hardware store. It, too, had changed, she saw at once. There was a new facade to the old red-brick building, and she could see household and kitchen utensils in the front windows. She remembered farm implements, plows and harrows, parked on the sidewalk.

"He's dead now, you know. God rest his soul."

"Mr. Carpozi?"

"Ah! Three winters ago. He died down in Florida. In his condominium. His son Gino has the place. Do you remember Gino, Cathleen? He was about your time at Wisdom. A fat little lad? The mother spoiled that child, God rest her soul as well. She passed away two years ago. A huge wake it was. Sixty-seven cars in the procession, all from the west side of Chicago. Gino gave Saint Pat's a set of kneelers in memory of his parents. He comes in at Christmas and Easter to try them out." The priest was grinning, glancing at Catty. "Ah, you know how those kind are, good to Holy Mother Church, but not faithful. But the kneelers, they're lovely. Three inches of thick foam rubber. Do you remember the bare-board kneelers in your time, Cathleen? Real penance, they were. Especially at Twelve, and with a full church."

"I remember Gino," Catty interrupted, trying to halt the priest's rambling. "He was a year ahead of me." Once he had chased her halfway home, trying to kiss her. She had been in the seventh grade then.

"He married a Jew. Can you believe it! A New York Jew at that. God knows where he met her. Not selling farm equipment, that's for sure."

Catty stretched her arm across the back of the front seat and, without turning, motioned Wendy to keep quiet.

"We have ourselves a Holiday Inn," Father O'Connor went on, "and I've gone ahead and rung them up. They've set aside some rooms for the family."

"I think we should stay at the farm," Catty answered.

"Well, Cathleen, I don't know if you want to do that."

"There's enough room, Father," she said nicely.

"But it isn't what it once was, Cathleen—the farmhouse, I mean. These last few years, you know, herself wasn't able to keep up the place. Then this winter, Emmett closed most of it down because of fuel costs."

Catty sank back in the leather seat, thinking through the problem. She didn't want to stay in a hotel. She had made up her mind to sleep at home one last time, as if that would be making a final payment on her past.

"Please take us out to the farm, Father. I'll speak to Emmett and decide later what we should do." She glanced over at the priest, kept smiling as she made her point. She didn't want to start arguing with the old man, not after all these years. But she wouldn't have him telling her what to do. He had done it when she was a child, but not now. Not any longer.

Father O'Connor turned the Cadillac onto the farm drive. Catty looked over her shoulder and said to Wendy, "When we get to the house, I want you to wait in the car a few minutes. Okay?"

"Sure, Mom."

"I'll go in first, Father." She did not pretend to ask the priest's permission. They were at her home, and it was her mother who was dead, shot to death on the kitchen floor. Catty began to grow angry again, thinking of that, of why she was back in Gatesburg.

As O'Connor drove slowly toward the house, Catty studied its outlines. The farmhouse seemed so small to her. She had let the place grow in her memory, she realized, let it become medieval and mysterious. But it was just a simple, southern Illinois farmhouse, three floors and a dormer on the top: her room. And later, Maggie's.

The place needed paint, she saw. And Emmett had tacked heavy plastic on all the windows and the porch. He had also lined the foundation with bales of straw, using them as cheap insulation. She was sorry Wendy was seeing it for the first time in such a run-down state.

Father O'Connor drove around the circle drive, past the apple orchard, then up to the porch at the back of the house. He stopped there but kept the engine running.

"I'm not sure if Emmett's here. He doesn't stay around the place much." He strained his neck to look toward the barns. "He could be seeing to the animals." He tapped the horn.

"Don't!" Catty objected. "Don't trouble him." She opened the front door. "I'll be right back, honey," she said to Wendy, and then stepping into the cold, went quickly across the brown grass to the back porch door, as if she were a kid again herself, hurrying home from school on a wintry day.

"Emmett?" Catty knocked on the inside kitchen door. Her whole body was trembling, but not, she realized, from the cold. God almighty, she thought, she was afraid of entering her own home, and she pushed open the door, almost defiantly, and stepped inside.

She looked at the linoleum floor the first thing. She couldn't stop herself. What was she looking for, blood? Signs of the last moments of her mother's life? The exact spot where she might have fallen?

The floor had been washed, she could see that, but not polished. There was a dullness to it, and she felt embarrassed for her mother, who had always kept a perfect house. Then she looked up and took in the whole kitchen.

"My God!" she said aloud, stunned by the upheaval, the squalor of the place. "What's happened here?" she asked herself, and stepped carefully around the table, went to the sink where dozens of plates were stacked haphazardly, pots and pans left standing in cold sudsy water. The white café curtains were dirty; the glass was grimy with wood-stove soot.

She poked her head into the spare room, the tiny, windowless square that the transient help had once used, the out-of-work old bums who wandered in off the highway looking for farm-labor jobs. The room smelled. Sheets and heavy blankets hung off the unmade single bed.

Turning back to the kitchen, she spotted another cot pushed into one corner and saw Emmett's clothes, some on chairs, some packed into large brown bags, all dirty laundry.

This is how they lived, she thought. In one room like Appalachian hillbillies. Like white trash, or poor blacks on Chicago's Southside. They lived in all this squalor.

"Oh, Mom, goddamnit!" There was pain in her throat; it squeezed out the words. Catty pushed open the kitchen door and escaped into the hallway; she felt the cold of the big, empty farmhouse whip across her ankles, rise between her legs.

"Emmett? Emmett?" she shouted. Her younger brother's name bounced off the walls of the empty place.

The downstairs rooms had been stripped. Most of the furniture was gone from the dining room and the front parlor. As she went slowly up the stairs, she saw that several pictures had been removed from the staircase walls—she could tell by the marks left on the flowered wallpaper—but the Infant of Prague statue still stood on a table on the first-floor landing.

"Emmett?" she asked, lowering her voice as she reached the second floor.

Her mother's old bedroom was at the head of the stairs. Catty pushed the door open slowly, frightened by the silence of the house, the emptiness.

Her mother's cherrywood bedroom set was missing, replaced by a cheap, used one. Now Catty was even angrier. In the back of her mind she had been planning to take that furniture back to Elk Grove, that and her own childhood bedroom set.

Catty crossed the hallway, looked into Mike's old room. It was the same as she had remembered, with the Notre Dame pennants still pinned to the wallpaper, the high school awards still on the bureau. Dust, in layers, covered the furniture, but the room hadn't changed or been used, she realized, since the day he'd left for the seminary. "So he'll always have a place here at home," her mother had explained, when telling the other children why they couldn't have his bedroom. Yet when he did leave the seminary, on vacations and holidays, he had always stayed with O'Connor at the rectory, driving out to visit the family as if they were just parishioners. Still, his bedroom remained intact, like a shrine.

The other room on the second floor was empty, the bed stripped, most of the furniture gone. Paddy had taken all his possessions when he moved, all his books and childhood belongings. He had even removed his high school golf prizes, she saw, or perhaps they had just disappeared with the other furniture.

Catty climbed the stairs to the top floor, the small dormer room that had been hers. She had claimed the room when she turned thirteen; it was the only way then that she could get away from her mother. She remembered reading for hours there in the window seat, high above the apple orchard. As she turned the doorknob, she realized she wanted Wendy to see the room. Before Wendy married and was lost to her, Catty wanted her daughter to see where she had slept as a little girl.

Catty opened the door and jumped in surprise. There was a man asleep in her small bed, a big man sprawled out across the narrow bare mattress. In one hand he clutched a pint bottle of whiskey. His face was turned away, buried, in a slipless pillow. The bedroom smelled of him, of his filthy clothes, the whiskey, and the farm dirt wedged into the cleats of his heavy work shoes.

It never changes, she thought with anger. The farm and everything about it would always be bitter to her. She crossed over to the bed and shouted down at him, tried to wake her drunken youngest brother without touching him.

Emmett rolled over and looked up at her.

"You!" he said. Catty was standing in the bright window light and it hurt his eyes to look at her. "Hey, what's going on?" He tried to get up, but his stomach erupted and he managed only to reach the side of the bed before vomiting onto the bedroom floor.

Catty jumped away, revolted. Even in the cold dormer, she could smell the bourbon. He was sick a second time, then jerked to his feet and ran for the bathroom. She could hear him retching into the toilet. Catty stepped over the vomit and followed him.

He was on the floor, crouched over the bowl. There was nothing left in his stomach, but he kept dry-heaving into the toilet. It sounded as if his insides were being scraped away. She thought of her own children, of having them sick like that. Never did she love them as much as when they were so helpless.

"Emmett," she said softly, "are you okay?"

He sat back on his heels and stared at her. His face was ashen.

"I'm going downstairs," she said softly. "I'll make you some tea. Clean up this mess, please." She moved toward the bathroom door.

"Hey!" he shouted after her.

Catty paused. "Yes?"

"This is my house, not yours. Don't start giving me any goddamn orders."

His farm boots stumped on the floorboards as he struggled to gain his feet and come after her. A moment before she had felt kindly toward him, but that emotion flipped over into fear. She didn't know her brother.

He rushed the stairs, stumbling, too big for the narrow hallway.

"Look!" he shouted, reaching the stairway. "You left us—her and me. You haven't stepped foot on this farm in twenty years."

Catty moved away from his reeking breath. "Yes, and I won't come back, not after the funeral. But we're staying here, Emmett. My daughter Wendy and myself. And the rest of my family is arriving tomorrow. Maggie will be with them. Joe is picking her up at O'Hare. So we're going to clean this house and open up the rooms, make all the beds. I want you to turn the heat back on."

"I can't afford the heat. I don't have any fucking money!"

"Stop swearing, Emmett. And don't worry about the heat or food. I'll pay for it. The family is all going to be home; there will be relatives in from Chicago. We have to make this place presentable. Now clean up your mess."

Catty stormed through the house, from floor to floor, then out the kitchen door and into the cold day. She held her breath until she reached the lawn, where she was able to breathe again without the smell of vomit and filth and death.

"Damn it!" she swore, walking toward the parish car. What had possessed her to take on Emmett? Why was she making a big thing of the family coming home to the farm? She only wanted it behind her, the whole family tragedy.

She reached the car and opened the front door. Wendy was sitting forward, listening closely to Father O'Connor.

The old priest was speaking, his brogue thickening as he went on. "And there's another old Irish saying that goes, 'May the road rise to meet you. May the wind be always at your back. May the sun shine warm upon your face, the rains fall soft upon your fields. And, until we meet again, may God hold you in the hollow of his hand.' "

"Hey, that's neat!" Wendy said, smiling, and then to her mother, "Mom, Father O'Connor is telling me all these Irish expressions. Tell her the one, Father, about the Druids and Saint Patrick."

"I know it, Wendy," Catty said quickly with an edge in her voice. "Get your things, honey." And then to O'Connor, "You knew how they were living, didn't you?"

"I suggested the Holiday Inn, Cathleen. I can still drive you there."

"No!" She would not let the priest dictate her decisions. "We'll stay here. But this house is a disgrace. Why didn't you do something about it, Father? She was your friend."

"And what was I to do, Cathleen?" He pulled himself up behind the steering wheel, as if to mount a defense. "Get you on the phone? Tell you they were penniless? And would you have come here and given them money enough for the heat? Food for the table? You haven't spoken a word to your mother in twenty years."

"But Emmett . . ." Catty began.

"The boy's done the best he could, but he's no farmer, not that lad." The priest shook his head, looked away from her.

"He's drunk, that's what he is."

The priest turned to her again, "And how would you be, finding your mother dead in the house, half her chest blown away with the God almighty shotgun blast?"

"Never mind," Catty managed to say, fumbling for the door. She had to get her daughter out of the car. She caught the shock on Wendy's innocent face.

"I'll call the Women's Sodality, have them send some ladies to help clean the place," Father O'Connor offered, softening his voice.

"No, I don't want any help," Catty said over her shoulder, stepping from the car. "We'll do this ourselves, Wendy and I." She didn't want anything to do with the women from the parish, or with girls she might have gone to school with. "Wendy, come on, sweetheart."

"Bye, Father," Wendy said softly, slipping across the backseat and opening the door.

"Bye now, lass." Father O'Connor cocked his head, smiled kindly at the girl, then said to Catty, "Call if you're wanting anything. I'm on my way to the airport to fetch the bishop."

"Ask Father Mike to call me."

"He'll be staying at the rectory, I should think."

"And where else?" Catty slammed the front door, then took Wendy's arm, walked her up the slight rise to the porch door as O'Connor drove away.

"He's not so bad, Mom," Wendy said.

"Please, Wendy, you don't know the man."

"He's kinda cute, you know."

"Enough, Wendy!" She opened the screen door and pushed her daughter ahead of her into the farmhouse.

"Do you know how Saint Patrick proved there were three persons in one God?" Wendy was asking as the screen door banged behind them.

# · CHAPTER 5 ·

"THE HEAT'S ON," EMMETT reported. He had come up from the basement and stood at the kitchen door. He had not changed or shaved, and stood there awkwardly, filling up the doorway; he looked like the family's retarded son, Catty thought.

"Wendy, this is your Uncle Emmett. You don't remember him, I'm sure." Wendy was already at the kitchen sink, her arms deep in sudsy water. "I don't think you were even six when Emmett last visited us in Chicago."

Wendy nodded, then said meekly, "Hi." She was embarrassed again, not knowing what to say to the strange-looking man.

"Hello, Wendy." Emmett brightened up. His niece was a pretty girl, and just having her in the kitchen made him feel better. He missed, he realized, having people to talk to.

"We're going to need sheets and blankets for those bedrooms, Emmett," Catty said loudly, noticing Emmett's interest in Wendy. Perhaps O'Connor was right, she thought; they should have stayed at the Holiday Inn. She did not know what Emmett was like. He might even be dangerous. "You have blankets and sheets, or were they sold off, too?"

"They've been packed away since the house was shut up. I'll get them later. I have to feed the animals first."

"Do it now, please. We'll be ready to start the bedrooms within half an hour." Catty dropped the mop back into the bucket and sighed, already exhausted from scrubbing down the linoleum. She never did floors in her own home; her housekeeper washed them every Thursday. But here she was in her mother's house—the home of the woman she had hated all her life—down on hands and knees to make the place clean.

"I'll make the beds, Mom. Uncle Emmett can show me." Wendy pulled her arms from the water and wiped off the suds. She recognized her mother's tone and knew that she was getting angry.

"Keep at what you're doing, Wendy," Catty said, and then to Emmett, "Go feed your animals. Then get the bedding. Do we have enough hot water? Wendy and I are going to need baths."

"In a half hour it'll be hot," he answered, stepping carefully where Catty hadn't yet scrubbed as he went toward the back porch.

"Where is mother being waked, Emmett?" Catty asked. "At Loughton's?"

"Loughton's is gone. He died maybe ten years ago. Bob Reese is the new undertaker. Do you know him? He was in school with Father Mike."

"I don't know. I can't remember the old names anymore. She's being waked tonight?"

"Tomorrow. Just the one night. And it's going to be out here, not in town." He took his army jacket off the door hook.

Catty spun around to look directly at her younger brother. "Here? At this house?"

"It was Father Mike's idea, I guess. He made all the plans with O'Connor. Hey, don't look at me like that. No one told me shit." He opened the back door and left the farmhouse, slamming the door behind him.

"I can't believe this! These . . . primitives!" Catty leaned the broom against the table.

"What, Mom? What's going on?"

"The wake!" Catty glanced at Wendy, thought about how to explain. "Your grandmother is being waked in this house. It's an Irish custom; they did it in Europe, and in the United States as well, a long time ago. Everyone comes to the house, and there's food and booze, and everyone gets drunk. It's disgusting and uncivilized and, goddamnit, I'm not going to let them do it." She was shouting, and Wendy, frightened, backed away from her.

"You mean they bring the body here?"

"That's right. In the front parlor. 'She was waked from home'; that's the expression."

"Mommy, I can't sleep here, not with a dead person. It's too gross!"

"Wendy, please! You'll only get yourself into a state," Catty said softly. It was her fault, Catty realized, blowing up and becoming hysterical. "Don't worry about the wake. I'll deal with Michael about it later, after we've finished cleaning these bedrooms."

"I'm not going in there," Wendy announced, indicating the spare room.

"No, I'll take care of it, sweetheart, or Emmett will." She would make Emmett clean the room, Catty decided, have him take the sheets and thin mattress and burn them down by the barns. Get rid of that stench.

"I don't see why we have to do this anyway," Wendy added, turning back to the soaking dishes. "This kitchen is filthy; he's filthy! Ugh!"

"He's your relative."

"I don't care. He's weird. Did you see the way he looked at me, and grinned!" She shook her body as a chill went through her.

"He's had a hard time, honey."

"I've had a hard time! You don't see me going around like that."

"I mean, he had a hard time in Vietnam. He joined when he was seventeen, and was captured. He was very young, and they tortured him, I guess."

"God, I saw this movie, *The Deer Hunter,* and they used to make the prisoners play—"

"I know, Wendy, that's enough."

"I still don't see why we have to stay in this house. I mean, what if, in the middle of the night, he comes busting into my bedroom thinking I'm a Viet Cong or something."

Catty smiled, in spite of herself, at how her daughter could dramatize her life. She was like Maggie that way, making everything some sort of adventure. She knelt down again to scrub and said calmly, "He's your uncle and he isn't crazy, and I don't want you saying anything like that to your brother and sisters, or your friends, or Jeff. . . ."

"Don't worry! I won't say a word to Jeff; he'd never marry me if he knew my relatives were crazy—"

"Wendy!"

"Okay! Okay!" She began to splash the water, then asked, "Was grandmother this . . . weird, too?"

Catty stopped scrubbing for a moment. She kept remembering her mother, flashes of incidents from when she was growing up. Yes, her mother had been strange, menopausal, Catty had finally decided. All that rage and anger could not have been normal. Yet when she found herself getting angry at her own children, Catty saw her mother in herself and that was terrifying.

"No, your grandmother wasn't weird, as you put it. But she had a hard life, and at times she was difficult to live with."

"Is that why you ran away from home?"

"I didn't run away, Wendy. I was out of college, on my own. And I had been married and was a widow. There's a difference, you know." Catty bent forward and began to scrub the old linoleum, throwing all her energy into the job. It was as if she was attempting to wash away all the years of the hatred she had felt toward her mother, wash away all the years she had lived with her own guilt.

# · CHAPTER 6 ·

IT WAS AFTER EIGHT that night before Catty and Wendy finished working. They had cleaned everything from the kitchen to the front parlor and all the second-floor bedrooms. They made the beds and washed out both bathrooms. Catty left the squalor of the top floor to Emmett.

"Why don't you take a bath, Wendy," she suggested finally. They had just finished the beds in what had once been Paddy Jack's bedroom.

"Where am I sleeping? I don't want to sleep by myself, Mom, not if he's going to be in the house." An hour before, Emmett had gone upstairs, not saying good night to either of them, nor offering to help with the housecleaning.

"Where do you want to sleep?" Catty asked. She was tired of making decisions. She had been doing that all day: decisions for herself, the family, the whole farm. All minor, of course, not the important things. Father Mike had already decided those—as he always had, and apparently always would.

"Here!" Wendy answered. "I like this room."

Catty nodded. It was settled. She glanced around Paddy's old room, trying to recall how it had been when the boys were young. She could not remember. They had never wanted her to hang around. It was only with Maggie that she shared some sense of family. All the rest, especially Emmett, were strangers to her.

"Well, go ahead and take a bath. Call me when you're finished. I need to wash as well, and then we both have to get some sleep. I'm exhausted."

"What about something to eat? Can we go into town or something? I saw a McDonald's."

"We don't have a car, honey. And I'm not going to ask Emmett to drive us anywhere in his truck. Don't worry. I'll go look in the kitchen and put something together. Take your bath."

"What about Daddy?"

"I'm telephoning him."

"I want to talk to him."

Catty studied her daughter. Now what was all that about, she wondered. "Okay, I'll wait until you're finished with your bath. You don't have to dress, just put on your robe and come downstairs."

"I'm going to be okay and everything up here, aren't I?" Wendy glanced upstairs, toward the dormer where Emmett was sleeping.

"Lock the bathroom door if you want, honey, but, yes, you'll be all right. I'm just going to be in the kitchen."

Wendy nodded. "Shut the door to the attic, okay? I don't want him looking down."

"Wendy, please!" She started to argue but then realized how strange all this was to her daughter, and just nodded and closed the bedroom door. At the end of the hall, before she went downstairs, she made sure that the attic door was shut. She could hear Emmett upstairs, moving around her old bedroom. She thought of saying something to him, of asking him if he wanted to eat, but the thought of him and Wendy having dinner together was too much, and she just went downstairs to the dark first floor.

She had forgotten to turn on the lights when they went upstairs to clean, and she paused at the bottom of the stairs and groped along the wall till she found the switch. She flipped it on. The light had burned out.

"Damn it!" she whispered into the empty hallway, and then feeling her way as she had done as a child, she worked herself around the banister and down the hallway to the kitchen, using the walls to guide her.

She remembered then an incident from her childhood, a brief moment that had been buried in her subconscious. She could not have been more than ten or eleven, and she had come down at night, barefoot and in pajamas, for a glass of water. When she reached the bottom of the stairs, she had seen an edge of light beneath the kitchen door and heard voices, muffled and unclear. Then her mother had laughed, and Catty had pushed open the door, rubbing the sleep from her eyes as she called out, "Mommy."

Her mother had been across the kitchen, partially in shadows by the back door. Catty had looked up, still sleepy and unfocused, blinded somewhat by the sudden light in the kitchen.

Her mother had come rushing from across the room, hit her across the face, and, spinning her around, slapped her a second time across her bottom and sent her sobbing from the kitchen. Someone had been with her mother. Someone had been standing back in the shadows of the porch, and Catty wondered now, after all these years, who had been with her mother. Who had her mother been trying to hide from the family?

A car turned into the driveway. Headlights swept the lawn and Catty pushed open the door and stepped into the dark kitchen. Perhaps it was someone who had read about her mother's death and, thinking the farm was deserted, was coming to break in. Or friends of Emmett's. Drinking buddies from the Crossroads Tavern. They'd come banging into the place, she was sure, tracking mud on her clean floors.

The car went behind the other side of the house, circled around the apple orchard, and came by the barns. It stopped near the porch, where Father O'Connor had parked his Cadillac. She wondered if it was him again, checking up on her.

Catty moved across the kitchen to sneak a look. She saw a man emerging from the car. In the wintry night he looked gray and shadowy.

"Oh, God," she whispered. She could hear the water running upstairs in the tub, and Wendy's footsteps crossing the bedroom floor. There had been a story recently in the *Chicago Tribune* of a farmhouse near Moline, where a family had been attacked by drifters, the new unemployed, driving their way back and forth across America. . . .

Stop it, she told herself. Where was Joe when she needed him? She was too dependent on him, she thought next, her mind ricocheting from thought to thought. She hadn't been this way when she was younger. Then she hadn't been afraid of anyone.

The car door slammed, echoing sharply on the cold night. The man came up the slight rise toward the house. He hesitated a moment on the bare lawn, then crossed the yard to approach from the front door.

Catty remembered the floodlight her mother had put in after their father left them, and impulsively she reached out and flipped it on, catching the man as he passed the windows. He stopped, startled, and turned his face toward the house.

"Paddy!" she said out loud, surprised at the sight of him. For a moment, it seemed incongruous, his being on the lawn and wearing a blue blazer, jeans, and boots. He looked like a photograph of himself, peering out at the world from the pages of a golf magazine.

She rapped on the window and waved into the night. Then, realizing he couldn't see inside, she flipped off the floodlight and went quickly through the kitchen door and out onto the back porch.

"Paddy!" she called him. "This way."

"Hello, Cat," he said, coming to the porch. He opened the storm door and stepped inside, bent down to kiss his sister on the cheek and hold her close.

Catty squeezed him back, though his embrace surprised her. They had never been an affectionate family and were always awkward at meeting.

"Am I the last to arrive?"

"You're the first. Emmett is here, of course. And Wendy came down with me this morning from Chicago. She's upstairs taking a bath. We've been cleaning all afternoon." She could hear her voice rising with anxiety as she brought him to the kitchen table. The room seemed smaller with Paddy Jack beside her.

"This is where it happened, Cat?" Paddy Jack asked, glancing around the room. He kept studying the kitchen, as if for detail.

"No—by the door of the spare room." Catty nodded toward the spare room. "Emmett found her late on Friday afternoon, according to Michael. He had gone out in the morning to do the chores, then left the farm. He didn't get home, he said, until early evening. She had been dead all day. I haven't asked Emmett about any of it. He's been . . ." She would have said drunk but did not want to start complaining, and said instead, " . . . in pretty bad shape since I got home this afternoon. I telephoned the local police, or rather Joe did. But Joe won't tell me anything. I guess it was pretty gruesome."

She slipped into one of the kitchen chairs, exhausted from the housecleaning and emotional strain. She looked a mess, she realized, and wished she had been able to clean up before her brother arrived.

"There's room here, Paddy, if you want to stay. The whole house was closed off and unheated; they couldn't afford the oil bills. Wendy and I put it back together this afternoon." She could hear herself racing on.

"I'll stay, Catty." Paddy Jack smiled. "It's okay."

"Thank you. I mean, I know it's silly and everything, but Emmett . . . he's so strange. He hardly talks. I mean, he just goes around in this goddamn trance or something, and—"

"Easy, Cat . . ." Paddy Jack whispered, going to her. Taking her gently by the shoulders, he began to massage the tight muscles of her back and neck. "I can handle some things, okay? What do you need done?"

Catty blew her nose, then wiped the tears off her face. "I'm sorry, but I just feel rotten. Coming home like this . . ." She looked up at her brother. How much did Paddy Jack know about her hatred for this farm, their mother? "Look," she said, "if you can handle Michael, that would be enough. I mean, he wants to have an Irish wake."

"An Irish wake!" Paddy Jack grinned. "I wouldn't have thought Mike had that much imagination."

"Paddy! This isn't the nineteen-twenties. No one is waked at home. He's doing it for his own purposes, I'm sure." Upset again at the whole idea, she looked up at Paddy Jack. He was built like their father, she saw. With age, he resembled him more and more.

"What does Maggie think about all this?"

"She doesn't know. She's flying into Chicago. Joe is picking her up about midday and they're driving down with the children."

"Maggie's the only one who can deal with Mike," Paddy Jack said decisively. "Besides, it should be up to her. She was closest to Mom, anyway."

"You don't care?"

Paddy Jack shook his head, not looking at her.

He seemed remote, detached, Catty thought, as if he were less than an in-law.

"She's your mother, too, Paddy."

"Hey, Catty, easy, okay?" He stepped closer to her, searched her face to see what was really troubling her. "You can't blame yourself," he said softly.

"I am not blaming myself!" She chopped off the words.

"Yes, you are. You're blaming yourself for not seeing Mom before she died. Blaming yourself for not having it out with her, for not getting a chance to explain yourself."

"There was nothing to explain. You know. I know. Everyone knows. We never got along and I don't know why. She just hated me, that's all." Catty shrugged, accepting her fate.

"I wasn't her favorite either, Catty. It was always Michael—"

"No, Paddy! She was different with me," Catty interrupted. "She had it in for me."

Now the tears came. As if a deep lake of pain and resentment hidden in some cavern of her heart had finally found passage to the surface.

Paddy Jack held her, crushing her face against his heavy jacket, letting her cry herself out. She clung to him.

Crying, and aware that she could not stop, Catty was startled by the violence of her own reaction and thankful that it had happened just with Paddy. Thank God she had not lost control in front of her children. It would frighten them to see their mother so helpless.

She pulled herself from his arms and began to wipe away the tears. She nodded, indicating that she was okay, and he let his arms drop. Catty went to the sink and turned on the cold water; she bathed her eyes, then took a clean kitchen towel to dry her face.

"Thank you. I'm sorry about this. I think I'm just exhausted."

"It's okay, Cat. We're all going to get battered this weekend. You lose a parent, and suddenly you realize that you're vulnerable, too.

Parents are always the buffer. Our hedge against death. Well, we've lost them both now, Cat."

"I didn't feel anything about Dad. I can barely remember him, really. He wasn't that much a part of my growing up here."

"I missed him. It was a lot harder farming, taking care of this place after he went back to Ireland. All I remember from being a kid is the goddamn work."

"Maggie and Emmett were lucky. Mom was a lot nicer, I think, when they were growing up."

"How is Maggie going to take this?"

Catty shook her head, sighed. "We talked briefly on Saturday. She was very upset. She's been having a tough time of it lately."

"She seemed okay when I saw her last August. What is it—the job?"

"No, it's not the paper," Catty answered. "She's involved with someone over there. She wouldn't say, but I think he's married."

"Did Mom know? God, that would have killed her."

"No, I know Maggie wouldn't say anything to Mom."

"Who is he?"

"I think it's the American ambassador. I guess that from reading over her letters. She mentioned him very early, when she first arrived, about what a wonderful man he was, and then, nothing. Never again. Then she started writing about some nameless man, and how 'difficult' it was."

"That poor kid. She's really snake-bit when it comes to guys." He stopped a moment, thinking, and then asked, "Does she ever say anything about McGraff?"

"Never."

"What went wrong with those two anyway?"

"Oh, Maggie was just too young. It was like me and Sal, except not so tragic."

Paddy smiled, remembering, then said, "When she left him and came on the tour with me that summer, when was it . . . seventy-four?"

"Seventy-three."

"That's right. Anyway, we had a hell of a good time, you know, the two of us," he said.

Catty slid down across from Paddy Jack at the kitchen table and asked, "Did she ever tell you why she left him?"

Paddy Jack shook his head. "Never! She wouldn't let me talk about him, or what had happened. Mike must know. I mean, he got the annulment for her."

"That was his idea, not Maggie's. She didn't care, but he couldn't stand the thought of having a divorced sister."

"I'm sure he did it for Mom."

"Mom liked McGraff, Maggie said. That's all she ever said about it when she called and told me. She was worried about what Mom would say."

"Mom liked him because he was Irish."

"Yes, but he was a left-hander. They never counted as Irish with mother."

"Like Joe."

Catty smiled. "First I marry a wop, then an Orangeman." She was amused at her own rebellion. "No wonder she hated me."

"She didn't hate you," Paddy said softly. "When I saw her last summer, I told her I had seen you."

Catty raised her head, finding that she was tense waiting to hear what her mother had said.

"She asked about the kids. Who they looked like. And she asked about you," he went on, looking directly at Catty. "She wanted to know how you were. She wanted to know what you looked like."

"Me? She never cared what I looked like. My God, she never once said I was pretty or anything."

"Oh, you know how she was. None of us ever got a word of praise. But I had this photo—remember the one Joe took on your back lawn? The two of us? I showed her that."

"And?"

"She looked at it for a while. She couldn't see it clearly, I guess, because she got up, walked over to the windows and studied it, and then asked if she could keep it. And I said sure, of course.

"But she still hadn't said anything. So finally I asked, 'Well, what do you think, Mom? How does Catty look?' And she just tucked the photo away in the pocket of that old smock she always wore and said, very cool, very detached, 'She took after me, now didn't she? I wasn't wrong about that.' She said it as if she were talking to herself, not me."

"What do you think she meant by that?"

"That you were a good-looking woman. You've seen pictures of Mom when she was young. She was beautiful."

Catty shook her head and said thoughtfully, "No, that wasn't it. She meant something else."

"Like what?"

Catty shrugged. "I don't know. I never could figure her out." She stood and went toward the door, remembering that she hadn't telephoned Joe. There was a small mirror on the open shelf of the cupboard, one Emmett had used for shaving, and Catty caught her profile and stood staring at it for a moment. "She didn't resent my looks. I think she took a lot of satisfaction in having a good-looking family. No, she was referring to something else about me."

"And you have no idea what?"

Catty shook her head. Then softly, as if she did not want Wendy to hear, she said, "Remember the time when I was in high school and wrote you for money?"

Paddy Jack shook his head.

"It was the senior prom at Wisdom and I wanted to go with Sal, of course, but Mother said no. She wasn't having anything to do with Sal from the moment she laid eyes on him.

"But I was determined to go. So I wrote and asked you for money, so I could buy a dress anyway. And that night, I sneaked out of the house, met Sal on the road. I didn't care what might happen. I just had to go to that silly dance.

"Well, Mom came down to school and got me. I was dancing with Sal and she just stormed onto the gym floor—in front of everyone, teachers, all the kids—and pulled me away from Sal. Without saying one word, she dragged me from the gym and back to the farm." Catty was silent for a moment, remembering how mortified she had been. "When I ran off with Sal, I thought I was getting away from her." She shrugged.

"She was afraid of losing you, too, Catty. I had left the farm at nineteen, and Michael was gone. She was there with the twins. She didn't want you to get involved with anyone, let alone Sal."

"No." Catty shook her head. "It goes back farther than that. I remember when Dad left for Ireland, that's when it started."

"Well, she'd lost him and here she was alone on this farm, being driven crazy by a houseful of kids," Paddy argued.

"She wasn't mean to you boys. Only me. I remember that. Even O'Connor realized that. Whenever he was out here, he'd try to make up to me, to explain away mother's resentment, anger. He kept telling me that mother would be all right, once she had a chance to rest."

"None of us had a chance to rest on this place. Mom especially."

"We had no money. But it did get easier after you started to send money home. But for years I could never buy any clothes. Remember how O'Connor would come into this kitchen with a box of old stuff from the Saint Vincent DePaul Society? God! I'll never forget the time in sixth grade when Johnny Maguire passed that note around class about how I was wearing his sister's old dress." Catty shook her head, weary from all her sad memories.

"It's over, Catty," Paddy answered. Her recollections had stunned him. He remembered only the hard work of the farm, not his mother's resentment. He had escaped from the work.

Catty nodded, agreeing. "I've got to telephone Joe. He'll be worried." She started through the kitchen door.

"Catty?" Paddy asked. "You don't have any idea why she was so hard on you, do you?"

"No. I don't know why she never liked me."

"It was because you were so much like her. The same strong will; your independence. She couldn't take it."

Catty sat quietly a moment, thinking of what her brother had said, then she answered, "I was never as strong as Mom. She always got her way."

"Yes, but you won at the end."

"I didn't win, Paddy. I ran away." And then she pushed open the kitchen door and went down the dark hall to the phone.

# · CHAPTER 7 ·

"Aunt Maggie . . . ?"

"Yes, sweetheart?" Maggie did not turn her head, but lifted her chin to indicate to Sara that she was listening. Since they had met her at O'Hare Airport, the children had been surprisingly quiet. Joe must have lectured them in advance, Maggie guessed, about behaving on the drive to Gatesburg.

"What was Grandma like?" Sara leaned forward, folded her arms across the back of the front seat, and put her head down. From the flatbed of the station wagon, Clare spoke up. "Sara! Don't bother Aunt Maggie."

"She's not bothering me, Clare," Maggie answered, and turned sideways in the seat so she could look directly at the seven-year-old. She spotted Joe glancing at her, frowning. What, she wondered, had Catty told him about their mother? How much did they know? Children had a way of sensing family secrets. She would have to be careful of the traps they'd lay.

"Well, let's see." She smiled at Sara. The girl had her father's gray eyes, and they made her seem older and knowledgeable. She was built like her father, too: small and compact, like a tiny fireplug. "Your grandmother taught me how to ride a pony."

"You had a pony?" the three children responded, in unison.

Maggie nodded. She had caught their attention.

"His name was Skipper."

"Skipper!" Sara sat up, exclaiming. A smile of delight swept away her serious expression. "Oh, Daddy! Aunt Maggie had a pony named Skipper," she repeated for her father. "Why can't we have a pony?"

From the flatbed of the station wagon, the other two—Clare and Timmy, the four-year-old—had tumbled forward to crowd the backseat.

"Was it Mommy's pony, too?" Clare wanted to know.

"No. Skipper was mine—and Emmett's. Your mother never wanted a pony."

"I want one!" Sara said at once.

"I know, darling, but you live in the city, not on a farm." Maggie reached out and touched the young child's cheek. It was as soft as a flower petal.

"Is he still there? Can we ride him?" Sara was shouting, and over their voices Joe demanded silence.

"Let Aunt Maggie tell the story, okay, everyone?" He glanced across at her, smiling, encouraging her to continue.

The children quieted down and Maggie said quickly, "Skipper has been dead for years, I'm afraid. He got to be a very old pony. Emmett has a horse, Mekong. But I'm afraid he's too wild for you. And besides, it's the middle of winter. We can't go riding in weather like this."

"Yes, we can," Sara said at once. "It's not snowing or anything. And horses have fur."

"Why didn't Mommy have a pony?" Clare asked next, sensing discrimination.

"You know Mommy doesn't like animals, Clare," Joe interjected.

"Your mother was away at college when Emmett and I had Skipper," Maggie said, not wanting the young girl to think something was wrong.

"Where did you get him?" Sara wanted to know. She leaned closer to Maggie, to get a better position for her question.

"At a farm auction, when Emmett and I were just Clare's age. We paid for him ourselves with the money we made raising rabbits."

"You had rabbits, too!" Sara cried, near tears at the thought of all she was missing.

Maggie went on to tell the children how they had raised rabbits, selling them at farmer's markets and saving money to buy the pony. She had not thought of the rabbits in years, or of the shed they had built behind the chicken coop.

"One year," she began, "there was a late winter ice storm. I think I was your age, Sara; it was before we had Skipper. Anyway, we must have had two feet of snow, and we lost the electricity.

"There were baby rabbits out in the shed, being kept warm by a small electric heater, so we had to move them up to the house. We must have had fifty bunnies, all less than a few weeks old. Your grandmother turned on the gas stove—that was the only way we could keep them warm—and we put the rabbits in covered boxes in front of the open oven doors." Maggie glanced into the backseat at the children. They were all silent, eyes bulging.

"After the others were asleep, I went downstairs again to make sure that the bunnies were okay." She looked at Sara and Timmy and smiled, knowing that this was something they, too, would do. "And, well, I forgot to close the kitchen door when I went back upstairs. Sometime during the night the sound of tapping woke me up. At least I thought it was tapping, on the bare floor of my bedroom."

Maggie paused, glancing at Timmy. The child was frightened, holding his breath. She shouldn't have made the story sound scary. She had forgotten how children worried about the night sounds. She went on quickly.

"Well, your grandmother woke as well. She, too, had heard the tapping. We still didn't have electric lights, but she had lit a candle and was coming down the hallway."

"The rabbits!" Clare said, solving the mystery.

"Clare!" Her father spoke up. "Would you please let your aunt tell the story?"

"Clare's right," Maggie went on. "The rabbits had all gotten out of the boxes and came upstairs to say hello! They ran into every room, and in all the open closets. Everyplace!"

"Did you get spanked?" Timmy asked, worried again.

"No, darling, I didn't." Maggie leaned forward and kissed the child on the forehead.

"Well, if I had let those rabbits out, Mommy would have had my hide," Clare announced. "You just do one thing wrong around our house and it's your life."

Joe glanced in the rearview mirror, started to say something, and then contained himself.

"It took us almost all night to find the rabbits and catch them again," Maggie went on, wanting to change the subject. "Your grandma said, 'No more rabbits in the house. Never again.' "

"Mommy said grandmother was a despot."

"Clare, that's enough! Your mother said nothing of the kind."

"Yes she did! She said it to you on Sunday. I heard you!" She was shouting at her father from the backseat. "You were in your bedroom, and I happened to be passing by and—"

"You were listening at our door again."

"I wasn't!"

"Yes she was, I saw her," Sara spoke up.

"I was not!" Clare reached over, trying to hit her little sister.

"That's enough!" Maggie turned completely around and knelt on the front seat. Her muscles ached from the fatigue of the long journey.

"All right, Clare." Maggie lowered her voice and spoke reasonably, treating the teenager as an adult. "That's enough, all right?"

"I didn't do—"

"I know. But for the moment, please be quiet. Everyone is very upset and tired from the car ride. And you all miss your mother. We'll be at the farm soon. Let's all try to be nice, okay? Do you want to play a car game?"

"No!" they all answered.

"Fine!" Maggie smiled. "At least we can agree on something."

"Did you see any wild animals in Africa?" Timmy asked in the new silence. His chin was resting on the front seat.

"Yes, I did, honey." That was a safe topic, Maggie thought. "At night I can hear lions roaring."

"You can?" Again in unison.

"There is a small zoo near where I live, and late at night, when Addis Ababa is very quiet, I can hear them roar. They wake me, sometimes."

She remembered her first night in Addis, waking at the sound of the lions, unsure of what the roaring was. She had been staying at the Ethiopia Hotel then, and she had awakened, alone in the strange room, far from home. Overwhelmed, she had begun to cry, hiding her head deep under the blanket, her face pressed against the pillows, afraid she would be heard.

"Did you see anyone get eaten by a lion?" Timmy asked.

"Oh, no, not eaten. They're all locked up."

"Like Brookfield Zoo. We have lions at Brookfield Zoo," Sara added.

"Which way, Maggie?" Joe asked, slowing the car.

Maggie looked ahead. They were approaching a stoplight. "Go straight," she instructed. "There are two ways, actually, but straight ahead is shorter." But she was no longer sure. New roads had been built since she had lived at home. It had happened gradually, over time, and coming home on one of her vacations, she had realized that the whole area had changed. Progress, she thought, feeling cheated.

"This was all farms once," she said, pointing to the rows of simple white houses, the tiny lawns and ribbons of black asphalt. "This was pasture land with cows and fields of wheat and corn. It was real country." She kept talking, as if to conjure up the past for the children.

"It looks tacky," Clare commented.

"It is, darling."

"I don't like it."

"You don't like anything," Sara added.

"I don't like you, that's for sure."

"Enough!" Joe ordered. "We're almost to the farm, and we're not going to arrive fighting. Are we?"

Maggie noticed that when pushed, Joe could be decisive. He was much firmer than Catty with the children.

"Your mother telephoned last night," Joe went on, including Maggie in this news. "Your grandmother is being waked at home."

"What does that mean?" Clare asked, sensing trouble.

"Whose idea was that?" Maggie asked, speaking softly.

"Father Mike's, I understand." And then to the children, "That means your grandmother's body will be on view at the farm. Her friends, and family, all of us, will pay our respects there. We won't have to go to a funeral home to say good-bye to your grandmother."

He was trying, Maggie realized, to soften the impact, to prepare the children—to prepare all of them. What a sweet man he is, Maggie thought. Catty didn't realize what she had in Joe.

He had begun to lose his fine, sandy hair, she noticed. She could see a shine on his pale forehead. And he was putting on weight. When she had first met him, after Wendy and Clare were born and they had moved from Texas to Illinois, he had been handsome, in the same rough, unkempt way as Jack McGraff. She wondered if Jack, too, would lose his looks, put on weight. No, she doubted that. Jack was too intense. He ate away his fat with nervous energy. But Joe was too easygoing, too much a nice guy.

"I'm not staying in any house with a dead body," Clare declared.

"I'm scared, Daddy, of being . . ." Timmy started to say, then lost control and burst into tears.

"Mag . . . ?" Joe began, but Maggie had already reached back and lifted Timmy up into the front seat. The small child was sobbing, trembling in her arms, and Maggie kissed his thick red hair, rocking him gently in her embrace.

"It's okay, Timmy. We're almost home. And your mother is there. You don't want to be crying when you see your mother, do you?" She raised his tiny face and smiled down at the little boy. Timmy shook his head, unable to speak, and she hugged him closely.

At that moment, she wanted a child of her own. She needed to get married, she thought, feeling more certain of it at that moment than she had ever been in her life. She wondered what had set it off. Was it Kenneth's offer of marriage? Or something even more obvious: her mother's death. Now she was truly on her own, without parents, without anyone.

"We're here," she said softly to Joe. They had crested a small hill, begun to descend. "On the right. See the mailbox?" She felt the car slowing beneath her and she took a deep breath, feeling her own tension building. Like the children, she was frightened. She bent her face into Timmy's thick mop of hair and let herself cry as the car moved slowly up the drive. She was home. Home for her mother's wake and funeral.

# · CHAPTER 8 ·

EMMETT WAS WAITING FOR Maggie. He stood at the front windows watching as Joe Duffy pulled into the circular drive. There was already a line of cars parked on the hard ground of the lawn. It upset him to have so many people around, so much noise. It made him feel out of place and not wanted. For so long he and his mother had been living alone, with just Maggie or Michael or Paddy Jack coming home for a few days, then flying off again, leaving them in the emptiness of the big house. Now all the noise bothered him, all the talking.

Catty bothered him the most. She never stopped talking, giving him orders. No one gave him orders, not anymore, not since the army. His hands began to shake thinking about her, and he jammed them into the pockets of his work jeans.

He shouldn't think about Catty, he knew. Nor about his mother. It would only cause a headache and send him into another rage. Still, he had to talk to Maggie when she arrived, make her believe him. Maggie was the only one who would understand, who would care.

Catty and Wendy had rushed outside to meet Joe and the family. Now they were coming back across the lawn, and Emmett stepped away from the windows, hid behind the heavy curtains. He did not want Maggie to see him watching. She would come into the house, he knew, and go straight to the front parlor, straight to the body of their mother.

He had only gone into the parlor once, the night before. It had seemed safe then, surrounded by his brothers. Now he was afraid to face his mother, laid out in the open casket. It would be better with Maggie. She had a way of always making things seem right, of solving his problems.

The house was different, Maggie felt, stepping through the door. Something was wrong, and it frightened her. She took a deep breath, braced herself. This was what she had feared: seeing her mother dead. Knowing she was gone from her.

"What is this?" Timmy asked, looking into the parlor. The room was filled with folding chairs facing the front. "There's a woman sleeping, Mom," Timmy said, spotting the casket.

Catty glanced at her husband, wondering what he had told the children. "Honey, that's your grandmother," she said.

Joe hoisted the little boy into his arms. "Come on, Timmy. Do you want something to drink?"

"I'm hungry."

"Well, we'll get something to eat then."

"Take the girls, too, Joe," Catty said, nodding at her daughters. When she and Maggie were alone, she guided her sister to the casket in the front parlor.

"Mommy looks at peace, doesn't she, Catty?" Maggie could feel tears on her cheeks and she reached out and slipped her arm into Catty's.

"Yes, she does." Catty pulled her sister closer and wrapped her arm around Maggie's waist.

Standing together, they did not look like sisters. Maggie was taller and thinner, more dramatic looking, with her hot-fudge–brown eyes and an angle to her looks. Catty seemed softer, rounder. She had the presence of a woman with family responsibilities. Yet she did not look like the mother of teenage daughters. Her age was noticeable only in the shadow of her dark brown eyes.

"I shouldn't have left her, Catty. I shouldn't have gone off to Africa."

"Maggie, you can't blame yourself." She hugged her sister as if she were her daughter. "It was an accident. Even if you were here, it might still have happened."

Maggie was sobbing now, her body shaking against her sister's. Then she pulled away, moved to kneel at the prie-dieu placed before the casket. Catty let her go, stepped back, and turned away. Maggie needed to be alone, Catty realized, and she had to see about her own family, get them fed and catch up with what had happened in their lives since she had left Chicago.

Maggie could not pray, could not find any words to offer God. She kept staring at her mother, searching the tiny, innocent-looking face, looking for, she realized, the breath of life, some suggestion that her mother was just asleep, waiting to be wakened, to be told it was time to get supper started.

Dear God, please take care of Mommy . . . She took care of me all those years. Helped me. Listened to me. Loved me always . . . Oh, why did you take her from me?

Mommy, I'm so sorry. I love you. I'll miss you. Why did you pick up that gun? To tidy up? To clear the table off? You poor sweet thing. . . .

Maggie bent her head and buried it in her palms. Her face was burning. In the cool room she was aflame with fever. She was sick, she realized. Her body was reacting to the long flight, the changing climates, her exhaustion. She needed some sleep. She needed to rest, or she wouldn't make it through the next few days.

She stared for a few more minutes at the open casket, unable to concentrate, too weak to kneel, too dizzy to stand, and tried to gather her strength. She could no longer cry. Her body was numb.

Well, Mom, she thought, what should I do? I don't have you to talk to, to share news with, to visit. I'm sorry that I went so far away. It was wrong. But I had to get out of Washington. I should have come here, I know. Emmett wasn't taking care of you. I could see that in September. He just wasn't able. I asked Michael to look after you, and he said he would. He said he'd visit and see that you were okay. I knew you were failing, but I didn't want to stay here, in Jack's state. I needed to make it on my own. I needed to make something of myself.

"Maggie?" Emmett said softly. He had come quietly up behind her, stood a few feet away from the kneeler.

"Oh, Emmett!" Maggie stood and rushed to her twin, wrapped her arms tightly around him, and let his strength hold her.

"I'm sorry, Maggie." He was in tears, though he had not cried before, not since finding the body. "I left the rifle on the table . . . I forgot it was loaded." He had thought through exactly what he was going to say, knowing that, of all the family, it was Maggie he had to convince.

"It's not your fault," she said. "It's not anyone's fault." Emmett needed to hear that, she knew; she needed to hear it herself.

He began to talk, compulsively, needing to tell someone in the family what had happened. He spoke in broken half sentences, gulping for words and breath. He talked for a long time. But he did not tell her, nor had he told the police, how he had crouched all morning in the corner of the kitchen, trembling on the cold floor beneath the sink, having lost control of his hands and feet and bowels.

Nor did he tell her how his shotgun blast had broken out the panes of glass in the window over the sink. How he had cleaned himself up toward noon, then carefully fixed the window before finally calling the police to tell them his mother was dead in the spare room off the kitchen.

"I left the place about eight . . . she was okay, you know . . . back in bed as usual . . . I thought I might hunt for a couple of hours over at

Barley's, and then I did the chores . . . I didn't come back up to the house till nearly three. . . ."

Maggie kept shaking her head, kept trying to hold back her tears. She bit her lower lip to keep from asking: Why did you leave her alone so long? Why didn't you look in on her before doing the chores? Why didn't you take better care of our mother?

"It was just a stupid accident, Emmett. It's not anyone's fault." She took his hand and walked him away from the casket, as if just the proximity of the body was troubling him. They sat down on the parlor's old formal sofa, which had been pushed against the back wall to make room for the folding chairs borrowed from Saint Patrick's.

"I'm sorry, Mag," he whispered, crying.

"We're all sorry, Emmett." She took her twin into her arms again and let him cry against her shoulder. Needing to be strong for him, Maggie forgot her own pain and concentrated on his. She remembered how he had been after Vietnam when he had come back to the farm, shattered from his imprisonment. He had been unable to sleep then and kept having nightmares. She remembered that first weekend on the farm when she had brought Jack home to meet her twin brother.

She had tried then to get Emmett into therapy, but their mother had been against it. "He needs rest, that's all," her mother had said, "the peace and quiet of this place. I'll take care of him myself." Even Michael couldn't talk their mother into having Emmett see a doctor. She had told them both, "What good are those people? They only fool around with your head until you're really crazy."

Emmett pulled away from Maggie to wipe the tears off his face and blow his nose. When the funeral was over, she decided, she'd find Emmett a doctor. And she'd pay for it, if the V.A. wouldn't.

"Do you want anything to eat, Emmett?" she asked, as if a meal might ease his haggard look.

He shook his head, staring at the bare hardwood floor.

He was not like his brothers, Maggie thought. He did not have Michael's massive chest, or Paddy's hawkish profile. Emmett was different—more like their mother, she suspected, when she was young. He belonged to another age, a gentler time.

"I don't want to leave the farm, Mag. They're going to want me to, I know. Mike will—"

"It's okay, Emmett. Don't worry." She took his hands in hers and squeezed, tried to stop his fingers from trembling. "I won't let them do anything. Promise." She smiled, lifted his chin so he had to look at her and know she meant what she said. It had been that way since they were children in grade school. She was the one who fought his battles.

"I don't have any money," he whispered, telling her his secret. "We've been broke all winter."

"Emmett, why didn't you write me? I asked you in September. Remember? I wanted to know then if you needed help." She could feel herself becoming angry and she stopped talking.

He looked away again, ashamed.

"I didn't want you to know. I mean, I thought if Father Mike or O'Connor knew, they'd want to sell the farm and put Mom someplace, and I'd have to . . ." He hung his head.

Maggie reached over and rubbed his neck, the tight muscles of his shoulders. "No one is going to sell this farm or send you away. It's yours, and mine, all of ours. Now don't worry yourself, Emmett." She spoke confidently, trying to pick up his spirits. It was her role in the family, she knew. The cheerleader, always rallying the family and carrying everyone along when they were down. That was one reason she said responded to Kenneth Graves: he was ready to take care of her.

Emmett nodded reluctantly, then asked, still with an edge of worry in his voice, "Tonight, at the wake, you'll stay with me, okay? I mean, I don't know all these people, and they're going to start asking me questions about what happened. I can't get into that. I mean, I'm not going to hang around if they start doing that." His voice rose alarmingly.

Maggie took his hands again, kept shaking her head to calm him.

"Shhh, Emmett," she whispered, "I'll stay with you, I promise. No one is going to get you alone." She stood up decisively. "Now, let's get something to eat."

She led the way down the hallway and he followed, as if they were children again. But as they neared the kitchen, he stopped.

"Maggie?"

"Yes?"

"It's Catty. She's been on me since she got home . . . giving me orders . . . bossing me around."

"She's upset, Emmett. Please don't mind her. This is very hard on her, coming home after all these years."

"I didn't ask her here. She could have stayed away for all I care—for all she cared about Mom."

Maggie sighed, weary of negotiating with him, with all the children. "Please, Emmett," she asked, "try to calm down, okay? I'll talk to Catty. Promise." She smiled, then turned and kept walking toward the kitchen.

Emmett took her arm, stopped her. "Okay," he whispered. "But if she keeps at me, I'll kill her. I swear to God I will."

# · CHAPTER 9 ·

WHO ON EARTH WERE all these people, Catty wondered, moving through the press of strangers. She knew the answer, of course. They were old Gatesburg friends of her mother, and relatives down from Chicago. Her relatives, though she had never known them in her life. Shanty Irish, she thought: cops and firemen, insurance salesmen and bartenders. The men were short and heavy, with thick necks, red faces, and loud voices. The women were overweight and badly dressed.

Seeing them depressed Catty; she could so easily have been one of them. Only being raised in the country, away from Chicago's Irish ghetto, had saved her. Maybe she would have escaped anyway, but most likely she'd have married some boy from the old neighborhood, another mick.

Catty glanced into the parlor. Emmett was there. And Maggie. Catty watched the mourners' ritual for a moment. They would come into the crowded room, kneel at the casket for a prayer, and then turn around to Maggie and say hello. They looked teary-eyed, offering condolence, and then they'd relate some incident they remembered about Caitlin DeLacy: the day she did such-and-such, or said some-thing-or-other. Already that evening Catty had heard a half-dozen stories of when her parents had first arrived in Chicago from Ireland. "They went to stay with Paddy Keane, God rest his soul, over on Loomis. He was a cousin of yours, you know." Then they'd glance back at the body and add, "Ah, your mother would have loved this, Catty, being laid out at home. It was mighty thoughtful of the bishop."

Catty had stopped listening. She watched Maggie, saw how grace-fully her sister paid attention to each of the relatives and neighboring farmers who had come out in the cold that night, all dressed up for the wake.

Maggie was good at it, Catty saw. But it wasn't fair to make her carry the burden all evening. Catty knew she ought to take her turn, go sit there in the first row, as one of the bereaved children, yet she couldn't. Being that close to the body upset her. Besides, Michael was in the front parlor, standing off to one side, looking imperial in his purple cassock. He, too, she thought, had dressed up for the occasion.

Catty glanced around for Paddy Jack. Down the hallway, men with drinks were coming out of the kitchen. The relatives had brought liquor with them and the partying had begun. It would start here and continue later at the Holiday Inn. It was as if they were away for a weekend football game instead of a funeral. Well, that was what Michael had wanted, Catty thought spitefully.

She turned into the living room to find her children. They were sitting on a padded bench before the fire, whispering to each other. They felt strange among the family, Catty realized, and that made her feel better. She didn't want her own to be like these relatives. She went to them at once, pushing past Paddy Jack, who was holding court, she saw, like the star that he was.

The crowd was tight around Paddy, and he was making small talk, reassuring his old neighbors that he hadn't turned snob. One of them, Doug Bauer, asked: "Is it true Tom Harris gave you your first set of clubs? That's what he tells everyone in town."

"I think he did. It was an old set of Wilson irons." Paddy Jack paused and winked, then added, "But I wasn't going out with his daughter then."

"Did you hear she's back at the club, Paddy?"

His head jerked up.

"Harris had a stroke last fall. He's okay—the bastard's too mean to die—but he can't run the country club anymore. Vanessa's home."

"Vanessa's in Gatesburg?" Paddy Jack asked quickly.

Several of the men nodded, then said together, anxious to tell him, "She's divorced now."

"I didn't know," he whispered. The men kept talking but he wasn't listening. He was remembering Vanessa and that summer long ago. That summer when she would come running barefoot out onto the golf course and meet him late on a warm summer evening as he finished playing the back nine. It was the year when they both were eighteen, and in love.

"She's still a looker," someone was saying. "How long since you've seen her, Paddy Jack?"

Paddy shook his head. "I haven't seen Van since I first went away on the tour."

"Well, now's your chance," one of men said, nodding toward the front door. Paddy Jack waited a moment, not sure what the man meant, then he glanced around.

Though there was a knot of people at the door, Vanessa Harris was the only one he saw. It had been twenty years since he had last seen her, but Paddy Jack knew her at once. However many years went by, he would always know Vanessa.

She was bundled up in a long fur coat, with the thick collar pulled up to frame her blond hair, her pale face. As she loosened the belt she was scanning the crowded room, looking for a familiar face. He watched her eyes pass over the room, circling, coming toward him, and he moved away from the crowd, stepped clear, and waited until her eyes found him.

She smiled, a little shyly. He knew just how much courage this had taken, her coming to pay her respects knowing he would be here.

He walked over and said casually, as he often had when they were teenagers, "I'll race you to the clubhouse. Loser buys the Cokes."

"Hello, Jack," she whispered. Her eyes were shiny with tears. She held out her hand and he stepped forward, took her into a soft embrace, whispering, "Hello, Van."

"I'm sorry, Jack . . . about your loss . . ."

He pulled back, still holding her by her arms, and said, "Thank you for coming. I just heard a minute ago that you were in town."

"Dad had a stroke in the fall. I came back, and"—she shrugged—"I'm divorced and free these days." She forced a smile.

"I'm sorry to hear that."

She nodded. "It was one of those midlife crises, I'm afraid. We have two children, both of them in college, and well . . ." She tossed back her head, clearing her blond hair from her neck.

"You look wonderful," he said, wanting her to know that she was still beautiful to him.

"Oh, Jack." She blushed and looked off. "I don't think so." Then she glanced back at him and asked directly, "What about you? How have you been? I've been watching you on television all these years, following your career. Oh, Jack, you're so wonderful!" She touched his arm, stepped close. "You did it, Jack. Just as you said you would. I was so proud when you won the Open. I must have cried all afternoon. My husband couldn't understand. . . ."

She laughed. "Remember how you used to play those imaginary matches? 'Hogan goes six under . . . Can DeLacey birdie the final hole and catch the Iron Man?' " They both laughed, remembering how he had looked striding down the fairway, pretending he was both players as well as the television announcer, keeping up a running commentary. And smiling his cocky, brilliant grin after he had hit a perfect wood into the green. Vanessa remembered seeing the ball against the pale sky, sailing to the green, touching softly, then rolling across the terrain contour toward the pin. As if it had eyes, he'd always said. As if it had eyes.

"Oh, Jack," she sighed, as if from a lifetime of regret. "I'm sorry.

I'm so sorry. We had such dreams." She looked up at him sadly. "That's why I was so proud of you. You showed them, didn't you? Showed us all."

"I was lucky, Van. I got onto the tour at a good time. I don't think I could make it today."

She shook her head. "No, you weren't lucky. Don't take anything away from yourself. You always knew what you wanted, and you got it."

"I didn't get everything I wanted," he added.

She nodded, kept her eyes on him as she replied, "We were kids then, Jack; we—I—didn't control my life. My father . . . You can't hold that against me."

"I don't. I might hold it against your father, of course. Except the Irish are such a forgiving race." He smiled, and Vanessa saw his eyes flash.

"Are you off to California next?" she asked to change the subject.

"No. I'm skipping San Diego. Emmett is going to need help around here for a few weeks. And"—he touched her shyly on the arm—"if you have time, I'd stop by the club. We could get a chance to catch up."

Vanessa nodded, agreeing.

Bishop DeLacey rocked back on his heels and scanned the front parlor, looking over the heads of the two men he was talking with, the mayor and the county supervisor. He wanted to see if anyone important had arrived within the last half hour, anyone he should make a point of greeting.

He spotted Paddy Jack standing in the doorway of the room talking with a woman. She looked familiar, but he couldn't place her face, then they walked away, toward the kitchen. Catty hadn't yet come to kneel and say a prayer. And she wouldn't, he realized with a certain admiration. He was damn lucky she was even there. It would have looked bad if she hadn't come home for the funeral. Everyone would have been asking questions. She had brought her kids, too, and that was good. They were cute Irish children, and they added a little life, he thought, to the wake.

He would have to say a few prayers soon. It was expected. Well, he would make it short. What with all the drinking, the relatives wouldn't be up for much praying. And they'd all be at church in the morning anyway. Time enough for prayers then.

There was a delegation of the Blue and Whites coming from Chicago, another from Saint Louis. The church would be full. And there'd be television coverage. He'd be able to talk about the family with all of them in the front pew—the strength of the Irish, he'd say, was in large families, and he could draw a moral from that about the Irish struggle and the Blue and Whites. It would work nicely, he thought.

"Excuse me, gentlemen," Bishop DeLacey said softly, "I have to have a word with the family." He nodded to the local officials and then stepped over to his younger sister and said, "I think it's time we said a few prayers."

Maggie glanced at Emmett as if asking for agreement, but her twin was staring down at the floor.

"I'll make it brief," the priest assured her. "You know Mom wasn't one for lengthy prayers." He smiled as he spoke, realizing the relatives sitting nearby were listening.

"She was just like Tommy McManus, Bishop," one of the aunts said. "Did your mother ever tell you about Tommy? He was from our place back home, from Tourmakeady."

"I believe she did, Aunt Peggy." The bishop straightened up, smiling. "He was the postmaster, wasn't he?" He smiled at the row of relatives sitting behind Maggie and Emmett.

"That's right! That's right!" Peggy smiled, pleased the bishop knew. She had a round, full face, flushed from the warm room and her excitement. "Father Leahy, he was the parish priest in our day. A good man, God rest his soul, but a bit long-winded. He had the gift of gab, that's for sure.

"Anyway, in those days you had to be in church for the gospel itself, or you missed Mass altogether. Well, Tommy McManus, he'd kneel there back by the door—the poor church was so small they couldn't hold everyone on a Sunday morning, and Tommy would kneel just inside the door. His heels would be soaked, I tell you, if it was raining. And when Father Leahy finished the gospel and started in on his sermon, out would go Tommy McManus." She snapped her fingers to show his speed.

"Ah, he would!" one of the old men in the row agreed, laughing now, remembering. "Many's the time I saw him. Many's the time I was with him myself."

"Indeed you were, John O'Cadhain!" Peggy leaned forward to catch his eye. "And wasn't my husband, Frank Cummings, God rest his soul, with you as well?"

In the first row, Maggie smiled at her aunt and tried to keep from crying. This was like listening to stories her mother had told, the endless, seamless stories of the old country, all rambling, episodic tales about one relative or the other. The faraway names of people and places had rolled effortlessly off her mother's tongue and sounded to Maggie like Irish poetry.

"Well, Bishop," Peggy Cummings went on, pulling the story back to her, "they had moonshine, you know, down by the river, hidden away."

"Poteen, it was." John O'Cadhain spoke up again, correcting her.

"Poteen! Moonshine! The same difference."

"Like hell it is," the old man answered, sitting back, shaking his head.

"The boys had it in jugs down by the river," Peggy went on, "and when old Father Leahy got finished with the gospel, out they'd go, you know, through the back door of the little church, sneaking away to have a nip. They'd stay down there, you see, until Father finished his sermon—and a good forty minutes that might take on one of his better Sundays.

"Well, one morning, Tommy McManus skipped out as usual, him and the lads, just after Father turned to genuflect before the altar. But this time!" She raised her finger, gaining everyone's attention. "Old Father Leahy was after them.

"I've never seen anything like it, Bishop." She looked up at the priest. "He must have been sixty if he were a day, but he leaped over that altar rail and down the center aisle, him in his vestments and all, and out the door, across the hay field. He caught Tommy before he reached the stone fence, grabbed him and Michael Sweeney by the ears."

"Mick Cobet, it was," John O'Cadhain spoke up from the end of the row. "Mickey Cobet was the one he caught. The rest of us got away. I know."

"He dragged them both right up before the altar," Peggy went on, "and made them kneel there from that Sunday on, he did. Ah, he was a great one for discipline. But Tommy, God love him, wasn't one for praying. It aged him, I think, having to hear Mass there on his knees at the altar rail."

Everyone laughed, appreciating her story. Maggie reached over and patted her aunt on the knee. Peggy was her mother's younger sister, yet Maggie had only seen her once before, at Father Mike's first Mass up in Chicago.

When she was a child, she had suggested to her mother that they take the train to Chicago to visit the relatives. They were doing dishes at the time, she remembered, and her mother had looked up from the sudsy water, glanced out the windows toward the barns, and said quietly, "Well, honey, I don't think that's possible." It was all she had ever said about seeing the family, and Maggie had known somehow, even as a child, not to press.

"I think we should get Catty and Paddy Jack for the prayers," the bishop suggested. "Would you ask them to come in, Maggie?" He spoke with confidence, like a man who expected his directions to be followed. Then he went to say his own prayer, kneeling down before his mother's remains.

But he could not pray. Instead he kept thinking of the day when he had last been with the whole family, when he had said his first Mass as a priest, at Christ the King parish in Chicago.

It was a Mass that Father O'Connor had arranged for him. A Mass, he had come to realize, that the old family friend had really arranged for his mother, not him. It was his mother's celebration. Her son had become a priest. The first one of the Rushes or the DeLaceys.

Well, Mom, you made it, didn't you? After all this time. You kept the secret from them, didn't you? You're gone now and none of your sisters or cousins, or even your children, will know. What shall I do? Tell them all tomorrow when you're laid to rest?

The bishop blessed himself, stood up, and turned to face the congregation. It wasn't a way to live, Mom, he thought. It wasn't a way to die. They were your children, Mom. Your sons and daughters.

In the front hall, Maggie glanced around, checking on the family. Catty was sitting with her children in the living room; Paddy Jack was standing with a blond woman in front of the fire, but before she could motion to them, the front door opened and Jack McGraff stepped back into her life, bringing into the warm farmhouse the chill of the cold February night.

"Hello, Mag."

"Jack," Maggie whispered, startled by the sight of him.

He stepped forward and kissed her on the cheek. She could feel his cold skin against her face. "I heard yesterday . . . I was in Chicago, and . . . I'm sorry, Mag." He kept hold of her, searching her face for a reaction.

Maggie nodded, still startled by the sight of him. But she was pleased that he had come, that he had remembered.

"Was she sick? Was it her heart?"

Maggie shook her head. "An accident. One of Emmett's guns . . . she moved it, and—"

"Jesus Christ! You poor thing . . . I had no idea."

"Father Mike is trying to keep it quiet. How are you, Jack?" She forced a smile, looking up at her ex-husband. It had been only six months since she had last since Jack in person, and then only fleetingly on a side street in downtown Washington. He had been with another woman then, and she had ducked into a store so that they wouldn't meet.

He nodded. "I'm okay, Mag. You don't mind that I came?"

"Of course not. You should be here. You were one of Mommy's favorites." When they had first gone out together, she had brought

Jack home for a long weekend and her mother had made Irish soda bread. Jack had never had it before, and he had been lavish in his praise. He won her mother over that night, and she had never, Maggie realized, gotten over the fact that Maggie had left him.

"I'm about to get everyone, Jack, for the prayers," Maggie said, seeing he was trying to decide what to do. "Why don't you say hello to Father Mike . . . and everyone." She knew that having driven down to Gatesburg, he would use the time to see people, be seen. It didn't upset her anymore. It was all part of the job, his life in the Senate.

"Can I talk to you later?" he asked at once.

"Of course. Everyone but the family will be leaving after the prayers. Why don't you stay for something to eat? Do you have staff people with you?"

He shook his head. "Is it possible to see you . . . alone?"

Maggie nodded, agreeing. She knew how compulsive he could become about practical matters. He wanted everything scheduled. "After the prayers, Jack, we'll talk." She pushed him toward the front parlor as if he were her child, sent him off to say hello to her brother Michael, to kneel before the open casket.

He looked like one of her brothers, she thought, and not for the first time. She had come to understand that it was what had attracted her when she had first seen him in the halls of Congress. Jack. Jack McGraff. Congressional aide John Peter McGraff then. Jackson. Her Jack. Darling Jack. Once. It seemed such a long time ago.

She had just finished her second year at Georgetown University and was spending the summer working on the Hill. Father Mike had gotten her the job on Capitol Hill, as a staff assistant to a subcommittee on famine in Africa. Jack McGraff, at twenty-six, had been the ranking aide.

From one of the press officers she had gotten hold of a photograph, a casual snapshot of Jack striding down the hallway, and she had it blown up to life size and pinned it to the back of her bedroom door. At night before falling asleep, she would whisper into the dark, "Good night, Jack."

She was in love with Jack McGraff before they had even spoken a word.

Yet when he finally did speak to her, it was Jack McGraff who was swept off his feet.

When he finally noticed her it was late August, a week before her job was over. She was leaving the Capitol building, walking across the length of the mall late on a warm Friday night, when she spotted him jogging toward her. It was almost as if his photograph had stepped from her bedroom door, and her heart slid off its safe shelf.

Yet she kept walking, kept her head up, looked blindly ahead, her vision blurry with fear.

He ran effortlessly past her and then shouted, "Hey!"

She turned slightly to catch him make a wide running turn and come back to her. He was wearing blue running shorts and a red T-shirt that said YALE UNIVERSITY. He looked taller and much more muscular than when dressed in street clothes.

She looked ahead and lengthened her stride, as if to outdistance him, but he jogged up beside her and fell into step.

"Excuse me." His voice still had its hard edge. "Aren't you what's-her-name?"

"No, I'm not!" she snapped back, her sudden anger pushing away any nervousness.

He paused a moment, then said, "You're Margaret DeLacey. Monsignor DeLacey's kid sister, right? I'm sorry. I didn't mean to be rude."

"Well, you were."

"I mean, I know you from the Hill. From our subcommittee. Right?" His voice softened.

"Yes, Mr. McGraff." She could feel her chin lifting, as it always did when she was upset. As if she were a slugger waiting for him to take a swing.

"Say, that was a nice job you did on Chad. How come you know so much about Africa?"

"We DeLaceys are all perverse."

Jack McGraff laughed. "Yes, well, that's true. I know about your brother's projects." He slowed his pace, expecting her to stop, but Maggie kept striding down the mall.

"What's the hurry, for chrissake?"

"Please stop swearing. And I don't have a lot of time. I'm late for an engagement."

"Okay! Okay!" He jogged back to her side, laughing now, intrigued by her hostility. "We can walk back to my place. I'll give you a ride home. Where do you live, anyway?"

"Thank you, but . . . I'm being met."

"Oh, where? I'll walk with you." He kept smiling, enjoying her displeasure.

"At the White House," she answered without thinking.

"No shit?"

"No shit."

"Hey, DeLacey, what's your game?" He jogged ahead, and then backward so he could watch her face.

"I have no game," she said quickly, keeping her eyes on the path.

"Well, why are you being so goddamn hostile?"

"Why do you swear so much?"

"I'm sorry. I forgot you were a good Catholic girl, with a brother who's a monsignor."

She gave him the finger and regretted it at once, realizing that it gave him an edge to let her anger show. But she was enjoying herself. She had his full attention, and she had him off balance about her.

"Truce," he said, offering his hand. "Détente."

Maggie shook her head. "No truce. No state of war exists."

"Then why are you rushing away from me?"

"I'm not rushing away from anyone. I'm late, that's all."

"Oh, that's right. You have a date at the White House."

"Correct."

"Say, who do you go out with at the White House? I mean they're all Republicans over there."

She wouldn't look at him. She let him sweat. Then she said airily, "A friend."

"Well, would you like to go out sometime?"

"You don't want to go out with me, McGraff. I'm not your type."

"Hey, who said so? I like all kinds of girls."

"You mean women."

"That's right, women," he said quickly. "I even like black Irish women. I'm Irish myself, you know. What about tomorrow night? Are you busy? There's a small party at the Indian Embassy."

Maggie stopped walking, turned, and asked him directly, "Why do you want to go out with me? You can have your pick of anyone on the Hill."

"How should I know why I want to go out with you," he demanded. "Is it that important?"

"Yes." She could feel her challenge begin to crumble and she walked off.

"Wait!" He caught up and touched her arm, then smiled. "You're cute. I mean, I think you're cute. Okay?" He had a sad little-boy smile, one that she had already seen, one that she would learn to mistrust. He stepped in front of her, lifted her chin. She felt like his kid sister.

"Yeah, sure, I date a lot." He shrugged, looked bashful. "But I haven't met anyone important . . ."

"Sunday," Maggie said, interrupting him. "Would you like to do something on Sunday? I jog," she added, as if to show they had things in common. Now her heart was flying.

"That would be terrific! I'll pick you up. Where?"

"School. I live in the dormitory," she admitted, feeling foolish.

"Hey, everyone's got to live in a dorm, once."

"I live in Copley. It's right on the quad. At ten, okay?"

"Sure." He kept grinning.

Maggie stepped away from him, went into the street to catch a taxi. She wanted to be alone, to let herself remember how it all had suddenly happened.

"Come at nine," she called back as a taxi pulled to a stop.

"Sure. Why?"

"We'll go to Mass, okay?"

He laughed. "Okay, Mass."

That week was the last time she had gone to Mass, and the first time she had slept with someone, all of it when she was nineteen years old. She had never put those two things together before, Maggie thought, watching the senator "work" the small front room of the farmhouse, shaking hands with his constituents as he moved toward the open casket. But it was Jack McGraff who had taken away her God, taken her virginity, and made her love him. No, that wasn't fair, she thought. Loving him was all her own doing.

She turned from the front room, from the sight of him, and told herself again how Jack McGraff didn't control her life. Nor was she afraid of him, or awed. Not anymore. And she was no longer in love with the man.

The doorbell rang, and glad for the distraction, she hurried to admit the last mourner.

An older woman stood on the porch in the glare of the front-door light. Beyond her, Maggie could see the town cab turn around in the drive and drive away,

"Is this the DeLacey home?"

Maggie pushed open the storm door and stood to one side, giving the woman room to come inside. "Yes," she said smiling. "I'm Margaret DeLacey." She did not recognize the woman but assumed she was another relative down from Chicago on the late train.

The woman stepped into the house and set down her small piece of luggage. She was not as tall as Maggie, and she seemed timid, uncertain of what to do next.

"I'm sorry that no one met the train, but I didn't know," Maggie apologized.

"Well, actually I came by airplane. By way of St. Louis, Missouri." She paused a moment, searched Maggie's face, and waited for a moment of recognition. Then she said shyly, "I'm Nora, Margaret."

"Nora? I'm sorry, but I'm just not very good at knowing all the relatives. My brother is in here . . ." She turned to look for Michael and spotted Father O'Connor coming from the kitchen. She nodded to him, then saw a look of surprise register on the old man's face. Something was wrong, Maggie realized, and then she heard the woman say softly, " 'Tis me, Margaret. Nora DeLacey. Your sister from back home in Ireland. Dad couldn't make the trip. It would just have been too much for him."

"Dad?" Maggie was having trouble focusing, as if she were being given too much information all at once. "I'm sorry . . ."

"Your father, Margaret Mary, your father back home in Tourmakeady. I know you're grieving now, but don't forget: we still have Dad."

# · BOOK TWO ·

## IRELAND
## 1940

# · CHAPTER 10 ·

THE MOTOR COACH REACHED the summit of the hill and Caitlin looked back toward the long green valley of Tourmakeady. "Oh, look, Cormac!" she said to her husband, "you can see nearly the whole of Lough Mask."

From the hilltop, she saw the dozen thatched roofs of Tourmakeady, their village, and the miles of low stone fences checkerboarding the remote valley. A fine winter day it was for the West of Ireland, cool and clear. On the steep mountainside beyond Tourmakeady, she saw their own sheep grazing, several hundred of them in a single flock, making a tight white mark, like a postage stamp, on the rocky cliffs.

They were finally going. After all the talk and worry, the day had come. They were off to Dublin to find work. Driven from their farm by Cormac's uncle. She felt a swift tug at her heart, but it wasn't because she was leaving the farm. She was leaving her little Nora, as well, leaving her baby, until they had a place of their own in Dublin. And to stop her swelling tears she said to Cormac, "I can see Maamstrasna."

"I won't be looking at Maamstrasna—not today, by God!" He crossed his arms and stared defiantly ahead. "It's a sad day when a man is driven from his place, and by his own people. I'm telling you, Catty, I won't be setting eyes on Tourmakeady or the Partry Mountains or Lough Mask itself until I can come home with enough brass in my pockets to buy the bastard out. It's a sad and sorry day when a man loses his farm, and to his own uncle at that, who had no rightful claim under God's good eyes to the property."

Caitlin looked out the coach window again, suddenly frightened that she would lose all her memories of this place, the lovely valley deep in Connemara. The coach crested the hill, turned with the narrow road toward Leenane and Galway where they would catch the train to distant Dublin.

She caught sight of her family's whitewashed cottage, where she had come into the world and been raised. She saw Cormac's farm deeper in the valley, the cottage where they had briefly lived as husband and wife, and where Nora had been born, and where she'd thought she would live and raise a family and pass away her life. She thought again of Nora. She had had to leave her baby behind with her sister, for there would be no hope of finding work in Dublin if she had to care for a child. Then the fear of what she was doing: of finding a job as a maid in Dublin, of living without Cormac in the city, crushed the thin edge of her confidence and she leaned against her silent husband and sobbed out her heart in his strong arms.

"You're Mairead Burke's cousin, now are you, child? God rest her soul, what a fine woman she was." The housekeeper, Mrs. Finnerty, peered at Caitlin across the kitchen table.

"Ah, I am," Caitlin whispered. "On my mother's side. They're from near Ballinahinch. Me mother was her younger sister, you see." She stood inside the kitchen door, too afraid to step closer. But it was the kitchen, not the woman, that overwhelmed her. Shiny copper boilers and side tables, all fresh with linen and trays of barmbricks. She had never seen such gleaming pots and pans, and gas stoves, and one pantry just for dishes. They could put the whole of her own cottage, she thought, into such a kitchen.

"And how do you find Dublin, child?"

"Oh, it's a wonder, isn't it?" she answered. "Why, there are more tarred streets in Dublin, I'm sure, than there are in the whole of Galway." Caitlin tried to speak up boldly, as Cormac had told her. "You're a Connemara girl, don't forget," he'd said. "Don't let any of them Dublin jackeens think they're better than you, with all their fine talk."

He had taken her as far as Merrion Road, leaving her to go the last few blocks on her own. "Mind you, don't let it slip that you're married," he had warned. "They're not likely to take that kindly, not Protestants, not these left-handers."

"And where would you be from then, child?" Mrs. Finnerty asked. She was a short, plump woman, with gray hair tucked neatly into a bun and a tiny, round face, smooth as a peach.

"Tourmakeady, ma'am," she said, forcing herself to speak up.

"Well, come closer, dearie. Lord, I won't be harming you, child," Mrs. Finnerty said softly, encouragingly. Caitlin stepped out of the shadows of the doorway and the housekeeper saw her clearly for the first time. She was a lovely child, Mrs. Finnerty thought, surprised. Connemara people were not handsome. They married late and the hard life of the mountains made them old before their time. But occasionally they produced a real beauty, and this girl was one, the housekeeper saw, though she was poorly dressed in a garish green dress.

There was more than a drop of the Spanish in her, Mrs. Finnerty noted, what with her black hair and dark features. The missus would appreciate that. Still, Mrs. Finnerty hesitated. She heard the independence in the girl's voice and spotted it in Caitlin's posture as well, the way she tossed her head and set her chin. Country people were that way, too independent for their own good. Well, she would give the child her chance, if only because of Mairead Burke, God bless her.

"Isn't Tourmakeady in the back of beyonds?"

"Well, to you I should think it is . . . but I never thought of it as being far away. Until I came yesterday by train, I hadn't been outside of home, except once, you know, to the fair at Clifden. Have you been to Clifden, ma'am? Now there's a fair sea on a clear day, but a fair day in Clifden, mind you, is as rare as a cool drink in hell."

The housekeeper smiled at the phrase. The missus would like that, she knew, having a simple girl still possessing her country language, her innocent ways.

"Have you ever worked out, Caitlin?" the housekeeper asked.

"Worked out?" Caitlin cocked her head. "Ah, you mean in the fields? Indeed now, why wouldn't I?" She sounded offended. "Wasn't it myself who looked after the cows? And fed the hens, besides the washing up and the cooking! My dear mother, God rest her soul, was crippled up with the rheumatism, and Da, why the poor man couldn't boil water if his life depended on it."

"That isn't at all what I mean, Caitlin." The housekeeper laughed. "But never you mind. You'll do fine. Come and wipe your feet, dearie, and straighten yourself up. The missus won't tolerate slouchers. Mind yourself and look sharp. Mrs. Steele is a wonderful woman, but she won't have laziness here at Vulcanus."

"They call the house Vulcanus, Cormac. Isn't that odd, giving a house a Latin name. And dear God, it's big enough for a king. The housekeeper, Mrs. Finnerty—she's from Glendalough in Wicklow, did I tell you that?—well, she took me upstairs to meet herself. And here the missus was still in bed, and it being after ten o'clock and all. I nearly passed away going right into the room and her still in her nightclothes. It's because they're Protestants. My cousin Sabha told me about them. She worked for a rich family named Breaffy in Castlebar. They haven't a bit of shame, you know, about staying in their beds half the day."

"Bloody aristocrats," Cormac said, cutting into his wife's breathless narration. She had been talking constantly since they met at the top of Baggot Street.

"Well, they're not aristocrats, exactly. Just rich, from the mills Mr. Steele's family started when they first came over from England, two hundred years ago, Mrs. Finnerty says."

"And what are they paying you, Caitlin?" Cormac asked.

"Thirty shillings a week, Mrs. Finnerty said. And my room and board," she said quickly, seeing Cormac's back stiffen.

"Jesus, Mary, and Joseph, we'll be on the dole before we have our own place again." He shook his head, a tight motion, as if his chin were being jerked by a string.

" 'Tis steady work, Cormac. And I have my own room under the slate; I don't have to share with the other girl." She went on quickly, pleased at the thought of spending time in the attic room, with the view of the Dublin mountains. Then, realizing what had upset Cormac, she stopped talking. Here she was in Dublin only a day and already she was working out, earning a pound a week.

"Have you gone by to see Tommy Keogh?" she asked, to change the subject.

"Bejasus, you wouldn't believe the place he's living in, Catty." He shook his head at his friend's sorry fate. "It isn't a house at all, not like we know, but a huge, ugly brick building. It's a factory, it is, with people stacked one on the other, like rabbits in a coop."

"Did he know of any work, Cormac?" she pressed, knowing his moods. He'd want to stop for a drink next, just to ease his pain. "I suffer more than most, Caitlin," he had told her when they first started walking out. She had thought it romantic then, his self-pity.

He shook his head. "Not at the docks. There's little shipping now, with England in the war and the U-boats on the prowl. Even though Ireland is neutral, we suffer just like the English."

"Oh, dear God above!" They would be destitute, she realized, if he didn't get work, too. And they were without friends or family in the whole of Dublin. It wasn't like Tourmakeady, where there was always someone to take you in or bring a pot of boiled potatoes and buttermilk if you were down with the chills. Here in the city, she knew already, one wouldn't even get a *"Conas ta tu?"* from a stranger.

"There was a bloke there, a Kerry man named Packy Fallon. He's living with Tommy in that flat, and he told me to go out to the building corporation. He has a friend working in Monkstown. There's some work to be found. But it's called under-the-hammer work, he said, for I won't be earning even the lowest wage."

" 'Tis something, Cormac," she said at once, cheering to the news. "Until better comes along."

"Ah, 'tis something."

She could hear the sorrow in his voice.

"It would be like working outside on the farm, wouldn't it?" she added, trying to dispel his dark mood.

"There's where I should be on a fine day like today, out in my own fields cutting turf. You can be damn sure that old gett Padraic isn't." At the thought of his uncle, he turned aside and spit into the bush.

"Cormac!" she scolded. They had left North Baggot and gone down the sloping path into St. Stephen's Green. The park on the midweek afternoon was quiet, with only a few nurses pushing prams the length of the green. She thought at once of Nora and a fist of pain caught her beneath her heart. It made her limbs weak, thinking of her child. She was thankful there were no young children in the Steele household. She couldn't stand it, having babies underfoot and none of them her own.

"That bastard's ruined my life and I'll damn well spit every time I say his name. Coming back like that from America. I curse the day I wrote to tell him Da was dead! You know as well as the day is long, he would never have set foot again in Ireland if he didn't have Granda's old will telling him the farm was his when Da died. Him and his bloody piece of paper!" He turned again to spit and Caitlin seized his arm.

"It does no good to get yourself into a fit, Cormac." But she knew it was no use. Once she went back to the house he would find a pub and get himself jarred at the thought of losing the farm. It was his only way of forgetting his luck, and for that she forgave him the half crown it would take to ease the pain. "Don't spend our time together being angry now, for I won't be seeing you again till Sunday."

He jerked around and she saw the new fear on his dark face. This was what she had worried about the most, their parting. What would he do without her?

"You won't be coming back to the boarding house?" She saw him brace himself, trying to accept the news that he was on his own in the city.

"I told Mrs. Finnerty I had to fetch my bag. She gave me till teatime."

"You mean you'll be off to work today?" he asked, suddenly realizing what Caitlin had been telling him.

"Ah," she answered softly. "Mrs. Finnerty needs me today, or the job's not mine."

"Jesus, Mary, and Joseph, aren't we something. A wife I can't even call my own, and all for a pound a week."

"I have to be at the Steeles' by half-three, Cormac. We don't have time to do more than pick up my bag from Mrs. Donohoe's." She looked away. She never spoke of their lovemaking, not with Cormac, nor with her sisters. She was afraid even to speak of it in confession, but going to bed with Cormac was not a joy for her. It was her fault, she knew. She had never liked making love to Cormac, not even on their wedding night. It wasn't at all like she read in books, and she knew it was a sin that a wife should feel that way about her husband and her marriage duty.

"Bejasus, I'm being denied my wife as well by Uncle Pat," Cormac said out loud, as if complaining to the passing nurses, the well-dressed strangers on St. Stephen's Green.

"Musha, Cormac, don't carry on so." She was wearying of his black mood. "I haven't time to be arguing more about Padraic DeLacey. I need to fetch my case from the boarding house." She turned back toward the street, hoping he would follow her.

Cormac cocked his head and looked over at his wife, squinting against the early afternoon sunlight. He hoped the squint would make him look tough, like one of the cornerboys they had seen earlier on York Street, but he knew it wouldn't. He wasn't tough like the cornerboys, or for that matter, like Caitlin. She wasn't afraid of Dublin.

Here she had already found work. Not a day in the city and already hired out at a guinea a week. He had to take a backseat to her. His mother had been right: grass wouldn't grow under Caitlin Grace Rush.

She glanced over her shoulder. "Coming, Cormac?" she asked softly, knowing she had been short with him. She tried to seem sweet and submissive, and let him have his way.

"Ah," he said, hitching up his loose trousers.

"Don't!" she asked, embarrassed again at his country ways.

"The divil I won't!"

"You look like a farmer," she answered back.

"And what am I, if not a farmer?"

"We're in Dublin, Cormac, not Connemara."

"I'm a farmer wherever I am, and if these Dublin jackeens don't like it, then it's too bad for them. And where would Ireland be without farmers, men like myself?"

Caitlin walked off, flushed with embarrassment, and Cormac followed behind, shouting after her in Irish, as if they were on a back road in Galway. She saw prams stopping and nurses, in their starched white uniforms, turning to giggle at this country pair.

She thought of how they must look. Cormac was wearing the black suit of his dead father. It was too small for him and his thick arms stuck out of the short sleeves. On his feet were his black rubber boots. He never wore his good leather shoes except to Mass.

She was no better, she thought sadly, in her green dress from Lipton's, the one she had worn to Salthill the summer they were married. She had lost weight since then, since the baby, and the dress looked like a hand-me-down.

"Cormac, you'll be the death of me," she said, and walked off, ignoring the giggles of the baby nurses. She noticed, though, how pretty and clean they looked in their white uniforms. How respectable.

"If it wasn't for the poor farmers like myself," he called after her, "De Valera himself wouldn't be Taoiseach, nor his party, the Fianna Fail, be running the Dail."

"You're not a farmer now, Cormac, nor I a farmer's wife. This is Dublin and I'm a servant girl, and you—well, God willing, you'll be working in the trades, or we'll both be living in a slum like Tommy Keogh. And little Nora will be out on the street with all those ragamuffins." She began to cry, thinking of the dirty slum children who had circled them on the back streets near the boardinghouse, begging for money.

"Never!" He brushed ahead of her on the path, striding off, his Wellingtons thumping on the soft earth. He walked as he had when crossing the bottomland to cut turf, planting each foot as if it were a fence post.

But they would never see their farm again, she suddenly realized, or the land that stretched down to the lake, or the blue-ink mist over the Partry Mountains. She would never again see Lough Mask or the Maamstrasna. Connemara was lost to her. She knew it as clearly as if it had been revealed by God.

"Cormac!" she called, frightened by her own thoughts. But he would not stop. She would not get a kind word from him, not after she had hurt his pride; she knew his ways. Silent now, she followed her husband out of St. Stephen's Green and into the city.

# · CHAPTER 11 ·

"HERE, DEARIE, LET ME have a look at you." Mrs. Finnerty positioned Caitlin in the center of the warm kitchen. "Did you wash now?" she asked, circling the girl, who towered over her. "I mean, all over? Did you wash your privates?"

Caitlin blushed and looked down in confusion.

" 'Tis nothing to be ashamed of, child!"

"Me mother taught me how to wash, Mrs. Finnerty," Caitlin answered back, letting her anger flash.

Then the woman stepped toward her and began sniffing. "It isn't your cleanliness that I'm checking, child," Mrs. Finnerty explained, when she saw Caitlin's expression, "but whether you went off yesterday to Woolworth's and bought yourself some cheap French scent. I won't have my girls smelling like bad women from Leeson Street." She reached out and tugged at the tight lace collar of the girl's uniform. The dress was too small, but until it was decided that Caitlin would stay, it did no good to let out seams.

"Well, it's time you earned your keep. I sent little Teresa off to Moore Street, so I'll need you to take up Master Adrian's breakfast. He came over from Holyhead last night." She glanced at the kitchen clock and added, "It's half-nine as it is, and time he was up."

She began to prepare the breakfast tray, taking a silver set from the cupboard. "Fry up a couple of eggs, child," she instructed, "and toast a slice of bread. He came all the way from England last night, and I always give the boy breakfast in bed on his first day home. He has a huge appetite when he's near my cooking." Then, lowering her voice to a whisper, she went on. "Mister Adrian is an actor. He was at Trinity, you know, but then last August he came home and told them he was finished there. He wanted to become an actor, another Barry Fitzgerald, mind you. And here the master had a place for him already at the mills. It broke the missus's heart, I know, but himself has a mind of his own, that lad." She shook her head, then said, as an afterthought, "Mind you, child, they'll be no telling stories of this household. We're a family here and I won't have our dirty laundry talked up by every scullery maid in Dublin. You keep what happens at this house to yourself."

"Yes, ma'am. But I haven't a soul that I know in Dublin."

"Ah, you'll meet girls from the other households. Not that many live in these days. They fancy their time off. Well, I won't have it. My girls live in, where I can keep a close eye on them. Now on Sunday you and little Teresa have time after dinner to make the last Mass at Blessed Sacrament and then take the tram to the park, if you wish. Teasy will show you about. She's a little slow, you know, but she has a heart of gold. Her people are from Donegal, some little place along the coast. Her older brother John was with my Arthur, God rest his soul, in the Gardai."

Caitlin thought of Cormac. They had planned to meet at St. Michael's and hear Mass before taking the train to Sandycover. A day at the beach, Cormac had promised her, to get them out of Dublin. "I'm to see my aunt on Sunday afternoon, Mrs. Finnerty," Caitlin said quickly. "She's a Poor Clare Sister, and I was going to stop by the convent and say hello. I haven't seen her since I was a little girl, before she took final vows." Caitlin kept building on the lie. It amazed her how easily she had thought it up.

"A Poor Clare, is she? Well, isn't that wonderful! Of course you should go by and see her. You don't want to waste your time up at the park when you have religious family in Dublin. Especially with your mother, God rest her soul, gone from you. Now, watch yourself, child, or those eggs will be hard as Connemara marble. He likes his soft," the housekeeper said, coming to the gas stove, and then under her breath, "like his head, I sometimes think."

Mrs. Finnerty arranged the tray, covering the hot plates with silver lids, placing a folded *Irish Times* next to the napkin ring, then nodded toward the back stairs.

"His room is at the end of the hall, Caitlin, away from the staircase. He's dead to the world, I'm sure, so just go ahead in and set the tray on the nightstand. But make sure he's awake before you leave. He's always been a hard one to wake in the morning."

As she gave the tray to Caitlin, she lowered her voice and said softly, "I was worried out of my mind, him living in London, what with Germany at England's throat. But now I can rest, knowing he's safe at home and under my roof. I raised that child myself, I'll have you know, and it would have killed me to have him hurt in London, not that he isn't trouble enough here at home. He's one of those socialists. Got all those funny ideas at Trinity. That's what happens when you send children off to college." She shook her head. "I did my best, God knows, but you never know what will happen to children once they leave you." She picked up her knitting, then added, "All you can do is raise them, as my late mother, God rest her soul, would say."

Cathleen knocked timidly on the bedroom door, then leaned against it, listening for any sound of Adrian Steele. The second floor hallway was quiet, as was the house, with the rest of the family already out for the day. She waited, building up her courage. She had never been in the bedroom of a strange man before. Balancing the tray on one hand, she slowly pushed open the door. The bed was at one end of the huge room, but she saw only the shape of Adrian Steele deep in the bedding. He had pulled the heavy blankets over his head and was hiding from the morning light.

Caitlin stepped inside and glanced about, looking for where she might set down the tray. Several leather cases lay open on the floor, with clothes picked out and dropped, and she had to move carefully to reach the desk. Pushing a dozen shirt collars and studs to one side, she set down the breakfast tray, then glanced again at the bed. He had not moved. She could hear him breathing deeply, like her own Cormac when he had had too much to drink.

Looking around, she appraised the bedroom. It was as big, she realized, as their entire thatched cottage at home, with a high ceiling, a wide dark walnut bed, and windows that covered one wall. Through them she could see the tops of the garden's chestnut trees and beyond the garden, Dublin itself, the winter sun shining off wet slate roofs.

The man in the bed stirred, reached up, and pulled down the top of the blankets, revealing a thick mass of black hair. Caitlin caught her breath. He was waking, as Mrs. Finnerty had said he should, so she could leave now without fear of doing wrong. She threw one more glance at the bed, and then as quietly as she could, carefully stepped toward the door.

"Do you expect my eggs and rashers to walk over here?" The voice was muffled by the cover of blankets.

Caitlin halted, glanced back. Above the blankets she saw only thick black hair, a forehead, and blue eyes, but she knew he was smiling.

" 'Tis me, sir, Caitlin," she offered.

"Musha, now who else would it be?" he answered, imitating her brogue. Then bracing himself on one elbow, he sat up and said, "Come here, lass," instructing her with his finger as if she were a child in school.

Caitlin moved one step closer, then halted, stopped by the sight of him, his bare shoulders and the thick hair of his chest above the blankets.

"Tell me, Caitlin—or is it Catty?" He kept smiling, encouraging her with the warmth of his blue eyes.

"Well, it's Catty at home, sir. Do you speak the Irish?" she asked shyly, then looked down at the carpet. She had never in her life seen anyone so handsome. He was dark and blue-eyed, like Cormac, but his eyes were a cloudy shade, like the color of the Maamturk Mountains on a rainy autumn day. He was Cormac's age, but he did not have her husband's hawkish face. He had the smooth features of a gentleman, the narrow nose and long fine lips that seemed as if they had been etched on the soft skin.

"Ah, I speak Irish," he said, answering her in that language. "And why not? Am I not Irish bred and born?" He shifted again in the wide, soft bed, sitting up further and showing more of his bare chest.

Alarmed, Caitlin turned half away.

"Now aren't you a shy one!" he said in English, but mimicking again the soft lyrical diction of the west counties. "Tell me, Caitlin, are you named after the virgin martyr Caitlin of Alexandria, or Saint Catherine of Siena?"

"Not a'tall! I'm named after my aunt Caitlin Taheny from Ballinahinch."

Adrian leaned back and roared, startling her with his loudness. She would be in trouble now, Caitlin knew. Mrs. Finnerty would hear him and think she had caused trouble.

"You're to eat your breakfast, sir," Caitlin said quickly, backing toward the open doorway. "Mrs. Finnerty said."

"Oh, Bridie," he sighed. "She'll be the death of me." He slid down again into the soft bed and, wrapping his arms about the thick pillow, swept her body with his sleepy eyes.

Caitlin felt the breath go out of her. She knew she shouldn't let herself be the cause of another's secret thoughts.

"Mrs. Finnerty will be wanting me," she answered weakly, looking away, then realized she didn't have the strength to leave the bedroom. "The rashers will be getting cold," she went on, trying to break the spell he had thrown over her, then rushed for the open bedroom door.

" 'Shy one, shy one,' " he said quickly. " 'Shy one of my heart; she moves in the firelight, pensively apart.' "

Caitlin flew out of the bedroom, nearly tripping on the hallway rug, and then free of the sight of him, she took a deep breath.

"Don't you know your Yeats, Caitlin?" he shouted after her. " 'She carries in the dishes, and lays them in a row. To an isle in the water with her would I go.' " His booming voice followed her down the back stairs to the kitchen.

"Is himself up?" Mrs. Finnerty asked, placing a new sod of turf on the fire.

Caitlin smelled its sweet aroma and she thought of home, of waking in the cold thatched farmhouse to rake the ashes in the hearth before making breakfast for Cormac.

"Ah." Caitlin's heart was pounding in her ears.

From the second floor, they heard him shouting out more lines of poetry.

" 'She carries in the candles, and lights the curtained room, shy in the doorway and shy in the gloom.' "

"It's him and his Yeats," Mrs. Finnerty said, smiling.

"And who is this Yeats, Mrs. Finnerty?" Caitlin asked.

"Sure, girl, even in Tourmakeady you must have heard of W. B. Yeats?" She peered over her glasses at Caitlin. "He lived near by, God rest his soul. Number Eighty-two Merrion Square. The family is great friends of the Steeles, and the boy." She nodded toward the second floor. "The poor man died last winter in France. He was a wonderful man." She leaned over the table, whispering. "It was Yeats that got the lad in at the Abbey. You've heard of the Abbey Theatre, haven't you?"

Caitlin shook her head, embarrassed again.

" 'Tisn't your fault, child," Mrs. Finnerty said. "You grew up in the back of beyonds, that's all." She sighed. "Well, you're in Dublin now, and you'll have your fill of news and politics and what have you in this household, especially with himself at home. He's a great talker, especially when it comes to harping about the English. When it comes to the English, he could quench a candle at the other side of this kitchen with his cursing." She lowered her voice and added softly, "As if the Irish aren't in enough trouble as it is." She shook her head, kept muttering. The speed of her knitting picked up.

"I'll put up the kettle for tay, shall I?" Caitlin asked, seeing the state the housekeeper had put herself in. She was thankful that Cormac wasn't that way, talking politics, getting all upset. "It's a waste of your strength," he had told her once. "You're better off planting spuds than talking yourself blue about De Valera and the Dail."

"Oh, thank you, dearie. Teasy will be back soon from Moore Street and I want the two of you to start on the downstairs rooms. They're a holy mess, and here it's an evening tonight. Would you be knowing what evenings are, child?"

"Well, evenings are evening, now aren't they?" Caitlin answered, embarrassed again at her ignorance.

Mrs. Finnerty laughed. "Well, I guess they are in Tourmakeady, but evenings in Dublin are something special. The family is at home on Tuesdays, for anyone who wants to visit. The Steeles are famous in the city for their evenings. You'll see Dublin's finest here tonight," she added with a note of pride. "Ambassadors and such, the foreign representatives, and senators from the Dail and Seanad." But then in the same breath, she said with scorn, "All of those fine ladies and gentlemen will be in the house with the likes of those poets and artists from Baggot Street, friends of himself.

"You'll be answering the front door, dearie. Little Teasy will serve up the coffee and tea, and I'll watch over the Jameson. Those Bohemians would filch a full bottle, given half the chance."

"Mrs. Finnerty?" Caitlin asked, coming to the table with cups, saucers, and a loaf of Barnbrack bread. "How in God's name will I know a Bohemian? I never in my whole life laid eyes on one."

The housekeeper smiled. "You needn't worry. You'll know them well enough by their home-woven coats. They're all for putting on Irish clothes nowadays. They think themselves grand at having gotten rid of the English."

"You're not for Britain, are you, Mrs. Finnerty?" Caitlin asked, surprised by the housekeeper's remark. She had never met anyone who liked the English. Certainly not in Connemara, where all the English were hated. She cut two thin slices of the Barnbrack onto plates and sat down across the kitchen table from Mrs. Finnerty.

"Indeed I am, child! The English are the finest people in the world, and we're a sorry lot for having chucked them out of this country. It was a damnable week, that rising. I lost my Arthur, God rest his soul, that day. Killed by the Republicans. He was in the police force, on duty at Cork Hill, when this Sinn Feiner rode by on his push bike. Easter Sunday morning, mind you, just before noon, and he shot my Arthur straightaway." The housekeeper paused, then went on softly, "They sent a boy around from Castle Hospital to fetch me, but by the time I got to Arthur he was gone." She was crying, the tears running freely down her cheeks. She wiped them away and added, "They laid him out in his uniform, and I tell you, Caitlin, you'd never seen such a handsome corpse."

"Your Arthur would be alive today, Bridie, if the bloody English had heeded our warning and quit Ireland."

Caitlin spun around, surprised by the voice. Adrian Steele was standing on the bottom step of the backstairs. He had carried his breakfast tray downstairs, and slowly he walked across the room to place it on the kitchen table. He did not take his eyes off the housekeeper. Caitlin stepped back instinctively, as if to give him room.

"It's his own people that cold-bloodedly murdered him!"

"I won't be speaking against your husband, Bridie."

"Then don't, Mr. Steele! Your opinion of my Arthur isn't welcome." She turned her head to wipe away the tears.

Adrian Steele glanced at Caitlin and said softly, "This is what the English have done, divided our country." He sounded in pain, sorry that he had upset the housekeeper.

"We were a peaceful country until you Sinn Feiners tore us apart."
The housekeeper stood and left her tea, as if by turning away from
him she could dismiss his argument.

"I suppose in Connaught you never hear such talk, am I right,
Caitlin?" His eyes caught hold of her, held her captive. "The west of
Ireland knows what Irish freedom really means."

She couldn't find her tongue. He was dressed like a boy from back
home, from the hills of Connemara, in a heavy fisherman's sweater
and baggy trousers. He still had not shaved, nor combed his thick
black hair. She wanted to touch him, to straighten his curls with her
own fingers. This sudden and unexpected desire frightened her, as if
a strange path had been burned through her heart.

"Leave the child be, Mr. Steele!" the housekeeper snapped.

"Caitlin is no child, Mrs. Finnerty," he said quietly. And then in
Irish, he added, "She's a young woman who knows well enough her
own mind."

"None of your Gaelic palaver in my kitchen, Mr. Steele!" Mrs.
Finnerty turned and addressed herself to Caitlin. "Time you started
in on the front parlor, my girl." She glanced at the clock. "The day's
half gone. Now where is Teasy? Oh, there she is!" She heard the
maid at the kitchen door. And then to Adrian, "Off with yourself, sir!
My girls have no time to be wasting. We have our 'evening' today, or
have you forgotten our ways since you've been to London?"

"I forget nothing about Ireland, Mrs. Finnerty. Not the stupidity of
our government, nor the beauty of our colleens."

The back door opened with a bang and Teresa rushed in, a draft of
cold, rainy wind behind her.

"Dear Mother of God, I was after thinking I'd never get home in
this weather." She dropped her wet bundles on the tile floor. "And
here I had left my galoshes in the broom closet. The wet is soaked to
me bones. I'll have turf growing between my toes." She glanced up
then and saw Adrian Steele. "Excuse me, sir, I didn't mean . . ." She
was in her late teens and had the pale face of a girl with a simple
mind.

"Not a'tall, Teasy! Not a'tall!" he answered, mimicking the young
girl's sharp northern accent as he made for the backstairs.

Mrs. Finnerty spoke up before he had planted his foot on the bottom step. "Don't you be giving my little Teresa any of your smartness.
Her English is as fine as any of your Trinity cronies."

"Indeed it is, Bridie." He smiled at all of them. "And don't we Irish
speak better English than the British themselves? Lenin's widow said
that her husband decided the best way to learn English was to go to
Irish political meetings in London—because the Dubliners speak
better English than anyone else."

"Off with you," the housekeeper ordered. "I won't be listening to anything about Lenin and his godless wife."

Caitlin saw now that, except for the subject of Arthur Finnerty, political talk was just banter between the young master and the housekeeper, a game familiar to them both.

"It is Lenin and Stalin who will save Ireland, Bridie. Long live the memory of our own dear socialists, James Larkin and James Connolly."

"Your father will have the back of his hand to you, Adrian Steele, with your talk of labor unions."

"Isn't it I alone in this whole household who truly believes in the Irish, in the greatest of our land? I'm not clinging to my English roots, Bridie, nor thinking that Ireland should be no more than another jewel, like India, in the British Crown. But you, Bridie, and your worship of the English! Your ancestors must be turning in their Wicklow graves, listening to you." He started up the stairs, taking them two at a time.

Mrs. Finnerty crossed the kitchen to shout after him, "I'm having a word with the missus! I've been with this family long before you were born, and I won't have such paddywhackery from the likes of you."

Mrs. Finnerty stood still a moment longer at the foot of the backstairs. Then, turning to the two parlor maids, she sighed and said, "And he was such a lovely child."

# · CHAPTER 12 ·

IT BEGAN LATE IN the afternoon, a heavy, wet snowfall sweeping across the Irish Sea. By six o'clock the square and the cul-de-sac lay under two inches. Caitlin had been sent twice to the curb to sweep the sidewalk clean and each time she came up the granite steps, she paused to glance in through the front windows at the drawing room, ready now for the "evening." She had never seen such grandeur before.

There was a fire lit, and candles as well, and the flames flickered over the golden wallpaper, figured with the silhouettes of graceful, costumed women. It seemed to Caitlin that the women in the soft light were dancing to music being played somewhere in the Georgian house.

Standing outside of the house on the top step, she watched as Mrs. Steele came into the drawing room carrying white chrysanthemums in a silver vase. Caitlin wondered where in the dead of winter the woman had found such flowers. But she was quickly learning that the wealthy had a way about them.

Caitlin swept the step again to look busy, then paused for another look through the windows at Mrs. Steele. She had only seen the madam twice, the morning before in her bedroom, and then a second time earlier that day when Mrs. Steele had come down to the kitchen, dressed in a tweed coat, boots, and breeches.

"Now why would she be dressing up like a jockey?" Caitlin asked the housekeeper afterward.

"God love you, child." Mrs. Finnerty shook her head. "Herself is just off to ride. They'll be up in the park today."

The Mrs. Steele that Caitlin had seen—first in her dressing gown, then gotten up like a boy—had not seemed like the lady of the house. But now, Elizabeth Steele was truly the mistress of Vulcanus.

She was not beautiful—that Caitlin realized. She had already seen in Dublin other women who were handsomer, and secretly she thought herself prettier. Mrs. Steele's face was all bones and angles that looked as if they had come together by chance, and her figure was equally spare. Still, tonight, for the evening, she looked beautiful.

Her gown was a white silk that swept the floor when she moved, and her hair crowned her head in golden waves that left her shoulders bare, ready for the long strings of pearls that were wrapped tightly around her slim neck.

Caitlin had never been so close to a beautifully dressed person before, and for the first time in her life she felt embarrassed by her own commonness.

Then, perhaps sensing she was being watched, Mrs. Steele suddenly looked up. Seeing her maid standing outside gaping at her, she smiled at once, and the smile softened her cold face. Though Caitlin could not hear her through the window glass, she saw her say, "Good evening, Catty," and felt accepted and welcomed at Vulcanus. She gave the steps one last sweep and went in out of the cold.

"Caitlin, where are your galoshes? You'll catch your death in this weather," Mrs. Steele said, coming out of the drawing room.

"I left my Wellies in Connemara, ma'am. I didn't think I'd be needing them here."

Mrs. Steele laughed. "Well, now, I think you're right about your Wellingtons. You'd have no need for them, not on our tarred streets, but you'll need rubbers in the wet weather. I'll have a word with Mrs. Finnerty." She paused again and glanced over at Caitlin. "Do you think you'll like working at Vulcanus, Caitlin? I know it must be difficult, so far from home and your family. We'll try to keep you busy, and happy. And Mrs. Finnerty, I know, will show you where your church is. And make sure you have time off for Sunday Mass, and devotions. Are you a Child of Mary?"

"No, ma'am. We don't have time, you know, for such things in Tourmakeady. But I make the First Fridays, and Mass every day in Lent." Caitlin did not know what more to say. She had never before carried on a conversation with a rich person.

"I want you to feel that you are free to do what you want, Caitlin— with regard to your church, I mean," Mrs. Steele continued. "We're Church of Ireland, as I'm sure you know. My mother's family goes back to Jonathan Swift." Seeing the blank stare on the girl's face, she realized that the parlor maid did not know who she meant. "Jonathan Swift was a famous writer and the dean of our Saint Patrick's. He was also a great believer, as we all are, in the Irish people. Such a believer that he had his footman buried near him on the south aisle of the cathedral. You must see his grave, Caitlin."

"Yes, ma'am," Caitlin whispered. She found she was not listening to what the mistress was saying, but rather to how she spoke English with a Dublin accent, the sharp, clean pronunciation of each word.

"What I want you to understand, Caitlin," she said, lowering her voice confidentially, "is that we, Mr. Steele and I, want you to be your own person here at Vulcanus. We believe in the self-determination of the Irish people. Our country has come a great distance in a short time. We have our independence, and the next step is to see that you young country people have every opportunity to better yourselves, and not feel you must emigrate to America or Australia.

"This is something I tell all the new girls in our employ, Caitlin. Mr. Steele and I feel that this is your country, too, as much as it is ours, and together we can build a wonderful world, free of all that warfare now taking place on the Continent. We have a Protestant now, Mr. Hyde, as our president, and De Valera, a good Catholic, as our prime minister. Together, Catholic and Protestant, we can make Ireland a wonderful new country."

Caitlin nodded, not believing a word of what the woman was saying. Like everyone in the West of Ireland, she knew the English Protestants were her enemy. Father Leahy had explained it to them from the pulpit—how Cromwell and his army had come to Ireland in the sixteenth century and driven the Irish from their farms and into the mountains of Connaught. "To hell or Connaught" was a curse Caitlin had grown up with.

But Caitlin knew when to keep her tongue, and she said instead to Mrs. Steele, "It's as Mr. Adrian says, ma'am, 'Ireland shouldn't be another jigsaw in the British puzzle.'"

"Quite right!" said Mrs. Steele absently as she moved past Caitlin toward the hallway, and then suddenly stopped. "So you've met my son, Caitlin?"

"Yes, ma'am."

Mrs. Steele studied her for a moment, then said quietly, her voice full of authority, "My son has gone to the west every summer since he was sixteen to study Irish. But at times his enthusiasm for the people is not tempered enough by the practicality of life. He's a dreamer, and I've raised him to be that," she added, as if proud. "But I must caution you. His ideas need time to season."

Caitlin nodded, agreeing.

Then Mrs. Steele brightened and remarked as she swept out of the hall, "You people from the west are so level-headed. It must have to do with living close to the land, all those rocks and bogs. Now hurry, dear, and fetch Mrs. Finnerty. Our guests will be arriving, and we mustn't keep anyone waiting."

"Here, dearie," the housekeeper said, handing Caitlin a silver tray of hors d'oeuvre. "Take these like a good girl and pass them about. Poor Teasy has her hands full just with the cups and saucers."

Caitlin was afraid at first, moving among the "evening" guests, but she saw at once that no one noticed her. They turned only to pick up a sandwich and kept talking. "With the help of God, we'll be free of the English soon," a large, pink-cheeked man said as he reached for a triangle sandwich. "As they say, 'England's danger is Ireland's opportunity.' "

"Dev won't seize the chance," answered another. "He's like an omelet that thinks it can get back and hide in the shell."

"I'll let him hide up there at the Dail, as long as he lets us trade with the Germans," the fat man added, speaking over the others.

"Churchill won't let you sell grain to Hitler, Richard. You can be damn sure of that," another replied.

"Winnie can't stop us. He'll have trouble enough just defending England's shores."

Caitlin circled the men and moved on to the next cluster of guests.

"There was a story going around the Gresham that Franco has captured Frank Ryan and turned him over to the Germans. Did you hear that one, Senator?" The men turned to a small quiet man dressed in a tuxedo.

"No, but what if it's true?" he answered. "We have no need for the likes of Frank Ryan back here in Ireland. Himself a Catholic, and fighting for those communists."

"He's not the only Red in Ireland."

"Well, that's true enough."

Casting an eye over the room, the man continued in a whisper, "I'm told your nephew is back from London, Richard. Is he done with ruining the poor English girls?"

"What of it?" answered the big man, angry now. "It would do those white-shinned wenches good to have the feel of an Irishman."

Caitlin moved on reluctantly, embarrassed to stay but sorry to miss what more they might say about Adrian Steele. Her tray was empty and she slipped through the crowd, back to where Mrs. Finnerty stood next to the liquor.

"They'll all be on their way soon," the housekeeper whispered. "Tanya Moisewitch is opening at the Abbey. They're wild for her in this household. Go into the front hall. You'll need to help the ladies with their coats. I'll send Teasy along when she finishes in the kitchen."

Caitlin circled the room and positioned herself at the entrance.

"Do you have such evenings in Connemara, Caitlin?" a voice behind her asked in Irish.

Caitlin jumped in surprise, then shook her head and looked down, nervous that Adrian Steele was speaking to her. He was standing well back, she noticed, so he could not be seen from the drawing room.

"Oh, no, sir, never." She was afraid to look at him, but stood as Mrs.

Finnerty instructed, with her back straight and hands clasped behind her.

"You have parties, don't you?"

"Aye, we do, but not a'tall like this one, you know, with people only standing around."

"You'd be off dancing, wouldn't you?"

"Aye. Down on the wooden bridge, or in Mr. Campbell's barn, if the weather was poor. How would you be knowing that, sir?" she asked, suddenly pleased to be speaking of home.

"I've been to Connaught. I know what it's like in summer when the students come up to the mountains to learn Irish. Have you got yourself a college sweetheart, one of the lads from National? Is that why you're in Dublin?" he teased, still hiding from the crowd of guests.

Caitlin could feel his soft breath against her bare neck, and she looked away, not answering. She thought of Cormac, alone somewhere at that very moment, and she knew she should feel guilty, but she couldn't keep from smiling. It made her happy to hear someone speak Irish—and homesick too, for the west.

"Or is it a Connemara fella, a farmer's son waiting for the old man to kick off so he can get the farm? You're too beautiful, Caitlin De-Lacey, to spend all your days cutting turf and planting spuds."

Caitlin glanced over her shoulder at him. "I'm after having my own life, sir," she answered sharply, afraid of where his prying might lead.

"Until you get a few pounds in your purse, and then what? Off to America? Do you have family there, Caitlin—a sister or two working as maids in New York? Are you for putting together your passage money and then being off, free of this cold island?" His voice was suddenly sad.

Caitlin looked directly at him, lured by the lament in his voice.

"Is it the gombeen man? Is that why you're here in Dublin, working out? Does your family owe the farm to the moneylender?"

"Not a'tall!" she said, surprised herself that she was daring to talk back. "We aren't poor people, sir, in Tourmakeady."

"It's a godforsaken place, Caitlin, you know that well enough. Connemara is a rocky, barren land." He seemed to be challenging her, wanting her to defend her home.

"I only know Tourmakeady, sir, and to me it is the finest place in the world."

"Good for you, Caitlin," he answered, and his voice lost its edge, but it was his blue eyes that showed the change of mood. They had been icy all evening. She had caught glimpses of him earlier, arguing with the guests, and the coolness of his look had frightened her. She was used to men who showed their rage and had done with it, but she saw that that was not his way. He was not like her Cormac, who would storm about the farm or stamp off to O'Cadhain's in the village and down six pints to ease his rage.

"Where do you get such fire, Caitlin DeLacey? How did you slip into Mrs. Finnerty's household? She's not one for hiring girls who might give her trouble. She goes for the likes of little Teasy. A simple girl who fetches without a complaint. You're not that way, are you?"

"I'm not one for hiding behind the door, sir," she answered proudly. She couldn't stop herself. She was being forward, she realized, but there was something about him that made her feel safe and equal.

"It's people like yourself, the farmers and fishermen of Ireland, who will save us." He nodded toward the crowded room. "Not the likes of them. They all think the chief will save us, De Valera and the Fianna Fail will keep us out of the war. Have you seen him, Caitlin? Riding to the Dail on his great big white horse, dressed up in a long black cape as if he were Chamberlain himself. They think it's all grand and great stuff, these bollixes."

"I won't know, sir, I'm not much for politics. We're free of England, thanks to the Dev, that's all I know. Back home we worry more about planting the potatoes and whether we'll have sun enough for the cows to graze. We don't have time to concern ourself with what goes on in Dublin."

"We're not free of the English, Caitlin," he answered quietly, still staring into the crowded room. "And if the Dev wasn't an old gett, he'd throw Ireland in with Hitler and we'd be rid of the English before spring."

"We have our parliament, sir. We are a free people."

"We won't be free, girl, until there is no more England, no more Empire. We are a free state, De Valera tells us, but doesn't England tariff our goods? You know that well enough even in Tourmakeady. Your father can't sell his cattle or crops to England for much profit, and now the English say we can't sell to the Axis either. No, Ireland will always be under control of the crown, as long as they do without our farm goods and won't let us ship out exports to her enemies. We won't be free until Great Britain is destroyed, which, thank God, the Germans will do soon enough."

His anger, she saw now, was always there, lying just beneath the calmness of his voice, the softness of his smile.

"You know what Lenin said about government?"

"I don't think I do," she answered vaguely, not feeling it necessary to add that she had no idea who Lenin was.

"He said government should be simple enough so that any peasant could run the country."

"God help us if Ireland needs me to run her!" Caitlin laughed. "I couldn't even find the house of Parliament, much less sit there."

"Well, I'll show you where Parliament is! One day we'll make a tour of Dublin's fair city."

"Oh, Mrs. Finnerty, she wouldn't—" Caitlin began fearfully. "Please, sir, I have me work to do."

"Mrs. Finnerty is in my employ." The hard edge slipped back into his voice. "She'll arrange the household as my parents and I please."

Caitlin saw Mrs. Finnerty motioning for her to bring the coats.

"Excuse me, sir." She stepped back to go around him, and he stepped back, too, blocking her way. Half his face was in the shadows of the dim light. "Mrs. Finnerty is waiting."

"It is people like Mrs. Finnerty, I'm afraid, that are the curse of Ireland," he called after her. "They're the righteous ones, wanting to keep everyone in their place so they may have petty dominion over parlor maids and charwomen."

"Is that Shaw you're quoting, Adrian?" Richard Steele asked, emerging from the drawing room. "I suspect you're all caught up on the English playwrights now that you're fresh back from the West End. Hmm?"

Adrian spun around, ready for the attack. "Nothing of the kind, Uncle Richard. It's Lenin. You heard the socialist cadence, I'm sure."

Caitlin reached out and swept half a dozen coats from their hangers, then begging pardon, scooted between the men, rushed back to the front entrance. Behind her, she heard the large man say, "You're not going to Eliza Doolittle this maid as well, are you, Adrian? Haven't you learned your lesson? It's the diet, I'm telling you. Those people eat only mutton and potatoes, at best the odd cabbage. Country girls are good only for domestic service, the men for day labor. You've seen them yourself down on O'Connell Street." The big man took a deep breath, paused, and then added softly, "No more experiments, Adrian. Please leave the downstairs help alone, if not for their sake, then for your dear mother's."

"Ireland's future is in this girl, Uncle. You'll see."

"I do see. I see her kind in every squalid slum of this city. And they are not our future! Please don't start on this socialistic nonsense, how we're all brothers under the sun. The Steeles are many branches higher than her kind on the Darwinian tree." He spun his black cape over his shoulders, plucked a silver-capped blackthorn walking stick from the brass stand, then said quickly, as if issuing an order, "Come along, now. We'll miss Tanya's opening."

"I'm no longer interested in Tanya, or the little revivals at the Abbey. These are not times for playacting and personal quests." He followed after his uncle, to join the crush in the front door. The door was open and the guests, standing under the green-gold blown glass of the fanlight, took their coats from Caitlin and went down the short flight of stairs to the front gate and the waiting cabs and limousines parked around the cul-de-sac.

"I am afraid, everyone, that Adrian isn't joining us," Richard Steele announced.

"Oh, Adrian!" a young woman called from the sidewalk. "Please come. It will be such fun, and we haven't seen you in ages."

"His calendar of social endeavors allows for nothing as frivolous as sonnets or Shakespeare," Richard Steele answered. A ripple of laughter came back from the crowd outside, and, having everyone's attention, he called out as he went down the stairs, "But, for my part—God save Frank Ryan!"

The other guests shouted back, "Up the Irish!"

"They're all fine patriots, your friends are," Caitlin said, stirred by the saying. It was one of the few things that evening that was familiar to her from home.

"No, Caitlin, they're just jarred," Adrian said disgustedly.

For a moment they stood, shoulder to shoulder at the columned doorway. "Half of that crowd won't be making it to the Abbey, not tonight. They'll be knocking back tankards of Guinness at the Bailey within a half hour. Or having brandy and soda at the Shelbourne while putting together their party for next week's hunt. There's not a revolutionary in that bloody lot!"

"Well, with the help of God, your Frank Ryan will be out of prison and home again." A week ago she had never heard Frank Ryan's name. Now she knew he'd been fighting against Franco and was in a Spanish jail. She had even read in the *Irish Times* how De Valera had telegrammed Franco for his release.

"Not with the help of God," Adrian said softly. He was whispering, though they were alone in the front hallway. "But with the help of ourselves."

He held her gaze with his blue eyes, as if trying to decide whether to say more, and then he said quickly, as if she'd understand, "They're waiting," and turning, he went out of the house, down the steps, and into the Dublin night.

Caitlin stood in the doorway, followed him with her eyes until he disappeared across the snowy park. She could hear Mrs. Finnerty calling from the drawing room, telling her to close the door before they all caught their death of cold. Adrian Steele was an odd one, she thought, trying to dismiss him. But she traced his footsteps with her eyes across the snowy square, and they seemed like traces not of a man but of a spirit, beckoning her toward a strange new world.

# · CHAPTER 13 ·

As Caitlin was leaving Switzer's Department Store, Mrs. Steele's new linen blouse under her arm, she saw Adrian. He was defying traffic on Grafton Street, waving motorcars and trams to a stop as he crossed the cobblestones. She stepped back against the stone, at once afraid that he would see her and thrilled that she was seeing him, out of the house and away from Mrs. Finnerty.

He was not dressed like the other young men she'd noticed in Dublin, the students at Trinity and National, who whatever the weather wore tweeds and gray flannels. Nor did he favor the heavy gray suits of Dublin businessmen. His clothes, she knew, were Irish made and bought in Dublin in Cleary's. Earlier in the week, Mrs. Finnerty had showed her his closets full of unused English suits, and shelves of linen shirts and silk ascots that his parents had bought him at Tyson's. He wouldn't wear them, Mrs. Finnerty said, because they were British made.

He reached her side of the sidewalk, but he walked with his head bent forward, both hands thrust into his trouser pockets, and didn't see her. He would be gone in a moment, she thought, and she would be safe. But as he stepped out of the way of a lady with a pram, he looked her way.

"Oh, good morning, Caitlin. Were you hiding out from the English in the corset department of Switzer's?" he asked, smiling.

"I beg your pardon, sir," she said, indignant. "I was fetching the mam's new blouse, that's what I was about."

"Now don't be insulted, Caitlin. You've heard of Maud Gonne, haven't you?"

"And wasn't she a leader during the troubles? And an actress as well at the Abbey in her time."

He nodded. "She tells of the time some British detectives were after her and she escaped by hiding in Switzer's corset department."

"I have no need to be hiding from anyone, sir, British or Irish," she answered defiantly, worried that he might think there was something sneaky about her.

"Did you by chance have time to pick up the foolscap and envelope at the stationer's?" he asked, taking her elbow as he led her away to where Anne Street went through from Dawson.

"Sure," Caitlin answered, pleased that she had thought of stopping first at the store on O'Connell Street. "And your stamps as well."

"Caitlin, you're a wonder. Come along and we'll have ourselves a cup of tea. There's a new bar here, I'm told; have you been there yet? I'm sure a girl like yourself is out and about Dublin on your Sundays off."

Caitlin looked away, embarrassed and frightened by the thought of having tea with her employer's son. It was something, she knew, that was never done in Dublin. "Well, thank you, sir. I don't have time to stop for tea now, but I'll be remembering that in the future," she said, recovering, and turned to leave, but Adrian Steele would not be left.

"Bridie Finnerty doesn't own every moment of your life, Caitlin. God almighty, don't give your soul to the likes of her."

" 'Tisn't my soul, Mr. Steele. It's me job," Caitlin answered back. "I'm not likely to find another position. There are plenty of girls looking to be parlor maids in Dublin. If you're wanting to have tea, then chat up one of those students from Trinity. They have time enough to sit about," she answered, angry that he was making it difficult for her to leave him.

"Bejasus, there's more than a bit of west country in you, after all. I should have known that shyness was put on. You'll have the back of your hand to me next, now won't you?" He laughed, mimicking her accent, then reached to take her arm and guide her down Anne Street.

Caitlin pulled away. "I'm not some heifer you can lead to the Galway Fair, Mr. Steele."

"Please call me Adrian," his voice softened.

"I told you, it won't be right. And you know that as well as myself, sir. Now I'm asking you, Mr. Steele, if you're concerned at all for my well-being, then don't be making my life difficult with the missus."

For a second they stood in silence, Caitlin as surprised by her outburst as he was. She was not used to speaking her mind, not even with Cormac. She was always careful with her husband, knowing how sullen her backtalk was apt to make him.

The moment of silence lengthened, but she did not move away from Adrian or look at him. She kept gazing off, watching but not seeing the shoppers going in and out of the small stores on the narrow street. What a nice day it had turned out to be, a clear February day, and the sky a bright winter blue, she thought, looking up. Adrian reached out and tentatively, gently, lifted her chin and turned her face toward his.

She knew it was wrong, letting him touch her, but when she felt his hand on her face, she felt only helpless and happy.

"I won't bullyrag you into doing my wishes," he said in Irish, as if to share another secret with her, "but I want you, and all the servants of these fancy Georgian houses, to know your day is coming. Soon you won't have to be doing other people's wash or running off to Switzer's for the likes of Bridie Finnerty. You'll have your own place up in the park, right beside the Taoiseach himself."

"I won't be having you make fun of me, sir."

"I'm only telling you what will happen to Ireland, once we rid ourselves of the English and those old men in the Dail." He was still speaking in Irish. "Have you seen the slums of this city, Caitlin? I know you have none back home in Tourmakeady, but here you need go only a little ways in any direction and you'll see the poor people living on those wretched narrow streets. You've been to the market on Moore Street and seen those Molly Malones selling their fruit and fish. Ah, it's a great little ditty: 'Sweet Molly Malone . . . A-live, a-live oh.' But she died of the fever, and there are thousands more Mollies just like her.

"And who's to help these poor people? Not our dear Taoiseach. Or the mayor, Alfie Byrne. Here he is dressing himself in evening clothes every morning he goes up to the Dail while families are living like cockroaches and sleeping six to a bed in Kevin Steet. You're better off in the wilds of Connemara, Caitlin. It's hell here in Dublin."

Caitlin thought of her home, the white thatched cottage on the green hillside, the sight of Lough Mask from her kitchen where she could smell the seasons of the year through the open half door.

"But there's new homes being built by the Dail, now aren't there?" she said, trying to cheer him up.

"Ah! A red-tiled dormitory city in Crumlin. It would break your heart to see those places, the bleakness of them, little stucco houses, row after row. Even so, they're better than what's here. But the Dublin slums will stay. Those Roman Catholic capitalists in the Dail think that slums are the will of God."

Caitlin stared up at him, amazed. Gone was the soft and charming young Master Steele, with always a joke and a smile for the ladies at home. Now his face wore the same strong expression as the fishermen of Ardbear Bay, who pitted their tar-black currachs against the Atlantic. Yet he was also beautiful, in the clear, pure way of the angels that appeared on Holy Picture cards and stained-glass windows. When they had talked at the evening, she had thought he must be daft. But now she was caught up, not in his message, but in his forcefulness.

Falling into step with Adrian as if she were mesmerized, she followed him obediently. She could envision Mrs. Finnerty in the kitchen, looking up from her morning tea to the wall clock and saying to Teasy, "Now what in God's name could be keeping that girl?"

Yet Caitlin couldn't pull herself away from Adrian, or the city. She had never been out in the middle of the day in Dublin. It was all new to her: the cabs of Burgh Quay, the crowd surrounding a three-card-trick man at Bachelor's Walk, and banks of people, more than the whole population of Tourmakeady, on the wide O'Connell Bridge.

They walked along the river. On either side of the Liffey there were gray stone buildings, and the sunlight bouncing off the winter river gave a silvery sheen to the stone walls. At the last bridge, Adrian paused again and in the distance Caitlin could see glimpses of the open, ruffled sea.

"When the Norsemen first came to Ireland," he began, as if telling a child a story, "they came up this river in their long boats. They intended to plunder and destroy, but Brian Boru defeated them in 1014. Then the English had their turn. All the kings and queens of England bit their teeth into Ireland, as if we were nothing more than sweetcake.

"But the worst of them were Cromwell and his army. His way of solving the Irish Question, apart from slaughter, was to send any Irishman with ten pounds in his pocket out of Dublin and across the River Shannon, into the wilds of Clare and Connaught."

"To hell or Connaught," Caitlin spoke up, knowing what Adrian meant and pleased to be able to impress him.

"Ah, to hell or Connaught," he answered sadly. "And the real Irish —the sons and daughters of the Celts—were left barren lands, unable to grow anything more than a few potatoes. For centuries they lived on the edge of starvation and then came the famine, the potato blight of the eighteen-hundreds, and everyone starved. Two million people died, while enough corn and cattle to feed the whole of Ireland was shipped across the Irish Sea as rent due to English landlords.

"And those who didn't die left Ireland. Over a quarter of a million left each year—the wild geese of Ireland."

Caitlin knew these stories. The men left Ireland to find work in America. They'd take only what they could carry in a single piece of luggage. Some took only their tea and a few loaves of bread and one good shirt and collar, all tied up in a bundle. She had memories herself of men leaving for America when she was only a child, of standing on the king's highway waiting for the jaunting car which would take the men as far as Ballinrobe, where they would catch the coach for Maam Cross and then on to Galway City; by night they'd be sailing for America. She remembered her excitement standing on the roadside, clutching her mother's leg. As the jaunting car topped the Hill of Weeping the men would turn for one long last look at Tourmakeady, the fragmented fields and stone fences, their farms and cottages. Then the weeping would begin. Her mother, too, clutching other women, and even her father. She could see her father's blue eyes glisten in the early morning cold and she, too, would begin to cry, not knowing then why, but caught up in the sadness as more wild geese left the mountains of Connemara.

They had reached the entrance of Trinity College, and Adrian turned in at the entrance. Caitlin stopped, unsure of what to do.

"Come along, Caitlin. We'll go by way of Lincoln Gate."

"But I'm not a student." She was afraid of being caught out of place, somewhere she did not belong.

"Don't worry. I'll protect you from the lads." He took her by the arm again, gently, and led her through the crowded sidewalk traffic. She had never had a man do that, take her by the arm and guide her, and the feel of his strong hand on her elbow made her dizzy.

"They eat Catholics, you know, all these Protestants," he joked as they went through the arched entrance and into the cobbled interior of Parliament Square. "You've never been to Trinity then?" he asked.

"And why should I? There's nothing here for me."

"Ah, there's your history, Caitlin, the Book of Kells from the monastery of Meath. Would you like to see it?" He stopped in front of the Campanile tower.

"I have no time to look at books, sir. I'm late as it is."

"You have not seen anything as beautiful as the Book of Kells. It was made by Irish monks."

"I wouldn't care if it were done by Saint Patrick himself, I haven't more time to be dallying."

"Would you come to see it with me another day?"

Caitlin paused and looked up at the young man, puzzled.

"Why, Mr. Steele, would you be wasting your time with the likes of me?"

"Because you're a beauty, Caitlin," he said quietly, thoughtfully, as if what she looked like had been on his mind. "There is a true beauty behind your dark eyes." He smiled then. "And rare beauty it is."

She looked away, unable to answer. No man had ever spoken to her so, said such beautiful things. His voice sung in her ear.

"We must carry on the dream, Caitlin, Yeats's dream, of a new Irish world. And Ireland must build her a new world with yourself at the very center. You, Caitlin DeLacey! Not me! It is the likes of me, with our university degrees, who must follow you. Do you know how beautiful you are in your simplicity, the directness of your ways? It is up to you to preserve what is truly Irish and rid us finally of everything English."

"I can't do such things, sir," she whispered, suddenly feeling responsible for his great schemes. "I haven't much learning at all. We had only but a national school at home."

"I'll teach you, then, myself. You don't want to go to the national school. They'll only misguide you. We must do as Jonathan Swift told us—'Burn everything from England except her coals.' It is our own folktales, our songs, and proverbs that you must study, Caitlin."

"And how would I do that, sir, what with my work at the house?" They had begun to walk again, out of Trinity and past Merrion Square. "I have just my Sunday afternoons off." She was beginning to worry, thinking he might take those few hours away from her and she'd never see Cormac.

"Ah, but soon enough you'll have all the time in the world," he said, slyly.

Caitlin looked up at him. "They won't be giving me the sack now?" she asked nervously.

He laughed. "Not likely! My mother thinks you're 'a charming child,'" he said, mimicking his mother's accent.

Caitlin giggled, then bit down on her finger, embarrassed to be enjoying a joke at the madam's expense. He went on then, still speaking in his mother's clear, icy tones.

"We—Mr. Steele and I—want you to freely practice your religion. We're Church of Ireland here, of course, but surely God—I mean, Mr. Steele and I mean—God must have liked you Catholics, for he has made so many of you."

Caitlin turned away, unable to keep from laughing out loud. Then she heard Adrian say calmly, all the fun gone from his voice, "It's the likes of her and my father that are your real enemy, Caitlin."

She glanced up, shocked to hear a son speak that way of his parents.

"It's their class, the Anglo-Irish of Dublin, who are holding the poor people down, stopping you from getting your own place in Ireland. Did she tell you yet that her family are descendants of Dean Swift?"

Caitlin nodded, afraid to speak.

"She's a great one for that, and at the same time telling how she wants you to better yourself. And here it was her bloody ancestors—the privileged Anglo-Irish, the landed gentry—who have lived grand lives off the incomes of confiscated lands and poor Irish tenants."

She would be in trouble, Caitlin thought, even for listening to such talk. It was something that she would never have heard among the Irish at home. They kept such opinions to themselves.

"Your mother is a fine woman, it seems to me," Caitlin said softly.

"And I'm thinking you shouldn't be carrying on like that about her to a perfect stranger."

"What I've said to you, I've told her, and father as well. It isn't them. It is what they represent. The last vestiges of colonial behavior."

They reached Northumberland Road and Adrian stopped walking, staring for a moment across the wide street at the row of red-brick houses. Caitlin was tired from the walking. At home, it was nothing for her to walk three or four miles up into the hills and bring in the sheep, but the cobblestone and pavement were hard on her feet. She sat down on the stone wall to catch her breath, wondering where he would take her next. It seemed as if they had walked the whole of Dublin.

"Do you see that house across the way, Caitlin?" he asked, sitting beside her.

She looked over at one of the double red-brick buildings.

"Do you see the window on the lower left? Can you tell me what flowers are growing there, in the pot?"

Caitlin looked at him. "Now why in the world would you be wanting to know a thing like that?"

"It's a hobby of mine, knowing about flowers." He kept smiling.

"A hobby is it! Well, you don't know the first thing then, sir, if you wouldn't be knowing what flowers they are. They're marigolds, and red roses and carnations; you have them in your own garden."

"Marigolds, are there?" He brightened with the news. "Are you sure, Caitlin?"

"And wouldn't I be having the same flowers at home in Tourmakeady?" she answered, puzzled by his question, then she saw what building they were staring at and her heart was swept with a rush of fear. She had been foolish, she realized, wandering around Dublin, being caught up in his grand talk about what Ireland would be like free of England and not knowing what Adrian Steele wanted of her.

"Are you sure, Caitlin?" he asked again.

She turned on him. "If you're thinking I'm blind, sir, or I don't know my flowers, then knock on the door of the German Legation and ask for yourself. And now, sir, I need to be getting back to the house. Would you please point me in the right direction?" She would not look at him. "You've walked me all over Dublin, and I haven't a clue where I am."

"I'll walk you home, Caitlin. We're just up the road." He stood as well, then glanced a final time at the stone residence before turning with Caitlin toward the Grand Canal.

"Now what would you be more interested in, sir, the marigolds or the roses? Or the Germans themselves?" she asked, wanting him to know she wasn't blind to his motives. "You know what the talk is in Dublin. How the Germans signal their Irish spies?"

"Where would you hear of such nonsense?" He laughed. "Is that what the priests have been telling you at Sunday Mass?"

"I won't be having you getting me into trouble with the Gardai, Mr. Adrian." She was frightened now, afraid they might have been seen by the police, and picked up her pace. " 'Tis the girls who told me about the flower pots on the windowsills, Mr. Adrian."

"Don't listen to the silly stories of the kitchen help, Caitlin. The Germans are clever enough not to signal the Irish underground by rearranging flower pots on their legation windowsills so that all of Dublin might know their business."

"Then you tell me, Mr. Adrian: how would the Nazis be contacting their spies?" She stopped on the sidewalk and challenged him.

Adrian stepped back a pace and put his hands in his trousers the way she had seen the cornerboys do. He kept smiling down, as if he were an older brother enduring her innocence.

"They'd send a young girl—a parlor maid, perhaps—into a stationery store on O'Connell Street," he said in Irish, "and ask that she buy a foolscap of paper and envelope, and make sure she told the clerk she wanted stamps as well, for the letter was to be posted to America. That's what an Irish spy might do, Caitlin DeLacey, and a message would be passed without a flower pot being moved on the windowsill of the German Legation."

"Oh, dear Mother of God," Caitlin whispered, her heart sinking.

But Adrian laughed then, and she decided he had been teasing her. A grin broke across his face, leaving him looking happy and young, like a lad in the school yard.

"Oh, Jaysus!" she swore, angry again, and also trembling in relief. "I should box your ears!" She stepped forward and hit his chest with the butt of her closed fist, saying, "May the hammers of damnation beat the soul out of you on the anvil of hell."

Suddenly, he pulled her into his arms, pinning her flaring fists and calming her at once with his surprise embrace.

"You curse like a poet, Caitlin."

"And you have no right teasing me in such a way. Putting the fear of God into me." She felt his tight embrace and knew how they must look to passersby on Northumberland Road, but she could not at that moment bring herself to tell him to let her go.

"I'm sorry," he whispered, but his eyes were still lit with amusement.

Now she pulled herself away and straightened her uniform, fearful that Mrs. Finnerty might see that the fresh starch was gone from the dress.

"Here I must be making a holy show of myself," Caitlin whispered, not looking up at Adrian. She realized again how strange it was for a parlor maid to be off in the middle of Dublin with the son of her employer.

"Oh, Caitlin, don't worry so."

"It's easy enough for you to say."

"I'm going back to Vulcanus to have a word with Bridie."

"I won't be putting a bother to you, sir."

"It is no bother, Caitlin, and I did kidnap you. I won't have you think I blackguarded you."

"I thought no such thing!"

"What do you think of me?" he asked, surprising her.

"Well, I don't think anything a'tall."

"You don't!" He sounded disappointed.

" 'Tisn't my right, sir, to be thinking about you."

"I'm always thinking about you, Caitlin," he said softly and not in English.

Caitlin was aware at that moment of the busy street and people around them, and that her neck and face were flushed.

"I'm a servant girl in your family's home, Mr. Steele," she answered in self-defense.

"In my world there are no servants."

"Well, you're a lucky man, sir, to be living in such a world. In Dublin—the only world I have—you're Protestants, Mr. Steele, high-up people, and I'm a Catholic." She answered him firmly, to put a stop to his talk, and was surprised at her own certainty. In Tourmak-eady she had never thought of such things, of whether she belonged or not, for she always had, she always would. But in Dublin she had already seen the difference between herself, a Catholic from rural Ireland, and people like the Steeles.

But Adrian Steele was not impressed. "We're both Irish, Caitlin. That's all that matters."

They had left Northumberland Road and ahead Caitlin could see Pembroke. She knew where she was now and that made her feel better, more willing to speak her mind.

"You know nothing a'tall about me, Mr. Steele. Not who I am or where my people are from. 'Tis easy enough, I'm sure, for you to talk grandly about the likes of me being able to rule Erin and govern the Dail, but the truth is we do well enough as it is to find work as maids at a pound a week.

" 'Tis harder on the men of Connemara. There's no work at home, not if they don't have a farm, so it's off to America or Dublin to find work under the hammer at the coal yards, or whatever odd job there is to keep body and soul together. And God help if they have little ones!" She began to cry, realizing how hopeless her life was in Dublin without her Nora, without even her husband.

Adrian stepped forward and seized her shoulders. The strength of his grip went through her with a force of poteen and she began to choke on her tears, embarrassed at having made a show of herself again.

"Caitlin," he whispered. " 'Tis true enough. I know about the poor people in the west, about all the Irish of Ireland. But soon we'll be free."

She broke away from his grasp and continued quickly along Pembroke, her fear turning to anger at his answer, more talk by those in power about what they'd do for the poor. She wiped away the tears as she walked, rushing to be away from Adrian Steele, but he seized her, spun her about on the pavement.

"There's a plan," Adrian said under his breath, "by those of us fighting England here in Dublin. There's a German coming to Ireland. His name is Oscar Plaus. He'll be arriving soon from Holyhead to help organize our attack on the Crown.

"Once we're ready, then our lads will rise up against De Valera and the Dail, seize control, and let the Germans use Irish airfields and seaports to invade England. In return, the Germans will help us get back the six counties and we'll set up a truly free country, with power shared by all the people." He was smiling, his eyes bright with pleasure.

"Dear God, why in the world would you be telling me?" Caitlin whispered.

"Because you're one of us, Caitlin."

"I'm a parlor maid, sir, and nothing more. I'm not a revolutionary!"

"Yes you are, Caitlin." He kept smiling.

Caitlin knew his way. She had learned already how when he cocked his head, looked at her from the sides of his eyes, that he was holding back something, and as she thought that, she knew what he meant.

"God almighty, you weren't teasing about the foolscap and stamp," she whispered, in a new rush of fear.

"I couldn't take the chance myself. The Gardai have their eye out for all of us home from London, and I had to get a message sent. You've helped us, Caitlin; you've helped Ireland."

"I've put the noose around my own neck, that's what I've done." She spun away from him and ran to the basement steps of Vulcanus House.

"I'll protect you, Caitlin," he called after.

"I'll have you mind your own business, sir." She thought of Cormac, of what he'd do to her if he found out how foolish she had been.

"I'll write it out in verse: 'Caitlin DeLacey, now and forever; wherever green is worn: all changed, changed utterly: a terrible beauty is born.' " Adrian Steele's voice followed her down the basement steps and she rushed into the kitchen and slammed the door behind her.

# · CHAPTER 14 ·

"THIS IS WHERE THAT fella Joyce lived," Caitlin said, nodding ahead toward Martello Tower. They had walked the length of the winter beach, from Sandymount to Sandycove.

"Who's that now, Catty? One of Tommy Joyce's people?" Cormac asked, finishing a choc ice.

"James Joyce! The fella that wrote about Dublin. Don't you know a thing, Cormac?"

"When would I have time to be reading books?" he answered back. "And when would you? Is that what they have you doing in Ballsbridge? Well, it's a different story, I'm telling you, in the building trades. At quitting time, I'm lucky if I have the strength to finish a pint." He stopped to study his wife, frowning. "Are you getting fancy on me, Catty? You'll be thinking you're too good for me next, what with your fancy white uniforms and indoor lavs. And here we've only been in Dublin a fortnight. I'll never get you home again to Tourmakeady."

They were alone on the hard sand; the schoolchildren and the couples had gone from the Sunday shore. The tide was turning. It was late. She would have to catch the train soon for Dublin to be home before teatime. Mrs. Finnerty had warned her about staying out late. "A decent girl isn't safe on Dublin streets nowadays, not since the troubles." It was only two o'clock but already the early February twilight had darkened the winter sky. She could no longer see the blue Welsh mountains topping the horizon of the Irish Sea.

"Now who's been giving you books to read? I should think you'd have enough work taking care of a place like that. You're not a slacker, I know that, Caitlin Rush." He cocked his head and smiled, trying to avoid a fight.

Linking her arm into his, she turned them both toward the shore. She was happy to make peace. They saw each other so rarely, only those few hours on Sunday afternoon, that a distance had opened up between them. He was becoming strange to her. If only they could find a small hotel in town next Sunday—Mrs. Donohoe's perhaps, one of the traveler places near the station. They had been strangers to each other for too long. But thinking of what she wanted made her feel sinful; she would have to tell the priest on Friday, she decided, when she went to confession.

"Come, Cormac," she said quickly, to escape her impure thought, "we'll have tea at the Pavilion."

"Ah, they won't have the likes of me at the Pavilion, what with my clothes. And it's Jameson's I need today, Catty, not a cup of tea."

The left the flat strand and walked along Hyde Road toward the station. Children were playing on the road, and as she and Cormac passed, Caitlin could hear them singing.

> Oul De Valera has a shop down in hell;
> He's selling ammunition and he's doing very well.
> Sixpence for a rifle, a ha'penny for a shell,
> Oul de Valera has a shop down in hell.

One of the small girls reminded her of Nora, and she wondered what her little girl was doing at that moment on the west coast, so close to her, only a half day's journey and yet so far away. Her suddenly longing for her baby left her breathless, and she turned to Cormac to keep from crying.

"Would you find us a place to go next Sunday? You know—a room?" she whispered.

"I was thinking you had forgotten me in that way, Catty." He pulled his arm from hers and slipped it around her waist as they approached the station. "I was thinking that once I got me a few pounds together we might rent ourselves a flat in Dublin."

"Sure, Mrs. Finnerty would never have that, Cormac. I'd be sacked, I know, if she found out I was married, and with a child at that."

"Are they treating you well there, Catty, at the Protestants'?"

"Ah, well enough. Teasy, little Teresa, is slow, you know, and Mrs. Finnerty is a bit of a fuss. The woman has a real tongue on her, like Molly Joyce from back home, but she has a kind heart, truly, and makes sure I have my Sunday afternoons out. I told her a bit of a fib, Cormac, and said I go to see my aunt, a Poor Clare nun. Do you think that was all right?"

Cormac raised his head and roared, startling the winter starlings in the sycamore trees. They flew off in a thick patch, like a puff of black smoke, and Caitlin, watching, realized how much she missed the out-of-doors. At home, working on the farm, she had never given it a second thought. Now she often found herself watching the birds in Herbert Park and noting the color of the sky.

"I don't mind you fibbing to have your time with me," Cormac answered. "We give our bloody souls as it is to the likes of them who live in those fancy houses."

They had reached the station at Dalkey and Caitlin sank down suddenly on one of the outdoor benches. She hated their partings. Their lives were so separate that she always tried to picture what became of him after he'd gone. He'd ride with her to Tivoli, then disappear into one of the massive buildings where he shared a flat— "a piece of floor," he told her, "not wider than a turf cutting"—with seven other lads from the west. The Sunday before he had pointed out his flat from the tram window, showing her the iron balcony where he hung his woolen underwear to dry. Once alone, she had cried all the way back into Dublin at the thought of him washing up and cooking for himself.

"We'll have a fine house ourselves someday, Cormac," she said. "One of those palaces like there is on Ely Place, with a mahogany door and a brass knocker."

"We won't, Catty—nor even one of those corporation houses in Crumlin," Cormac answered calmly. "That's not for the likes of us." He sat beside her on the bench and took out a tin of Carreras. Smoking was new to him, and he lifted a thin cigarette carefully from the pack.

"But we will," she said stubbornly. "Mr. Steele said as much." She had to talk about him, had to mention his name to Cormac in some way. She had been thinking about Adrian Steele a lot, comparing him with her husband, and now she had to say his name out loud, if only to be free of her secret thoughts.

"Who's that, love, one of those high-up people?" Cormac asked, striking a wooden box match against his boot.

"Himself's son. Adrian Steele. He's an actor with the Abbey. I talked to him at their evening. You know what an evening is, don't you?" she asked, knowing he didn't.

"Mr. Walsh was there, the Dev's minister. He's a good friend of the family, Mrs. Finnerty says." She was showing off, she knew, but she wanted to impress her husband. At home in Tourmakeady he was always the one to bring home the news from the village. Now it was she who could speak of the great world.

But Cormac didn't notice. "Ah, Walsh's people are from the west, down near Kerry. I met a cousin of his once at the fair in Galway. The bloke was hitting up everyone in this pub for a drink, telling them how he was close to De Valera because of his cousin." Cormac laughed, shook his head, remembering. He went on quickly then with another story of that fair, how he had met English tourists on the Galway Road and given them the wrong directions on purpose.

He was enjoying the recollection, so Caitlin kept quiet. She had heard the story often, of how he had bested the English on the Galway Road, but she knew it made him feel better to talk of home. It was Connemara that interested him, not what was happening to her at the Steeles'.

She saw the Dublin train approaching. She would not see Cormac for another week, but that thought did not strike her with as much terror as it had at first. She knew she could find her way back to Ballsbridge, do her job, and earn her keep. It made her feel important, but also guilty that she was no longer so dependent on her husband.

As they approached the train they were surrounded by other couples like themselves, down from Dublin for an afternoon at the seashore. The men were all digging in their trouser pockets for change, but Caitlin had her fare ready, as if she were a girl on her own, coming home from a day at the Booterstown Fair.

Cormac was still telling his story of the English tourists. "I tipped my cap to them, I did, and one of the men—those chinless uppity kind—gave me sixpence, and asked, as if he were J. D. Rockefeller himself, 'Which way to Maam Cross, my good lad?' "

Moving quickly ahead of him, Caitlin hurried to two empty seats. Cormac lowered himself into the space beside her.

"I sent them up by way of Cornamona," he concluded, and laughed aloud, still amused by the thought of the tourists driving off, their Daimler struggling up the narrow mountain road.

Caitlin looked out the dirty pane as the train cleared the station. Over the slate rooftops she tried to get a glimpse of the sea, some blue patch of sky and foam to carry back with her to Dublin.

"Now what did this fella say, Catty, this left-hander of yours, about the likes of us owning one of those Georgian houses?"

"It was nothing, Cormac, nothing a'tall," she replied. It was too late to talk of Adrian Steele, of his fine thoughts, and of how he had sent her into the stationer's on a dangerous errand. She had thought to ease her mind by telling Cormac, but now she realized she was afraid.

Caitlin shifted in the wicker seat. The train had picked up speed and they were rushing toward Dublin, past Monkstown and Seapoint with its well-kept garden, and the whitened stones and the station's name written with shells in Irish. Then onto Blackrock, where from the train windows she could see the public park and bandstand, and the high-platformed diving tower high above the saltwater baths. She would be in Dublin soon, Caitlin thought, and there would be another week without Cormac—another week with Adrian Steele.

"Cormac." She leaned closer to her husband and whispered. "We'll go to the rooming house, to Mrs. Donohoe's. She knows us and won't be asking about luggage."

"Ah." He nodded, not fully understanding.

"We'll go today, and not wait till next Sunday." She would have to lie to Mrs. Finnerty about why she'd missed tea—but she could say her aunt, the Poor Clare, had asked her to stay for vespers. Would Mrs. Finnerty believe her? At that moment, it hardly mattered. This was the only way she could think of to save herself from Adrian Steele.

Cormac had fallen asleep, as he always did after they made love, but Caitlin was wakeful. She moved his heavy arm off her and slid from the bed. Once he awoke, she wanted to be dressed and ready to leave.

Caitlin felt better dressed. She was feeling guilty and she wondered why. Perhaps it was that she had made love to her husband on a Sunday afternoon. In Tourmakeady they made love only at night, and then just once a week.

Once, when they were newly married, she had tried to coax him into bed on a Saturday night after a dance in Campbell's barn. But he had turned away from her, saying that he wanted to receive Holy Communion the next morning. She had never tried to seduce him again, and after Nora was born, he seemed less interested in her. She glanced back at the bed.

All she could see of Cormac was the back of his head and his undershirt. He would never take that off, and she was the same way. It pained her, being undressed. As a child she had learned how to slip into her nightgown first before taking off her clothes, for there was little privacy at home, with her father and brothers always about.

She was learning about privacy now, in her small room at the Steeles'. It was a lovely feeling, she had begun to realize, to sit in her window at the top of the house and look over the wet slate roofs of Dublin. To watch the sun in the early afternoon cross the city and shine on the Liffey. To do nothing at all but daydream and be quiet and alone and happy with herself. She had never had that before.

Perhaps she should have been a nun after all.

Father Leahy had spoken to her father when she was eleven, coming out to the farm on his push-bike. She had been sent off to play in the fields instead of doing the washing-up after dinner, but instead of disappearing she had hidden behind the turf stack and heard the priest suggest that the convent would be "a good place for little Catty." She would have a good home the priest said, and be taught cooking. "The convents and parish houses are always in need of a girl like Catty."

She had held her breath for fear that her father would say yes, held her breath until she thought her heart would burst. Then her da had answered, "Sure, but we won't be wanting to lose our little Catty.

She's a pleasure, that child. And I don't think the sisters could handle the likes of her, God love her."

She realized then her father knew she was listening, and she ran out into the haggard, frightened that she still might be sent away. She hid all afternoon in the rock shelter of the Druids, but when it turned dark, her da came to find her, as if he had known all along where she would be hiding.

He came up the slope singing so she would know it was him, and carried her home, telling her while they were still outside the cottage and away from her brothers and sisters, that he'd never let anyone take her away from him. Then he set her down and sent her inside, saying, "Go dry your tears, girl, and cut yourself a slice of ginger-bread. And don't worry about the priests and nuns. They'll never have a child of mine to turn into an English lackey."

Before she went into the cottage, her father kissed her on her fore-head. He rarely showed such affection. It was the Irish in him. Her Cormac was the same. Cormac never told her if he loved her. To such men, Caitlin knew, it was a kind of weakness to tell women what they felt.

Caitlin was dressed now, but Cormac was still asleep, as if their brief lovemaking had exhausted him. But she knew better. It was the work on the buildings. He was a strong man and he had worked hard at home, but that was his own place, and his heart was in the labor. It was different with the hammer work, the ten-hour day for wages of eight hours.

She closed her eyes to the dreariness of the room, to the sight of her husband on the bed, and remembered how Adrian had looked the day before when he had surprised her in the library.

It was not her task to dust the first-floor rooms, but Caitlin was doing it anyway, letting Teasy stay downstairs with Mrs. Finnerty for an-other cup of tea. Once alone in the library, she put down her duster and began searching the shelves for books to read. She had been taking books up to her room for the last week, reading them late at night, after Teasy and Mrs. Finnerty were asleep.

"Ah, you're the one who's been reading my books!" Adrian Steele said from the doorway.

Caitlin dropped the book she had just pulled from the shelf.

"It's all right, Caitlin. I want you to read Irish writers," he spoke quickly, coming into the library.

Caitlin glanced up at him, her face flushed. He was dressing for riding, wearing boots and his astride coat.

"I'm sorry, sir, but I should have been asking the missus's permis-sion."

"You have mine," he said quickly. "Now what have you there?" He came closer to glance at the book she had pulled from the shelf. "O'Sullivan it is, and in the Irish! Have you been reading Yeats?"

"I've tried, sir, but 'tis a rare poem that makes sense to me. He mixes his words, you know. You'd think with his people coming from Sligo and all, he'd be able to say what he was thinking straightaway. His poems are like trying to follow a cow's path through the pasture."

Adrian laughed, then reaching up high in the shelf, pulled down another leather-bound volume. "This is by James Stephens. He's a grand writer, and tells all the old Irish stories."

"Have you read all these books, sir?" She nodded to the shelves.

"Not all, but most." He walked the length of the bookshelves, running his fingers lightly along a row of leather volumes. "Swift and Shaw, Oscar Wilde, James Stephens, Synge, O'Casey and Edmund Burke, George Moore and Oliver Goldsmith. And James Joyce and William Butler Yeats." He spoke the names, Caitlin thought, as if they were a litany of saints.

The sun had come out and it filled the room, pouring over his fine clothes and Spanish boots. She did not think anyone else could ever look so handsome.

"This is Ireland's greatness, these men," he said. "But there are others as well that Erin should be proud of. Men who never wrote a verse or a book. Forgotten men, like those in the Wexford Rising of ninety-eight. That rebellion was put down by Prussian mercenaries. The colonel who led them had the Irish rebels flogged across their stomachs instead of their backs, so they would suffer greater pain."

He paused a moment to look at the high shelves, bathed now in the yellow winter light, then turned to her and said softly, "I'm sorry, Caitlin, for having compromised you last week. It wasn't right, involving you without explaining."

She was unable to take her eyes off his face. The morning sun lit his face and thick black hair, as if he were a portrait on the library wall, a painting of Parnell himself. Or one of God's archangels.

"Well, I can't be writing a book, sir, or even a poem," she said softly, feeling herself being swept up by this man.

He stepped closer and searched her face. "Would you be willing to help Ireland, Caitlin?"

"Ah, sir." But she knew in her heart it wasn't Ireland she wanted to help.

"Please don't call me 'sir.'" He smiled down at her, edging her into agreement with the warmth of his look.

She blushed. "Adrian it is then."

"I need you to do me a favor, like before."

Caitlin nodded, hardly hearing, caught up as she was in watching his lips move and feeling his hand on her shoulder, touching her, pulling her gently into his conspiracy.

"Catty, what time do you have?" Cormac said from the bed, stirring like an ox from the deepness of his sleep.

She turned from the window, her mood broken by his voice.

" 'Tis time I'm getting home," she answered slowly.

"I'll stay a bit longer in these clean sheets, now that they're paid for. It's a better sleep than I'd get in Tivoli. But come here, love, and give me a good-bye kiss." He lifted his arms to her.

"Ah, you've had enough kissing for one day," she answered, as if to make a joke of her refusal, and swiftly slipped into her coat. She stopped at the door, feeling selfish and guilty. "Next Sunday it is?" she asked, looking back at the bed. The room had darkened and she could not see his face, just the bulk of him.

"At Sandymount. We'll go up to the Pavilion if the day is good," he offered.

Caitlin nodded. She knew he was trying to make amends, as if he, too, felt the coldness of her reply. It was because they spent too much time apart, she told herself, and nothing else. That was why there was a strangeness between them. But the truth had come clear to her that day, for it was Adrian she had dreamed of when Cormac had made love to her. In her heart she knew she had already betrayed her husband.

# · CHAPTER 15 ·

CAITLIN WAS ALMOST HOME, walking up Serpentine toward Claremont Road, when she heard the noise. At first, caught up in her worries over Cormac, she was too startled to realize what she was hearing. But as she glanced over her shoulder she saw the motorcar lurching down the empty street. Caitlin kept walking, then looked back at the auto again. The gray sedan was speeding toward her now, and its headlights were dark. She began to run, frightened without knowing exactly why. The car caught her before she reached the terrace, cutting sharply into the cul-de-sac to block her way. It missed striking her by inches and she stumbled against the bonnet, terrified that she was about to be kidnapped, as she had heard often happened to girls in Dublin. Then, nerving herself to confront her pursuer, she looked through the windscreen and saw Adrian grinning at her.

"Are you daft?" she shouted angrily, then yelped with pain as she struck one of her legs on a bumper.

"You're hurt!" He popped open the right front door.

"It's lucky I'm alive with the likes of you at the wheel. Didn't you see me on the walk?"

"Shh! Come along."

"I'm late as it is, Mr. Steele."

"Yes, but come along anyway. I've spoken to Bridie." He had her by the elbow, pushing her into the wide front seat of the Bentley. "And where did you tell her you'd be taking me—if it isn't too bold of me to ask?"

"I'll tell you in a minute. You said you'd help if I needed you. Well, I do. So for now, please hold your tongue." He swung the sedan around, bouncing the front tires on the curb, and raced back toward Ballsbridge. They drove silently for several minutes before she realized they were leaving the center of Dublin and heading south, back toward Dun Laoghaire. It had stopped raining, and Caitlin could see something of the new moon. It lit their way, like a dim gas lamp, on the damp, empty road out of the city. She wanted to ask where they were going, but she wouldn't risk being shushed again like a child. They were out of the city before he spoke.

"We're to pick up a man, a Mr. Thomas. He's in Dun Laoghaire and needs to go down to Dalkey."

"Dun Laoghaire? But I've just come from there—" She stopped talking at once, suddenly realizing that she might give her secret away. But Adrian Steele was concerned only with his own affairs.

"I need a woman with me."

"Ah?"

"Mr. Thomas won't come to the door, I'm told, unless he sees a woman. He's staying at a Miss Shane's boardinghouse."

"And who would he be now, this Mr. Thomas?" Even as she asked, she began to fear the answer.

"He says he's a commercial traveler, but he's no more that than you or I," Adrian said softly, with a hint of pride.

"Is he a spy, then?" she whispered, afraid even to say the word out loud. Every day in Dublin she heard a new rumor of a German spy being sent ashore by a U-boat or dropped into Ireland by parachute.

"He is. Caitlin Brugha herself rang me up and asked if I'd collect Mr. Thomas."

"Is she Cathal Brugha's widow, God rest his soul?" Even in Tourmakeady they knew the story of Cathal Brugha, who had fought alongside De Valera in the Easter Rebellion and the civil war. The story was that he had been the last holdout in a hotel on O'Connell Street, refusing all offers of surrender. Then when the hotel was set on fire, he ordered his troops out and stayed behind in the burning building. Not until his men were safe did he come to the doorway with a revolver in each hand, his face black with smoke, and start firing on the free-staters, only to die in a hail of bullets.

"The same. She gave her husband to the cause of Irish unification. And now, they say, she's giving the profits of her business, Kingston Shirts, to the German ambassador. All in memory of Cathal."

"But why in God's world would she choose you to fetch a German spy in the middle of the Dublin night?"

"I know her daughters, Noinin and Neassa. Noinin is reading philology at the National and Neassa is a medical student. When I was home from London at Christmas, Noinin invited me out to their house, Ros na Riogh, for a party.

"Mrs. Brugha heard me talk that night about using the war to get England out of Northern Ireland. And as I was leaving, she asked me if I would be willing to help the cause. I told her I would be proud to, especially for the likes of her, the widow of a great patriot."

He took a small torch from the seat and, leaning forward to smother the light, read the directions off a slip of paper. Then he started up the car again and drove another few blocks, explaining as he drove, "There's a woman who usually collects Mr. Thomas, Kinsella's daughter, Maisie."

"Sean Kinsella?"

"The same. The deputy in the Dail." Adrian glanced over at her. "See, Caitlin? All kinds are involved in the resistance, high-up people as well as the likes of those living in the slums behind Merrion Square."

"And the likes of myself, who should know better." She sighed restlessly.

"It's simple enough," he went on, as if to overcome her unwillingness. "All you need do is go up to the house and knock. Miss Shane will answer the door. You ask for Mr. Thomas. Say that you're a friend of Maisie Kinsella. That will do it." He gestured up the empty street. "What you do is take Mr. Thomas out the kitchen door, cross the garden, and knock on the kitchen door of the house behind. It's a family by the name of Mahon. They'll let you in. Go straight through and out the front. I'll be waiting on Park Place."

"And why in the world would you be doing that?"

"We don't know, but the G-Two might be watching the place."

"Jesus, Mary, and Joseph."

"Don't be worrying. You'll be in and out of the place in minutes." At the corner of Corrig Road he stopped the Bentley. "It's the third house on the right. Go ahead," he whispered in the darkness.

Caitlin could hear his fear. For all his grand talk of revolution, she thought, Adrian was as innocent as herself. She had her hand on the handle but could not push the door open. She knew it would not be as simple as he said. Something would go wrong. She would be arrested and sent to prison. She had already heard on Radio Eireann how the Gardai were taking down rural road signs so German spies parachuting into Ireland wouldn't know the way to Dublin.

"I can't do this, Adrian," she whispered, ashamed that she had agreed to help.

For the moment both of them were silent in the dark automobile. Would he become so angry, she wondered, that he'd push her out and leave her to find her own way home?

If she could just tell him about her baby, she thought. If he knew about Nora, he wouldn't ask her to risk her life for Ireland's freedom. It wasn't fair to demand so much from someone like her. She knew well enough that the high-up people never went to jail.

"Please, Caitlin, the man's waiting," he whispered. The rain drove against the car with the force of the sea behind it.

"I'm afraid of the coppers, Adrian."

"Now why would the coppers be out on a night like this?"

"You said yourself the G-Two might be watching the boarding-house." She was buying time, trying to marshal her arguments. True, she had agreed to help him—but not on this particular evening, not on this particular mission. If luck were habit, she'd be at home, up under the slate in her warm room, far from danger and the wet weather.

"And what if there are coppers around? They'll think you're just one of the boarders yourself, just back from the Dublin flicks. Now hurry—go while the rain is up."

She went. Against her better judgment she went because against his determination she had no will. He was so sure of himself that he compelled her faith—though in one corner of her country mind, she knew that running down the short street to Miss Shane's was the most foolish thing she had ever done.

She ran with the wind, oblivious to the deep puddles she splashed through, rushing only to have it done with, for she could not turn back. Adrian had already driven off, leaving her exposed to the weather and everything else—like one of their lambs at home, she thought, left behind on the rocky hillside. She reached the boarding-house and, still refusing to think of how foolish she was, pushed open the iron gate, ran up the walk, and rang the bell.

Only then did she glance about and see the other automobiles parked on Corrig Road. Was there a G2 policeman in every car, she thought—or were they watching from the windows of the houses across the street? She had seen Jimmy Cagney movies at the Tivoli Cinema; she knew how the FBI had cornered him in *Scarface.*

Then the door to Miss Shane's creaked open and she swung around, afraid of what she could see. But instead of a dangerous German spy, there was a small gray-haired woman, peering around the edge of the door, which she kept on its chain. The light in the hall behind her was lit and on the wall Caitlin could see a framed picture of the Sacred Heart. She had one herself at home, over the mantel of the hearth. There was no trouble here, she thought. She was among her own.

"Miss Shane?"

"And who would be asking?" The tiny woman made no hint of opening the door further, but there was no fear in her voice either.

"I've come for Mr. Thomas. 'Tis Maisie Kinsella that sent me. Would you be taking me to him?" Caitlin asked, smiling down at the woman. From inside the house, Caitlin could smell sausages, bacon, and onions cooking. It made her hungry at once for Dublin coddle, and she remembered she hadn't had a bite to eat since her high tea with Cormac at the country shop in St. Stephen's Green.

Without replying, the old lady shut the door and unlatched the chain, then opened it again and said quickly, "Come in, missy, before I catch the death of cold." She closed the door behind Caitlin and, locking it, said, "He's out on the side porch. Go get him, then leave by the kitchen door, go through the garden, and knock on Mrs. Mahon's door. She'll let you out onto Park."

"I know," Caitlin said quickly. She hated being treated like a child. "A car is waiting," she added, to show she knew the plan.

But Mrs. Shane wasn't listening. Behind Caitlin someone was banging on the front door.

"Did you come alone, girl?" the old woman whispered.

Caitlin nodded and felt a surge of fear. She said quickly, "That might be my friend . . . the car driver." She began to pray that it was Adrian.

"Who is it?" Miss Shane demanded and waved Caitlin toward the rear of the house.

"Open up in there!" a man shouted through the locked door.

"Go, child!" Miss Shane demanded, and then raising her voice, said, "Coming! I'm needing to find my housecoat."

Caitlin ran into the back parlor and stood trembling in the darkness. She could see nothing, but she knew the door had opened. She felt the wet cold of the rain blow down the hallway and sweep against her legs. Then she heard men demanding that Miss Shane unchain the door, the landlady asking meekly what in the world police could be wanting on a night like this, stalling with her act of innocence.

There was no hiding from them, Caitlin realized, no cowering in the dark. They would find her.

She bolted from the parlor, slipping between two upholstered chairs with white crocheted linen doilies pinned to the arms, and ran through the dining room toward the kitchen. There were no lights on in the back of the house and she stumbled against the cupboard, hurting her knee. The house was confusing, and she realized she had never been in anyone's home in Dublin, except for the Steeles'. She did not know how normal people lived.

"Here!" a voice called. Caitlin saw the silhouette of another woman standing in the kitchen doorway. The woman motioned frantically as Caitlin limped across the kitchen, disregarding the pain in her knee. Behind her, the police were running down the hallway, their heavy shoes shaking the small house. She had no time to get Mr. Thomas, Caitlin realized. She had to get away from the police.

"You have an auto?" the woman asked in a harsh, angry whisper.

Caitlin spotted the back door, the one leading to the garden. If the police were waiting in back, they would get her. But the ones in front had reached the parlor. She ran for the kitchen door.

Outside, the garden was dark and the rain had come up again in a sudden swell. She raced directly to the door of the house behind, as if she were a girl at play, and burst into the warm lit kitchen without the courtesy of knocking.

A woman at the stove spun around, raising the ladle in her hand.

"Are they on to you?" the woman asked, then, without pausing for an answer, pointed toward the hallway. "The front door is un-latched."

The other woman had followed Caitlin, but now she sprinted past, as if she were accustomed to fast exits. Pounding along behind her, Caitlin passed a man in the front parlor. He was reading the papers and looked up in astonishment as the two women darted by. For a moment Caitlin fantasized that she could just stop, slip into an empty chair in the small room, and be perfectly at home. That all this fleeing from the G2 was only some silliness that had nothing to do with her at all.

But the woman did not pause and they ran through the front door and out into the driving rain. It blew against them in waves, as if the tide itself had come ashore.

"The auto!" the woman demanded as they reached the curb. The street was deserted.

Behind her, Caitlin heard Mrs. Mahon slam shut the front door. They were alone in the street, and the police, she knew, would be following, tracking them across the garden.

Then she saw Adrian. The huge car spun onto the wet tarred side street and raced toward them.

"There!" she shouted, running for the car.

Adrian slowed the Bentley but did not stop. Caitlin jumped onto the running board, pulled open the door, and fell into the rear leather seat. The woman was behind her, and they tumbled over onto the floor.

"Keep down," Adrian ordered, picking up speed.

Caitlin closed her eyes and waited. She waited for the police sirens and the end of the chase. Waited to be caught and taken to prison. She waited for the shooting to begin, waited to die in a hail of bullets as Cagney had in *The Roaring Twenties*. But nothing happened. She listened to the car's engine, to the panting of her own breath and that of the woman, who lay on top of her in the dark backseat. Adrian kept speeding. Caitlin could feel the auto lurch, skidding on the wet pave-ment, as he went one way, then another. She closed her eyes and prayed for it all to be over, for her to be safe and home again.

Gradually the automobile slowed. Adrian was cruising to a stop, and Caitlin raised herself up and glanced out the window. They had reached the wall of People's Park. She had been there the Sunday before with Cormac.

"We've gotten clean away!" Adrian shouted, laughing. "Caitlin, are you all right?"

"Yes, thanks be to God. But no thanks to you," she said at once, letting her fear turn into anger. " 'Tis a fine mess you've gotten me into!" And then to the woman, "Would you be getting off of me, ma'am? I'm not some old rug that's laying around."

The stranger moved and Caitlin saw then who it was.

"Ah, Jaysus!" she whispered. It wasn't a woman with her on the floor. The long black wig had twisted on the man's head, and the heavy rouge had been ruined in the rain. She saw it was a young man dressed cleverly in a woman's dress.

"I'm sorry," he said softly. "Did I hurt you?"

"You're English?" Caitlin asked.

"No, German, but I went to school in England as a boy. I am sorry there has been trouble. We did not know the house was being watched."

"I am a friend of Miss Brugha, and Noinin," Adrian said at once.

"And you?" The young German turned to Caitlin.

"She is a . . . friend," Adrian answered quickly.

"My name is Caitlin DeLacey," Caitlin spoke up, at that moment feeling proud to identify herself.

"You were very brave in the house. And now we will let you go home."

"Yes," Adrian agreed. "Caitlin, I'll leave you at Seapoint. You can catch a train."

Caitlin said nothing. It was what she wanted—to be safe. Yet now that it was over, she liked the idea that the German had called her brave.

They rode a few blocks through the dark residential area of Monkstown, and when they reached Monkstown Circle, she said quickly, "I'll be going along with you."

"No, Caitlin! They know he's escaped and there will be roadblocks before we reach Dalkey."

"You'll never get past any roadblock, just the two of you."

"No," Adrian said firmly, dismissing her offer. "I won't risk your safety a second time." He drove into the railway station and stopped. "Hurry and be off."

"Thank you, Miss DeLacey," Mr. Thomas said after her, when she opened the door. "I will remember what you have done for me, our cause."

She paused a moment, waited for Adrian to say some words of appreciation, but he had already turned to Mr. Thomas and was speaking to him in German, as if what lay ahead for them did not concern her. She slammed the car door and ran for the arriving train, leaving the men, the underground, and the secret war of Adrian Steele behind her.

He had made a fool of her again, she thought, running through the rain. Was it only her help he wanted, and nothing else? Did he not care for her feelings? And here she had risked her life for him and his German. She reached the station and stopped running. For a moment she couldn't stop her tears, nor the way her heart ached, torn to shreds by his cavalier ways.

Then she pulled herself together, wiped the tears off her face. She wasn't just another country culchie who could be bullyragged about by the likes of Adrian Steele. No, he hadn't heard the last from her. She owed him a piece of her mind. And he'd be paid in full, she promised herself.

# · CHAPTER 16 ·

"Is there something you're wanting to tell me, Catty?" Cormac asked, setting his elbows on the small tea table.

Caitlin turned her face away from him, looking toward the white-capped sea. She was crying; the tears were warm on her cold cheeks, and heavy like the rain and wind that blew against the Pavilion windows. A set of doors to the boardwalk banged open, suddenly sweeping the tearoom with a draft, wet and salty, like her own tears.

"Nothing, no," she answered.

"Sure, you haven't said a word all afternoon. I might as well be talking to myself." He hooked his thumb toward the teapot. "And you haven't touched your tay. Is it Nora that's got you upset? All those little ones come down with the croup in winter, don't you be knowing that? She'll be better, come the fine weather."

He took from his pocket the letter they'd received from Catty's sister Joyce. "She's a crepe hanger, that sister of yours. If there was anything really wrong with the child, we'd be hearing more than a few lines by post." He peered at the letter again, holding it at arm's length so as to read without his glasses. "If you're asking me, I'd say little Nora is suffering from your sister's cooking. I feel sorry for the likes of Joe Flaherty, having to make a meal out of Joyce's coddle. Aye, the child will be fine. You know Nora; she's a strong one." He folded away the letter, as if done with the problem, then added, "I'm thinking we'll bring the little one here to Dublin by the new year. A pub mate of mine was saying I should sign up for one of those corporation houses in St. Begnet's Villas."

The wind died away, and the rain ceased driving against the high Pavilion windows. For a fleeting moment Caitlin could see a patch of blue in the wild black clouds, and she wondered if the day had cleared in Connemara and if Nora was well enough to lie in her cradle in the sun behind the cottage. And was her sister giving Nora enough porridge, especially now with the winter dampness soaking through the cottage walls? Her heart ached at the thought of the meagerness at home. Adrian was right. It was the poor farmers who suffered, whoever was governing Ireland. And it was up to country peasants like herself to bring justice to her own kind.

Caitlin wiped her tears away with a tea napkin and said fiercely, "I won't have Nora live in one of those places, without a piece of turf of her own and playing in the street with slum ragamuffins and tinker children. Cormac DeLacey, where's the sense the good Lord gave you?"

His wife's sudden bolts of anger were new to Cormac. At home she rarely raised her voice, and never at him. He recalled then how at the close of day she would come to the half door of their cottage and look for him. She'd be waiting with a pitcher of milk in her hands, the late afternoon sun catching on the white walls of the cottage, catching, too, on her golden face. And he had thought then, coming down the slope, that he was the luckiest man he knew. For she was the most beautiful woman in all of Connemara, and having her for his own made him feel secretly guilty, as if he had stolen her from his betters.

But in Dublin, this feeling had disappeared. The sun seemed never to shine on them, and they could not spend even a few hours together of a Sunday without words. She seemed to hide her thoughts, as if he were someone to fear, a stranger to her.

"It's a farm we should be saving for," she went on, "and not an ugly little red-tiled house in the likes of St. Begnet's Villas. You'll be having us living out with the tinkers next."

She seized her purse and stood, but did not march off. Her fear stopped her. It was not the fear brought on by Nora's croup or Cormac's talk of bringing the baby to Dublin. It was the fear of what was happening inside her.

She thought of Crazy Michael back in Tourmakeady, who ran after the sheep on the hillside, thinking he was one of them himself. "Crazy Michael is touched by God," everyone said, and tipped their cap to him, as if they were passing the Blessed Sacrament. But it wasn't God who had touched her, Caitlin knew, although she, too, was chasing after someone not her own kind.

"I'll be going now, Cormac."

"There's time enough before the train," Cormac protested. "It's only half-three. I had a mind we could walk along the East Pier to the lighthouse."

"Are you daft?" she asked, buttoning up her old coat. "We'll both drown in this downpour." She was always harsh with Cormac now, but she couldn't help it. It was as if she wanted to provoke him, to make him lash back and bring her to her senses. "That's all we need do but come down with the death of cold. We'll end up in Mercers Hospital without a florin between us."

"Sure, never mind the walk then. We can go along and see what flick is playing at the Adelphi."

"We have no money for cinemas, not after spending two and six for tea and buttermilk scones." She walked away from him. The tearoom was crowded, with more couples and children rushing in from the blowing winter rain. At home in Tourmakeady, she wouldn't have gone out on a day like this, but kept close to the warm hearth. It was Cormac's fault, she thought suddenly, and for the first time. He had ruined her whole life with his silly letter to his uncle. He would have been better to keep quiet about his father's death—as she had advised him—and not be writing Yankee relatives, long gone from Connemara.

At the door she paused, stopped by the driving rain. She would be soaked, she realized, before she reached Ballsbridge—but she would be home early and have time for a hot bath, time to soak herself in a tub full of sweet-smelling bath soap before putting on a fresh uniform. The Steeles were entertaining titled people that evening for dinner.

Caitlin finished serving the roast beef and red currant jelly, then picked up the mashed potatoes from the sideboard and circled the table again, serving Mrs. Steele first and then Lady Lambert. Mrs. Finnerty was ahead of her with a serving dish of carrots and parsnips, and there were still Swedish turnips to be served, as well as the watercress, and wine. It would have been easier if Teasy were allowed at least to bring in the food from the kitchen, but whenever guests were invited, especially titled guests, she was kept out of sight.

"We'll make do ourselves," Mrs. Finnerty had told her before the guests had arrived, and then for the tenth time that day showed her how to serve the dinner guests, bending from the waist with the heavy plate secure against her elbow. "You're to be like a spirit in the dining room, Caitlin. Don't be drawing attention to yourself."

Caitlin had no wish to be noticed. She liked the fact that no one, not even Adrian, seem to be aware of her as she moved around the table. It made it easier for her to watch Allison Lambert and listen to their conversation.

She bent forward and presented the plate of potatoes to Allison Lambert, who had turned to her right and was saying to Adrian, "But don't you think, Adrian, that the problem in Ireland is Catholicism? I mean, if it weren't for this religious fanaticism, the natives and the Anglo-Irish would intermingle freely. It's just that the Papists—" She stopped speaking, aware of Caitlin at her left shoulder. Turning her blond head, she glanced at the serving platter, then slowly looked up at Caitlin and said coldly, "I don't care for potatoes."

Caitlin stepped back, her face flushed, and moved quickly down the long table. But she listened for Adrian's reply, waiting for him to put Allison Lambert in her place.

"Religion has been a divisive force throughout history," Adrian answered vaguely.

"Not the Church of Ireland," she persisted. "Just the Catholics. It's people like that Catholic Truth Society who want everything Protestant banished from Ireland."

"Oh, Allison, dear, let's not talk religion or politics tonight," Lady Lambert interrupted, from the end of the table where she sat next to Mr. Steele.

"I'm only asking Adrian for his opinion, Mummy," Allison answered, leaning forward and into the light of the candle.

Caitlin glanced at her as she presented the plate of potatoes to another guest. Allison's face was beautiful in the candlelight, soft in a way that she knew hers would never be. Of course, she thought angrily, Allison Lambert had never spent a day digging turf or herding sheep in the heat of summer.

"Well, if you must have Adrian's opinion, ask him about his trip to London. Tell us, Adrian, what plays must we see? We'll be going over right after we see you race at Glennamain."

"Oh, Mummy, you want to talk about the theater when Ireland is slipping away right under our noses. Don't you agree, Adrian?"

"Yes, you might look at it that way," Adrian murmured, not looking up from his plate.

"Well, I won't let De Valera and his sharpies drive *me* out! Ireland is as much mine as it is theirs. Mummy and Daddy's ancestors came here in the fifteenth century. We didn't steal our property in Meath; we paid for it. I won't give up my inheritance just because a pack of commoners have taken over this government."

"No one is asking you to leave," Adrian said quietly.

"Yes, but everyone we know is leaving—not just because of the war but because of all the new laws coming from the Dail. I don't think it's right that when I get married my children must speak Gaelic. If those people in the west want to learn an archaic language, fine, but what good will it do them once they leave Ireland?"

"It's a lovely language, Allison."

"I think it's horrible! Besides, if they're spending all day learning Gaelic, they won't have time for English." She was leaning toward Adrian, pressing her point. "It seems foolish to me, all this interest in Gaelic. What great books have been written in that language? All the great Irish writers wrote in English—Burke and Swift, Yeats, Synge, and Shaw. If you took away those Anglo-Irish writers, why, Ireland wouldn't have a cultural heritage. And besides," she said, summing up, "it is a silly, rudimentary language, not one on which to build a culture."

Caitlin held her breath, waited for Adrian's reply. She knew what it would be: his favorite saying, that the Irish language was the spike on which all of Ireland's future would hang.

"Well, Allison, I don't think it will come to that. It will be voluntary, I'm sure. But you have a good point, I must say, about Yeats and Synge." He reached for his wineglass, and then smiling, asked, "Will you see Sarah Hester in London? Give her my best if you do, and tell her I'm terribly sorry I didn't get a chance to drive out to Hampstead."

Caitlin flushed angrily. Was this to be his entire defense of the Gaelic revival? Well, she would not let it go so easily. Bypassing Mr. Steele, she went directly to Allison's elbow and presented her serving platter. When the girl ignored her, Caitlin did not move on. Instead she cleared her throat, causing Allison to look up in surprise.

"Potatoes, miss?" Caitlin said, smiling.

"No, I told you," said Allison, "I don't care for potatoes."

"That's a shame, then," Caitlin continued, ignoring Mrs. Finnerty's frantic gestures from the kitchen. Picking up the ladle herself, she dropped a large dollop of potatoes on Allison's plate; it fell with a startling *plop*. "Sure, 'tis the potato, miss, that's the strength of the nation. I thought you'd be knowing that, you being so Irish and all."

"Caitlin!" Mrs. Steele had risen to her feet. "That will be all. Ladies," she said, turning to the Lamberts. "Please join me in the drawing room for coffee. And my apologies for our maid. She's fresh from Galway, and we're still trying to civilize her."

"Mother!" said Adrian. But this time Caitlin did not wait for his defense. Tossing a scornful look at Allison Lambert, she sailed through the swinging doors and into the kitchen.

Hours later Caitlin was still cleaning pots and pans—Mrs. Finnerty's punishment for her outburst—when the swinging doors parted and Adrian appeared.

"Can we talk later?" he whispered in the darkness. Caitlin had turned off the gas lamps in the room and was working by candlelight.

"And what will we be speaking about," she asked in Irish, "the Gaelic League?"

"What do you mean, Caitlin?" he asked impatiently.

"I mean we should discuss Allison Lambert and her fear of learning Irish. Sure if she had said Ireland should be building a palace for the king, I think you'd be agreeing with her."

"Allison Lambert is a ninny," he answered.

"Then why wouldn't you give her your talk about how great Ireland will be once we have a culture of our own, free of English speech?"

"I have better things to be doing with my time than converting Allison Lambert. The girl is a fool, but I promised my mother I'd be polite to her. You, of course, made no such promise." He smiled at her in the candlelight, and after a moment Caitlin had to laugh, too, at the memory of Allison's astonishment. "I need to speak to you tonight, after the Lamberts leave. Meet me here at two. Everyone will be asleep. 'Tis wonderful news, Caitlin. It's what the whole of Ireland has been waiting seven hundred years to hear. Two, then?"

"Aye, and to be made a fool of again," she said quickly, ready now to give him a piece of her mind.

"What do you mean?"

"You left me in Monkstown to take the train, and after I had risked my life."

"And you had, Caitlin. You were so brave. Mr. Thomas said so himself."

"And what does yourself say, Mr. Steele?" She challenged him. She didn't want to know what the German thought. It was for Adrian that she had risked her life, yet he still seemed blind to that fact.

He stepped closer to her in the shadowy light of the kitchen and said softly, "I didn't want you taking a second chance at getting caught. Not when the G-Two were on to us."

"Aye, but now it suits your wishes for me to risk my life again." She was still upset with him, but her resistance was melting in the warmth of his voice.

"You're the only one I can trust, Caitlin," he said in Irish. "And Ireland needs you."

She cocked her head and looked up at him. The yellow candlelight played against her pale cheek, hid half his face in darkness, and concealed the look in his eyes.

"Do you need me, Adrian?" she asked.

"More than Ireland needs you, Caitlin," he whispered, and as if to seal her fate in his, he reached out in the darkness and touched her gently on the arm.

She nodded yes, agreeing to help. She did not have the strength to voice her own fear, not at the dangerous course she was taking for Ireland, but because the path she was on with Adrian, she knew now in her heart, was taking her away from her husband and her marriage vows.

"It's the German eagle," Adrian said to Caitlin, pointing to the wax seal. He pulled the green booklet from the envelope and placed it on the kitchen table. "The code name is Fall Grun—Operation Green." He tapped the thick document. "What this contains, Caitlin, is Germany's invasion plans for Ireland. There's seventy-eight pages, as well as photographs of the ports and landing beaches. I read it today, on the way back from Donegal."

"Dear God almighty, where in the world would you be getting such a thing?" Caitlin whispered, frightened just by the sight of it. It was two A.M. and they were alone in the kitchen.

"There's a German who owns a hotel at Inver in Donegal. His people used to own property, but in the last war, the English took it from him, so he has no love now for Great Britain. They say in Donegal that he supplies the German U-boats. They come at night by rowboat into Inver Bay and he gives them fresh eggs and butter. It's them that gave him the plans to pass along to Mr. Thomas. Hitler is planning to strike from Ireland and France, squeeze the bloody English as if they were nothing more than a pimple." He opened the document and began to scan the pages.

"Listen to this!" he said, translating the German. "Four thousand troops are leaving from L'Orient, St. Nazaire, and Nantes. They'll land along the southeast coast, between Wexford and Dungarvan. Once they have the harbors, the infantry and commando units will go thirty miles inland and form a front line from Gorey on the Wexford-Dublin road, across Mount Leinster, through Thomastown, in Kilkenny, to Clonmel in Tipperary. They'll be given air cover by the Luftwaffe's west and the German navy from Brest. It's a grander plan than I ever had hoped for, Caitlin."

"And we could go to jail, just for looking at the thing."

"The Gardai haven't a clue this document exists."

"And what would you be doing with it?"

"Of the underground lads who read German, I'm the highest ranking. I need to translate the plans by Thursday for the meeting at the Red Bank, then get the underground's reply to Mr. Thomas. A boat is coming ashore to pick him up at Coulagh Bay. He's reporting back to the Abwehr, the German espionage division."

She leaned forward into the small bowl of light to read the German title of the booklet—*Militargeographische Angaben über Irland.* She thought of the Brown boys who had just joined up with the Irish Maritime Service. They were stationed in the southwest of Ireland, she knew from their mother, patrolling the Celtic Sea.

"But some of our own will be killed. You said yourself, we can't have Irishmen killing each other and not the British."

"Well, if the Irish army is smart enough, they'll throw their lot in with the Germans once they land. But I can't be worrying about who might get hurt. My job is to get the Germans our reply."

"But why you?" She reached out and touched his arm, as if by holding him she would keep him safe. It was the first time she had ever touched him, and she felt in the tips of her fingers the strength of the man. It surprised her. She had thought his strength lay only in the passion of his talk. But his arm was as lean and strong as that of Cormac, or any of the boys who had held her close and danced with her on the wooden bridge in Tourmakeady.

"I'm not known as a Sinn Feiner, so the Gardai hasn't my name. And I've a reason for going down to Kerry—we're opening the country house there for the races. It will be easy enough for me to slip away, meet the train in Kilgarvan, and take Mr. Thomas to meet the U-boat."

He spoke confidently, as if it were all easily done.

"The races?"

"The point-to-point. It's Mother's affair. We don't hunt, we just race over the field. Everyone from the village is invited, and friends of the family as well. It's a great social event for Mother. Her way of showing support for Ireland—you know, letting the locals have a day of it on the grounds, drinking free Guinness. But come night and the formal dinner! Well, back up go the ancestral gates to close out the Catholic riffraff, just like the old days."

"And why should she invite the villagers? They'd only feel out of place with Dubliners, I'm sure. They'd rather be among their own kind."

"That's not the point, Caitlin." He sighed. "This is another example of what Lenin calls the class struggle. How one people think they're better than another."

"Sure, I don't think anyone is better than myself," Caitlin answered back.

"And no one is!" he said, smiling. "That's what so grand about you. You're not like some of those country culchies from Mayo—bogtrotters who want nothing more out of life than a jorum of Jameson. I could see that for myself when you came into my bedroom. It was the way you held yourself. Another Emer the Discreet. Do you know the six maidenly gifts of Emer?"

Caitlin shook her head. She knew only that Emer was the wife of Cuchullain, Ireland's legendary king.

"Beauty of person, beauty of voice, the gift of music, knowledge of embroidery, knowledge of needlework, and the gift of wisdom and virtuous chastity."

Caitlin smiled with pleasure, then looked down, embarrassed by his attention. He could charm the eyes out of a potato when he wished, she thought. She was silent for a moment and let him gaze at her, then made a gesture of fixing a loose comb in her hair so that her arm was raised and her breasts outlined. It was sinful, she knew, but she could not keep from making a show of herself.

"You are very beautiful, Caitlin DeLacey," he told her in Irish.

She could hear the tightness of his voice. She had never known any man but Cormac, yet she knew how men looked at her, and she had always shunned such attention. But now she wanted to display herself to Adrian, and felt no shame or sin in it.

"I'll be driving to Glennamain on Thursday to help the O'Sheas open the house for the guests on Friday. Usually Teasy comes along to help. Should I be speaking with my mother about your going instead?"

Caitlin nodded, not looking at him. Her head was bent, as if she had already submitted to his advances. She felt a thrill; her whole insides seemed to be burning away. He went on, talking of all the work that needed to be done by Saturday and how much better it was for her and not Teasy to go, building, it seemed to her, layer after layer of excuses for their deception, their chance of being away together and by themselves, free of his parents, free of Mrs. Finnerty, free, too, if he only knew, of her husband.

"And on Saturday night, we can slip away, the two of us, to meet Mr. Thomas and take him to meet the boat." His voice picked up with excitement. "I'll need your help."

She nodded, not knowing how to refuse him, and wondered if it was her help he wanted and nothing more. Her soaring passion fell away, and her heart dropped like a tar-black currach cresting an ocean wave. She would have to wait until Glennamain to find out.

# · CHAPTER 17 ·

GLENNAMAIN LAY IN THE lap of the hills, with open fields and woods surrounding, and the drive curved through the trees, which on that day were leafless and brown black. Beyond the house the hills were blue, and beyond the hills, the sky and horizon gray as monk's cloth. The setting reminded Caitlin of her own valley in Tourmakeady, but the land here in the south of Kerry was richer, she saw, and it would be easier, she realized at once, to graze sheep on such green pastures.

They passed through the gates and Adrian stopped the car.

"Would you know what they call this wall, Caitlin?"

"A famine wall, now wouldn't it be?"

"Yes. From the time of my great grandparents. They built it high and locked the gates, and then backed the wall up with a thick line of trees—all for keeping the sight and sound of the starving peasants out of their grand lives. But they knew all of Ireland was dying. In the morning they'd send servants down to clear away the dead women and children whose bodies pressed up against the gates."

"Wouldn't they even take care of their own neighbors, the people from the village?"

"My great grandmother, they say, came down with baskets of bread and would talk to the dying women. If they promised to convert to the Church of Ireland, she'd give them bread for their children. She'd take their names and made sure to check with the minister before the day was out. Unless the women made good and really did convert, there was no food the next morning."

"Soupers," Caitlin said, remembering what these Catholics had been called who changed their religion for something to eat.

Adrian started up the car again and they went ahead slowly.

"There was a small house on the grounds," he explained as he drove. "My great aunt lived in it. She was a bit queer in the head, I'm told, but a true fighter for Irish independence. During the troubles she opened the front gate one night to let a lorry onto the grounds. It was full of petrol, and they were planning to crash it into the big house, where the Black and Tans were bivouacked. But the driver had no lights, and he didn't know the drive. He misjudged the road —see how it turns?—and overturned the lorry near the little house instead. The petrol exploded and killed Aunt Elizabeth. The Black and Tans came out and just watched the house burn down."

"Oh, dear Lord," Caitlin whispered. "What a shame."

"Yes, it was," Adrian agreed. "If they had only gotten to the house, they could have done some real damage."

"Oh, Adrian, that's not what I meant! Why would you be wanting your own home destroyed? Don't you love coming here from Dublin, where you can see the sky and feel a bit of ground under your feet?"

"Yes, but that isn't important. I'd have the house leveled, Caitlin, for what it represents. For all the peasants who died out there, on the king's highway. Isn't that what you'd want, too?"

She was silent. She could see the house now through the bare trees. It was big as the railway station in Galway City, she thought, bigger than the Steele house in Dublin, and made of quarry stone. Wild ivy grew thick up the front of the house, encasing even the top-floor windows, reaching to the tile roof. It made the house look abandoned and gone to seed.

Adrian spun his Invicta into the drive and pulled up before the front doors. It began to rain, just as he shut off the engine.

"There's no one about," Caitlin said, looking at the closed house.

"Sure, they're somewhere. Mrs. O'Shea is never far from the place. We'll go in and I'll have a look about." He started to open the door, but the rain swelled up and blew against the car. He quickly closed the door to wait it out. They were familiar with such early spring weather and knew the worst would be over in minutes, as the storm passed across the Derrynasaggart Mountains.

For a moment they were both quiet, listening to the rain. Being caught in the car with Adrian made Caitlin aware of him, the closeness they shared. It had been different on the open road; they had been driving, and Adrian had spent the time explaining point-to-point racing.

Now, Caitlin realized, they were alone and far from Dublin. She glanced out the side window at the locked house. They would be alone again that night, she realized, not even the O'Sheas there with them in the big house.

"Do you keep the whole house open?" she asked, wanting to break the silence.

"Oh, no. We have half the place shut up, even in the hunting season. We'd need all the turf in Kerry to keep the place warm."

"How many rooms do you have?" She kept her head turned from

him, as if studying the mansion, but the glass was steamy and opaque from her breath. She wiped the windscreen.

"Twenty, I should think. Or more. I've never counted them, you know. Sure, don't worry, Caitlin, we'll find a room big enough for you, and with its own warm fire."

"I'll sleep where I belong, up under the slate," she answered quickly, as if to remind him of the distance between them. And then she pushed open the car door and impulsively stepped into the rain, bothered less by getting wet than by being alone with him any longer.

Adrian came after her and ran up the stone steps to unlock the front door.

"There's no electric," he said, leading her into the dark front hall, "just these gas lamps." He lit several in the hallway, but they did little good. Caitlin could smell the wet turf of dead fires, smell as well the dampness of the stone walls. The cold went through her whole body and she shivered, clutching her sweater.

"I'll make a fire," Adrian offered.

" 'Tis my job to make fires. Mrs. Finnerty didn't send me down here so that you might be waiting on me hand and foot. You have your own business, I'm sure, what with your horse, and the race and all." She set her small purse on the chair and went at once to the huge hall fireplace. The stove had been swept, she saw, and turf stacked in the grate, ready for the match.

"It would please me, Caitlin," he answered in Irish, "to wait on you. You do nothing but care for me in Dublin."

" 'Tis me job," she answered coldly.

"This house is the O'Sheas' job, not yours," he answered back, suddenly upset. "My family employs them year round to look after this place; you would think they'd have it heated and ready when we arrive. Well, I won't be taken advantage of this way. If the O'Sheas don't wish to work, I'm sure others do."

Caitlin had seen him behave that way before when he didn't get what he wanted. He was like a child, quick to take offense and be angry.

"Yes, these country culchies and bogtrotters are a trial," she snapped back. "You're a great one with your talk of helping the Irish people, Mr. Steele, but God help them if they inconvenience you." She knelt before the open hearth.

"I'm sorry," he said, coming up to stand behind her. "I am my mother's child, I'm afraid, and sometimes find myself behaving just like her."

"Don't be blaming your mother, Adrian. You're old enough to be standing on your own two feet." She lit the turf fire, adding, "There, that was simple enough, now wasn't it? No need for getting all in a rage over it."

"You will forgive me, Caitlin?" he asked in Irish.

"You've done nothing to me, Adrian. Though if you find fault with country people, I'd just remind you that I am one myself."

"It isn't you! It isn't them! I'm just upset with everyone these days. I think it must be all this tension, what with our plans . . ." He lowered his voice, though they were alone in the hallway. "I don't think I could even be doing this much without your help."

Caitlin shot him a glance. "I don't understand, sir. I've been doing nothing myself, just going along as best I can."

"You do more than just go along, Caitlin. With you I have someone to share my ideas, to listen, and dream. Everyone at the Red Bank Restaurant, all the old pro-Nazis, well, they're thinking of themselves, or trying to settle old scores from the time of the troubles and the civil war. It's different for you, you and me. We didn't fight those battles. We can think about Ireland as it is today. As it should be tomorrow."

An old woman's cracking voice interrupted. "Would that be yourself, Mister Adrian, raising cain here in the front hall?"

Caitlin turned and saw a tiny woman peering at them from the other end of the dark hallway. She looked like Caitlin's grandmother Nora, in a long black dress with a black shawl wrapped tightly around her shoulders.

"Mary O'Shea! Faith and beglory, where have you been?" Adrian went to the old woman, his arms outstretched. "If you aren't still the most beautiful creature in Kerry."

"Would you listen to him, missy? And me with a face like a plateful of mortal sins." Mrs. O'Shea had a round, perfect, fair face, as white and pure as bone china. She must have had admirers in her day, Caitlin thought, and she was flirting with Adrian, giggling as she tried to evade his arms. "Now none of your paddywhackery," she ordered as he caught her in a gentle embrace.

Caitlin smiled. Irish men were not affectionate, and to see Adrian caring for the older woman pleased her immensely.

"Have you decided yet, Mary née Dillon O'Shea, to leave that husband of yours and run off with me to the seashore?" Adrian went on, imitating her brogue.

He was playing to both of them now, and Caitlin laughed at his silliness. He could be so wonderful and kind, she saw, when his head wasn't full of revolution and war, and she felt sad that all their time together couldn't be so happy.

"Musha, it's the old people's home I'll be running off to, not the seashore." She pulled away from Adrian and stepped closer to Caitlin, peering at her curiously. "Now, you've a lovely face on you, missy," she said, taking hold of Caitlin's hands. "And what would they be calling you?"

Caitlin could almost feel the old woman's brittle bones, twisted from age and arthritis, and she thought at once of how she, too, would end up, destroyed by a lifetime in the cold, damp weather. The old were never warm in Ireland, she remembered Grandma Nora saying.

"This is Caitlin DeLacey, Mary," Adrian said. "Caitlin has been with us since February. She's come down early to help with the cleaning." He was talking rapidly, as if telling a lie.

"Where would your people be from, Caitlin?" Mrs. O'Shea said, her eyes not leaving Caitlin.

"Connemara, ma'am. I'm from a little place called Tourmakeady. Would you be knowing it?" Caitlin asked, smiling, trying to endear herself.

Mrs. O'Shea shook her head, sighing. "Sure, I wouldn't be knowing what's on the other side of Annagh Bog if my life depended on it. In my day we didn't go gallivanting around as does the likes of himself here in his big car. We stayed where God put us down, and thought ourselves blessed at that. But nowadays!" She shook her head. "The young ones can't keep a penny in their purse, or be a day out of Dublin. The same is true, I'm sure, of the likes of yourself, dearie." She nodded up at Caitlin. "There's nothing a'tall to keep you in Connemara, is there? I'm surprised you're not off to America like all the rest from the west. I'm told you can't turn around in Boston without bumping into someone you know from Connaught. Well, come along, child. There's work to be done before herself arrives." She moved slowly toward the hallway door, her slippers scraping the cold stone floor.

Caitlin glanced at Adrian. She was willing to work, but it wasn't possible for the housekeeper and herself to clean the big house in one day.

As if he knew what she was thinking, Adrian said quickly, "I'll telephone the convent school in Killarney. The mother superior sends over her top-form girls to help out every year, and Mother gives the convent a donation. All you need do is supervise." He nodded discreetly toward the old caretaker. "Keep Mary from confusing them utterly." And then raising his voice, he asked, "Mary, is your Frank out in the barns?"

"God knows where that man is. Frank O'Shea is like a shadow without substance. I need only to open my oven door, though, and he's by my side, as if the devil himself were his tour guide. But to find him when there's work to be done, well, you'd sooner be pinching a leprechaun." She paused at the doorway. "Come along, Caitlin

DeLacey. You're not in Dublin now where you can be enjoying your leisure like one of those silly girls that follow himself around on the day of the race." She didn't look at Adrian, but her eyes were twinkling.

"Mary O'Shea, the devil's got your tongue today!" He began to blush as he fumbled to stir the fire.

" 'Tis true enough, Mr. Adrian! There's half a dozen of those Dublin ladies that have their cap set for you. And 'tis time you did get yourself a wife."

"And you know yourself, Mary, that the lot of them are all ninnies," he said, and led the housekeeper away.

Caitlin picked up her bag and went after them, through a dark hallway and into the long cold dining room. There was a fire in the hearth, but she could not feel its heat. The ceiling was high and decorated with fine plasterwork, but she saw that it needed paint, and the blue walls needed a wash. A table long enough for twenty was layered with turf ash and dust, and walking by, she ran her finger along the dull top and left a dirty streak in the dust.

Glennamain was a pigsty. That was why Mrs. Steele had agreed so quickly to let her drive down with Adrian. Even with convent girls, Caitlin knew they'd be two days getting the place clean—just in time for the guests' arrival Friday night.

Through the windows she saw part of the garden and a path that went straightaway between yew hedges. Beyond the garden wall and near the barns, men were erecting a canvas tent, working through the steady rain. Well, she thought, trying to put the best face on her work, at least she'd be inside and dry, and not sloughing through mud as she might be at home.

The weather cleared after dark, and Caitlin stopped dusting the dining-room woodwork and stepped outside for a bit of air. There was a garden just beyond the French doors to the dining room. It was not set off from the house with a square wall of hedges, as most Irish gardens were, but built close to the big house, with a path between clipped yew hedges that started at the doors. It was a garden with hidden places, a spring garden, and a summer one, all bare and brown between the high shrubbery.

She followed the path between the hedges, letting it lead her away from the big house, which soon lay behind her, lit with lamps and candles and full of schoolgirl voices. Their talk and laughter flowed through the open windows of the top floors, filling the night air. It was a party for them, Caitlin knew, being out of class and away from school. She felt momentarily jealous of their freedom and their innocence. Though she was their age, she felt a generation older, with a husband, a child, and now this strange and frightening feeling for Adrian Steele.

It was wrong, she knew, yet she could not keep herself from day-dreaming of Adrian, watching for him, or wanting to be with him, if only as his maid. And when he actually reached out, as he had in the dark kitchen in Dublin, and touched her arm, she felt her body ache for him as she had never ached for Cormac. She was afraid she could not save herself, that her heart no longer had the will, or her soul the grace, to keep her body pure.

Caitlin found a stone bench hidden in the box hedge and sat down so she could look back at the house, silhouetted against the night sky. It was a bright night, which meant a fair day tomorrow for the race, she guessed. And she thought how she must be sure to sprinkle holy water in Adrian's boots the next morning. It was the best way of protecting hm.

He had showed her earlier how the racetrack was set out, with the hedges, stone fences, brooks, and streams serving as natural jumps. The course was two miles around the big house and barns. It would be a miracle, she thought, remembering the height of the hedges, if he wasn't killed. She would ask the Blessed Virgin to watch over him, but she wondered if the Blessed Virgin, or Christ Himself, would even listen to her prayers, now that all her secret thoughts were sinful.

"Are you looking for a leprechaun, Caitlin DeLacey, under the box hedge?" a voice behind her whispered in the darkness.

She was startled only for a moment. "And haven't I seen enough leprechauns in my day?" she answered, and smiled.

"Would you be knowing now how to catch a leprechaun, then, and have him show you his pot of gold?" Adrian asked next, thickening his brogue.

"My father told me there's only one way to catch the man, and that's when he has stopped to mend his brogues. He runs about so much that he wears his shoes thin, Da said, and when he feels his feet on the ground, he sets under a hedge or behind a wall and takes them off to mend. You'll know by the tapping of his hammer, and the trick is to come up as quiet as a cat and catch him up in your arms, then demand his pot of gold.

"But the leprechaun is full of tricks, and if you don't keep your eye on him, then he'll be off like a flash, and you'll never see him again. Nor have another chance in your lifetime to get your pot of gold. At least that's what the old people say in Tourmakeady."

"Well, I've found my leprechaun," he said, moving closer to her on the bench.

"Aye, but that's just the start then," she said, turning away nervously, "for I've heard many a story of catching the leprechaun, but no one has ever gotten away with his pot of gold."

"It isn't gold I seek, Caitlin DeLacey," he whispered, the brogue gone from his voice.

Dear Mother of God, please help me, she thought, and turned her face further from his, for if she saw his eyes, she knew she could not resist him, whatever the sin.

"I'll be going back to the house," she said next, "for there's still work to be done."

"There's convent girls enough to do the work, Caitlin."

"I'm feeling a bit chilly as it is," she went on, though despite the breeze on her face, the truth was her body felt aflame. "I'll be saying good night," she whispered, and went to stand, but he slipped his arm quickly about her slim waist and pulled her easily into an embrace, finding her lips with his own.

Her arms closed around him, her fingers combed his black hair, as she responded for a moment to his passion. Then in panic, and breathless, she pulled her lips from his and cried, "No, Adrian, no! I can't!"

"I love you, Caitlin," he said. "I'm mad for you, girl."

"It's wrong!"

"It isn't wrong if I love you." He seized her again and fought until his mouth touched hers.

Caitlin felt her body melt away, dissolve in his strong grasp. She no longer had the strength of will to defy him. His hand stroked the curve of her neck, smoothed the cloth of her shoulder. As it moved down to touch her breast, she felt her eyes close and her head go back.

And then she thought of Cormac, of her marriage vows, of gaining an eternity of hell in exchange for this moment, and she shoved against him, shouting, "Dear God almighty! Damn you!"

The sound of her own voice gave her strength enough to break his hold, and she ran from Adrian Steele, down the dark hedge path to the house, where even in her fear and tears, she saw that some of the convent girls were looking out the upstairs windows to see who it was in the garden that had called out God's name in vain.

# · CHAPTER 18 ·

CAITLIN CAME OUT THE servants' hall at dawn and looked both ways, furtively, as if she were being pursued. It had rained in the night, and the path was muddy. Already her shoes were wet. She slipped out of them and tiptoed barefoot across the soft fields until she reached the canvas tent where the jockeys were already assembling.

The dress she wore was not her own. It was made of fine French cotton with a high lacy collar and had a full skirt that swept down to her ankles. She had found it in an upstairs closet, in one of the bedrooms they had cleaned. The label was from Harrod's in London, and Mrs. O'Shea said it had been left by an English girl who had come for the races the year before. When the cleaning was done, Caitlin smuggled the dress upstairs to her attic bedroom. She wanted Adrian to see her in something besides a maid's uniform.

He would be out early, she knew, exercising his horse, Nightfall. She had to find the canvas tent, the unofficial racing headquarters that had been erected near the paddock, but the mist was down and nothing was visible beyond the hedges of the garden. She could hear the voices of stable hands and grooms but could not see them. She wondered if Adrian was there, too, somewhere in the thick morning mist.

Caitlin kept walking in what she hoped was the right direction. A moment later the mist lifted and she saw she was beside the tent. She stopped then and, with both hands, piled her long hair up on her head, pinning it there. Then she slipped back into her shoes and went into the tent. A turf fire had been started and village women were already at work. Caitlin could smell rashers and eggs, and brown bread baking. It made her think of home and of getting up in the dark to make breakfast for Cormac and little Nora. Some of the stable boys stopped by the tent for a cup of tea and a slice of bread on their way to the paddock with their horses, still steaming from their morning exercise. Everyone talked excitedly about the race ahead.

"Tim O'Neill is bringing his big black, Samhain, to give him his chance on the double jumps," one of the grooms announced to all.

"I'll have a shilling on him then. I knew his mare, Irish Queen, saw her myself at Kildare when she took the Conyngham Cup," another answered.

"For shame," one of the women said, slicing brown bread as she spoke, "why would you be betting on anyone but Mr. Adrian today?"

"For spirit, I'd bet it all on himself and Nightfall," said the first groom gallantly.

"But for money," chimed in the second, "I'd have to go with Timmy O'Neill and the Conyngham Cup."

Everyone laughed but Caitlin.

"Would you be looking for someone now, miss?" an old man asked, eyeing her.

Caitlin shook her head. She was about to explain how she'd come with Mr. Adrian to organize the cleaning when suddenly she thought better and kept silent. She felt daring in her borrowed dress, a little mysterious. Why let the old man hear her Connemara brogue and know instantly that she was just a country culchie, a bogtrotter like himself? They would think she was down from Dublin, one of the Steeles' houseguests, unless she spoke.

"Sure it will be a fair day, don't you think?" a groom said politely, putting a finger to his cap as he spoke to her. "The year before last, miss, when Tommy Burke took the day on Black Clare, you couldn't see the course, what with the rain."

"You've come from Dublin, have you, missie?" the old man asked, keeping his eye on Caitlin. He had pushed his tweed cap up on his forehead as if to see her better. "Or would you be one of those London lasses that himself seems to favor?"

One of the village women turned on him then, warning him in Irish to keep a civil tongue or he'd have the lot of them chucked off the place.

Caitlin moved away, smiling, then went to the long trestle table to pour herself some tea. Before she could, one of the women did it for her and handed her the cup with a smile and a quick bow. Caitlin nodded her thanks, realizing that she liked the deference. It wouldn't be so bad, she thought, never so much as buttering your own soda bread. Well, these villagers would know the truth about her soon enough, once Mrs. Finnerty was up and around. But for the moment she enjoyed her secret.

She sipped the tea, not as she had all her life in Tourmakeady, but as herself did in the drawing room. The townsfolk were still watching her, though they had gone on to talk about the race and how the course had had to be altered because of flooding in the lower pasture. "We'll be taking the hedge higher, up by the tennis court, and finish on the flat," a groom observed. "The speed ponies will do fine today, if, God willing, it clears."

The soft rain stopped then, as if on command, and the mist parted for a moment, revealing several horses and riders cantering through the fields. Among them was Adrian, taking Nightfall over the jumps. Afraid the old man would be after her soon with more questions, Caitlin ducked under the side flap and went out to lean against the judge's cart. But then it occurred to her that if she stayed there, the judge would come over to chat her up, so she walked out into the field toward the place where she had seen Nightfall taking the hedges. She could see nothing through the mist, but she heard the horse's hooves on the soft earth as he raced from hedge to hedge and then a brief silence as he cleared each jump. She found herself holding her breath as she walked, listening until he landed again and went racing off, his hooves striking the meadowland as if it were a muffled drum.

Then there was silence. She stopped to listen, turning slowly in the misty field to determine which direction they had taken. She realized that she had also lost the voices from the tent. A sudden isolation like this had happened to her at home, when she had been out cutting sedge for thatching and was caught by low mist drifting in over the mountains. She knew better than to move. This mist would clear, and she had not come far. But Mrs. Finnerty would be awake soon, and there was breakfast to make and serve for the family and guests. She should give up seeking Adrian and just return to the kitchen. She would see him at breakfast anyway she told herself—though in the house, of course, she would not speak to him, never even lift her eyes to glance at him, afraid that Mrs. Finnerty or the missus herself might notice.

She stepped into the heavy mist, heading back, she hoped, toward the judge's cart and the tent. The fog was so thick she could not even see the ground, and she kept stumbling in the uneven field. She was trying to remember what the land had looked like the day before when suddenly she heard a horse again, this time galloping toward her. She spun around and around, frantically trying to catch its direction, but with each turn she grew more confused, till in the end she knew only that the horse was coming at her from out of the shrouded field.

Terrified that the rider would not see her until it was too late, she plunged off to the left, where she hoped she remembered a cover of trees, only to have Nightfall break from the mist directly before her.

She dove to the soft earth, sank into the wet grass and mud as the horse's hooves, barely clearing her body, kicked chunks of turf back into her face.

"Jesus!" Adrian swore, reining in Nightfall. "What in God's name are you doing here, girl?"

All Caitlin could think was that the dress was ruined, and as she pulled herself to her knees she thought of what a fool she had been, wearing what didn't belong to her. It would take six months of wages to pay for it.

"Are you daft, strolling through the middle of the course?" Adrian shouted, running to her. He reached down and, seizing her by the arm, yanked her up. "Nightfall could have killed you!"

"Let me go!" She pulled her arm free and, still stumbling in the rocky field, turned away from him. The mist had blown off the hillside and the villagers in the canvas tent could see them clearly. "I came out only to wish you well in the race. And to say I'm sorry for upsetting you last night, with all my carrying on." She lowered her voice to a whisper and kept pulling at the chunks of clay that stuck to her dress.

"Here, let me!" he said, reaching to help.

"Are you mad, with half of Kilgarvan looking on?" She backed off, not looking at him. "I'll fend for myself, thank you." She was furious at him for yelling at her, for making her look foolish, and she turned and ran for the fence gate.

"Please, Caitlin, I didn't see you! It wasn't my fault." He ran back to get Nightfall, then tramped after her across the muddy field.

Ahead of them and coming out to the judge's cart, Caitlin saw Allison Lambert. She was dressed in a royal-blue velvet astride coat, with breeches tucked into high black leather boots. She wore her long corn-silk hair loose, so that when she turned her head quickly to search the field for Adrian, it swept out behind her like late summer gorse. Caitlin realized how foolish she looked, dressed in a long cotton dress. It wasn't something a Dublin lady would wear to a country race, and as Adrian went off to greet Allison, she ran through the mud to the servants' hall, wanting only to get away from him.

The race began one hour after breakfast. All the servants rushed to finish the washing up so they could get their places at the starting gate on time. But Caitlin was not among them. Instead she went around the big house and down the drive toward the entrance of the estate, to a small rise near a stand of chestnut trees. There she was high enough to catch sight of the horses as they first came out of the woods. She was also safely distant from the other house servants, who stood on the bank by the final jump. She did not want the others to see her reactions to the race—nor did she want Adrian to see her watching.

As she was still climbing the rise to the chestnut trees, she heard a cheer go up from the crowd and knew the race had started. She ran the rest of the way, looking back toward the starting gate all the while. The horses were going over the ridge, disappearing from sight. Reaching the crest, she scanned the fields and woods below, hoping to catch sight of the jockeys as they approached her end of the estate.

She heard them first, from deep in the woods, then caught sight of their bright colors flashing through the bare branches of the trees built to hide the famine wall. She stood on her tiptoes, but all she could make out was the flashing ribbon of the riders' colors. And then suddenly the racing horses broke out of the stand of trees and into the bright April sunlight.

Adrian was ahead on Nightfall. Caitlin saw that at once, and had to force herself not to cheer. The horses raced past her, down the yellow gorse-covered slope to the pond's edge, then followed the shoreline toward the road, took the hedge between the drive and the tennis court, turned again and crossed the plowed land, then circled around behind the house and were off again to the ridge for the second lap.

Nightfall was still in front as they crossed the hill. She followed his blazing gold colors on the high green slope, but there were a half-dozen horses close behind, their bright colors bunched together like a knotted rainbow.

The horses pounded over the ridge and into a cotton-wool mist, and all Caitlin could see were the Derrynasaggart Mountains in the distance, shiny with late winter snow. For a moment the day was quiet. Then faintly she heard the horses' hooves, like faraway thunder, and she followed the sound, as back in Connemara she might listen to a storm gather over Lough Mask.

As she turned to the point where the horses would come through the trees, she took a deep breath and realized that she had been holding her breath in excitement.

Nightfall burst out from the trees. He was running freely, having left the other horses a distance behind. Caitlin had never seen horses racing and jumping before, not in Connemara. City folk—the English had the Anglo-Irish from Dublin—came into the mountains only to fish. Horses were used to till land, pull sidecars, and haul turf carts out of the bog, not for racing across pasture land on cold spring days.

Now, watching the horses fly by, seeing the rainbow of their colors unravel and re-form as they passed each other and jockeyed for position, Caitlin was caught up in the thrill of the race. It left her breathless as the jumpers came by her a second time. She couldn't take her eyes off Nightfall as he thundered past below her, his muscular flanks glistening in sweat, and Adrian up in the saddle, leaning forward, his own face nestled against the horse's wild mane, as if they were somehow lovers.

The other horses followed, hunters and mountain ponies, small farm horses, the kind Tom Campbell, their one Protestant neighbor in Tourmakeady, might buy for his children at the fair in Galway City.

Adrian and Nightfall were easily ahead, galloping away from the other jumpers. In spite of herself, Caitlin shouted with delight and ran down the little slope, as if to follow them, her eyes on Nightfall and Adrian in his golden racing colors. Then she stopped and watched as the horses crossed the field, jumped the tennis-court hedge, circled the country house, and ran straight for the stone fence and the judge's cart. As they went into the final lap, she looked over the other horses, trying to spot Tim O'Neill's big black prize winner, Samhain. Far back in the pack, she saw only one horse big enough to be likely. He was bunched in with a half-dozen other small farm horses and ponies. He was no challenge to Nightfall, she thought with relief.

A cheer went up from the crowd gathered by the finish. It came back to her on the April breeze and for a moment she wished she had stood with the rest of the household near the judge's cart, so she too could have shouted as Adrian raced by. She was sorry now she had fought with him earlier in the day. It had been her fault, going out onto the racecourse in the midst of fog.

But perhaps he had seen her after all, she thought, standing alone, dressed in her new trim uniform and white apron. Mrs. Finnerty had insisted she and Teasy wear them to the race. "I won't be having you taken for country culchies," she said. "And besides, I want you ready right afterward. Herself will be serving tea and scones to the Dublin guests up at the big house. See that you get yourselves back to the kitchen. Don't be lolling about with all those lads from Kilgarvan."

The hills grew silent again. The horses had slipped beyond the ridge, though Caitlin could see from where she stood that a few of the ponies had pulled up lame and others had tossed their riders on the last jump. There were boys from the village running across the open field to help them. She was thankful then that she had remembered the holy water in the boots. It had never failed her.

Wanting now for Adrian to see her, she climbed up and stood on the stone wall so that he might spot her when he came around on the last lap.

Caitlin saw him deep in the wood that ran the length of the famine wall. In the distance, only his racing colors flashed through the brown-black leafless trees. The sun had come out, appropriately for the end of the race, and in the late morning it filled the woods with shadows and yellow light and deepened the violet green of the winter's heather. She could hear Nightfall's hooves hitting ground that was smothered with fallen beech leaves, and the thunder of his hooves quickened as he came closer and then burst from the trees and raced down the yellow slope to the water's edge.

But he was no longer free of other horses. Tim O'Neill had come up through the pack, and as they went down the slope to the pond for the hedge jump between the driveway and tennis court, Samhain moved up beside Nightfall, running, it seemed to Caitlin, as if he were fresh from the barns.

"Oh, dear Mother," she whispered, and blessed herself. How awful for Adrian to lose now, on this final lap. Then she saw Nightfall veer suddenly to the right, cutting off Tim O'Neill on Samhain, and take the hedge on the inside. Her heart went into her throat. It was a dangerous move, she knew. He would gain a few yards on the other horse, but the lads in the tent had spoken earlier about the flooding, and the turf being soft on that edge of the jump. She lost sight of them for a moment as they landed beyond the high hedge, and then she saw Nightfall, riderless, bolting away. An instant later she saw that Adrian, caught in the stirrup, was being dragged behind him, bumping violently across the stubby field.

Leaping off from the stone wall, she ran down the slope toward the tennis court, where Nightfall had come to a stop. The slower horses were still coming out of the woods and she ran into their path, heedless of the danger as they sped by her. She was aware only of Adrian lying motionless by the tennis court, his leg twisted and caught up in the stirrup.

She slowed as she approached Nightfall, afraid he might bolt again. Speaking softly, as she would to her animals at home, she moved close enough to the horse to gently stroke his neck, gain his trust, then seized the reins. The horse jerked back, eyes wild in his head, but she held on to him, steadied the animal.

Others were coming. They, too, had seen Adrian fall, and Caitlin heard a half dozen shouting as they circled the big house and came running toward the court. If she didn't hurry, they would frighten Nightfall again, and this time it might be even worse for Adrian, lying helpless beneath the horse's hooves. Holding the reins tightly, she slipped under the horse's neck and with one hand ungirthed the saddle and pulled it off the sweating animal. Nightfall bolted away, kicking free of the leather and blanket, as Caitlin let go of the reins. Then she carefully loosed Adrian's foot from the stirrup and set his leg down. Kneeling beside him, she gently turned his body so that he lay flat and at rest.

He moved. "Christ!"

Caitlin sighed with relief, seeing that he was all right. "You're sound enough, I see, to use the good Lord's name in vain," she said.

"Nightfall?" he asked.

"Your horse is fine. He's there on the slope, though God knows he could have killed you, dragging you like a cut log half across the field."

He sat up, brushing the dirt off his jacket.

"Don't you be moving! The lads are coming and they'll help you."

"There's nothing wrong with me."

"Be still, Adrian Steele," she told him, taking pleasure in giving him an order. She wished that the lads were not running for them.

"Yes, ma'am," he said, smiling, then added, "I could have won if I had made that jump. Timmy O'Neill would never have caught me in the plowed field. Nightfall is too fast for the likes of that one."

"You could have killed yourself just as well."

"Were you worried then?" He was smiling at her.

"I won't be wanting any of the lads to be hurt on those jumps," she answered vaguely. "Some went down, I saw, in the flax field."

"Were you worried about myself on Nightfall?" he pressed.

Caitlin glanced up. The lads from the starter's gate had slowed to a walk as they rounded the tennis court, seeing that Adrian was all right. She stood and stepped back, embarrassed at having been seen so close to the master's son.

"Were you worried I might hurt myself, Caitlin?" Adrian said in Irish, pushing himself up and standing.

"Aye, and why wouldn't I be?" Caitlin said quickly.

He nodded, saying nothing, for the lads had arrived. The last exchange between them was a lingering look that meant more than the charade of their talk.

# · CHAPTER 19 ·

"I CAN'T SEE ANYONE," Caitlin said, so frightened by what they were doing that she had to speak. They had driven Adrian's Invicta to the ocean's edge and pointed it toward the sea. It was not yet midnight.

"We're safer that way," Adrian replied calmly. He was not afraid and that made her feel better.

She thought next of Cormac and wondered how he'd react if he picked up the *Irish Times* and saw a photograph of her dead on the rocky beach of Coulagh Bay. She let her mind dwell on that, taking a perverse comfort in the notion of his grieving.

"They patrol the waters, do they?" Mr. Thomas asked from the backseat. He was leaning forward, looking out the front window toward the sea.

"Not as much in this bay," Adrian answered. "There's no harbor, so the patrol is left to the local defense. We have our own man with them. He'll keep them away from the bay until after one A.M. By then you'll have boarded the U-boat."

"You've spoken to your man?"

"Yes. He's a constable in Glengarriff. I visited him yesterday."

"A policeman?" Mr. Thomas exclaimed.

Caitlin, too, looked quickly at Adrian, surprised.

"There are more than a few policemen among the Gardai who are supporting Germany. We needn't worry about the local defense force tonight."

"But there's the Irish navy!" Caitlin said, thinking again of the Brown boys from back home.

"There's nothing at all to the Irish navy, just two old patrol vessels. I've seen the both of them piered at Bull Bridge."

"What about torpedo boats?" Mr. Thomas asked, his interest perked.

"We haven't a one, though I hear the English are shipping over half a dozen to patrol the Dublin coast. Right now there's nothing more to the navy than a training ship and a barge they're fixing up to plant mines in the mouth of the Shannon. And a few fishing boats."

"How would you be knowing all this?" Caitlin asked, surprised again at how little she knew about her own country.

"One of the lads has a fitter's job at Bere Island."

"It isn't the Irish forces we need worry about," Mr. Thomas said. "It is this weather. Will they see our signal out at sea?"

"I worry about their coming ashore in a rowboat on these rocks. It would have been wiser to land near the Ards Peninsula, which is flatter."

"You're right," said Mr. Thomas. "This location wasn't my decision. But the U-boat should be here soon. Is it time we went down the cliffs?"

Caitlin heard the tension in his voice as he pulled together his few belongings. He had changed into his German uniform and Luftwaffe jacket on the drive from Killarney. If he were to be captured now, Adrian had told him, he would be protected by international law, with the rights of a soldier.

"Fraulein, tell me again what you are supposed to do," the German said.

"Beginning at twelve midnight, I'm to flash the auto lights every minute for fifteen minutes. Then I stop. If Adrian hasn't returned by half past the hour, I flash again for another fifteen minutes," Caitlin said, repeating her instructions.

"Very good!" The German smiled, as if she had nothing more to worry about.

"Mr. Thomas?"

"Yes, Caitlin?"

"But I have no watch," she whispered.

"Here, take mine," Adrian said quickly.

"No, take mine," said Mr. Thomas. "It's English. The Abwehr gave it to me. And these English pounds. I'll have no need of them in Hamburg." He handed her the pocket watch and slipped a tight roll of money into her fingers.

"I can't be taking this," Caitlin protested, feeling the weight of the notes.

"Please do," the young German said. "I know how the English have made your people suffer. Send it home to your family. The high command will think I spent it on Guinness." He kept smiling, and she thought what a handsome man he was, and how young. He seemed younger than either she or Adrian, yet he was not afraid to go out into the stormy sea. The English had no chance against such men as him. The Germans would win this war. It would be, as Adrian kept saying, all over by the fall of the year.

"I will save your money for you, Mr. Thomas. Until the next time you come to Ireland. And God willing we'll be at peace, and the day will be fine, as we say at home." She turned to smile at him and whispered, "God bless you."

"May He bless all of us," the German whispered.

Looking at him, Caitlin was suddenly aware of the fear in the young man's eyes. But it was not something he could share with her, or Adrian. His fear was just another secret to be kept. She wished she had the courage to say she understood, and that he would be home soon with his family. But she wasn't confident enough herself. It was as if they were playing a game with their emotions, hiding themselves from the truth of their lives.

" 'Tis time," Adrian said, and opened the car door. Then, to Caitlin, he said, "Come around to this side so you can switch the lights."

Caitlin stepped into the dark. It was cold above the bay; even on such a night, there was a wet breeze from the ocean. She ran around the big car and slid into the driver's seat. Adrian showed her the headlight switch on the wooden panel of the car's interior.

"All right, Adrian?" Mr. Thomas asked.

"All right. Here, Caitlin, the torch." He passed his heavy flashlight through the open car window.

"We'll be off," Mr. Thomas said. "Good-bye, Caitlin, and good luck to yourself." Turning, he ran for the bare rocky cliffs. They disappeared instantly down a narrow path and Caitlin realized that she was alone at the edge of the sea. She tried to make herself think of home, for she was never afraid of the night in Tourmakeady. Often she'd go off and climb to where she had a clear view of the lake, and sit there in the long twilight to watch the night sky change the water of Lough Mask into silver.

She turned Mr. Thomas's watch over in her hand and snapped open the cover. It was a wealthy man's watch, she saw, beautifully made with diamonds set in the hours of the day. Not right for the likes of her, she thought, nervous again at the thought of being found with it. She turned the torchlight on the roll of pounds and saw they were all five-pound notes wadded together.

"Dear Mother of God!" she exclaimed. It was nearly a thousand pounds, more money than she would earn in a lifetime at the Steeles'.

Looking out the side window where the two men had disappeared, she wondered if she should run after them and return the money when she saw the two of them reemerge on the cliff. She was about to climb out when she realized that it was not Adrian she saw silhouetted against the night sky, nor Mr. Thomas either. And then there were more men at the cliff's edge, appearing as if from nowhere, until a half-dozen dark figures stood together. They were dressed as the G2 men in Dun Laoghaire had been, wearing overcoats and carrying rifles.

"Oh, God help us," she whispered, and slipped down in the front seat of the Invicta, burying her face in the leather seat. They had not spotted her, she realized, but they must have seen Adrian and Mr. Thomas on the path down to the bay. They would all be caught and taken to Mountjoy Prison.

She had to run, she thought next, her mind whirling, trying to catch on some fragment of hope. She could head across the bog fields and find her way to Castletownberg. Driving through the dark village on their way down to the bay, she had seen where the bus stopped by the post office. If she were alone, the police would probably think nothing of her. She could take a bus home, for she had money now, a fortune of English pounds. For a moment she gathered herself together for flight. But then she thought of Adrian, caught between the bay and the rocky cliffs. There would be no getting away for him, unless the rowboat came and took him as well. But the rowboat would not come, she suddenly realized. She had not signaled the submarine offshore.

Caitlin forced herself to raise her head and peer out the side window to where the G2 men had been standing. There was no one now on the cliffs. She rolled down the window and listened for voices, but all she could hear were ocean waves crashing against the rocks below. Turning around, she glanced out the rear window to see if they were circling her. But the small promontory was deserted, except for the misshapen trees, twisted by the constant Atlantic winds. She could escape, Caitlin realized, run down the empty country road past their big cars, which had to be parked on the road below. But then she stopped thinking of escape. What had alerted them, she wondered. Had someone seen the Invicta speed through the empty streets of Ardgroom or Eyeries and telephoned the police?

Or had she and Adrian been spotted meeting Mr. Thomas in Killarney, when he got off the train? Perhaps someone had noticed that he waited until the very last moment before swinging out the coach door, jumping down into the gravel bed of the railway station as if to be sure no one was following after him. Or had Adrian's constable friend in Glengarriff been a G2 informer after all?

Caitlin slowly opened the door of the sports car and stepped out. She circled the car, keeping down so she couldn't be seen from the edge of the cliffs. She wasn't a true Irish woman, she thought, if she couldn't protect her own.

Gathering her courage, Caitlin stood and reached inside the open window of the Invicta for Adrian's flashlight. Guided by its slender beam, she ran toward the edge of the cliff to where the path led to the beach. In the darkness, she saw nothing, heard only the Celtic Sea crash against the black rocks. She pointed the small torch toward the beachhead and snapped it on and off quickly. Adrian might see it, she thought. And if he did, what would he make of it, this too-rapid signaling?

Now she spotted movement! She ran down the steep slope for a half-dozen yards until she reached another vantage point and, crawling out on the ledge, lay flat across its smooth broad back. A rowboat was coming in from the U-boat, its dark shape topping the white-capped waves. There were two men in the boat rowing hard against the tide. At each cresting of a wave the boat seemed to teeter, as if it might lose its balance and capsize, and then just before it was swallowed by another wave, it tipped forward into the wave's trough and raced for the shore. Her heart leaped . . . and then she realized that they would be killed, too, along with Mr. Thomas, and her Adrian, all gunned down by the G2 agents.

She flashed the torch, hoping Adrian or the Germans might see it and realize something was wrong. She snapped the torch off and peered over the edge of the ledge in time to see a man dive into a cresting wave and swim for the tiny boat. It had to be Mr. Thomas, she thought; he had seen the G2 men and decided not to wait for the boat to come ashore.

The shooting started immediately, rapid firing from a half-dozen places below her on the cliff. The sound of the shots came to her distorted by the swirling ocean wind that battered the cliffs. She grabbed the ledge, praying with all her heart, and then she saw the boat turn away from the shore, leaving Mr. Thomas adrift in the open sea.

Dear Mother of God, she thought, he would die there in the water. She stood up, heedless of her own safety and searched the black waters for Mr. Thomas. She saw he was still swimming away from shore, not having seen that the boat had turned and the Germans off the U-boat were pulling out of Coulagh Bay.

Then, from out over the water, she heard an explosion, and a flash of light lit the shore and Coulagh Bay. Rapid machine-gun fire started farther down the cliff, and Caitlin fell to the smooth ledge, lest she, too, be seen in the bright flash. But no one was shooting at her, she realized, or knew she was behind them. The G2 men were sending up flares, and in the light of another exploding flash she saw a machine-gun tracer crisscross the water and rip into the swimming figure. Mr. Thomas crumpled in the tide, and she saw his body was caught up in a whitecapped wave and tossed back toward the beach.

The G2 men on the shore climbed down from the rocks and ran to the edge of the water, where Mr. Thomas's body would wash up.

Others were still shooting out to sea, trying to hit the tiny boat before it disappeared into the darkness.

Caitlin backed away from the ledge and ran to the top of the cliff, ran past Adrian's car, ran down the deserted road toward town. She ran without thinking, ran with only the image before her of Mr. Thomas's body being tossed about in the sea. Caitlin did not want to die like that. She did not care enough about Ireland's freedom, or England's defeat. Those things had nothing to do with her. She was just a servant girl from Connemara, with a husband back in Dublin, a little girl at home. What in God's world was she doing mixed up with spies?

Then her heart almost stopped as the headlights of a car picked her up. She darted down into the shallow roadside ditch and fled into the field, the soft turf of the bog.

The car skipped to a halt on the road as she slid behind a turf stack, waiting with thumping heart for the bright flares, the relentless hail of shots.

"Caitlin! Caitlin!"

It was Adrian shouting for her.

"Come back! Come back!"

He was alive! He hadn't been killed or caught. She raced back the dozen yards to where he waited, standing in the beam of the headlight.

She ran into his arms and he swung her off her feet and into a tight embrace, then rushed her into the Invicta. Wordlessly, they raced away from Coulagh Bay toward Castletownberg, the Caha Mountains, hoping to reach the safety of Glennamain beyond.

They speeded along the empty country roads of Kerry, afraid that at each turn a roadblock would be waiting. Finally Caitlin could bear the tension no longer.

"I tried to signal," she whispered, ashamed that she hadn't done more, that she had run in panic for her own life. But Adrian was concerned with other matters.

"Some bastard in Dublin betrayed us. We'll find out who he is; the G-Two has heard its last from him."

As the car raced through Glengarriff, Caitlin forced herself to look back to see if there were police cars chasing them, but the town's street was deserted, the road empty. She began to breathe more easily, and she looked over at Adrian, marveling at how he had kept the presence of mind not only to escape but to save her. She owed him her life, she thought.

"And Mr. Thomas?" she whispered, feeling the weight of guilt at being alive.

"He's dead. The man never had a chance once they set off those flares."

"He was afraid, too, before you went."

"He saved me."

"What do you mean?"

"We were still hidden in the crags when he saw your flashing. We didn't know why you'd be signaling, and we were climbing back up to find out when they opened fire. He ran for the water, and the G-Two went after him, ran right past me in the rocks. I crept back up to the top of the cliff."

"Oh, dear God, I killed him," Caitlin said.

"You killed no one. It was the G-Two."

"He could have surrendered. They'd have put him in Mountjoy, that's all. Not killed him like a wild animal."

"And if he had, they would have gotten both of us and no one left to give the next agent a hand." He glanced over at her. "You did your best, Caitlin. It was very brave of you to signal."

"I was running for my life, I was. I didn't have the courage to stay and help you."

"You've courage enough for the both of us," he answered, his throat sounding tight. "And what did I do myself but run?"

He was crying, Caitlin realized, as he pressed harder on the Invicta's accelerator, speeding the car away from the bloody mess.

"I left the lad to die, when here he had come from Germany to help us."

"You did what you could, Adrian," she whispered, knowing she had to bolster his spirits. " 'Tis more than either of us can do, fight these G-Twos."

"We'll fight them again, Caitlin, and the next time it will be ourselves who will win the day on those bastards!"

He would not quit, she realized. It was in his very soul, this need to free Ireland from the English. It was this passion of his that drew her to him, she realized. How could anyone not love a man who cared more for his country than himself?

She kept quiet as they climbed the twisting mountain road. They were going through thick mountain fog, but Adrian did not slow his car. She would die here instead, she thought, plunge over the edge of the narrow road, and she made an act of contrition. It would be better, she thought, if they died together in a flaming wreck. Then at least Adrian would die a hero to his cause and she would be still faithful to her husband. But then the Invicta broke through the fog and ahead of them she saw Glennamain, brightly lit behind the famine wall.

"There!" he exclaimed. "We're home, Caitlin. We're safely home."

"Aye, home," she whispered, "thanks be to God," but she realized she could never be safe at Glennamain, nor in Dublin, not now, not ever again.

# · CHAPTER 20 ·

As they drove through the gates of the famine wall and raced up the drive, it looked to Caitlin as if the whole of Glennamain was lit with lights. The party seemed to have spread through the house like a summer fire.

Adrian pulled the Invicta to a stop while they were still in the trees, and they sat in the shadows watching couples dance on the terrace.

"Mrs. Finnerty will be looking for me," she said, suddenly remembering her duties.

"She has help enough with the village women, there's no need for you to work yourself to the bone," Adrian answered back. "Besides, I told Mother you deserved the night off, what with cleaning the whole place yourself."

There would be no one upstairs in the servants' room, Caitlin thought next. She would be alone at the top of the house, with not even Teasy to keep her mind off what had happened to Mr. Thomas.

"Please, Adrian," she said at once, "I can't be alone, not after what has happened." She reached over and seized his arm, as if she were afraid he might run from her. "Would you come with me into the garden? For a little while at least, until I feel better. You can't be going to the party, not after what has happened."

"I'll stay with you, Caitlin," he whispered, leaning over to her in the car. "But I have to be seen by everyone. They'll ask questions of my mother if I'm not about. The police would have seen the Invicta, and there's not many of them in the south of Ireland. I'll have a walk about, tell everyone I was resting, because of the fall, and then be with you within the hour by the spring garden. Will that be all right, Caitlin?"

She nodded, though she did not want to be alone for even a moment. She felt safe only when he was with her.

"An hour then in the spring garden."

"Aye," she whispered, as he started the Invicta and drove it slowly around the house to the garage.

Caitlin went up the dark back servants' stairs to her attic room and, taking off her clothes, slipped on her nightgown. She had always felt warm and secure wearing her nightshirt, and she had time before she had to meet Adrian. Just knowing she would be seeing him later made her feel better. In the morning, she thought, they would be off to Dublin. She took a deep breath, thinking that soon everything about Kerry, Coulagh Bay, and Glennamain would be behind her, as if it were only a long, terrible nightmare.

Sounds of the party rose from the terrace. The guests were hidden by the sloping slate roofs of the house, but she heard the music, the sound of talk, and women laughing.

She should be home in Tourmakeady, she thought, home with Nora and Cormac, not here among these people, all these Dublin jackeens with their snooty accents and their fancy British clothes. She shouldn't be risking her life, as if it were nothing at all, what with a child of her own. It was different for Adrian. He lived on the edge of the day, without a care, as if he were a child himself. But she was not like him, or his fancy friends below her on the terrace.

She thought of Tourmakeady and her peaceful life before Dublin and the Steeles. How easy it would be to pack up her few things and go down the back stairwell, through the kitchen and out across the lawn to the fence gate. It would be morning before Mrs. Finnerty or any of the others knew she was missing. They'd come upstairs to the attic and find the bed made, the closet empty.

How would Adrian act, finding her gone and out of his life? Would he come to Tourmakeady, she wondered. Drive into the mountains and search her out on the banks of Lough Mask? She could see herself in the cottage, baking round cakes on the griddle when he'd drive up in his car and find her with little Nora, sitting peacefully before the hearth.

Oh, dear, Adrian, what would you say? What poem would you find to tell me how your heart is broken, knowing I am already spoken for? Would you think yourself deceived, even though I often reminded you we were nothing more than parlor maid and master's son?

Caitlin could feel tears briefly warm her cheeks. She should not be thinking of him, she told herself. Cormac was her husband, a part of her real life, in Connemara. She remembered the day of their engagement. The dowry negotiations had taken the whole of an afternoon and evening. Her father and brothers had gone to O'Cadhain's public house in the village to meet with Cormac and his friends in the back room of the bar. Six of them on each side. Tommy O'Cadhain had put out brown bread and butter, a bottle of whiskey, and a barrel of porter.

Her brother Packy had stood in for her since she wasn't allowed to be present, telling Cormac and his friends what a fine wife she'd make. "And didn't she knit this fishing sweater for me herself?" he told them. Caitlin smiled, recalling the story as Cormac had told it to her later.

Timmy Joyce had spoken for Cormac, praising him as a fine, industrious lad, with his own farm and livestock, and not yet twenty-one. "He's a wealthy man, Cormac DeLacey, and with no brothers to share his good fortune."

The bride bartering went on until the moon was up over Lough Mask, with her father making an offering and Cormac's friends not asking for more, but saying across the wooden table, "Jesus, Mary, and Joseph, Paddy Rush, where is Caitlin going to find a fella half as good in Tourmakeady? Would you deny the girl a lifetime of happiness by giving such a meager dowry?"

They finished the whiskey, brown bread, and butter, and still they talked. It was after ten o'clock before her mother saw little Michael running up the hill to the house, carrying the news that the dowry was set at a hundred pounds. Caitlin and Cormac were free to marry.

She had gone down to the pub then with the women, her mother and sisters and female cousins, and by the time they reached O'Cadhain's the word had spread through the valley. She could see the neighbors coming in from the hills, their torches bright as stars. And then she had stepped inside O'Cadhain's to the cheers of the townsfolk and danced till dawn with Cormac and her brothers, and all the lads of Tourmakeady whispering in her ear that Cormac DeLacey was a damn lucky fella, and never before in her life had she been so happy or dazed with joy.

The banns were announced the next Sunday. She had felt proud in church, hearing her name and Cormac's read aloud by Father Leahy. She wasn't just another lass in Tourmakeady, a girl to be eyed by the lads and watched over by her mother, whispered about at dances down on the wooden bridge. She had been spoken for, chosen.

Yet she was afraid of what would happen to her at her wedding, on their short honeymoon in Salthill. On the Friday before she was married, she had asked her mother, shyly, about what to expect from Cormac. "I haven't a clue," she whispered, following her mother into the cowshed.

"Ah, musha, don't be worrying. Your husband will be knowing well enough. Father Leahy wouldn't like our talking about such matters in the middle of the day, and this being the Feast of Saint Fainche! Be off with you, girl, feed the pigs, and leave well enough alone."

But Cormac had not known. In the little boardinghouse on Galway

Bay, he had turned away from her in the bed and gone to sleep without a kiss or an embrace or a gesture of love on their first night together as man and wife.

She had cried herself to sleep that night, trying to keep him from hearing her sobs and knowing that in some way it must be her fault, her failure as a woman that he would not even look at, let alone touch, her body.

It was cloudy and cool the next day, but they had gone to the beach anyway, afraid to be alone together in their room. She remembered sitting on the black sand staring at the ocean and thinking she had made a terrible mistake, that she should have gone to America with her friend Mary Kilcourse, to Chicago where she had relatives on her mother's side—gone anywhere but to Salthill with Cormac DeLacey.

He said nothing to her that morning, simply sat and tossed pebbles into the surf. It wasn't until time to take the bus back that she built up enough courage to ask, "Is there something you're finding wrong with me, Cormac? If you don't want to have me as your wife, then give my da back his hundred pound sterling, and he'll see Father Leahy writes Rome and annuls this marriage."

"Well, I didn't want to be getting you pregnant, Catty. It could happen easy enough, I know. I had myself a talk with Father Leahy in the confessional."

"Jesus, Mary, and Joseph," she whispered. "Cormac, we're married!"

"Aye, we are. But what will the lads be saying at O'Cadhain's if you begin to show? They'll have a good laugh on me, now won't they?" He glanced at her and Caitlin could see the sudden anger in his eyes. "I won't have my wife bullyragging me into fatherhood."

"Why did you marry me if we weren't going to be a true husband and wife?"

"We'll be husband and wife soon enough," he said quickly.

"But isn't that what marriage is for? Didn't Father Leahy tell us so when we went to sign the parish book?"

"There's more to marriage than my having my way with you not half a day after the wedding."

"Is that why you're thinking I married you, Cormac DeLacey, just so I could have permission to sin?"

"No, but everyone at home will know soon enough if we have it off at Fitzstephen's boardinghouse."

"Is that what you're afraid of?" she asked, smiling at his innocence. It had never occurred to her that he would be so strange. Away from Tourmakeady and his friends, she'd thought, he would be different with her, more affectionate. But she was wrong. He thought all of Ireland had ears and eyes only for them.

"We'll have time enough once we're on the farm, and by ourselves. No one will know our business then," he said, as if making an offering to her.

"Then why did we spend good money coming here to Galway Bay? To Salthill, too, when you can't put your toe into the water without it being frozen up like a lump of ice?"

"Sure, I won't be having them riding by our place on their push-bikes and thinking we're inside and having a go at each other."

"Bejasus, Cormac," Caitlin flared up. "Then we might as well be living out-of-doors, so no one will even think we're making love!"

She turned away from him then, ashamed of what he thought of their marriage, and ashamed that he felt the love between them was something to be made fun of by the lads at home, and a corner of her heart shut itself forever from her husband.

Adrian would not force himself on her as Cormac had, getting himself drunk first at O'Cadhain's, needing the drink to arouse his desire. Suddenly she hated her husband for everything that he had put her through, for humiliating her with his inept lovemaking. Would Adrian be the same, she wondered? Were all Irishmen, Protestants or not, so useless?

Behind her, Caitlin heard a soft knock on the attic-room door, and then a cold draft wrapped itself around her thin ankles. The door, she knew, had opened and silently closed. She did not turn from the open window, just listened as his footsteps crossed the room to where she stood. She waited for his hands to touch her shoulders. Then she found herself listening to her own heart, marveling that it was not beating wildly. She was that way, she knew. At times of trouble or excitement, her whole body calmed itself down. She gained control by becoming a stranger to her own feelings.

"Caitlin?" He spoke without touching her.

She could feel his breath on her bare neck, knew by the tremor of his voice how much he desired her. She could send him away now, she thought.

"I've come to see if you're all right, Caitlin," Adrian whispered.

She shook her head, unable to find her voice and not daring to turn to him. If only he would touch her gently. Then everything would be all right. Please God, let him hold me, she asked, then thought how curious it was to ask God's help in her adultery.

" 'Tis you that had the terrible time," she finally managed to say. "It was terrible, hearing the shooting. I thought you were dead." She began to cry, unable to hold her tears in check any longer.

"It's the price of freedom, Caitlin," he whispered.

"I think it is too grand a price."

She moved now, turned to him. He had changed clothes and was wearing his dinner jacket; his stiff white ruffled shirt seemed to shine in the darkness. She was pleased it looked so well on him, for she had taken care in its starching. He looked so handsome, she thought, his shirt showing off his dark face, his dark eyes.

"I thank you for coming, but you shouldn't be worrying about me tonight, what with your friends all here at the house." She found she could not look at him and talk, yet she knew his eyes were on her face, and she slowly turned her head to show her profile in the shadows.

"They're my family's friends, not mine."

"I'm thinking that Miss Lambert is a friend of yours."

"Allison Lambert is a ninny!" he answered quickly.

"Indeed? You seemed not to think so this morning when you left me in the racing field to have a word with her."

"I didn't come here to talk about Allison Lambert."

"Then why did you come, instead of meeting me in the garden as I asked?"

She locked her eyes on him, holding him to account.

"I'm in love with you, Caitlin." He said the words in Irish, as if the language could keep his love a secret between them.

Now the words were spoken, it all seemed clear and reasonable, and the ache she had felt in her heart since she first saw him vanished. Yet she felt she had to test him, test herself.

"I dust parlors, Adrian. Surely you can't be in love with the likes of me."

"I can be in love with whomever I damn please." He took hold of her, seizing her shoulders, then gradually relaxed his grip, and his fingers stroked the silkiness of her inner wrists. She was trembling in his hands, as if he had captured some brilliant feathered bird in the wild. Her softness took him by surprise. Always she had seemed his equal, with her sharp tongue and quick replies. He felt her tense, and she pulled away.

"I'm not the one for you to be loving, Mr. Steele. I'm no fine lady like Allison Lambert or Olivia Dawson."

"Olivia Dawson?"

"Aye, her cap is set for you as well."

"The girl's an addlebrain," he declared.

"Sure, are we all ninnies and addlebrains, Mr. Steele?" she asked, teasing.

"No, dear Caitlin, you are nothing of the kind. I have never met anyone as wise as yourself, or as kind and loving."

"Don't embarrass me with fine words," she said quickly, glancing away, frightened by what was happening between them.

"I want to be embarrassing you, mavourneen. I want to be loving you."

Gently, he pulled her into his arms. Caitlin resisted, held herself stiff, but then she fell into his embrace, as exuberantly as a country girl might leap into a stack of hay.

It was his desire that startled her most. Cormac had never hungered for her that way, and at first she was afraid of his need. He lifted her off the floor and carried her effortlessly to the narrow bed and she felt the length of his body on hers.

"Adrian, I mustn't," she managed to say, but as she spoke, she uncontrollably kissed the soft flesh of his neck and cheek. It was her own desire she was frightened of now.

"Oh, my darling, darling Caitlin," he kept saying, moaning as his mouth canvassed her face, sought out her bare skin.

"Shhh," she whispered, frightened by his talk. Cormac and she had never spoken when they made love. Talking did not seem right. Love was a thing to be done in dark and silence.

"I love you, my darling. I love you," he kept repeating, not heeding her, and then his hands swept beneath her nightgown and found her breasts, smothering them beneath his palms.

Caitlin awoke before dawn. She had slept for only a few minutes after they first made love. And then Adrian, aroused by her stirring, had wanted her again, and they made love a second time with the same passion. That time, realizing how unlike he was to Cormac, she had surrendered herself fully. That had excited him more, and for a moment, in the back of her mind, she was afraid Teasy or the other girls might hear the bed shake under them.

But she forgot her fears and concentrated on the lovely music coming from the terrace, and what Adrian was doing to her, how desperate he was to hold and have her. It made her dizzy with delight, this newly discovered power, this knowledge that a man could be so taken by the pleasures of her body. This was what real sin was like, she thought. No, it could not be, she thought next. Nothing this good and lovely could be a sin in God's eyes, and she held her lover in a tight embrace, whispering his name into the dark.

He slipped away into a gentle sleep and she kept him in her arms, lying beneath him and loving the weight of his body. But though she could see his face, she could not touch him as she wished, and slowly, as carefully as she might set Nora down in her crib, she moved him to the pillow beside her, pulling away so she might watch his profile in the moonlight.

Asleep, he seemed younger and less angry. His brow unfurrowed and the edge he had about him, the jutted chin and glancing look, slipped away. He seemed untroubled. She smiled and, dipping her head, kissed his ear. His head jerked, but he recovered, settled again, and slept on. Caitlin put her forefinger between her teeth and bit down to keep from laughing. She did not want to wake him, not yet. It was still dark, the terrace was quiet, the country house silent. She heard only the frogs from the lake. Their faraway choking carried clearly in the night air.

Fog had moved in and she loved it for its concealment. Yet the mist through the open window was cold and the dampness chilled her, chilled Adrian. He stirred and quickly she lifted the sheet to his chest, tucked it about him. Seeking warmth, he turned to her body and she slipped down on the soft goose mattress to place her breast against him. He settled at once, finding contentment against her.

It startled Caitlin, this freedom she had with the man and her abandonment of modesty. She wanted to give herself to him, to let him have her body. She wanted him to be her master, to serve him in this and every way. And then she heard the jew's harp.

The sound of the harp came from far off, from beyond the famine wall. Quickly, frightened once more, she slipped from the bed and went to the open window to see if in the early morning light she might see who was playing the tiny instrument—though in her heart she already knew there was no one below her on the lawn, that the lovely melody did not come from anyone at Glennamain.

"Caitlin?" he whispered, stirring in the bed. When she did not answer, he sat up and rubbed the sleep from his eyes. "Come to bed, my love?" he asked.

"Did you hear the jew's harp, Adrian?"

On the small maid's bed he shook his head.

"Do you know what it means?" She was no longer frightened. Having heard the harp, she felt only peace, as if her life was beyond her will. She walked back and sat down beside him on the bed. "Have you ever been to Lough Mask, darling?"

He reached up and pulled her into an embrace. "Yes, when I was younger, I fished there. I'd go with the boys from school, and my father. He's a great one for fishing."

"Would you be knowing then the story of the fairy island of Lough Mask?" she whispered.

"Is there a fairy island now?" he asked, mimicking her soft brogue.

"Aye." She smiled back, not minding his teasing. "I've not seen it, but others in Tourmakeady have. Sean O'Rahilly, God rest his soul, had been there, I know. I heard his story told often enough in the village. He died before my time, but they tell of how once he was coming home from Clonbur, crossing the lake late in the day when a heavy mist came up. He rowed for hours without a notion of where he was, and then he began to hear music. It was summer, you see, and often in fine weather there are dances down on the shore. He followed the sound of a jew's harp and found himself on an island, there in the middle of Lough Mask.

"But there is no island in the Lough, Sean knew. Yet when he stepped ashore, he found young people dancing, and music as well, and poteen, he said, that was sweet as spring water, and he sang and danced and had his way with girls as lovely as any that walked the streets of Dublin. Then, drunk with poteen and pleasure, he fell asleep on the soft turf, happy, and thankful he was alive and safely off the lake.

"In the morning, the fog was still there, but he struck out again and had only rowed a hundred yards when he was finally free of the mist and could see the shore of Tourmakeady. He rowed for land as if the devil himself were behind him, and when he came safely into our bay, he looked back at the lake and there was no mist on Lough Mask, nor any island, or young people dancing to the music of a jew's harp."

While she was telling the story, Adrian had raised himself up on one shoulder. He kept smiling, gazing down at her, amused by her story and wondering what it all meant.

"He never saw the fairy isle again, though he was caught often enough in the mist of Lough Mask. But then—it was during the troubles—he woke one day and said to his wife, 'Were they dancing last night down on the bridge? I could swear I heard a jew's harp on the night air.' And he went off that morning with his slan to cut turf.

"It wasn't but half past nine that his wife heard the jew's harp while she was carding wool, and she ran to the turf field and found him. He had been shot in the head and left to die like a goat. It was the Black and Tans that done it, a roving band of those murderers."

She lay her head against his chest and Adrian could feel her tears on his bare skin.

"And what are you telling me, Caitlin?" he asked, though he knew the point of her story.

"I heard my jew's harp, dear, when I woke this morning. It was calling to me."

He stopped himself from making fun of her. He knew superstition was strong in the west. Instead he asked, "But didn't the jew's harp save Sean O'Rahilly on Lough Mask?"

"Aye, it did. But the jew's harp is God calling. It called to Sean O'Rahilly to save him, but then he sinned on Lough Mask. And so have I."

"There's no sin in our love, Caitlin," he said firmly. The sun had reached the slate rooftop and came through the small attic window, lighting her face gloriously.

" 'Tisn't you that I've sinned against, darling." She touched his face. "And if I had, I'd gladly do it again, a thousand times." She smiled through her tears. "I've sinned against people you do not know, and for that the jew's harp played its tune." She turned her face from his and stared up at the open window. She needed to hurry, for the maids would be up soon and Adrian would have to leave.

"Caitlin, you have sinned against no one for loving me." He bent and kissed the soft nape of her neck.

He was so innocent, she thought, and not for the first time. He was never troubled with his life, with what he did. He felt blessed with good fortune, a perfect life. Perhaps it was the Protestant in him, this feeling he could not be judged by God. But she knew better. Her adultery had stolen something from Cormac, and someday she would pay with her life. She knew this. For she had heard the jew's harp in the morning.

# · CHAPTER 21 ·

ON A CLEAR JUNE morning two months later, Caitlin was on her way to the fish market. She was still two streets away when she caught a whiff of that day's catch and her insides erupted. She fought to get her breath, but right there on the corner of Moore Street she had to brush other pedestrians aside to reach the gutter in time to vomit.

"Caitlin, are you all right?" Mrs. Finnerty asked, appearing behind her. They had both been shopping and had agreed to meet at the fish market.

Caitlin nodded.

"A bit of a sick stomach? Come along, child, and I'll put you on the bus. Can you be walking as far as the GPO?" She had Caitlin by the elbow and was steering her away. "It's Hitler that's doing this," she explained, leading the way. "He's sprinkling a virus from the air, they say."

Caitlin knew what the housekeeper meant but was too weary to argue. For days she had been feeling tired; the night before she had actually fallen asleep over supper.

"It's those German airplanes. They fly over at night and drop the viruses while we're in our beds. Don't be buying flowers from those sellers at the pillar, Caitlin. 'Tis easy enough for some spy to sprinkle buds with the stuff, and the next thing you know, we'll have it in the house." Mrs. Finnerty sighed. "Sure, I wouldn't be surprised if we weren't all dead by the end of summer."

Caitlin did not respond. It was an old argument with Mrs. Finnerty. She said instead, "We best be getting on with the marketing."

"Look at yourself, child! You're as white as a sheet." Mrs. Finnerty reached out and felt Caitlin's forehead for fever, but there was none. "Have you been eating properly? That's the trouble with you young things, going off and starving yourselves half to death so you can look like one of those film stars."

"I've not been starving, Mrs. Finnerty. You know well enough." Early that week, Caitlin had been surprised to find she no longer fitted into her maid's uniform. She and Teasy had spent an evening letting out the seams.

" 'Tis true." They had reached the bus stop at O'Connell Street and the housekeeper stopped to eye Caitlin for a moment. "But sure you can use the extra pounds. You were thin as a rail in February when you came up from the country. Here's a bus. You go ahead home and start dinner. I'll finish up with the shopping. There's just ourselves tonight, what with herself and Mr. Steele down at Glennamain." She pushed Caitlin toward the bus queue.

Caitlin did not protest. She knew what Mrs. Finnerty would do, once on her own: spend the afternoon at the Ladies' Public House. In recent months, the housekeeper was finding time to socialize at "The Ladies," the only pub just for women in Dublin.

Caitlin stepped onto the bus feeling better, as she always did when she was away from Mrs. Finnerty.

Back at Vulcanus Caitlin had some tea and went to work. She finished putting the potatoes up and started washing the pots. With the water running, she did not hear him come into the kitchen, nor know he was there until she felt his arms around her waist, his lips kissing the soft flesh of her neck.

"Have you no sense?" she asked, upset at once with him.

"The house is empty. We're alone, love." He still held her, his arms linked around her thin waist, as if they were a lock.

"Teasy's here!"

He shook his head, grinning. "I gave her a fistful of shillings and sent her off to the Booterstown Fair."

"You didn't!"

"I did."

"Mrs. Finnerty will have a fit, and poor Teasy, she'll be the one in trouble, not yourself. Teasy doesn't have the sense to say no, with you dropping coins into her palms."

"I'll handle Bridie Finnerty. Don't be living in such fear of the woman, Caitlin. Yeats was wrong. We're not a priest-ridden nation at all. It's the housekeepers of Ireland that keep our people underfoot."

"You're a queer one, master." She smiled at him despite her anger. "Don't be blaming the priests and housekeepers. 'Tis yourself who is demanding and imperial. Now leave me be!" She pulled loose from him, wondering how in the world she would tell him her news.

"Oh, stop calling me 'Master Adrian'!"

"And what else would I be calling someone who behaves like a lord?"

"Dear God, how in the world did all this happen?" He ran his fingers through his hair and began to pace the kitchen, talking as fast as he could. "I don't think your work is 'beneath' me. It isn't that my work is better than yours; it's equal. We're equal. We're more than equal, you and I." He stepped closer, but she moved aside so he could not touch her.

"If our work is so equal, then, why is it I sometimes read poetry, but you never cook potatoes?"

"I don't have the time, my love," he said softly.

"Time!" Now she was in a rage. "You're in your bed half the day as it is! I swear, you only get up at noon so you won't be missing a meal. It's boiled potatoes and buttermilk today, by the way. Mrs. Finnerty said not to be fixing anything special, what with your mother and father down in the country."

He touched her. Took her hands and pulled her to him, though at first she resisted. He needed to touch her; there was a wonderful beauty, he thought, in her fierceness.

"Caitlin, I'm up half the night going to meetings. And there's letters to be written, letters to the *Independent*. When I leave you, I don't return to my own bedroom and sleep. I would never leave the warmth of your body, except to do the work of Ireland."

"Stop this," she whispered, and glanced around, expecting someone to be watching.

" 'Tis true. 'O woman, shapely as the swan, on your account I shall not die.' "

She cocked her head, letting herself be swayed by his fine words. "Would you be writing that poem yourself?" she asked.

"Would you love me less if it was Yeats?" he answered. He stepped closer and slipped his arms around her waist.

Caitlin let herself fall gently into his arms and be lifted off her feet and carried through the house, to her small room under the slate. It was not his poem, she realized, but it didn't matter.

He set her softly on the narrow mattress and knelt beside the bed. Slowly, carefully, he unbuttoned her white blouse, her skirt. He slipped away her clothes as if they were silk. She turned her cheek into her pillow and closed her eyes, held her breath. Each time they made love, she felt she was taking a great voyage out to sea, sailing away in the fairest of weather.

He was beside her, naked now himself; she slipped her arms about him, and he whispered, "You make me so happy."

She smiled but did not speak. Instead she let her fingers answer him, slowly and softly etching her fingertips down the length of his back, over his buttock. He shuddered when she touched him so.

"Darling, darling, I love you so," he said, and kept talking, declaring his love.

"Shh," she whispered, still embarrassed by his speaking out loud as they made love.

"Would you be talking to yourself, Caitlin DeLacey," a voice said from the hallway, and then the door of the gabled room pushed out and Mrs. Finnerty came inside. Her face was flush from too many ginger beers at the Ladies' Public House. It was a moment before she realized what she was seeing: Caitlin DeLacey and her master, naked together in bed. Then she cried out, "Curse o' God," and lurched back to the hallway, stumbling from the drink and the surprise.

When the door was safely shut, she shouted through it, "Caitlin DeLacey, may the devil swallow you sideways! Get on with your clothes, you hussy. And get your bags. I won't have you in my house a day longer."

Mrs. Steele refused to look at the parlor maid, though she had driven up from Kerry as soon as Mrs. Finnerty telephoned with the shocking news.

She sat behind the library desk and nervously fiddled with a stack of letters as she asked, "Do you have anything to say, child?"

"I'm sorry," Caitlin whispered.

"You have brought a terrible disgrace to this household." Mrs. Steele then looked up at her parlor maid. "I can only pray that what has happened can be kept among us. As a Catholic, Caitlin, you must realize you have committed a grievous sin."

"I love Adrian," Caitlin spoke up.

"Yes, I'm sure you do, in your innocence, but that doesn't matter. What you have done is beyond the bounds of all propriety. I know I must take some of the responsibility. My son, I regret, has a wanton nature, and Mr. Steele will deal with him. It is my task to say what is obvious even to yourself, Caitlin, and that is that you must leave this house. I have paid you until the end of the month, and I have included the price of a train ticket back to Galway. Also, I've written a letter to your family explaining why you have been dismissed. It is only right that they know of your transgression." She pulled a sealed envelope from a cubbyhole of her desk.

"I would like to speak to Adrian," Caitlin said quickly, summoning up her courage.

Mrs. Steele paused a moment, and then said, "Yes, you may see my son and say your good-byes. Perhaps it will make an impression on him, since so very little else does. He behaves irresponsibly without thought for other people and their lives. He should understand now how his actions have destroyed your life. Pack your belongings, child, and come back to the library. I'll have Adrian meet you."

He was waiting in the library when she returned, standing at the bookshelves with a book in hand. The late afternoon sun lit his face, and Caitlin thought at once how wonderful he must have looked onstage at the Abbey Theatre. Then he turned and saw her and smiled, and she took her first real breath of the day. Everything will be fine, she realized. No matter what else they did to her, she still had Adrian.

"Oh, my love," she whispered, and could only say, "they're sending me away," before she began to cry.

"You'll never be away from me, Caitlin," he said in Irish, holding her wet face in his hands and smiling. He bent to kiss away her tears.

She could smell his English cologne, and she wondered, How could he go on with normal living after what had happened to them?

"They're sending me home, Adrian."

"I know. I'm sorry, darling." He kept smiling at her, as if he thought he could cheer her with that alone. "But it isn't the end of the world. You'll only be in Connemara. I can be there in half a day." He slipped his arms about her waist, as if they were still carefree lovers.

"Can't we go away together, Adrian? To England? Or Germany?" Her mind whirled with the wonderful possibility of flight. In time, she thought, once they were settled on the Continent, she could send for Nora and raise her daughter free of her own country's repression. It was what all great Irishmen had done: flee Ireland. Yeats had done it, and James Joyce. Surely Adrian would want to do the same.

But Adrian pulled back. "There's a war on, Caitlin. And I have work to do, for Ireland's freedom. We can't be thinking of ourselves at a time like this."

"But they're throwing me out, Adrian! What will I do?"

"Sure, there's plenty of work in Dublin. This isn't the only house that has parlor maids."

"But no one will be hiring me in Ballsbridge, or in Rathmines, for that matter, not after Mrs. Finnerty finishes telling the other housekeepers all about this."

"The hell with Mrs. Finnerty!"

"The hell yourself, Adrian Steele! I'm the one who needs work." She pulled from his arms, feeling cold in the sunny library. It was all crazy, anyway, she realized. They couldn't live together in Ireland or England without marrying, and how could she do that? She had a husband and child, and there was no divorce for anyone in Ireland. Then she had an inspiration. "Adrian, we can be together. We can emigrate to America!"

He was shaking his head before she stopped speaking. "I can't leave the struggle," he said. "You know that."

"I need you."

"Others need me, too. Besides, there'll be time enough for us. The war will be over by the fall, and Germany will win. And if I were to marry you today, my father would cut me off without a shilling. I need to give them time to get used to the idea. We've never had a Roman Catholic in the family."

"I love you, Adrian," she whispered.

"If you love me, Caitlin, you will go to Connemara and wait until the war is over. We'll be married by Christmas, I promise."

"I can't marry you in Ireland, Adrian," she said quietly.

"Yes, you can, once we're free of England." He came to her again and they stood quietly a moment, both looking through the window curtains at the square, where two nannies were pushing perambulators across the small park.

"I can't marry you in Ireland, Adrian, because I am married already." She said it as calmly as she might tell him the day's weather.

"Married?" Adrian whispered. "Married?" he repeated, as if trying to learn the word in a foreign language.

"And I have a child living in Tourmakeady, a little girl."

"A child?" He turned away, staggered by the news.

"You have to go away with me, Adrian," she told him, "for I am now carrying your child." The final secret was revealed to him, and she sank down on the window seat. It had been such a strain, hiding the truth.

"How could you do this to me?" he shouted.

" 'Tis both of us who did it, Adrian," she answered back.

"Don't you have any sense of decency?" he went on, not listening to her. "I would never have . . . a woman with a child!"

He was stammering in his surprise and in that she found some satisfaction. For once he was not ready with a quick reply, or a bit of poetry. But now she knew, as clearly as if he had already said the words, that this would be his excuse. He would never leave Ireland, nor marry her. He would never leave Dublin, or his family, or this grand house in Ballsbridge. She had been a fool, she thought, as Cormac had been a fool to write his uncle. But Cormac had only lost their farm. She had lost much more than that.

"I gave you my heart, Adrian," she said softly.

"You gave your honor to another man, Caitlin DeLacey, not to me," he said grandly, as if he were clean in the whole affair.

"Aye," she said. "But 'twas you, Adrian Steele, who had no honor at all to give."

And then she left him. She picked up her bag in the hall and went out by the front door, the door she had never used before. She left it open behind her, as if to say, all is abandoned here. She did not turn at the sidewalk to look back, though she knew well enough that Mrs. Finnerty would be watching, peering out from the kitchen windows.

She walked the length of the River Liffey until she reached Phoenix Park and then wandered aimlessly through the fields, from Old Town Wood, to White Fields, to the Wilderness. She kept moving, for she knew the Gardai were on the alert for loiterers, ever since the Irish army's ammunition had been stolen, right out of the magazine fort. She wondered if Adrian had been part of the underground team that had pulled it off. He had a Thompson submachine gun in his bedroom —he had shown it to her. But when she asked if it had come from the magazine fort raid, he had just smiled and told her to never mind. She had been sure then that he had been among the brave lads. But now she doubted it. Raids on the British, right in the heart of Dublin, were carried out by heroes. Writing letters to the editor had always been more in Adrian's line, she thought bitterly.

It began to rain when she left the park, so she caught the tram at Park Gate and rode down to O'Connell Street. She stopped for tea in a basement restaurant, but found herself ordering whiskey instead. She drank it down in one quick swallow, then trembled as it spread through her like a turf fire. Feeling stronger, she ordered a second, then a third. She paid for them all with a five-pound note she peeled from the wad Mr. Thomas had given her.

It was still raining when she went back into the street. She paused at the corner, her brain hot and fuzzy, and forced herself to decide what to do.

She had to see Cormac. She had to catch the train to Tivoli and be at his flat when he came home from work. But, dear God, what would she tell the man? That she had been sacked for adultery with the master's son? She sank down in the curb and felt her stomach, sour from the three whiskeys, rise up. She vomited into the gutter, while passing ladies drew themselves aside and hurried by her.

When she did find the strength to stand, it was after six and there were crowds of civil service workers going home. It was colder, but her mind was clear. She knew what she had to do.

She waited for dark to fall and the streets to clear of anyone she might know. Then she walked to the old post office on O'Connell Street, where the Sinn Fein had first struck for freedom in 1916, and from the anonymity of a public call box there, she struck back at Adrian Steele.

"Constable Ginty, here!" said the officer who answered the telephone.

"I'm calling to report on a traitor, sir," Caitlin whispered.

"Well, lady, I can't be hearing you. Speak up, dearie."

She told him again why she was calling, turning her face into the booth so as not to be seen or heard in the vaulted post office building.

"And who would the traitor be now, ma'am?" he said, as if humoring her. But he would find out soon enough, she thought, that she was no daft old lady, imagining spies on every back street of Dublin.

"His name is Adrian Steele, from Ballsbridge."

"And who might you be, ma'am?"

" 'Tis no matter who I am, sir." In a firm voice she told him quickly about Adrian's Thompson submachine gun. " 'Tis from the magazine fort, up in the park."

"Where's he keep this Thompson?" the constable asked, serious now.

"Under his bed. I've seen it myself. The gun and ammunition. He has a box of it, with 'forty-five-caliber' stamped on the wood."

"Ballsbridge, you say?"

"Off Serpentine Avenue. Vulcanus, the house is called."

"And who is it that's telephoning? We can't just be believing everyone who rings up the station."

Caitlin smiled into the black telephone. "Tell Mr. Steele it was a country culchie that told on him."

Then she slammed down the phone and fled the GPO, knowing now that she must leave Ireland, for once Adrian was taken by the Gardai, the bloody Sinn Fein would be on her. Even in Tourmakeady she would not be safe from the revenge of the IRA.

She'd use the English pounds to book passage to America, for Cormac and herself. And once settled in the States, with jobs and a place of their own, they'd send for Nora. A dead German had done for her what Adrian would not do: made it possible for her to leave Ireland forever.

# · BOOK THREE ·

## PAST AND PRESENT
## 1954–1982

# · CHAPTER 22 ·

## GATESBURG: 1982

THE MORNING AFTER CAITLIN DeLacey's wake the farmhouse kitchen was silent, except for the crackle of the bacon Catty was cooking. She was absorbed in her thoughts, but looked up as Maggie came in. "Good morning, Mag. You're dressed already!"

Maggie nodded. "I thought I'd better get into the bathroom before the rush began. We have to be at Saint Pat's by ten?"

Catty nodded. "Yes. I couldn't sleep, so I started getting breakfast for my gang. Coffee?"

"Yes, thank you." Maggie yawned and went to sit down at the kitchen table, letting Catty pour her a cup of coffee. "Are we the only ones awake?"

"If you mean, have I seen our new sister this morning, the answer is no." Their eyes met and they sat down at the same time, ready to begin.

"Talk about family secrets!" Catty said, reaching for her cigarettes. Lighting one and taking a deep drag, she shook her head.

"But I don't get it," said Maggie. "If none of us knew about Nora, who let her know that Mommy had died?"

"Oh, I'm sure O'Connor sent a telegram to Ireland. Although even he probably never imagined Nora would turn up. I don't think O'Connor believes in airplanes."

"No, it wasn't him. He was shocked when he saw her in the doorway."

"Well, Michael must have known about her, then."

"What makes you think Father Mike knew about Nora?" Maggie asked.

"He's the oldest. He was always closest to Mother. And he's been to Ireland."

"Yes, but not to Tourmakeady, where Dad was. Michael went directly to Belfast; I was there! We didn't see any relatives."

"Why are you so proud of the Ireland trip, Maggie? It's unlike you," her sister asked. "I know they attempted to kill Michael. And one of the IRA hunger strikers died in his arms. But did his trip do any good? They're still killing themselves over there, and now Michael is just as bad—an Irish fascist, with his right-wing organization."

"The Blue and Whites support Irish freedom, Catty," Maggie answered, "not killings!" She stopped herself. She would not get involved in a political argument with Catty, not with any of the family. Now was not the time for arguments. Instead she said, "Do you see any family resemblance?"

Catty shook her head. "No, nothing. Nora's heavyset. Looks old. She has beautiful skin, though."

"It's that Irish diet and weather. It kills most people." Maggie paused a moment to sip her coffee. They hadn't had a chance the night before to talk with their new sister. After the wake Nora had gone off to bed, exhausted by the long trip from Ireland. Maggie promised herself that after the funeral, she would sit down with Nora and get to know her.

"I still can't believe that Father Mike knew about Nora all these years. Knew Dad was alive!"

"Michael knew, Maggie. Of course he did." Catty stubbed out her cigarette and immediately lit another. "When Dad went back to Ireland in fifty-four, I was told that he was killed in a car accident. It was O'Connor who told me, not Mom. He pulled me out of class, I remember. That was all. And I was afraid to ask Father O'Connor or Mom how it happened."

"Mother didn't say anything to you?"

"She never told me anything. Everything I found out about this family I learned from Paddy Jack."

"Well, Mom and I talked all the time about Ireland, what her life was like growing up, and still she never mentioned Nora, or anything about Dad. She just said Dad was killed in that accident."

Maggie remembered how as a child she and her mother would sit on the front porch during the summer and watch the sunset over the river cliffs. There had always been a soft breeze in the evening that brought with it the scent of the crops growing south of the house, apple blossoms in the orchard, and ripening strawberries on the bushes down by the creek. It reminded her mother of Tourmakeady, she had told Maggie, and growing up on the shores of Lough Mask.

"I think Mom changed after you left for college, Catty. I mean, it could have been you instead of Sal. I think that frightened her."

"No. If she changed, it was because not having me around meant the thorn was gone from her side, that's all." Catty raised her eyebrows. "Did she tell you why she hated me so?"

Maggie shook her head. "She just said you were wild. She kept warning me not to turn out like you, and here you are, a mother and homemaker." Maggie smiled wryly. "I'm the wild one, the black sheep."

"Come on, Maggie, Mom never thought that."

Maggie shrugged. "She would have if she'd known the truth."

"What do you mean," Catty asked, "that you've gotten involved with the wrong sort of man?"

Maggie nodded.

"This guy in Africa is married?" Catty asked.

"I'm afraid so."

"Well, that does complicate things."

"It's even worse than that," Maggie went on. "He's our ambassador."

"Oh." Catty set her elbows on the table.

"He wants to marry me."

"And?"

"God knows what I want!" Maggie laughed. "I'm afraid, especially after McGraff."

"I can't believe Jack showed up last night!" Catty stubbed out her second cigarette, then got up and emptied the ashtray in the trash, as if the butts were evidence.

"I didn't mind."

"He spent the whole evening working the room."

"That's just Jack. He's always on. Actually, he liked Mom. God knows why. They never agreed about anything. She always kept asking me, 'When's he going to do something for his own kind and stop helping the colored?' "

"His own kind?" Catty asked.

"The Irish. Everyone you saw here last night from Chicago's old Southside."

"Ignorant micks. Narrow-minded racists. I hope this black man, Washington, wins the mayoral election in Chicago. That will fix the Irish!"

"Catty, they're victims of their environment too. They've never gotten out of the Irish ghetto. We were lucky. Mom kept us away from all that."

Catty leaned across the table. "Well, why did she stay on here after Dad went back to Ireland? She had to work the farm herself, with just us to help out. We never had anything. The boys wore each other's clothes. Michael was the only one who ever had anything new. You wore all my things, remember? And I got used clothes from the Saint Vincent DePaul Society. Kids in school would tease me when I'd show up wearing their older sisters' dresses. Jesus!"

For a moment they sat in silence, both upset by the memories of their childhood. Then Maggie asked, "Where could she have gone?"

"Chicago."

"Not Mother. One of her driving passions was for us to do better than 'marry another mick.' I remember how she never wanted me to hang around with kids like the Mahons and O'Haras. Shanty Irish, she called them. That was one thing about Mom. She wanted us to do better than she had. She was very proud when I married Jack Mc-Graff. She thought he was the right sort of Irishman. I know it broke her heart when I left him."

"And I drove her wild when I ran off with Sal. We're both guilty, Mag."

"Well, if she had ever known your Joe, she would have loved him," Maggie said, reaching over to take her sister's hand.

"Perhaps. But I don't think so. Joe wouldn't have been good enough for her. She'd have found fault with him just because he wasn't better than us. Mom had a lot of self-hate inside her."

"Catty, come on!"

"Come on, yourself! I'm like her. I hate my background. Be honest —didn't that crowd at the wake embarrass you? They've all been here in America forty years and they still talk and act as if they just got off the boat. It's people like them that hold us back."

"Catty, I've never felt held back because I'm Irish."

"Nothing ever could stand in your way, Maggie."

"It's not just me, Catty. I've never felt any of the prejudice that you're talking about. Not in Washington."

"Well, I guess even my kids feel less restricted than I did. After all, I'm going to have a Jewish son-in-law."

"You are? Wendy?"

"She says she's in love with a boy at school. His name is Jeff Golden. He's very nice. I know the family. They own a jewelry store in Elk Grove."

"Wendy isn't old enough to get married."

"You tell her that, please!"

Maggie shook her head. "These kids! Why do they want to get married? Why doesn't she just sleep with him?"

"She's already done that."

"You're kidding!"

Catty smiled, amused by her sister's reaction. "Welcome home, Maggie. They've got the pill in the midwest, you know."

"Does Joe know?"

"About her sleeping with Jeff? No. He'd kill her. He'd kill me."

"What are you going to do?"

"Do? I'm a parent, Maggie. There's nothing I can do. She's seventeen. She thinks she knows everything. Just like I thought I knew everything. How can I blame my daughter? She didn't exactly lick it off the grass, as Mother would say."

"I'll talk to her," Maggie said firmly.

"Thank you. She might listen."

"Well, I'm not so sure. Have you ever known any of us to listen to anyone? It's a family trait."

"At times I wish we weren't so headstrong. It only gets us into trouble."

"DeLaceys have done very well, Catty. And we're not in trouble."

"Emmett DeLacey is."

"Emmett, well." Maggie sighed. "Emmett is just Emmett."

"You don't think Emmett is strange?"

"Oh, for God sakes, no!" Maggie set her cup down, spilling coffee as she did. "Emmett has single-handedly been taking care of Mom since he got home from Vietnam. It has been tough on him, I know. And I feel terrible about that, about not doing more for him, for both of them." She became teary suddenly.

"Maggie, this place was an absolute sty when I got here on Sunday. You wouldn't believe the squalor they were living in. There's no reason for living like that." Catty's voice rose as she thought again of how the kitchen had looked. "Wendy and I worked all day just to make it decent. You remember how neat and tidy Mother always was? It was terrible of Emmett to make her live like that."

"It's my fault," Maggie insisted. "I knew when I was home in September that she was getting too feeble to handle the place. Emmett doesn't care what the house is like. All he worries about are his cows! What I didn't realize was how bad off they were financially. That's what he kept from us. He didn't want us to know he couldn't make the farm pay."

"I would have given him money if I had known."

Maggie glanced at her sister. She wanted to say: But you had nothing to do with Mom for twenty-five years. Then she thought better of it. The past was past.

"It wasn't Emmett's fault," Maggie said again. "He did the best he could. Remember, he was here by himself, without hired help. When we were growing up, all the boys were home. No! It isn't his fault. Emmett has problems, sure, but he's worked hard. Every time I came home to visit he'd be out at the break of dawn, working all day. He never seemed to rest. It's just that when Mommy got really sick, well, he couldn't take care of her and the animals, and everything else." Maggie could hear her voice racing to justify her twin.

"Maggie . . . Maggie . . ." Catty whispered. "All right, honey." She spoke softly, as if she were trying to calm one of her own children.

"We know it was an accident. All of us are overreacting. This is a hard time for us as a family."

"It's bad enough that Mommy is dead, but I know how this town is. They'll be blaming Emmett next."

"Maggie, what does it matter? You don't have anything more to do with Gatesburg. And now we can sell the farm."

"We're not going to sell the farm."

"Why keep it? I don't care about the money, but—"

"We're not going to sell it because of Emmett, and because, well, I might come back here to live someday."

"Maggie, you're just being sentimental. You'll never live here, not in this place . . . what did Mother call it?"

"The back of beyond."

"That's right!" Catty smiled. "We're the back of beyond. No, you'll marry your ambassador and never think of Gatesburg again."

"But I'd want him to see it," she blurted.

"Just the way Jack did?" Catty answered, then wished she hadn't.

Jack. Maggie thought of Jack's first visit to the farm.

She had been in school, and he was still a congressional aide when she had brought him home for Thanksgiving. They had gone for a walk down by the river and doubled back to Henry Nob. She wanted to show him her secret spot, where she had always gone as a child, to sit in a grove of maple trees and look down at the farm.

They had talked then of getting married, and of having their own farm someday, with cows and sheep and horses, an apple orchard and garden, a side porch and swing, and, of course, children and a lifetime of happiness together.

Some of that had come true. They had married, the very next summer. Paddy Jack had given her away and Father Mike said the high Mass at Saint Patrick's in Gatesburg. The reception had been at the farm, with tables set up in the orchard so the guests were showered all that lovely afternoon in pink apple blossoms. Jack ran for Congress from upstate Illinois and won. Maggie flew to Illinois with him almost every weekend and drove down from Rockford to visit her mother on the farm. But she and Jack had never got around to a farm of their own, or any kind of a home, for that matter. And certainly not to children, or a lifetime of happiness.

"Anyway, I'm not marrying the ambassador, Catty," she said. "At least . . . I can't think about it now. I have to fly back to Addis Ababa for a few days and pick up files and notes. Certain Ethiopian rebels could be in danger if these files got into the hands of the Marxists. But for the moment, neither my personal life nor my job is important. What's important is getting this place in order. Getting Emmett in order. Straightening out his life."

"You can't straighten out Emmett's life, Mag. He's in very bad shape."

"I know he is." Maggie was angry at once and it showed on her face, in the hard jutting of her chin and in her brown eyes, deepening in color. "He's been on his own, with huge responsibilities, and no one to help. Not you, Catty—" she met her sister's eyes—"and not me. I'm his twin. He needs me."

"Okay, Maggie, okay. But it won't be easy. Emmett isn't just a bad housekeeper, you know. He's sick. When I got here, he was dead drunk. His clothes were filthy and he stank. Wendy was frightened to death of him."

"All right!" Maggie spoke up quickly, trying to stop her sister. "But what do you expect? He was a POW for almost two years. He's never gotten over that."

"Maggie, we're not just talking about Vietnam. Emmett has always been . . . different. He was even odd as a child. I can remember the two of you as children. You were twins, but you were like night and day."

"There's nothing wrong with Emmett!"

"You sound like Mother."

"Fine! I don't care who I sound like. I know my brother. I know him better than anyone. My God, you haven't even seen him in what . . . twelve years?"

"All I needed was ten minutes. When I came in here on Sunday, I saw immediately that he was out of touch with reality. I don't blame you, Maggie. You were in Washington, and then Africa. I'm not saying Paddy Jack should have spotted what was wrong when he was here last summer. Mother, I'm sure, was protecting Emmett, concealing his problems. But when she began to fail, Emmett crumbled.

"If there's anyone to blame, it's O'Connor. He was around; he should've spoken up. And isn't Michael always coming back to Gatesburg? Why didn't he realize something was wrong? It doesn't take a Freudian analyst to recognize that Emmett is seriously ill."

Catty had not raised her voice. She spoke slowly, carefully, as if she had already thought through the problem. The seriousness of her tone, the logic of the conclusions, frightened Maggie. She glanced at her sister. "Do you think he could have harmed Mommy?" She asked the question quickly, afraid of the answer.

"It's possible, yes. But I won't believe it until it's proven to me."

"What do the others think?"

Catty paused a moment, deciding how to answer, and then, tired of all the secrets her family had been keeping, she said, "Joe has talked to the police, and they said there are some discrepancies in Emmett's story. Something about the time of death. The coroner said Mother died around eight in the morning. Well, it was after five P.M. when Emmett finally telephoned the sheriff."

"Oh, God," Maggie whispered, feeling the weight of the revelation. Then she forced herself to reason, to remember that there was no hard evidence, no admission of guilt. Nor was he guilty, she reminded herself. Emmett didn't kill their mother even by accident. She would have known, sitting with him before the open casket.

"No!" she said, looking over at Catty. "There may be some mystery about what happened, but I know one thing: Emmett didn't harm her."

Catty nodded. "I think there's going to be more trouble, though, Maggie. Michael . . . I think Father Mike believes Emmett did it."

Maggie stared at her sister. Nervously, Catty went on. "I gather there isn't enough evidence to bring charges . . . or so Joe says . . . but Michael told him . . . he thinks Emmett did kill Mother."

Maggie stood up and walked over to the kitchen windows, looking out, with her arms crossed as if she were hugging herself against the cold weather.

"Remember what Emmett did to you, Maggie," Catty said, still sitting at the kitchen table.

"Oh, for godsakes, Cat! We were kids at the time; he never saw me." Involuntarily, she touched the old scar between her breasts. For a moment she closed her eyes, remembering. And then she heard a sound in the driveway and looked out the window again.

The hearse was moving slowly on the gravel drive, appearing ominous and out of place—a long black limousine in the clear, cold morning, driving slowly past the old farm equipment, the closed-up barns, and the naked apple trees. Soon it would be time for the final prayers, the closing of the casket, and the funeral procession into town.

"No," said Maggie, her eyes on the hearse. "Michael will not do this." After all her mother and Emmett had been through together, after all their years on the farm, she would not allow a wedge of doubt and guilt to obscure the fact that they had loved each other. They had all loved each other—she, Emmett, and Mommy—and she would defend her brother even if it meant she had to fight them all, all of her brothers and sisters.

# · CHAPTER 23 ·

BISHOP DELACEY PAUSED IN his sermon to survey the crowded church. Looking over the heads of his brothers and sisters, and the relatives, all gathered in the first rows of Saint Patrick's, he saw the rows and rows of Blue and White delegations from across the state. The church was packed with its members. But when he spoke, he addressed the TV cameras that had been set up in the choir loft to film the funeral service for his cable program.

"Our mother came from Ireland, from the shores of Lough Mask, from the small and beautiful village of Tourmakeady. She came to America—to this small and peaceful town of Gatesburg—and here for over forty years she raised her sons and daughters in hard times, when there was little money in the house and little food beyond what the farm provided. Yet in all those years she kept her faith, and she kept her children safe within the warm embrace of the Catholic Church.

"And because of her faith and her love for America, her chosen land, and Ireland, the land always of her dreams and fond memories, we today do not simply have the sorrowful task of saying our final farewells. We are also celebrating a great life.

"Not a great life in terms of public honors or recognition. No, but a great life in what mattered most to her: raising her family, making them take one step further in life. This was her achievement: the success her family made in America.

"I am a priest and a bishop today because of the sacrifices my mother made for me. I know I can speak for all my brothers and sisters when I say that what we achieved in our careers, we owe to Mom. She encouraged us, pushed us, fought for us, and saw that we had the opportunities that were never given her. Our fortune is her fortune. Our success is her success. This is the great Irish-American adventure: how a poor woman from rural Ireland can come to rural America and achieve for her children the life denied her at home.

"Yet she did have her own great adventures, her own achievements. In her youth when Ireland needed her the most, she fought beside the other great Irish heroes to rid the nation of its English oppressors. This was the past she never spoke of, not to us—her children—or to her friends and neighbors. In time, I hope everyone, all her family and friends, and those even who might have misjudged her, will understand, that like the great Maud Gonne, she stood with Ireland when Ireland needed her.

"It is only fitting then that we send her on her final journey with this song of Ireland and lost love."

The bishop bowed his head. And from the back of the church, high in the choir loft, a soft tenor voice began to sing:

> She is far from the land where her young hero sleeps,
> And lovers around her sighing;
> But coldly she turns from their gaze, and weeps,
> For her heart in his grave is lying.

> He had lived for his love, for his country he died,
> They were all that to life had entwined him;
> Nor soon shall the tears of his country be dried,
> Nor long will his love stay behind him.

Maggie turned her head and glanced down the row at Catty, to see how she was reacting. Her sister was staring into space, her eyes resolutely dry. Poor Catty, Maggie thought. It must be terrible for her to come home at last, but too late to make peace with their mother.

Nora was crying. Sitting beside Paddy Jack, with her fingers wrapped tightly around a string of black rosary beads, the tears ran freely. She looked like a nun out of habit, Maggie thought, a missionary sister back from Africa. She recalled how every spring a new Chevrolet from Wenzel Motors would be raffled off by the nuns, so pagan babies in Africa might be saved.

Maggie smiled sadly, remembering. Her mother would drive them out east of town in the truck so they could ask farmers, all Lutherans and southern Baptists, to buy the nuns' raffle tickets. They'd have buttermilk and cookies on the side porch of the big old Victorian farmhouses, sitting quietly, Emmett and herself together on a swing, while their mother and the farmer's wife talked poultry and egg prices. Then the farmer's wife would go inside to fetch her purse and come out to buy fifty cents' worth of chances on the Chevy.

Maggie began to cry, the warm tears falling on her clenched fingers like candle wax. Then she looked up, brushing away her tears. Father O'Connor had stepped forward with the altar boys to bless the casket. He was unsteady on his feet, and one of the boys held his arm as he filled the thurible with incense. They were all aging, she thought, all dying. She remembered Father O'Connor from her childhood, all the Sunday afternoons he had played ball with her and Emmett and their mother. Now the old man could barely move. His voice was hardly audible. He would be next, she thought. She would be back again to Gatesburg for another funeral soon.

Catty watched as Nora DeLacey unwound the rosary beads from her fingers and slipped them into a plastic case. A glossy picture of the Blessed Virgin was stamped on the cheap material of the case. Irish Catholics were known for their summer pilgrimages, and Catty wondered if Nora had been to Lourdes. How little she knew about her sister. Was she married? Did she have her own family, children at home in Tourmakeady?

Catty heard her children squirming in the seat behind her. Being in church was all new and strange to them. She had hoped the novelty would keep them quiet through the funeral, but now she felt Timmy's breath on her neck. He was standing on the kneeler and leaning against the back of her seat. In a moment, she knew, he would whisper for her attention. She waited for Joe to pull him back into his seat.

Catty had hated church as a child. It had seemed as if they were always at Mass. They went every day before school, as well as on Sundays when their mother took them to the earliest Mass. There were never more than a dozen other parishioners in attendance at the six o'clock, and the stone church was cold and dark in the winter months, hot on summer mornings. Father O'Connor never turned on heat or used fans until later in the day, when the Masses were crowded.

"Too bad for you," her mother had told her once, when she complained of the cold church. "Offer it up. You do little enough in the way of penance." Catty had turned her face away from her mother's rebuff and stared out the truck's window at the bleak winter landscape. Through all the years, she could still hear the tone of her mother's reply, colder than the day itself. She stared at the sealed casket as she remembered the long-ago incident.

"Mummy," Timmy whispered in her ear, "can I have a baby rabbit, please?"

"Shh." Catty turned to get Joe's help, but Nora, sitting to her right, had already handed Timmy her rosary case, which immediately silenced and fascinated him. Catty looked over at Nora and smiled, then bowed her head and tried to say a prayer, to make some gesture to her dead mother. But no prayer would come. Nothing returned to memory from her years of Catholic school. She had forgotten it all, as one does forget whatever one has been forced to accept without ever believing.

Father O'Connor circled the casket, blessing the remains, then stood at the altar rail and faced the congregation. His voice was thin, and in the big church he had to make an effort to be heard.

"Caitlin DeLacey's life speaks for itself. Her family, who, God love them, are all here, bear witness to what a wonderful, grace-filled life she lived. Bishop Michael DeLacey! You all know him as a friend and as a leader of a great cause, the Blue and White Battalion. Padraic John, our own celebrity. Many's a time, Paddy Jack, your mother would have me saying an extra prayer at the Sunday Masses so that you wouldn't get beaten by that Protestant, Jack Nicklaus."

The old priest smiled at the family. He looked almost shy, Catty thought, and she wondered if with age the man had lost his toughness. His hair was all white, his eyes had lost their sharp blueness.

"And Cathleen Ann! A wonderful family she has, and married to an Irishman, she is." The old priest kept smiling, looking over the congregation. "And then we have our little Maggie. God love you, child." The old priest had moved down the first pew and impulsively, kindly, he reached out and touched Maggie's wet cheek. She was crying openly, and did not try to stop her tears.

"Many's a time I can remember being out for Sunday dinner at the DeLaceys', when Maggie and Emmett were no taller than the wild yellow daisies in the field. I'd be sitting on the side porch with their mother having a glass of ice tea and we'd spot the pair, brown as berries, coming home with the cows. And then the twins, those little tykes, would hook up the milkers and do the milking themselves, separate the cream, and feed the animals for the night." His expression changed as he switched into his Sunday sermon voice.

"There was no sitting around watching television, wasting their time. Not with those two! Nor with any of the DeLaceys. Caitlin DeLacey knew how to raise children. And I'm sorry to say, we don't have enough mothers like her today, who know their children need the habit of hard work, not the habit of smoking and drinking, which, dear God, we've come to see leads directly to drugs and heroin addiction." He paused for a moment and blinked, as if he'd forgotten what was happening. Then he looked around.

"Emmett! Where are you, lad?" In a moment he saw him, sitting with the other pallbearers at the end of the second pew. "Emmett, dear boy, you were with your mother to the very end. God bless you, son. What more can a mother ask than that her children be with her in her last days? And Emmett was—living at home, working the farm, taking as fine care of her as she took of them during the years."

The priest made a sweeping gesture with his hand. "Michael, Paddy, Cathleen, Maggie, Emmett—your mother always loved your faithfulness. For years she attended that early Sunday Mass, because she said she had to be home in the afternoon to answer your long-distance calls."

The old priest paused again and looked down the family pew. Then he said softly, his voice for the moment lost in the crowded church, "Nora Agnes, God love you, child; you who have been denied all these years the love of your own mother."

He stopped abruptly then, and when he spoke again, his voice was louder. "There's a wonderful line of the late John F. Kennedy's that some of you may remember: 'To some generations much is given, of other generations much is asked.' 'Tis the same, you know, in families. And of Nora Agnes DeLacey, much has been asked. As an infant Nora was left behind in Ireland when Caitlin and Cormac sailed to America. It was during the war, and they had barely enough money to get themselves to Illinois. Of course, Nora was fine. She was with Caitlin's sister in Tourmakeady, and you know how great Irish families are when it comes to taking care of their own.

"It was 1954 before Caitlin and Cormac saved enough money so Cormac could go back to Tourmakeady and claim their firstborn, Nora Agnes. I took Cormac myself up to Chicago, to Midway Airport, and put him on a TWA flight for Shannon. It was the last I ever saw of Cormac DeLacey."

Saint Patrick's was hushed, Catty realized. This was all news to the locals, secrets the DeLacey family had kept from the town.

"Cormac DeLacey couldn't bring himself to return to America. From the beginning he was never himself here. He couldn't get the feel of this country, he once told me. He missed the Partry Mountains and the shores of Lough Mask. He missed the mist of the mornings, the peaceful life of County Mayo. His heart had never left Tourmakeady.

"And in Tourmakeady, he had Nora. She was just a child when he went back, and once he arrived he realized that he couldn't take a girl that age away from all that was familiar to her. He'd only be away a year, he wrote back to Caitlin, but you know what a thief time is, and how the years slip away. And then, Cormac suffered a heart attack, you see, and the doctors in Galway City wouldn't let him fly. Not then, and not now. If he could, he'd be here with us today to bury his dear wife whom he loved all these years, though time and duty kept them apart."

It was all Catty could do to keep from laughing. That was the story Father O'Connor had told the family after the wake; now he was telling everyone in Gatesburg. First, her father had died in a car crash, next he had a heart attack. She didn't believe a word of it. But O'Connor would keep going, she knew. It was his way of getting a story out, of dispelling all the rumors that would start about Caitlin DeLacey and her family.

"And now these brothers and sisters—divided by war, and then by lack of money—are finally a family. A few months ago Caitlin asked me not to forget Nora when her time came. She wanted me to get word to Tourmakeady. But it was Bishop Mike who provided the money for his sister to fly to America. And so God has granted Caitlin DeLacey her final wish—that all her children be together at the end of her life." The old priest smiled out over the church, but there were tears in his gray eyes.

Catty glanced at her older brother, sitting up on the altar, towering above them. Michael's head was bowed, as if in prayer, but Catty knew better. It was so he didn't have to meet their eyes while O'Connor lied for him. That bastard, she thought, of course he knew! He knew all those years when they were young. He knew about Nora; he knew their father was alive in Ireland. And their mother and O'Connor had told everyone that Cormac DeLacey had been killed in Ireland so no one would know he had abandoned his wife and children.

"Now we send our dear Caitlin Rush DeLacey to her final reward," Father O'Connor was concluding. "Born into time on August ninth, 1921, she is now born into eternity."

The old priest bowed slightly, signaling the pallbearers to come forward.

Snow was falling when they stepped outside and Catty turned to Maggie immediately. "It's too cold to take the kids to the cemetery," she said. "They're not dressed warmly enough to stand outside in this. I'm sure they're already setting up the lunch Paddy Jack ordered at the country club—Joe and I will just take them there and meet you."

"Oh, come on, Cat," Maggie said, slipping her arm into her sister's. "Joe can take the kids. You come to the cemetery with me." As she spoke, she reached over and linked her free arm into Nora's, saying, "And you, too, Nora, come along with us." Maggie felt ashamed that she and Catty had not put themselves out more for their new sister. She had been touched by what Father O'Connor had said, and realized for the first time how terrible Nora's childhood must have been, growing up without a father and mother.

"No, Mag," Catty insisted, slipping free. "I'll go with Joe and see that everything is in order at the club. My presence isn't required at the grave." She spoke firmly, determined not to go farther with their mother.

Maggie studied her sister, wondering how much further she could push her, knowing that Catty was in pain. Catty hadn't had a chance to make her peace with their mother and letting go would be almost impossible.

"Okay, Cat, I understand," Maggie whispered, embracing her sister. "Go with Joe and the kids. Tell Vanessa we'll be at the club by noon." She kissed Catty on her damp cheek and wondered if her sister had finally cried, or was it just the wet snow, blowing against them on the church steps.

"Come along, Nora," Maggie said next, helping her down the stone steps. "We'll ride in the first car."

"Maggie!" Catty called, just before they reached the limousine. "I counted the cars. Fifty-six," she said, smiling.

"That would have pleased her," Maggie answered. Turning to Nora, she said, "When you get home, tell Dad that fifty-six cars were at Mommy's funeral. It means that she had a big funeral."

"Oh, 'tis the same in Ireland," Nora answered, stepping into the limousine. "Though I must say, in Ireland a successful funeral is also counted by how many days the party lasts."

As soon as she reached the country club, Catty went to the empty bar and ordered a Bloody Mary. The clubhouse was deserted on the snowy winter day, but she could see that the small dining room was ready for their family brunch.

Turning to look for Joe, Catty noticed Vanessa Harris standing in the doorway of the bar. She was wearing the same black Nipon dress that she had worn to the wake the night before. It was a dress Catty had seen at Marshall Field's in November and decided she didn't have the waist to wear. But she didn't envy Vanessa. The woman looked too thin, almost gaunt, and for a moment Catty thought with sympathy of Vanessa's problems: her divorce, her father's illness, financial troubles at the club. It was Catty's rule, however, never to worry about the rich. As her mother had often observed, the rich always had money enough hidden away to carry them through hard times.

"Hello, Vanessa!" Catty crossed the carpeted bar to greet her. "Thank you so much for arranging this at the eleventh hour. Maggie and I are very grateful."

"Cathleen, it's the least I could do for Paddy Jack and your family." She smiled sadly at Catty, and then said softly, "It seems like yesterday that we were all kids. Now your mother is gone, and Dad is so terribly ill." She shook her head. "When we were kids, we thought we'd be able to control our lives as adults. But they just sort of get away from us without our noticing. A decision here. Another there. And, well . . ." She shrugged, then laughing, added, "Suddenly we're forty!"

"Come on," Catty suggested, "let me buy you a drink before we get any older."

"Thanks, I'd love to," Vanessa answered. "But first let me run into the kitchen and check on things. Your family will be here soon, and I want to make sure the cook hasn't chosen this moment to get temperamental. I'll be right back."

She touched Catty on the arm and was heading for the bar entrance to the kitchen when she suddenly remembered something. "Oh, the police called. Detective Larry O'Hara; he's a club member. He was trying to locate the family. He didn't realize your mother was being buried this morning. I told him he could phone here later."

Catty nodded, frightened by what that might mean, and then she heard Joe scolding and Timmy wailing. Next it would be Clare; she sighed and went to see what the matter was, feeling sorry that her husband and children all had to go through this long ordeal because of her.

"I shouldn't have come," Nora said, as the cars left the cemetery after the burial. " 'Tisn't right. I feel like a stranger among all of you."

"Of course you should have come. She was your mother, too."

"No. I can't say that. She left me."

"What's Dad like?" Maggie said at last, trying to divert the conversation.

"Oh, a good man, I guess. I never think of what he's like. He's just Dad, that's all."

"I'll see if it's possible when I fly back to Africa, to stop in Ireland and see him. Do you think that would be all right, Nora?" She asked politely, not wanting to sound presumptuous.

"He's an old man, Margaret. Most days he's not, you know, really with us."

"He's my father, Nora. I can't just let him die in Ireland, not when I know he's alive. I never had a father."

"And I never had her, so we're even, it seems."

"No, not even. Not until I know why he really left."

"But didn't Father O'Connor just tell us?" Nora was a stout woman, and when she turned to look at Maggie, she rocked back in the seat.

Maggie paused to stare through the front window at the heavy, blowing snow. They had left the cemetery and were heading for the country club. If the snow kept up, she'd be snowbound on the farm by nightfall, something that hadn't happened to her since she was a child. Finally, she answered her new sister.

"I don't believe Father O'Connor," Maggie said, suddenly realizing that it was true: she didn't trust him. He was like Father Mike, always trying to control how she saw the world, hiding family secrets from her, from all the family. And reminded of what Michael had said, she asked Nora, "What about all of Mother's IRA involvement! Did you know about it?"

But before Nora could reply the car pulled into the country-club parking lot and Maggie saw there were police cars by the front entrance.

"What is this?" Maggie said out loud, and her heart did a sudden flip. Something was wrong. There had been another tragedy.

As the limousine stopped, Maggie rushed out. Catty, who was standing, waiting, in the open breezeway between the locker rooms and the main clubhouse, ran down the gravel walk toward Maggie when she saw her.

"What happened?" Maggie asked. "Are the children all right?" She could not keep herself from thinking the worst.

"The police," Catty said. "They've come to arrest Emmett." She took hold of her younger sister by both shoulders, as if to embrace her.

"What for?" Maggie asked, suddenly defensive, pulling free.

"A detective is here. They have witnesses."

"Witnesses? What are you talking about, Cat?" She spun around, looked for Emmett, who was stepping out of Paddy Jack's car.

"The detective says they have statements from some people who know Emmett. He told them, Maggie, that he was going to kill Mommy."

# · CHAPTER 24 ·

## ADDIS ABABA

MAGGIE WOKE IN A sweat, the heavy quilt of her bed twisted about her body. She had dreamed of the Serengeti lions. Dreamed of the female she had seen while on safari in November. The lion had broken her jaw attacking a wildebeest and retreated to the shade of thorn trees, where, the guide told Maggie, she would die alone, unable to eat and abandoned by her cubs.

The nightmare must have been produced by the valium she took when she had reached her home in Addis Ababa, Maggie decided, and for several moments she was disoriented. In one week she had traveled from Africa to Gatesburg and now back to Africa again. She did not feel as if she were wholly there, in her bedroom, but as if her body itself was stretched from Illinois to Africa.

She had arrived in Addis that morning, hoping that Kenneth had received her cable and would be waiting. But only Tedesse was there, bearing the message that the ambassador had flown to Lalibela for the day. Kenneth had gone to investigate new reports of famine in northern Ethiopia and would not be able to see her until the evening when he returned to the capital.

Maggie rolled over and in the darkness of the shuttered room felt around for her watch. It was four P.M. She would have to get up soon, she told herself.

Lying back, she stared up at the bedroom ceiling. It had begun to rain and the corrugated roof of the house amplified the downpour, so she felt as if she were inside a tin drum. She could hear nothing else, not the heavy traffic on Mulugeta Buli Street, not even her heartbeat. The rains would make Kenneth late, she thought. In fact, if the airport at Lalibela was fogged in, he wouldn't even be able to get back to Addis. Damn it, why did he have to be absent when she needed him?

She was being unreasonable, Maggie realized. Although he knew of her mother's death, Kenneth knew nothing of Nora or the case against Emmett. She hadn't written or telephoned. And he would only be upset when he learned she had just flown back to Ethiopia to clear out her office and pack up her things. But Emmett needed her. If she could have trusted someone else in the Addis office to sneak her notes and articles on the neighborhood kebeles from the safe and get them to her, she wouldn't have come back at all. But she knew that if her research notes got into the hands of the communist government, it would mean certain death to the Ethiopians who had risked their lives to talk to her.

She had to admit she had come back to see Kenneth, too, to see if she really was in love with the man, enough to go through the pains of his divorce to marry him.

The rain slackened, then stopped as unexpectedly as it had begun, and in the sudden quiet Maggie heard the back door open and close. She listened for his familiar footsteps, but she heard nothing. The silence made her instantly afraid. She reached up to turn on the bedside light, but before she could snap it on, a pistol shot hit the lamp.

Maggie jerked away as the lamp shattered beside her. Then the fluorescent overhead light blinked on to reveal Virginia Graves standing in the doorway.

"I could have killed you," Kenneth's wife said calmly, lowering a silver pistol. She stepped into the room, then paused a moment to survey the bedroom, as if to calculate the occupant's taste, before moving closer. "Do you mind?" she asked politely, and sat down on the end of the bed. The pistol swung loosely in her fingers. "I'm not crazy, Margaret," she said, smiling tightly. "I don't want to go to jail for murder. There's no diplomatic immunity for ambassadors' wives, though God knows, there certainly should be."

Maggie had curled up in the far corner of the wide bed and pulled the heavy quilts to her neck.

"You must leave my husband alone, you know. Kenneth is incapable of breaking it off. He hasn't the willpower. He's never been able to leave young women alone, not in any of our posts. Not in Kenya, or Saigon, or Dakar." Virginia began to cry quietly, without attempting to conceal her tears.

"I . . . I have no idea what you're talking about," Maggie whispered.

"Of course you do! Don't embarrass yourself. Did you expect this little affair to go unnoticed? Addis is full of gossips. Your good friend Ann Merrill just for one. And Kenneth has never been able to hide anything from me. I've always known when he has taken a new lover." She looked away from Maggie, stared off, and began to speak slowly.

"I should have left him years ago, but I had no real money of my own, and living overseas, with servants, made life easier. Especially with children. I didn't mind his affairs at first, when we were both

younger. To be honest, I had my own lovers then." There were tears
in her eyes, and bowing her head, she began to sob. "But now . . . it's
embarrassing. Humiliating. It is bad enough here in Addis with Kenneth sneaking over to your bed after dark, but to flaunt it, going down
to Lake Langano together, sleeping openly . . ." She raised her voice.
The tears were gone.

Maggie slowly moved one leg toward the edge of the bed. The
ambassador's wife leveled the small pistol at her and Maggie stopped
moving. "Wasn't the senator enough for you, Margaret DeLacey?"
she asked. "Do you have to ruin my life as well?"

"I am not trying to ruin anyone's life, Mrs. Graves." Hearing her
own voice gave Maggie confidence. "I've already decided to stop
seeing Kenneth."

"Of course you have, my dear." Virginia Graves gave the handgun
a quick shake. "That's what you all say when I coax you."

"I'm sorry I've caused you any pain," Maggie said quietly. She
could see the older woman's eyes now, and realized the ambassador's
wife had been drinking.

"In Kenya he actually slept with an African. Not a local, mind you,
but a third country national. A secretary from Madagascar. She was
quite beautiful, really." The older woman paused a moment to stare
at Maggie, then asked, "You're Irish, aren't you?"

Maggie nodded.

"I've always hated the Irish. Such grubby little people."

In one move, Maggie threw her blanket back and dove across the
bed, flinging her arms around Virginia Graves, covering her with the
quilt. The silver pistol dropped to the rug and Maggie went after it,
letting go of the woman.

Virginia tried to reach the gun first but couldn't move fast enough.
As Maggie scooped it up, the older woman slipped to her knees,
sobbing and clutching the wooden bedpost. Maggie stepped back,
the gun in her hand. She was gasping for breath, suddenly frightened
by what she had done and by the realization that she might have been
killed.

"Go ahead, shoot me!" the ambassador's wife demanded.

"I'm not going to hurt you, Mrs. Graves," Maggie said. "But I am
going to call your husband."

Virginia Graves lurched at her, throwing Maggie against the soft
straw-and-dung wall. Now that she had the pistol, Maggie was no
longer afraid. She thought only how desperate Virginia Graves was,
how sad her life must be, and felt guilty that she had caused some of
her pain. Suddenly the woman picked up the poker from beside the
fireplace and started toward her. Maggie sighted the pistol and said
quickly, "Stay there, Mrs. Graves, or I'll use this pistol of yours."

"There's no need for violence, Margaret," Kenneth Graves said from the doorway. "Put away the gun!"

Maggie turned on him. "I'm trying to keep your wife from bludgeoning me."

"Fine. I'm here." The ambassador strode into the bedroom, as if this were just another diplomatic crisis he had been summoned to solve, took the poker, and said quietly to his wife, "Virginia, we'll go home now." Then gently, he gathered the helpless woman into his arms. He glanced over at Maggie and said, "I'm sorry this happened, Margaret. I'll explain later."

"There's nothing to explain. Please just get out of my house, both of you." She felt cheap and sordid.

Kenneth studied Maggie for a moment, as if he knew he should do more for her, but his wife was clinging to him, choking on her tears, and he said lamely, "We'll talk." Then he began to lead his wife out the bedroom door.

"Here! Take this." Maggie tossed the silver pistol onto the bed. "Your wife may need it again."

There was a delay at Bole Airport. A Lebanese merchant from one of the shops off the piazza was caught trying to smuggle gold out of the country, so the flight to Rome was being held up while everyone else's luggage was opened and searched. Peering through the long lines in the departure area, the ambassador found Maggie sitting on her suitcases, waiting her turn.

"I went by your house this morning," Kenneth said, "and Kelemwork said you had left. I don't understand. You've just returned." He was standing above her, trying to appear nonchalant as he struggled to make himself heard over the noisy crowd around them.

"I am leaving." Maggie stood and stepped behind her suitcases, using the pieces of luggage to separate her from Kenneth. She did not look up him as she said, "There's a problem at home. Mother was killed by one of Emmett's shotguns. It was an accident, of course, but some young detective in Gatesburg wants to prove Emmett killed her. I'm returning home until the whole matter is settled. The *Post* is sending Jim Thompson out to take my place."

"Oh, Maggie, why didn't you tell me?"

Maggie glanced quickly at Kenneth and answered, "You have troubles of your own."

"I can explain all of that," he said.

"I don't want to hear anything about any of it." The long line through Customs began to creep forward and she pushed her luggage ahead with her toe.

The ambassador bent to pick up the heavy pieces, saying, "Here, let's get out of this cattle call. I'll find the station manager and have him cut through this goddamn red tape."

"Please, Kenneth, leave me alone," Maggie snapped, then glanced around to make sure that no one who mattered heard her chastising the American ambassador. But they were surrounded only by Ethiopians, all oblivious to them.

"You're not being reasonable, Margaret," he answered coolly.

"Your wife threatened to shoot me. Under the circumstances, I think avoiding you is the least I can do." She thought of what Virginia Graves had said: a woman in every overseas post. It had seared Maggie's heart, made her incapable of even simple courtesy.

As an Ethiopian army official, flanked by officers, pushed through the crowd of passengers, Maggie felt a brief flash of panic. She was carrying the articles and notes in her purse, all concealed as personal correspondence, and she wondered how thoroughly Customs would search passengers on the Rome flight.

When he saw the American ambassador, the general stopped. They greeted each other and exchanged a few words of Amharic before switching to French. The general carried a riding crop in one hand and he was nervously clapping it against his thigh. Maggie looked away, trying not to appear concerned. General Yohannes Kifle was head of the CID, Ethiopian intelligence, and it was always best to remain anonymous with intelligence people. He might recognize her as the *Washington Post* reporter, but more likely he would think she was simply an American tourist, a friend of the ambassador visiting the Horn of Africa.

"Gold smuggling," Kenneth said under his breath as the general and his guards moved on.

"Yes, I know, a Lebanese."

"You're all right, aren't you?" he whispered. "If you like I can use the diplomatic pouch."

Maggie shook her head. She was through relying on his help, the power of his position.

"Don't be foolish, Margaret," he insisted, as if he had guessed she was taking a risk. "You don't have diplomatic immunity. They might be waiting for a chance to rifle your bags."

"I'm not smuggling anything, Kenneth. I'm not even taking souvenirs. Kelemwork will pack up my things and Jim Thompson can ship them home when he arrives in country."

"I'm not talking about Coptic crosses, Margaret. Where are your notes?"

Maggie did not answer.

"You know they're more valuable to the Ethiopian secret police than a hundred kilos of gold."

Still she did not reply or look up.

"All right, have it your way." He sighed. "But come with me into the VIP lounge. I'll have the station manager clear your bags through Customs. They'll be less likely to search you then."

She began to shake her head, but he had her by one arm and was reaching to collect her bags, as if she were his ill-behaved daughter.

"All right," she gave up. "But I'd still better go through Immigration. You take my bags and I'll meet you in the lounge once I have my boarding pass." She took her passport and health card and went ahead, leaving Kenneth to carry her three pieces of luggage and her straw basket from Harrar, in which she had slipped all her notes and interviews of dissident Ethiopians, as if they were nothing more than letters from home.

"I'll stay with you until the plane boards," Kenneth said, when Maggie joined him again inside the VIP lounge.

"There's no need." She would not look up at him.

"Margaret. Are you really going to leave Addis Ababa, and me, without a word of explanation?"

"You have had plenty of explanation," she answered, moving away to sit down. She realized too late that she was sitting on the same sofa where a week ago she had told Kenneth Graves that she loved him. "If you need more, well, ask your wife."

She was being unnecessarily cruel, but she couldn't stop herself. She wanted to get back at him for making her feel like a fool in front of his wife. Even Jack McGraff, for all of his faults, would never have compromised her heart in such a way.

"My wife is a drunk, Margaret." He had followed her to the sofa but sat down in a chair across from her. "She has been a drunk and valium addict for years," the ambassador went on, speaking softly, "and she is not responsible for what she says. She shouldn't be here in Africa. It's too difficult for her. The woman needs rest. I am sorry that she embarrassed you."

"Shot at me, you mean. I can't blame her. I'm the one who's violated her life. I'm the sinner."

"Oh, for God's sake, would you please stop with your Catholic morality. Sin is not an issue in our situation. I wasn't cheating Virginia by becoming involved with you. I told you, Virginia and I haven't had a sexual relationship in half a dozen years."

"She's still your wife. And I'm still the other woman."

"I'm leaving Virginia and I want to marry you, Margaret. Doesn't that mean anything?" He was leaning forward, drumming the coffee table with his thin fingers.

Maggie looked away, not responding. She wanted only to be alone, in flight from Africa and the mess she had made of her life. Only days before she had been anticipating her return to Addis and Kenneth, looking forward to his being the one sure part of her world. It was lousy, she thought, finding out you couldn't count on anyone.

"Margaret, are you listening?"

"I can't marry you, Kenneth," she said coolly, without a hint of the regret she felt.

"A week ago you said you loved me. Here in this room." He tapped the tabletop.

"Loving you has nothing to do with whether or not I want to marry you."

"What in God's name did that woman say to you?"

"Ask your wife," Maggie answered, standing. She spotted the station manager returning to the VIP lounge with her passport and, beyond him, saw that the Rome flight was boarding. She was off again, she thought, a woman without a home. But she did have a home, she reminded herself, and her responsibilities waited there, like an albatross. She began walking toward the Ethiopian.

"My wife is a pathological liar," the ambassador said, following.

It was unseemly, Maggie felt, being pursued by Kenneth from one end of the Bole Airport to the other. She stopped at the exit and, accepting her passport and boarding pass from the manager, thanked him in Amharic. As she prepared to gather her bags and pass through the gate, the head of the CID came out of the Customs Office and walked quickly up to her.

"Madame," General Kifle asked in French, "I am terribly sorry, but it is a necessity that I inspect your carry-on luggage. A formality, you understand." He bowed slightly, smiling.

Maggie glanced at Kenneth, trying not to let the general see the panic in her eyes. She should have given the notebooks and articles to Kenneth in the first place and let him pouch them out for her. But now it was too late. Because of her foolish show of her independence, the secret police would discover the evidence, the names and plans for a revolution, as they had found the soft Ethiopian gold strapped to the skin of the Lebanese merchant. It would have been far better never to have returned to Addis Ababa, to have chanced letting Jim Thompson handle the pieces as routine mail. But then, she would have never learned of Kenneth Graves's promiscuous past.

"Of course, General." The ambassador stepped forward and took the bag off her shoulder. It was stuffed with books, her makeup kit, and several small gifts for Catty's children, and all the notes and names of her contacts, the dissident Ethiopians and their secret organization. Kenneth quickly presented the bag to the Ethiopian official, as if Maggie had nothing at all to hide.

The general fingered through her things, pulled out her stack of correspondence, and began to open and examine each letter. Maggie turned away, unable to look. It was suddenly clear to her that the CID had been on to her, that they did know she was meeting rebels in the capital. He kept looking, searching deep into the bag, while another army officer looked into her handbag. Then, finding nothing, he stepped away from her and said curtly in English, "Have a good trip. *Woizerit.*" This time he did not give the customary Ethiopian bow.

"*Ameseghinallehu,*" Maggie replied in Amharic and, feeling the slight pressure of the ambassador's hand on her elbow, let herself be led toward the waiting jet.

When they were out of hearing, he said softly to her, "I took the liberty, Margaret. I have your notes and will get them out of the country in the state department weekly mail pouch."

"Thank you," she whispered.

"You have to always be certain of what you're doing when you're dealing with such people. They respect authority. Never show vulnerability. If you do, they'll pounce."

It was his personal code, she knew, the way he conducted his life. She wondered if they'd taught him that at Groton, his prep school, or was it at Yale that he learned to mask his feelings. Well, it wasn't the way she wanted to live her life, keeping her true feelings hidden, as if they were some sort of depravity.

As they approached the boarding ramp, Kenneth asked, "Where are you staying in Rome?"

"I don't know. I'll only be there overnight."

"Try the San Montesi. It's a very quiet hotel and you'll get some rest."

"Thank you," she said, not looking up.

"Will you come back?"

Maggie shook her head.

"And what about us?" he asked gently.

"There isn't any us!" she said, summoning up her courage. Then, moving slowly under the weight of her luggage and handbag, she turned and started up the steep boarding steps.

"I won't let you get away from me, Margaret," he said after her. "I'll be in Washington within the month. We need to get aid to these famine victims in the north of Ethiopia. I'll telephone you when I reach the States."

She turned on the ramp and stared down at him. "Don't call, Kenneth. If you have any decency left, don't ever trouble me again." And then she rushed into the open hatch, leaving Africa for good, and leaving Kenneth Graves for the last time.

# · CHAPTER 25 ·

## ROME

TORRENTS OF RAIN MADE getting out of Fiumicino Airport difficult. The traffic was logjammed on the tiny Roman side streets. Maggie sat near the back of the bus, numb and exhausted from the long flight out of Africa. The plane had stopped in Asmara, then in the Sudan, and again in Egypt. She had been unable to sleep, even after taking a valium. Now she was furious at the continual delays, the stop-and-go traffic.

The bus lunged forward and, defying a chorus of horns, burst into an open lane. Maggie looked up and saw they were passing the Colosseum, empty now on the rainy afternoon.

She closed her eyes and listened to the slick sound of the tires on the wet street, feeling cold, hungry, and unhappy. God, why was everything going wrong. Mommy . . . Kenneth . . . Emmett being arrested . . .

When she opened her eyes again, she saw they had come into another large open piazza. The bus whipped around it in a wide circle. People were standing in the aisle, pulling down luggage. They had reached the railway station and bus terminal. She would be at the hotel soon, where she would be able to warm up and get some sleep. She could almost feel the comfort of the bed, like an embrace.

"We have had a cable from your embassy in Addis Ababa reserving a room," the hotel manager told Maggie when she presented her passport. "I have selected one on the courtyard. It will be quiet. You'll be able to rest." He spoke English with a soft and charming accent.

"Thank you," Maggie said, surprised. Kenneth had cabled ahead, she realized, to make sure she got a comfortable room. She felt guilty, but also relieved. It was so much easier to travel, she thought, with someone taking care of you, even at a distance.

"Your luggage, signorina?"

"I have only this overnight bag. Everything else I left at the airport."

"No worry." The small man kept smiling. He snapped his fingers for the bellboy, then walked with her to the elevator. "Room five-eleven. If you wish anything, signorina. Please."

"*Grazie*, signor."

They paused in front of the old-fashioned elevator with its iron grille. Maggie took notice of the black marble columns and pink marble floors of the lobby, the rich wood paneling of the walls. Kenneth had chosen well, as always.

"Oh, I am sorry, signorina. I have forgotten. A message from your embassy here in Rome." He handed her a sealed envelope. "It came a few hours ago."

"Thank you, signor." He bowed, clicked his heels, and departed over the marble floor.

She tried to guess who might be contacting her. Kenneth again, from Addis? Or was it more bad news from home? She cut into the embossed stationery with her fingernail and pulled out a thick note card.

She recognized the blunt printlike writing at once:

> I'm here. In Rome.
> Dinner at nine?
> I'll pick you up.
> Love, Jack

Jack in Rome? How was that possible? She felt disoriented—she had traveled through too many time zones.

The bellboy ahead of her in the hallway opened a door and stepped aside. Dismissing him with a tip, Maggie went into the room and locked the door. The room was small and cozy and furnished with antiques. She liked it immensely and her spirits lifted immediately. Lovely hotel rooms always made her feel special.

As soon as she could, she began to undress. She felt as if she had been in her clothes forever. Just that morning she had been in Addis Ababa with Kenneth . . . but now, all that seemed in another world.

Naked, Maggie slipped into the soft bed and closed her eyes. She needed to get some sleep before she decided whether it would be smart or stupid to meet her ex-husband for dinner.

The ringing telephone brought Maggie back from the safety of sleep. She struggled toward consciousness, knocking over an aspirin bottle as she reached for the receiver. "Yes?"

"Mag? It's me. I'm downstairs." Jack sounded sheepish, realizing he'd woken her. "May I come up?"

"No!" She flopped back into the soft pillows. "What are you doing in Rome?"

"I'm in Rome for a conference on terrorism. And I happened to be at the embassy when a cable came from Ethiopia. I heard one of the secretaries mention your name when she made the hotel reservation. Why are you headed back to the States?"

"They've arrested Emmett."

"When?"

"On the day of the funeral. The sheriff said they had evidence . . . you know, there was no suicide note, or anything. They said Emmett killed Mother."

"Jesus Christ, Mag! You poor thing . . . I had no idea."

Maggie listened to the disbelief in his voice. It made her feel better to realize he was upset. This was one tragedy in Emmett's life for which Jack McGraff couldn't be blamed.

"There's no chance he—"

"It was an accident, Jack!"

"I know, but still, sometimes these things are hard to prove."

"We'll get the proof."

"Okay. If you need help, I'm here."

"Thank you." She sighed.

"You'll have to fill me in."

"I don't know very much."

"Will you have dinner with me?"

She nodded in the dark room, realizing with some astonishment that she was giving in to Jack McGraff. He had always had his way with her—except, of course, when it came to her brothers and sisters.

Jack was not in the lobby when Maggie stepped out of the elevator. How like him, she thought, immediately angry. He had gone off somewhere to make a phone call, she was sure, or had met some constituent from home.

She walked across the lobby, checking her reflection in the mirrors. Rested and with her hair combed, she looked better than she had expected. She was wearing her one good dress, one she had bought before leaving Washington. Jack had never seen her in it, not that he was ever aware of what she wore, even when they were married.

There was a small bar off the lobby, and she paused a moment at the entrance, searching the dark room. He wasn't there. She would find a comfortable chair, she decided, and give him a few minutes. She was accustomed to waiting for Jack. She recalled, resentfully, all the hours she had spent waiting for him to finish a meeting, waiting for him to have time for her, and their life together.

She spotted him then, in one of the telephone booths built into the paneled wall at the rear of the lobby. Who in the world could he be calling at that hour in Rome?

"Signorina?" A young man in a white coat stepped over to her, holding his serving tray flat against his chest.

"Oh, yes . . ." Maggie paused a moment to think of what she wanted to drink, trying to guess how much longer Jack might be. Then, carefully, she made the request in Italian. *"Vorrei una tazza di caffe. Per piacere."*

The young waiter grinned at her and, bowing, turned back to the bar.

"Mag, I'm sorry. I got hung up on this call . . ." Jack reached her sounding breathless, as if he had jogged across Rome.

*"Un attimo!"* she said to the waiter, and then to Jack, "Do you want anything to drink? I just ordered coffee."

She looked up at him and realized that they were each searching the other's face. To break away she turned to the waiter and said quickly, in her phrase-book Italian, *"Devo partire immediatamente."* The young man bowed, flashed another smile.

Jack reached for her arm, helping her up. "God, you smell wonderful! Arpège, as always . . . I had forgotten."

"Thank you, but doesn't Helen use Arpège as well?"

"Mag, hey . . ." He sounded hurt.

"I'm sorry. That was unfair."

She moved away, too aware of his body. She knew she would begin to criticize him just to short-circuit her own feelings.

"Which restaurant are we going to?" She spoke quickly to conceal her nervousness.

"Well, I asked at the desk for someplace close. A quiet place, you know, and out of the way. They suggested something called a *trattoria.*" He searched his pockets, then produced a sheet of yellow legal-size paper. "Here! It's called Senese's and they say it has great food. The owner's wife does the cooking."

"Good! Let's go. I'm starving."

"Wait—I have a briefcase."

"Pick it up later, Jack." She grabbed his arm, frowning. "If you bring it along, you'll only be pulling out files, showing me your work. I just want to talk to you, okay?"

He didn't argue, just followed her out into the cold. It had stopped raining but the night was raw, and even though she had put the lining in her raincoat, Maggie was shivering.

"We can grab a cab," he offered.

Maggie shook her head. To make amends for being rude, she took his arm and leaned into him, using his body to shield her from the wind. He was shorter than Kenneth, she realized, and did not have

Kenneth's long, loping stride. She found herself shortening her pace to keep in step.

"Mag, I'm really sorry about Emmett." He squeezed her arm.

"Thanks, Jack," and for a moment she felt close again to him. "I know everything will clear itself up, once I'm home."

"Can I do anything?"

"We'll talk about it later, after I've had something to drink." She did not want to talk about Emmett. Instead she asked, "Now who do you know in Rome to telephone at ten o'clock at night?"

"Dave Meyer of *Time* magazine. We're having breakfast in the morning. Do you want to join us?"

"No, thank you. I'm catching an early flight to Heathrow and then going on to Shannon. I want to see my father before I fly back to Illinois."

Jack nodded and then said softly, "That must have been a shock. I mean, finding out your old man is still alive in Ireland. Mike knew, didn't he?" He glanced at Maggie.

"Father Mike told us after the funeral. He said Mom told him years ago, but she didn't want the rest of us to know. She was ashamed, I guess, that Dad had left the family."

"The Irish are great when it comes to hiding the truth, aren't they?"

"You don't do badly yourself, McGraff."

"Why? What do you mean?"

"Well, for one, you could have written and told me you were planning to marry Helen Fisk."

"I'm not marrying Helen Fisk," he said quickly, his voice rising.

Maggie stared at him, startled by the news. "But what about all the gossip I read in the paper? The stuff about Helen telling her girl friends that she was going to be the next first lady?"

Jack sighed and shook his head.

"Well, McGraff?" Maggie demanded. "Don't try and tell me you two were just good friends."

"We were destroying each other. It was a marriage that looked great on paper, but otherwise . . ." He shrugged, looking beaten.

Maggie released his arm and shoved both hands into her raincoat. The bottoms of her pockets were wet.

"I was going to write to you," he said. "I was even planning to come out to Africa and see you. I want to marry you, again, Mag. We made a mistake, not trying to make it work, in spite of everything, about Emmett, and . . ."

She kept walking, staring down at the sidewalk.

"Maggie, I love you."

Maggie thought: he means it. She had learned to read his voice, to understand when he was telling the truth. But why? Why, suddenly, did he want to marry her? The thought frightened her.

Maggie looked up. They had reached a crossing, a complex inter-section with half a dozen streets feeding into a wide piazza. It re-minded her immediately of Addis Ababa, the crazy patchwork of streets that the Italians had built during the war. And she thought next of Kenneth, of how lonely he had looked standing on the tarmac.

"Where are we?" she asked.

He held up the sheet of paper and tried to read the sketchy map with the aid of the street lamp.

"Here, let me." She took the paper from him and checked the street signs. "We've gone too far. We have to go back a block."

The side street was nothing more than an alley, crowded with cars and sloping away from the piazza. Halfway down the dark block, Maggie spotted the neon sign for the *trattoria*.

"There it is."

"Is this place safe?" Jack stopped at the narrow entrance.

"Come on, you're in Rome, not Washington." She smiled at his caution. "Don't worry; I'll take care of you." She linked her arm into his, feeling friendly again.

"I don't like these foreign countries." He smiled, still resisting. "I like the United States, where I'm recognized."

"Oh, come on, Jack," she said. "You risk your life flying in air-planes, but you're frightened of a simple dark alley." Maggie opened the door and stepped into the tiny restaurant. It was a simple room, with fluorescent lights, metal tables, and no tablecloths. Old paintings of the city, reproductions of the Arch of Titus and the Villa Borghese, hung crookedly on the walls.

"This place is a dump," Jack said loudly. "Let's get out of here."

"Shh."

"*Buona sera, signorina . . . signor . . .*" A waiter approached with two large menus and gestured toward the half-dozen empty tables.

"Let's go," Jack whispered. "We'll get sick eating here."

"Be still!" Maggie silenced him, and then, smiling to the waiter, said, "*Buona sera, signor. Non parlo bene l'italiano. Parla inglese?*" She spoke slowly, carefully pronouncing each word.

"*Si! Si! Va bene. Va bene.* I know *inglese*," he offered haltingly.

There were a few older people sitting in the rear of the restaurant; they looked up at the American arrivals and then returned to eating. All of them were wearing overcoats. It was cold in the *trattoria* and Maggie wondered if they hadn't made a mistake after all, but she wouldn't leave, not after standing up to Jack.

"Some recommendation," Jack said as they sat down. "This looks like a set for a Mafia movie. I can see it now: U.S. SENATOR AND EX-WIFE GUNNED DOWN IN PIZZATOWN WIPEOUT!"

"Stop it, Jackson!" She laughed. In a minute, he'd be spinning out a whole novel, elaborating the details. She was feeling better now, she realized, beginning to relax.

She glanced at her menu and, at that moment, felt inexplicably happy. Perhaps it was just because she was rested, and could already smell the food. She would not let herself think that she was happy because of Jack, that they were together in Rome, in a tiny, out-of-the-way place where no one with claims to make could find them.

"Do you want me to order?" she asked, scanning the menu.

"Yes, please, but nothing strange." Jack closed his menu, happy to be free of the responsibility.

"Jack, they should never let you out of Illinois. How in the world did you ever get to be a senator?"

"Because of you. You were wonderful to me. It gave me strength."

She was afraid of his smile, his good nature. Eventually he would wear her down. It was only when he was jealous or angry that she could resist him. She had learned to make him mad at her just to keep from being seduced.

Maggie caught the waiter's eye and nodded. He came quickly, flashing a pad of paper.

"*Signor, potremmo avere piatti locali, per favore?*"

"*Si. Zuppa alla veneta . . . lasagne al forno . . .*" He began to gesture.

"You know I'm never happier than when I'm with you," Jack said, speaking as if they were alone in the restaurant.

"Quiet, Jack, please," she said quickly, glancing at him. "What do you want for a main course?"

"Whatever you're having. Just being with you is pasta enough."

Now he was being silly. She made herself forget that once she had found that endearing.

"*Potremmo avere . . .*" She searched the long menu, looking for a recognizable dish.

"Veal?" the waiter suggested. "*Cima alla genovese . . .*" He pointed to the dish on her menu.

Maggie shook her head. Jack never ate veal. "Do you have . . . *avete manzo?*"

"*Si, bistecca alla fiorentina?*"

Maggie nodded.

"*Grazie! Grazie!*" The waiter reached forward and quickly lifted the large menus from the table, paused again and asked, "*Vino?*"

"*Si. Una caraffa—rosso.*"

"Water? Bottle water?" Jack asked, speaking to the man.

"*Acqua minerale,*" Maggie added.

"*Si, si!*"

Maggie sat back in the chair, exhausted from the effort to pronounce the Italian correctly.

"What are we having?" Jack asked, now curious.

"Don't worry. I got you a Big Mac and a Coke."

He smiled, then said seriously, "Can we talk about us?"

"And spoil my dinner?" She reached for the bread. Her stomach was growling. It had been over eight hours since her last meal. She had been in the Sudan then, she thought—a lifetime ago.

"We need to talk." His voice had leveled; he wasn't teasing anymore.

"Not now, Jack. Look, just once can't we behave like two normal people, off in some nice, ordinary, freezing-cold *trattoria?* You know, I've had a tough time this last week, and once I get home, I have to deal with getting Emmett out of jail." She buttered the hard bread.

"I hate to say this, but it's possible he did do it. . . ."

"Jack! I don't want to hear any more such talk. And not from you!" She was angry at once. After all, they had fought before about Emmett.

"Okay. Okay." Jack backed off. "Well, if you want, I could have someone on the staff look into the . . . situation. It might help having the Senate's office put pressure at the local level."

"Thank you. That would help." She knew the value of inquiries from his office to the police in Gatesburg.

"What do you know about the death?" He took a pen and an envelope from his suit coat pocket and began to jot down notes on the back of the envelope.

She told him what little she did know, what she had been told by Michael and Catty, and explained how Emmett had been arrested on the basis of his barroom declarations. "He might have said it. But he was probably drunk and sounding off. I'm sure it must have been difficult for him, living with Mom, without money, without friends."

"Easy, Mag." He reached over and carefully touched her arm, as if still not sure how far he could go with her. "Let me see what I can do. I know the county prosecutor."

Maggie nodded, suddenly relieved, as if the total burden was no longer on her shoulders, and she thought how odd it was to be with Jack again, involved with her brother. Perhaps this time he would save him.

The waiter brought the red wine and two small glasses. Maggie filled them both, then handed one to Jack. He was smiling his million-dollar smile, as Dan Rather had once termed it, and his face was all she could see.

"Let's get drunk, Jack," she said.

Maggie reached out and felt for Jack, wanting him again and dreaming of how gently and kindly he had made love to her when they came back to her room. But the bed was empty; the sheets were cold. She woke at once, thinking, This is what it means to be someone's mistress: to always be alone at dawn. Once such abandonments had hurt her, but she had rationalized them as unavoidable when one was involved with a public figure. Long ago she had accepted the fact that she would always be second in Jack's life.

As she reached for her watch on the night table, she found his note, explaining in his familiar large print that he would return at ten o'clock with the embassy car to pick her up. There was no signature, no avowal of love.

Well, she wouldn't be waiting. She would go ahead on her own. She did not have to waste her life away waiting for Jack McGraff.

Crumpling the note in her fingers, she jumped out of bed and went quickly across the room. The phone rang before she reached the bathroom.

Jack, no doubt, pressing her to have breakfast with him after all. She picked up the receiver and said quickly, "No, Jack, I don't want to."

"Margaret?"

The voice sounded far away and somehow different, so that it took her a moment to get her bearings. Even on the phone, it was odd of him to be so hesitant.

"Kenneth! Oh, Kenneth, it's you."

Maggie slipped back onto the bed.

"Margaret, were you expecting someone else?"

"It's nothing." She thought of lying, but there was no reason to lie. She and Kenneth were through. "Jack McGraff is here in Rome. We had dinner last night and he wanted me to have breakfast with him this morning."

"Jack McGraff?"

"Yes." She paused.

"Oh . . . well, I thought I might telephone and make sure you arrived safely. I know it's terribly early, but . . . did you have a good flight? I mean, there weren't any problems, were there? It's always so damn hard flying out of Africa, anything at all can go wrong."

It was so unlike him, she thought, to ramble on that way. She had done this to him, caused him so much pain.

"Yes, the trip went fine."

"I just wanted to catch you once before you left this side of the pond. I have your . . . package. I will forward it to Washington. Also, I had a talk with Virginia. I understand what you must have thought."

"Please, Kenneth. I'm sorry, but I don't want to talk about it, especially now."

"I'm not at liberty to speak, but there will be some changes."

"I'm sorry, Kenneth. Don't tell me anymore." She could hear herself shouting into the phone. The connection was poor, and his voice was fading. "I must go, Kenneth. I have to catch my flight."

"I'll telephone you when I'm in Washington. And if you need help, financial help, I mean, please let me know," he shouted before the line went dead.

She sat for a moment with the receiver pressed against her bare body. She was no good at this, she thought. Even for a day, she couldn't handle the two men in her life. Slowly, carefully, she replaced the phone and stood up, eager to get dressed and out of Rome, to get on with her life without her ex-husband or her married lover.

# · CHAPTER 26 ·

## TOURMAKEADY

MAGGIE SLOWED THE HERTZ rental car and stopped at the crest of the hill. It had rained all day on the drive north, but now, suddenly and spectacularly, the sun came out. Below her on the left was a lake, silvery bright in the sunlight, and beyond the green hills, the end of a thick rainbow disappeared over the green mountains. Maggie smiled at the sight. The Irish Tourist Board couldn't have done better.

Still, she had no idea where in Connemara she was. The road signs were all in Irish. One had said TUAR MHIC EADAIGH, 10 KM, and she guessed that was Tourmakeady. According to her road map, she was south of Tourmakeady, on the eastern shore of Lough Mask. The long silvery lake was to her left, behind the stone walls.

Ahead of her she spotted a tall, stoop-shouldered man crossing the narrow road. He was wearing a gray cap, suit coat, and tie with his knee-high black boots. The Irish, she thought, must be the only people in the world who dress up to work in the fields.

Stopping the car beside the farmer, she lowered the car window and asked, "Pardon me, but am I on the road to Tourmakeady?"

The old man leaned on his wooden hay rake.

"And where else would you be, miss?" he said in a surprisingly strong voice. Half his teeth were gone, Maggie saw, but he had fair pink cheeks, crystal-clear blue eyes, and thick white hair.

"Sure, we're not like America a'tall," he went on. "We're a poor country, you know, and need only one road to find our way to Tourmakeady." A smile began in his blue eyes and swept across his face like a surprise. It made him look years younger, Maggie realized, even mischievous.

"And how far down this one road is the village?" Maggie asked, enjoying the old man.

" 'Tisn't far a'tall. I'd be on my way there myself, if I had half a mind."

"Would you like a lift?"

"You wouldn't mind, would you, miss?" He cocked his head,

squinting at her, and when she shook her head, he set his wooden rake against the stone fence bordering the road and got in.

"Your rake," Maggie said. "Aren't you afraid someone will take it?"

"And who now would steal an old rake like that one? Sure, there's not a good day's work left in it." He eased himself into the tight front seat and, once settled, studied the dashboard. " 'Tis a marvel, isn't it?"

"What's that?" Maggie asked, turning over the engine.

"All these gauges and gadgets. Why, I wouldn't know where to put the key."

"Do you drive?"

"I did in my day. Now Nora does the driving."

"Is Nora your wife?" Maggie glanced at the old man.

"No, my eldest daughter."

"How many children do you have, sir?" Maggie asked, watching the road. She drove by the Lough Mask Inn, then up the hill toward a church. There were sheep grazing on the hillside above the lake, but the thatched-roof farmhouses were gone, and she could see modern homes built beside old stone ruins.

The rainbow shifted then with the sunlight, and the bands of color slipped over the horizon beyond the lake.

"They're in America," the old man said, "all but Nora. She's a dear girl, Nora is."

"And your wife?"

"She's dead now."

Maggie felt a chill go through her as she let the car slow again and stop by the side of the road. "Was your wife's maiden name Rush, sir?"

The old man stared at Maggie. "Would you be knowing her?"

"I'm Maggie, Margaret Mary DeLacey. I'm your daughter, Dad."

He stared at her, confused, his blue eyes watery. Then he whispered, "Jesus, Mary, and Joseph, is it you, Maggie? You were in diapers when I saw you last, child."

She began to talk quickly, nervously, saying she should have cabled ahead, told him and Nora she was coming. She kept explaining, but the old man just stared at her, looking stunned by her announcement.

Then he said softly, kindly, "And don't I see your mother, God rest her soul, in your eyes?"

"I'm told I resemble her," Maggie whispered. "Both of us do, Catty and I."

"Catty," Cormac whispered, then looked off. "Little Catty," he said, and fell silent.

"Where's Nora?" Maggie asked, to pull his attention back from the past.

"At home she is," he said. "You haven't been to the house then, girl?"

Maggie shook her head.

"Well, we'll go there instead of into town. We can go to town any old time." He seemed suddenly impatient, eager to show her the farm. "Here, turn your little car about and we'll go out to the place. Nora's there, you know. At home." He leaned forward, anxious to be on the way.

Maggie was glad to be busy with the driving. She did not know what more to say to her own father. He was like a figure from a photograph, an ancient Connemara farmer who might appear on an Irish calendar. But he was her father, her own flesh and blood, and she prayed that after all these years, they could mean something to each other again.

"Go there by the gate," he said, waving his thin hand toward a break in the stone wall. She saw the narrow road, not much wider than her small car, and turned off the tarmac. "We don't get many autos back here," he said, by way of explanation. "Nora has her bike. And my two feet are good enough for myself. Sure, I haven't any- where to go, to tell you the honest truth."

Maggie smiled. He sounded like Father O'Connor. The thick brogue, the choice of words. She glanced over and saw he was leaning forward, perched at the edge of the seat, looking ahead. He looked so old, she thought, yet at the same time strong. He was like an African acacia tree, bent and twisted by the weather, yet ageless. Of all the family, Paddy Jack resembled him the most. They had the same gauntness, the same hawklike look.

"There now," he said, raising his hand, gesturing.

The day had cleared, leaving a cloudless blue sky beneath which Maggie could see the length of the horseshoe valley. It stretched for several miles before sweeping up the steep slopes. But just ahead, where the road turned into the valley, Maggie spotted the thatched roof of a small cottage. Her father, she realized, had not abandoned his old home for a new house. She remembered her mother's stories of going into those hills to gather sedge, the long grass used to thatch roofs.

"It's beautiful," Maggie said. Smoke curled from the stone chim- ney, golden-yellow gorse bushes grew against the whitewashed walls, and the winter afternoon sun caught the setting as if it were a still-life painting. Maggie parked by the front gate.

"Well, it's home," her father commented, hurrying to open the car door as soon as Maggie stopped.

Maggie stepped from the car, too, staring at the farmhouse as if she were afraid it would disappear from sight. And then she saw Nora appear in the upper half of the Dutch-style front door. She was clutch-ing her hands together at her waist and seemed puzzled to see a car, and her father home from the village.

"It's me, Nora," Maggie said. "Margaret. From America."

"Dear Mother of God, if it isn't!" Nora said, opening the door and coming out to them. "You gave my heart a fright when I saw your car and Da. Maggie, dear, it is you!" Her face beamed and she rushed to embrace her sister. "You said you'd come, God love you. It's Margaret Mary, Da!"

"And sure I know that well enough myself. Didn't I meet the girl on the road?" the old man answered, pushing forward and going up the short walk to the front door. "Come along the two of you. Nora, put up the water for tea. Have you had your dinner, child?" He was full of questions now that he was on his home turf.

Maggie laughed, happy at his bossiness, happy that he and Nora had welcomed her. She had been tense all morning, secretly afraid that her father and Nora wouldn't accept her into their house. Daugh-ter or not, she was an intrusion into their lives. They had managed alone all these years. Her father might have been resentful; Nora might have been jealous of Maggie interrupting her special relation-ship with their father.

"Where are you coming from, Maggie?" Nora asked.

"I left Ethiopia Monday morning."

"Did you, indeed!" Nora pulled away briefly to look at Maggie's face. "Airplanes are a wonder, aren't they? Africa one day, Ireland the next. You'll be staying with us awhile then?"

Maggie shook her head, feeling guilty. "I can't, really. I stayed last night at Ashford Castle."

"Oh, isn't that a grand place? We were down in Cong ourselves a while back for a funeral. A friend of ours passed away, God bless his soul."

Maggie nodded, waited for Nora to finish, and then she explained how she had to get back to Gatesburg because of Emmett.

"I haven't said a word to him," Nora whispered, nodding toward their father. "He won't understand, you see."

Maggie nodded. "I won't mention anything. But he seems fine . . . your . . . our father."

"He's always a bit better in the fair weather. Come along, we'll have that tea and you can visit. You'll stay the night?"

"Nora, I don't want to be any trouble . . ."

"Oh, dear girl, you're no trouble at all. It's a joy having you."

Maggie followed the two of them into the kitchen. The house was smaller inside than it had seemed from the road, with a low ceiling and tiny windows. The kitchen was clean, but without charm. Maggie's eyes swept around quickly, but she was afraid to look too closely because she did not want Nora to notice. Still, she couldn't stop herself. She kept thinking, This might have been my home. She tried to imagine herself as a child, an Irish girl home from the church school.

Cormac had already sat down at the table and taken off his cap. His forehead was milky white, and without a cap, his face lost its sharpness, the eyes their strength. He looked meek. The house seemed to humble him.

"Sit down, girl!" he said, waving Maggie toward a chair. The voice was loud, but his tone was gentle. He didn't know how to talk to her, Maggie realized, so she smiled and did what he told her, sitting across from him. The table was in front of the kitchen windows, and Maggie again drank in the beauty of the valley and the steep mountains in the distance.

"You have nothing at all like it back home, have you?" her father said. He was watching her closely, trying, it seemed, to learn everything about his daughter just from the sight of her.

Maggie smiled back at him. She could see tears glisten in his eyes.

"I can see Caitlin in your face," he said again, softly. "Aye, she was a beautiful woman."

Maggie nodded, catching the lump in her throat before she began to cry. She turned her face away and looked out the window again.

"Is that the salmon river?" she said, needing to speak, and pointed to the small creek that crossed the field below them.

"There was salmon once in it, but I don't see the lads fishing."

"And the bridge!"

"Your mother told you then about the bridge."

Maggie nodded. The tears in her eyes streamed down her face and she couldn't stop herself. She was crying because she was in her mother's house. The home she had gone to as a young bride a lifetime ago.

"It was a wooden bridge in her time," Cormac said. "We'd have dances there at night in the moonlight. The boys and girls would come from miles around Tourmakeady. Everyone walked over the hills, for there were no cars here in them days."

"Mom told me about the dances," Maggie whispered, wiping at her nose with her napkin.

"Your mother's place is farther in those hills. I'll take you there after we've had our tea. There's nothing to her house now but a few stone walls still standing. The Rushes, you know, they all left Tourmakeady. Went off to England and America after the war. Joyce Flaherty, that would be your mother's oldest sister, she died last spring. God rest her soul. It was Joyce who took care of Nora here when she was a little girl."

Nora came to the kitchen table with the pot of tea. "We'll let it sit for a bit," she said, smiling over at Maggie. "Can I cut you a slice of soda bread?" She spoke quickly, anxious to be kept busy.

Maggie was not hungry but she could not refuse, knowing how much Nora wanted to serve her, to make her feel welcome. "Thank you. Please."

"Aye, you know, it was a sad day long ago when we left this place, your mother and me," said Cormac. "I remember it clear as if it were yesterday. We went off in winter. A day like today it was, cold and sunny, after the rain. We took the bus as far as Galway. They called buses motor coaches in them days.

"Your mother said to me when we reached the hill, 'Look at Maamstrasna. You can see the mountains.' But I wouldn't look, and many's the day in Gatesburg, I cursed myself for not taking a last look at my mountains. I ached for the sight of them. You can see Maamstrasna there yourself across the valley. Aye, the sight of it makes my heart pound. There's not a mountain or a hill in the whole of that bloody Illinois." He shook his head, a quick jerk of the chin, remembering.

Paddy Jack made the same gesture, Maggie realized, recognizing a family trait.

"Is the tea ready, girl? It's had time to grow old in that pot." He reached for it, but Nora took the pot and began to fill the cups.

"Why did you leave America, Dad?" Maggie asked. "Why did you leave the family?" She had not meant to ask the question. Her bluntness surprised even her, but she couldn't stop herself.

He did not look at her or answer, and for a moment she thought he hadn't heard. She glanced at Nora, who simply shook her head and frowned.

Their father took his cup of tea and sat back in the chair. He looked small, and old.

"Your mother, now, she never said a word to you?" he asked. He had cocked his head, as if to catch a new angle on his youngest child.

Maggie shook her head. She would not say anything, she told herself. Having been brave enough to ask the question, she would now force the old man to speak, if it took her the whole of the afternoon. She desired to know the truth, after all these years, after all the secrets kept from her, and the rest of the family.

"Your mother would have nothing to do with Ireland. With coming home to Tourmakeady," he said finally.

"Then why didn't you stay with us?"

He nodded toward Nora. "The girl here."

"Nora could have come to America. Thousands of girls her age have traveled over from Ireland."

He sat forward, put both his thin elbows on the table, and sat squinting, as if pulling ancient memories back to mind. "Aye, she could, I know. But I wanted to see Ireland, Tourmakeady once before I died. You were in diapers when I left. Do you remember me a'tall?"

Maggie shook her head.

"Why didn't you come back?" she asked next. She could see what he was doing, talking around her questions to keep from answering the hard ones. "We were all told you were killed in a car accident on some mountain road."

"Tell her, Da," Nora said, becoming impatient.

Maggie glanced back and forth between her sister and father.

"Your mother, God rest her soul, we weren't getting on, you see." He looked embarrassed, telling his child. "I thought it best, you know, if I stayed away." He sat back and hooked his fingers in his black suspenders.

She looked around the tiny kitchen, taking it all in: the plastic cloth on the table, the fading black-and-white photographs, a calendar from Saint Mary's church, the pieces of palm, dried in the months since Easter, caught behind the painting of the Last Supper.

Now it was her father's house, the home of her sister Nora. It could never be hers. She belonged to another time and place, to her father's other life, which had nothing to do with Ireland or this farm overlooking Lough Mask.

Her father was a stranger to her. The time he had had with her mother was a life that meant nothing to her. She and her father had never been a family. Still, he was her own flesh and blood, and she prayed that after all these years she might find a way to know and perhaps love him, as she had always loved her mother.

"Drink your tea, Maggie dear, before it gets cold," Nora said to break the silence.

Maggie smiled over at her sister and then, picking up the cup, said to her father, "Dad, would you please take me to see Mom's house? I want to see where she was born and lived as a little girl. She told me so many wonderful stories of being a child in Tourmakeady."

She would try, Maggie told herself. She would try to bridge the years and the distance that he had put between himself and his American family. "And if you don't mind, I think I'd like to stay with you for a couple days." She glanced at Nora and went on explaining. "I think it's time I got to know my sister, and you, too, Dad," Maggie added, reaching out to gently touch her father's hand. She would try, she promised herself, though she felt only anger at the loss of years, a lifetime of years lost to her, lost to all the family, and on both sides of the ocean.

# · CHAPTER 27 ·

## GATESBURG: 1954

CORMAC FOLDED THE SUNDAY edition of the *Chicago Tribune* carefully so that the death notices were showing and then tilted the page to catch the morning light. He had been sitting at the kitchen table for over an hour, since the family had returned from six o'clock Mass at Saint Patrick's in Gatesburg.

"I see there's a Helen Tighe mentioned here. She died on Friday at Saint Elizabeth's Hospital up in Chicago. Would she by any chance be one of the Tighes from Ballinrobe? I knew a Paddy Tighe. He worked with me in the building trades that time in Dublin. He talked then of coming out. It says here she was the widow of Patrick James Corcoran of Ballinrobe, County Galway."

Caitlin didn't answer. She had come back into the kitchen after feeding the twins and putting them down to sleep and saw that the breakfast dishes were still on the kitchen table.

"Where's the girl?" she asked at once.

"Now that I think it, the Paddy Tighe that I knew in Monkstown came from down near Waterford," Cormac went on, not responding to his wife. He was reading without his glasses and held the paper at arm's length. "He was a little fella, but, by God, he could put the drink away. She's being buried from Christ the King."

Caitlin went through the kitchen door and into the hallway. She closed the door so as not to wake the twins, then called up to Catty, telling her daughter to get downstairs at once. When she came back into the kitchen, Cormac asked, not looking up from his paper, "I thought Christ the King had gone colored."

"Will you be sitting there all morning, Cormac DeLacey?" she demanded. "Michael will have all the milking done by the time you finish with the notices."

"And what if he does? He's old enough to be handling the milking." He turned the page and studied the next column. "There's a Joe Lyons dead as well. Do you remember Joe Lyons who went out with one of the Boyle girls?"

"What in God's name are you talking about?" Caitlin asked, stirring the chicken soup.

"I'm talking about the Boyle girls. Annie Boyle, I think it was. She had met this fella Joe Lyons in Galway City one Saturday, and he came up to see her at Christmas. He came into O'Cadhain's that time, to be asking directions, you see, for her father's farm, and Liam Devlin speaks up and tells this fella that Annie Boyle is dead and buried a week past. Drowned, he said, crossing Lough Mask. Aye, he was a great one, Liam was, when it came to pulling your leg. And Joe Lyons! The blood went out of his face, and him standing there with a little gift wrapped all up in shiny paper. And Dev, he's going on about how it was two days before the body came ashore below Trean." Cormac started to laugh then, remembering.

"You'd think, after all this time, you'd be done with your stories of Tourmakeady."

"Well, I'm thinking of going back and getting some more," he said quickly, keeping his eyes on the death notices. "Going before my name is added to this list." He tapped the newspaper. "They're some my own age now, them dying. If I wait much longer, I'll be dead and buried before I lay eyes again on Lough Mask."

Caitlin stopped what she was doing to watch her husband a moment, and then she said quietly, "And why in the world would you be doing that?"

"You know well enough why. Have you forgotten our Nora?" He did not look up at her.

"Going to Ireland, are you, with the twins still in diapers? And a third cut of alfalfa still to be done?" She held up her wooden spoon as if it were a club to beat back what was coming.

"And just when is a good time to be going, Catty?" he asked. He spooned sugar into his morning tea and stirred it quickly, sloshing the tea and milk onto the oilcloth that covered the table.

"Mind what you're doing! You're worse than the kids when it comes to making a mess." She turned to the stove to taste the soup, then put the cover back on the pot.

"Too bad for you," Cormac muttered.

"We'll send for the child," she said after a moment, "as I wanted you to do years ago."

"We had no money years ago."

"We could have all the money we needed from your cousin, Dermot O'Connor, and without a question asked, I might add."

"I won't be taking money from the church like one of those colored," he said.

It was an old argument, and Caitlin only raised it as a way of giving herself time to think. She was frightened just by the thought of Cormac back in Ireland, even for a short time.

"She's old enough to come herself," Caitlin finally said. "There's others who have come in their day, and without a family waiting either."

"I won't be having her coming on her own," Cormac answered, pouring his tea into his saucer before sipping it. "When I get the corn picked, then I'll be going. I had a letter from Michael McNutley last week. He said they were over there in the spring, him and Jean. They took a plane. TWA right there from Midway. He said it was nothing a'tall to fly into Shannon. They have a grand airport there, Michael said."

"How in God's name can I be milking twenty cows twice a day, with the boys and Catty in school and the two little ones at home?"

" 'Tis time Mike left school. He's had enough of school." Corman bent over the saucer to sip his tea.

"What are you talking about?" Caitlin stepped away from the stove. A lock of her graying hair had slipped loose, and with one hand she pinned it in place.

At thirty-five, and the mother of six, Caitlin DeLacey still had some of her young girl's figure, though her breasts were fuller and her waist had thickened. Farm work and caring for the family had kept her slim, made her stronger. And the years, and the children, had added depth to her brown eyes, softened the lines in her face. But her manner had hardened and there was an edge to her voice.

"I said, if you didn't hear me, that I'm thinking it's time the boy was done with school," Cormac announced.

"Jesus almighty, I never heard of such a thing. You'd take your son out of school and destroy his future so you can be going back to Ireland for no good reason at all. Do you think that gang over there will still be waiting to buy you a pint at O'Cadhain's? You're a bigger fool than I thought, Cormac DeLacey." She went to the sink full of dirty dishes, saying flatly, "I won't let Michael leave school. Michael has better things to do with his life than end it here on this farm."

"And what's wrong with farming? 'Tis good enough for the likes of myself. There's many a fine man who spent his days farming. My da for one. No finer man lived than Michael DeLacey!"

"Don't start again about your father, or Ireland, and what a grand place Connemara is for farming. You can't plow two feet without hitting stone, or have you forgotten all the rocks you dug from your father's land?"

"Aye, but when you cleared those fields, the soil was as rich . . . why, spuds grew without planting."

"And nothing else, by God!"

" 'Tis a damn sight better land than they have here in Illinois."

"And you want Michael to give up school so he can be out there in the fields with you, breaking his back, trying to make corn grow, and a few potatoes? Is that the life you want for him?"

He did not answer her. Caitlin looked out beyond the orchard, where she saw Michael crossing to the barns with two buckets of pig slop. She had never seen such a boy for working. How unlike his father he was. Michael never rested, never idled away his time in daydreams. He was like her in that way, she thought with pride. Her son was not afraid of hard work.

He was the only one of her children like that. Paddy Jack hated farm work. She knew Michael would do Paddy's chores next, and without a complaint. And she knew without asking that Paddy was at the golf course, trying to get work caddying. But he was good boy, Padraic, and that night he would be home with what he had earned, two or three dollars to give her, and never thinking of keeping the money for himself.

Suddenly she remembered Catty—the girl still hadn't stirred from bed. It was always the same, every morning the same struggle to get her up. Caitlin got angry just thinking of Catty's laziness.

"He can read and write and do his numbers." Cormac pushed back his chair, blessing himself, and stood, adding, "I won't be in Tourmakeady for more than a few months." Then he flipped on his cap and twisted it into place with a quick tug.

"Cormac DeLacey, you haven't listened to me."

"I hear you well enough." He moved toward the back door.

"You won't take Michael out of school. I won't have it! He'll finish at Wisdom and then go to college. He won't be like us, without an education, and having to work himself to the bone just to make ends meet. You get nowhere in America without a college education. You know that well enough yourself!"

The back-door screen slammed and Caitlin watched her husband walk off toward the barns.

"Did you hear me, Cormac DeLacey?" She went to the screen door and shouted after him, but she knew he would have nothing more to say. He would go and she couldn't stop him. But, by God, she promised herself, he wouldn't ruin Michael's chances in the process. She would see to that.

From the spare room off the kitchen came the sound of the twins beginning to cry, first Maggie and then Emmett. Caitlin grabbed a towel and was wiping her hands as Catty pushed open the kitchen door.

"What time is it, Mom?" Catty asked, yawning.

"Time enough for you to be down here to help."

"It's Sunday, Mother!"

"There's no Sunday for me, or your brothers. Michael has been out in the barns since we got home from Mass. You're the only one who's gone back to bed, like some Hollywood star." The twins were screaming, and she had to shout for Catty to hear her. "Get upstairs, girl, and dress. There's work to be done."

Catty turned away, still yawning. Impatient with her daughter's insolence, Caitlin leaned over and slapped Catty on her bottom, snapping, "I don't have time for your complaining. Get dressed. I need you to look after the twins. I'm going to town."

"But I told Kathey, I'd ride my bike over to her house. All the Handleys are going to some dumb family picnic, and Kathey has to stay home because she has the mumps."

"Oh, now you'll be bringing mumps into the house so the twins can catch it! And you with all the cleaning to do. By the time I get back from Gatesburg, I want the dishes stacked clean and the wash hung out. It's going to rain tomorrow."

"But, Mother! I told Kathey!" Catty stamped her foot.

"That's too bad for you. Now be off! I haven't all day for your whining." She pushed open the door and went to the crying babies.

"Look at the two of you," she said sweetly to the crying babies. "And I gave you both bottles just a half hour ago."

The door swung shut on her daughter Cathleen Ann, who turned and ran from the kitchen, tears streaming to her face.

"Well, to be honest with you, Caitlin, Cormac did have a word with me. About a month ago it was now. I thought it was just one of his notions, you know, and I didn't pay him mind." Father O'Connor fingered the papers on his desk.

The pastor's residence was quiet. It was after one o'clock and all the church traffic had gone from the side street of Gatesburg. Like his cousin Cormac, the priest wouldn't look at Caitlin, but tried to hide behind the papers stacked on his cluttered desk.

"I know Cormac. He has his ticket bought. He wouldn't have said a word unless his plans were made," Caitlin insisted.

Father O'Connor nodded. It was warm in the first-floor study, and the priest paused a moment to turn on the small desk fan. He aimed the breeze at Caitlin, as an offering. But it only stirred the heat of the hot August Sunday afternoon. Caitlin could hear Mary Quill, the priest's housekeeper, in the kitchen, and smell fried chicken. The priest would be sitting down soon for his noontime meal.

"We don't have the money for air tickets, Dermot. And Cormac hasn't sold off any of the livestock to pay for it, I know that for sure."

She watched the priest, waiting for him to say something, and when he didn't, she asked, "You gave him the passage money now, didn't you?"

The priest nodded, still not looking up at her.

"Jesus, Mary, and Joseph, the two of you in it together. What's a woman to do?"

" 'Tis time the child was here with you in Illinois. Nora's sixteen now, isn't she?" He raised his voice slightly.

"On the twenty-second of the month." Caitlin kept her eyes on the priest. "If we'd had the money, Dermot, she would have been with us years ago. There's no reason Cormac has to fly home. We can send Nora the money for an airplane ticket. My sister Joyce will go with her as far as Limerick."

The pastor nodded. "Well, that's true enough." He was a small thin man, like her husband, with the same blue eyes and thick shock of black hair. But he had none of Cormac's hawkish features, the sharp nose or jutting chin. There was a softness to Father O'Connor, as if he were hiding a weakness. "Cormac wants to see Tourmakeady again, Caitlin, you can understand that. He misses Ireland. There's many like him, you know."

"And he's willing to sacrifice Michael's future just for one sight of Lough Mask. What rubbish! Did he tell you he wants Michael to quit school and work full-time on the farm?"

The priest shook his head. "And what does the lad want?"

"The boy's too young to know what he wants," she answered back, "but he's staying in school. He's a smart one, Michael is, and I won't be having him ruin his life spending it on the farm."

"Aye, he does have a good head on his shoulders. Sister Saint Stephen is putting him up for the Knights of Columbus Award. He'll be getting the hundred-dollar scholarship if he wins." The thin priest leaned forward, said softly, nodding to her, "I'm sure Michael will be winning, Caitlin."

"And what will we do with a hundred dollars? Michael can't go to college with a hundred dollars, Dermot."

Caitlin looked away from the priest. The small office was at the front of the parish house and she could see through the screen window, across the porch and into the elm-lined street. It was a hot and still Sunday afternoon. No children played on the sidewalk, nor was there any traffic, but she could hear a radio, and the sounds of the Chicago White Sox baseball game being broadcasted. Michael would be listening at home, sitting on the screened-in front porch, drinking the iced tea she had made for him before driving into town.

Baseball made no sense to her, but she liked the sounds of the broadcast. She often turned the radio on when the children were in school, when she was alone in the kitchen on a quiet afternoon. She found it comforting to hear the game being played in the background. And she always remembered the final score so that she could tell Michael when he came home from school.

"You know how Cormac is, once he has his mind set," Father O'Connor said, speaking softly. "Why don't you have the boy stay home for a while? 'Tis only a few months. And he's smart enough. He'll catch up soon. I'll have the nuns set out special work for him."

"If Michael quits, he won't be going back in a few months. Cormac will take his own sweet time returning to America. He knows well enough that Michael is a better worker than himself."

"Michael's a good lad." Father O'Connor nodded. "Don't be worrying about Michael's schooling. I'll find a place for him, get the lad a scholarship," the priest added, as if adding another enticement.

Caitlin studied the priest closely while she waited for him to continue.

"Up in Chicago. At Quigley High School, our preparation seminary."

"Michael's never said a word to me about the priesthood."

"He can go to school there, make up his mind later," the pastor whispered.

"I won't have him become a priest," she answered back. "He's smart enough to go to Harvard, one of those big, fancy schools out east."

"Oh, Mother of God, and how would you pay for that? You don't even have the money to keep him in high school if it wasn't for Paddy Jack bringing in a little extra every summer. Michael will be lucky to graduate from high school if Cormac goes off. And, Caitlin DeLacey, hear me now because Cormac *will* go back to Tourmakeady."

Caitlin glanced out the windows again.

Through the thick summer leaves she could see a woman sitting alone on the front porch of the house across the street. The woman was fanning herself with part of the Sunday paper. Caitlin envied the woman's peace and quiet and wondered then if she shouldn't sell out the farm and move to town. Buy herself a house like that on a side street near the Catholic church so she could rest on a Sunday afternoon and have time again to herself, as she had once in Dublin.

It would be easier for the children, too, she thought, easier on Michael. He wouldn't have the chores day in and day out. And she could find herself work as a housekeeper for one of the rich families that lived on the country-club road.

"Have you thought, Caitlin, of going home yourself?" the priest asked. "You could sell the farm for a pretty penny. And in Ireland, what with the land being dirt cheap, you could find yourself a nice farm, a little place somewhere in Connemara. Aye, it would be fine raising the twins in Ireland, wouldn't it?"

"I'll never set foot in that country again," she told Father O'Connor, staring back at him. "And it's my money that bought that land. It's my place, not Cormac's. My name is on that deed, and the bank mortgage as well. I was the one with the thousand pounds to make the down payment. Not Cormac! My God, we'd be on the dole today in Dublin if it weren't for my good fortune."

She reached for her purse. It was no good spending her time here. She would get no help from this priest.

"And how did you get such a grand amount anyway?" O'Connor asked, standing with her. "At the time, I remember, when you first came from Chicago, Cormac said you got the money from this family in Dublin where you worked."

"That's true enough."

" 'Tis an odd thing, you know, those left-handers giving you such a grand amount. Why, 'tis like winning the sweepstakes itself," the priest said, following her onto the front porch of the old Victorian parish house.

"They were wonderful people, Mr. and Mrs. Steele." Caitlin reached to open the screen door, but the priest stopped her hand.

Caitlin's cotton blouse was sticking to her shoulders, and she felt perspiration on her face. The priest was smarter than Cormac, she knew, and could not be easily fooled. Hearing confessions for twenty years had taught him about people. She could feel the priest's hand lie heavily on her arm.

"I did the family a great favor," she said carefully.

"And they rewarded you with boat passage for two, and enough money to buy a farm in Illinois," O'Connor replied. "Well, now, it must have been some favor you did those Protestants."

"I saved their son from prison." Caitlin turned to stare at the man. "He was one of those Protestants who supported the Sinn Feiners at the beginning of the war. There were German spies everywhere in Dublin. They'd be parachuting into Ireland at night, and the boy, Adrian Fitzstephen, they called him, was one of them in the Irish underground.

"The G-two, the Irish army intelligence branch, came around Ballsbridge to make inquiries. I told them Adrian had been at home all evening, that we had listened together to the news on the BBC, when I knew as well as I know my own name that he was in Westmeath picking up a German spy.

"When madam heard what I done, it was she that made the offer. She told me I could have what I wished, for saving their son, and I told her I wanted to go to America."

Father O'Connor cocked his head, as Cormac might.

" 'Tis a wonder you had so much good sense about you, Caitlin," he said. "'Tis a grand thing you did, helping a left-hander."

The priest did not believe her, Caitlin realized. But he could not prove she was wrong. The Steeles were gone from Dublin. After she and Cormac were safely in America, Caitlin had written Lily Mc-Gonigal, one of the girls who worked across the square from Vulcanus. Lily answered Caitlin, writing that Adrian had been arrested and sent to Mountjoy Prison for aiding German spies and stealing arms from Phoenix Park for the Sinn Fein.

The Steeles had sold the house in Ballsbridge, Lily wrote, and moved down to the house in Kerry. Mrs. Finnerty had retired, and only Teasy had gone with the family to Glennamain. Caitlin never wrote to Lily McGonigal again. She needed no more news of Dublin once she was sure Adrian Steele was where he deserved to be.

"My sister Agnes knows a family named Steele. Did I ever mention that to you, Caitlin?" The priest followed her out of the rectory, down the sidewalk to where she had parked the pickup truck. "Agnes is a nun, you know, the mother superior of the convent school in Killarney. I understand from Agnes the Steeles have been terribly kind to the convent and great supporters of the secondary school. Do you think they'd be any relation to those employers of yours, Catty?"

Caitlin climbed into the front of the truck. "Oh, Steele's a common Anglo-Irish name, you know," she answered back.

"Agnes mentioned to me sometime back that a son of theirs had been in a bit of trouble with the law. She said he was a fine lad, a bit wild, though, and he had spent a time in Mountjoy Prison."

Caitlin turned the key in the truck, but the batteries of the old pickup were low and the engine wouldn't catch.

Father O'Connor stepped closer and, bracing his arms against the passenger door, ducked his head into the open window.

"Agnes said the family was shamed by the lad. He got himself involved with a servant girl in Dublin at the time of the emergency."

"There's plenty of young girls, I'm sure, who are misguided by those Dublin jackeens," Caitlin replied. She pumped the pedal again and, mercifully, the engine took off, roaring in the silent street.

Father O'Connor waited for the engine to settle. He did not step away from the cab, and before Caitlin slipped the gear into first, he said softly, "Let Cormac go back to Tourmakeady, Caitlin, and see his home again. You owe that to the man, for all he has done for you. Leaving Ireland was a terrible blow to him. I'll see that Michael gets into Quigley. He'll have his college education. And we need to have a smart lad from this parish go into the priesthood. 'Tis a great honor for you. And myself, I might add." The priest stepped back from the pickup. She was free to leave. His deal was made.

Caitlin watched him in the rearview mirror as she pulled away from the curb. He looked like a black exclamation mark in his clerical trousers and short-sleeved black shirt, standing before the old white Victorian houses.

The bastard, she thought, and the breath went out of her, as if he had her by the throat. She wondered how long he had known about Adrian Steele. She did not wonder why he had kept the secret. He had saved it for now, for just this moment when he could take Michael away from her.

# · CHAPTER 28 ·

## GATESBURG: 1982

"SEE, THERE'S A QUESTION of eight hours," the detective said, spooning more sugar into his cup.

He was like an Ethiopian, Maggie thought, the way he doused his black coffee with sugar. She left the kitchen table to heat more water.

"Those are unexplained hours," he said softly, as if he were speaking confidentially, though they were alone in the house. "The coroner is very clear about the time. Your mother died between seven and eight o'clock on Saturday morning. They can tell by body temperature, skin coloring, and coagulation of the muscle protein. That's rigor mortis, you understand."

"Emmett did not kill our mother, Lieutenant O'Hara," Maggie said evenly. "I don't understand what we've done that everyone should wish us such ill."

"If your brother didn't do it, Mrs. McGraff, I'll be damned if I know who did," the young detective answered calmly.

His name was Larry O'Hara. He and Maggie had gone to the same high school, he had reminded her when he arrived at the farmhouse. She was a senior and he was just a freshman. But he had been a freshman-class escort when she was homecoming queen.

Maggie couldn't quite place him. The family, she knew, had lived across the river, behind Holtz's Brewery and at the edge of East End, the black part of town. Shanty Irish, her mother had always called them.

"I'm not Mrs. McGraff, Lieutenant. I never was. When the senator and I were married, I didn't change my name." She gave him a quick, tight smile. "I'm still a DeLacey. And you may call me Maggie, unless there's some rule against it in your police manual."

"This isn't any cross-examination, Mrs.—Maggie."

"Then what the fuck are you doing, Larry?"

The detective coughed into his cup of coffee.

"I make my living as a reporter, Larry. I know something about murder investigations, and if you're not looking for evidence, then why are you out here, snooping around?"

"Well, you know, there are always some loose ends—"

"My brother's in jail," she said, cutting him off, "and he'll be in jail until we can get the bail reduced to something reasonable. Why in the world was it set at five-hundred-thousand dollars? Jesus Christ, there are war criminals walking around with smaller bounties. What does Judge Boyer think he's doing—protecting an innocent world from my rabid little brother? Emmett is a Vietnam vet, a POW, a goddamn war hero! He should be out on his own recognizance. Even a two-bit judge like Boyer should know what constitutes appropriate bail."

She sat back, embarrassed by her outburst. Larry O'Hara was very tall, very thin, all elbows and knees, and had the emaciated look of a marathon runner. His white shirt was loose at his neck, and his tan polyester suit jacket too short in the sleeves. He wore a wide multi-colored tie, tied in a thick knot the size of a fist. Maggie had forgotten how badly men dressed in Gatesburg. Even the police wore leisure suits.

"This is a small town, Maggie. You've forgotten," O'Hara said quietly.

"You, and everyone else, seem to have forgotten that Emmett is a small-town boy!"

"Hardly a boy."

"Certainly not a big-city gangster. You and I know that even if there was a crime here, it comes under the heading of small-time stuff, no megabucks involved, no unnatural practices, just an old woman and a boy and a family tragedy."

O'Hara moved restlessly in his chair. "You don't have all the facts."

"I suppose the police do?"

"Well, one at least that seems to have escaped your notice. This does come under the heading of police business, Maggie, so I urge you to think carefully before answering."

Maggie flushed. "Don't be ridiculous. You're not on television. What do you want to know? None of the DeLaceys have anything to hide from the police, or this town . . ."

"Do you know, or did you at any time know, of a two-hundred-and-fifty-thousand-dollar mortgage on this property?"

"Of course not. My mother paid the mortgage off years ago. And it wasn't anything near that amount."

O'Hara pulled a scrap of paper from his pocket and consulted it. "It says here that a mortgage for that sum was issued by Gatesburg National. It was signed by your mother and Emmett. A lot of people would consider a quarter of a million dollars motive enough for murder."

"I don't believe it." If Maggie was nonplussed, she was determined not to show any reaction to Larry O'Hara. "Of course you realize this is a valuable farm property and it costs a good deal to keep running properly. My mother and Emmett may well have decided to make some capital investments."

The detective glanced around the kitchen, then added, offhandedly, "That's one of the reasons the district attorney's office recommended that bail be set high."

"One of the reasons?" Maggie watched O'Hara gazing out the kitchen window at the unpainted barns and broken equipment littering the yard, and she thought, Oh God, what now?

A silver Mercedes was circling the farmhouse; it stopped behind the kitchen door. Someone who knew their way around the farm, she realized. The front door was never used in winter and had not been opened since the funeral.

"There's talk around the courthouse that there was pressure. It's just a rumor," O'Hara continued as Maggie stared at the Mercedes, "but there's talk your brother, the bishop, had something to do with the amount of bail."

Maggie's head snapped around. "Don't be absurd! That doesn't make any sense."

"Well, it does if the rumor is right—that the bishop . . . your brother . . . wants Emmett kept behind bars."

"Our family, Lieutenant, doesn't conspire against each other. You do watch too much television—" Maggie stopped. A woman stepped out of the front seat of the 380SL. She was wearing L. L. Bean gumshoes and jeans under a full-length red fox fur. Vanessa Harris.

"Our mother killed herself by accident. There's nothing more to say."

"The evidence doesn't support an accident, Maggie. We could consider suicide, naturally, but there's no note. There usually is." The detective stood. His height made the room appear smaller, and she remembered then that her high school had gone to the state basketball finals a few years after she had graduated.

He followed her to the back door.

"You know, I used to play ball with Emmett when he first got back from Vietnam. He was a damn good power forward."

"Well, what do you think? Do you really think someone like Emmett could kill his mother?"

"I'm sorry to say, Miss DeLacey, but I think he could. We had a run-in once, out at the Crossroads Tavern. He can be a real mean sonofabitch, that brother of yours."

Vanessa Harris knocked at the porch door, calling Maggie's name.

"I don't think you know Emmett." Larry O'Hara lowered his voice. "I don't think you know how crazy that guy can be." He shoved open the door and stepped into the cold morning without a word of good-bye.

Vanessa rushed in, talking nervously.

"Paddy sent me over. He's gone up to Chicago for me, for the country club, I mean. He knows the president of the Illinois PGA, and he went to see if he can get them to hold their tournament this year at the club. It would make all the difference for us if we could get the championship here in Gatesburg."

"Damn it," Maggie said. "He said he would help with the animals." She was suddenly furious with Paddy Jack.

"May I help?" Vanessa offered. Relaxed now, she slipped out of her fur coat. She had on gumshoes and tight-fitting jeans, but she was also wearing a light blue cashmere sweater set and tiny sapphire earrings.

"Thanks, Van, but I think I can manage for another day. I'm trying to get one of the Grange boys to work for us. It's too much to handle by myself, even with Paddy's help." Maggie smiled quickly, then asked, "Would you care for a cup of coffee?"

"Yes, please." Vanessa paused a moment, studying Maggie, and then she added, "And maybe it would help if you told me what has upset you. Was it Larry O'Hara?"

Maggie forced herself to smile.

"Actually, my whole morning has been a problem. The telephone rang at dawn—somebody else trying to jump on the DeLacey troubles, I thought. But this time it was actually an offer to help. A telegram from Washington offering me bail money, but with plenty of emotional strings attached." Maggie shook her head. "I'm sorry, Van, you don't want to hear all this. It's just that I hate it—all these god-damn intrusions into our family's private business.

"Then O'Hara came out about an hour ago to snoop around and tell me that he knows Emmett is crazy and killed Mother."

"He's trying to make a name for himself," Vanessa explained. "A case like this gives O'Hara a chance to get known, and next election he'll run for sheriff. Gatesburg hasn't had a murder trial since that drifter raped and killed the Olsens' girl, Barbara Anne. You remember?" She took a cup of coffee from Maggie.

"Maybe you're right. But there was an element of vindictiveness about O'Hara that was frightening."

"Oh, I can't believe that!" Vanessa placed her coffee cup on the kitchen table and then sat down herself.

Maggie shrugged. "Well, that's what I got."

"Don't worry about it. They're always saying something about the DeLaceys in Gatesburg. If not your family, then ours. I'm sure the whole town knew how much I got from Brad Adair when we divorced."

An edge of anger had slipped into Vanessa's tone. It surprised Maggie; she had never heard the woman raise her voice. It made her feel closer to her.

"You can drive yourself crazy worrying what Gatesburg people think. They're jealous for the most part. You have a very successful family, Margaret, and all of you have done it on your own."

"Well, If I'm so successful," Maggie said, laughing, "then why am I out slopping pigs at six in the morning?"

"Oh, you know what I mean . . . Foreign correspondent . . ."

"Divorcée . . ."

"Well, who isn't!" Vanessa glanced over at Maggie. "Sometimes I think that's the mark of real achievement. Having survived a marriage and a divorce."

"I'll drink to that." Maggie suddenly felt much better. She was glad now that Vanessa had dropped by the farm and realized how lonely she had been since she'd returned from Africa and Ireland.

"Well, Van, why don't we quit talking about the DeLaceys and all their problems." She laughed. "What about your problems? Tell me about your husband."

"Oh, God, no! I'll just get depressed. He left me for a woman half my age. An airline stewardess. They kept meeting on the same overnight trip. He's handsome enough, and . . . No! I don't want to talk about Brad."

"All right!" Maggie paused. There was something she did want to know, had always wanted to know, and she wondered now if Vanessa would tell her. "What about . . . tell me, Van, what happened between you two, Paddy Jack and you?"

Vanessa smiled sadly. "You do ask the tough ones, don't you, Margaret Mary?" She sighed. "Well, I guess you're old enough. And there's certainly no reason why you shouldn't know the truth."

# · CHAPTER 29 ·

## GATESBURG: 1961

PADDY JACK HIT A screamer. Using a four wood, he drove down on the tight lie. The golf ball stayed low through the trees, but once over the creek it caught the late afternoon breeze and took off, cleared the cluster of bunkers in the right rough, and dropped safely on the narrow fairway. It was a great shot, leaving him less than a soft wedge to the eighteenth green.

"Damn you, DeLacey!" Craig Evans angrily slammed his wood against the ground. He thought Paddy Jack was trapped in the trees and would have to waste a shot by playing his ball safely out into the fairway.

Paddy smiled. Craig Evans was the son of a club member. Paddy Jack always felt terrific beating rich kids—the ones who thought their fathers' money made them special. "Okay, Craig, catch me!" he shouted, and grabbing his golf bag, he swung it easily onto his shoulder and strode from the deep rough.

On Monday afternoons the course was officially closed, but Mr. Harris allowed Paddy Jack to play golf. And all summer long, he had been challenging members' sons, offering each of them Monday matches at five dollars a hole. Evans, three years older than Paddy Jack, was on the Yale golf team. But Paddy Jack wasn't worried. He knew Evans did not have enough club to reach the green, unless he got lucky.

Evans got lucky. He hit a thin three wood from the short grass. The shot duck-hooked to the left and caught the front bunker. But then the ball hit a metal rake left in the sand and, bouncing forward, ran to within ten feet of the pin, leaving a makable birdie putt.

Evans shouted out, laughing, then turned and gave Paddy Jack the finger. "Finally!" he yelled across the fairway. "Finally I got a god-damn break!"

But Paddy Jack was already striding off, concentrating on the distance between his ball and the cup, deciding how to play his wedge shot to the green.

Paddy Jack had not yet lost a Monday match. "I only take money from these guys so I can spend it on you," Paddy had told Vanessa early in the summer. And it was true. He gave his mother his pro-shop salary, keeping only the members' tips himself. Even that money he shared with Catty and the twins.

The money he won from the members' sons was never mentioned at home. He needed it for Vanessa. Spending money on her made him feel older. It made him feel free from everyone. And he liked the idea that he had won it at golf. He liked knowing that none of the members could beat him. And he couldn't let Craig Evans win today.

Paddy Jack pulled up his wedge from his bag and dropped the clubs. He had more confidence in his wedge than any other iron in his bag, and knew exactly what he needed to do: hit the shot high, over the top of the flag, and with enough spin so it would draw back toward the cup. He played quickly, not letting himself get tense over the shot. His goal was to get his ball closer to the cup than Craig's so that the pressure of the match would shift back to the member's son.

Opening his stance, he took a long, loose swing, making sure he hit through the shot. As soon as he touched the ball, he knew it was on line and would play. His only worry was that the ball might catch a hard spot at the top of the green and not spin back to the cup, but it didn't—the ball went six feet beyond the flag, then spun back, rolled down the steep green and into the hole.

Craig Evans threw down his bag and slammed his putter to the ground. "If you aren't the luckiest sonofabitch!" he swore, bending to pick up his scattered clubs.

"What do you mean, luck?" As Paddy Jack grinned he saw Vanessa running toward them. "What are you doing here?" he called, pretending, for Evans's benefit, to be surprised. But he knew. As always, she had been watching the match from the clubhouse. And as always, when he made a spectacular shot, she was coming down to retrieve the lucky ball.

She scooped it out of the cup, held it up, and pretended to kiss it. Then she ran down to where he and Evans were standing in the fairway.

"What are you doing, Van?" Craig called as she approached. "I can't believe you're one of this guy's fans."

As an answer, Vanessa ran into Paddy Jack's arms.

"You could have beaten Arnold Palmer today, darling," she said, and, in front of Craig Evans, kissed her father's employee.

"Your father's not going to like it when he hears you were making out with me on the eighteenth green," Paddy Jack told Vanessa as they drove home from the movies later that night.

"It's okay. Dad likes you. Yesterday at dinner he said that the best thing he ever did was hire you to run the pro shop even though you've only been to high school."

"Yeah, I can run the shop and keep the members happy—but he'd still like it a lot better if we weren't going out."

"He's just protective, that's all." She smiled to dismiss his worry. "Daddy knows I'm going to date whoever I want. He just thinks I shouldn't get crazy about anyone. I'm nineteen. I have three years left at Vassar. And he has these grand plans I'm going to become a lawyer or something. You know how fathers are."

"No, I don't. I haven't seen my old man in years."

"Well, don't take it out on me, okay?" Why did he want to spoil the best part of the evening, the part she had been thinking about all week? "If you're going to have a chip on your shoulder about everything, then I don't want to go out with you!"

"I'm sorry," he said, turning the car east toward Gatesburg. "But it makes me mad when people hold it against me that the old man left us and died, or the fact that we don't have much money. Shit, when I get on the tour, I'm going to be winning maybe five thousand a week. Then what do you think this town is going to say? They'll be kissing my ass, that's what. Your old man, too."

"Don't talk like that about my father. Don't talk like that at all in front of me."

"I'm sorry," he said quickly.

"No you're not," she answered, not looking at him. She was concentrating on the narrow road and the gray light the headlights made against the concrete. She rolled the side window down and turned her face into the night breeze. "I've never done anything to you," she went on in a low voice. "It's not my fault Daddy owns the country club. And he has helped you. Given you time off to play in tournaments, letting you practice on Mondays."

"I'm not talking about your old man."

"Well, I don't know anything about the other people in this town. I didn't go to school here; I only know a handful of kids, and they live on the point."

"It's the kids from the point I'm talking about. All those rich assholes! Sukie Hoyt and her crowd."

"I don't hang around with them."

"I didn't say you did." He hated arguing with Vanessa. She had the knack of always being right.

"I think Sukie Hoyt is a jerk, too."

"You should be there when she comes down to the pro shop. She thinks her shit doesn't stink."

"Paddy, please, don't be vulgar!"

"I am vulgar. I'm Irish, aren't I?" He raced the Chevy into the country-club road, then immediately slowed down. It was a warm June night and he knew that the members who lived in the houses lining Country Club Road would be sitting on their terraces, enjoying the summer night. Any one of them would be eager to tell Tom Harris how that DeLacey boy had raced his wreck of a car down the drive just so he could get Vanessa home before midnight.

"Why are you always putting yourself down?" she asked.

"I'm not! What do you mean?" He kept driving slowly, realizing that all too soon they would be at her home, the huge white rambling Victorian mansion that was built on a rise behind the tenth tee.

Vanessa shrugged. "You do, you know. Put yourself down. It's like you're afraid someone will do it, so you beat them to it. I don't think 'the Irish' are vulgar people."

"You don't count. They do." He nodded toward the houses on both sides of Country Club Road.

"I know one thing, DeLacey." She turned suddenly and, pulling her legs up under her, slid over next to him in the front seat. Lacing her arms around his neck, she touched the inside of his ear with the tip of her tongue. "I don't want you to take me home."

"It's almost twelve."

"I don't care."

"Your old man will be pissed enough at me."

"He went out to the point for dinner, he told me. And he never gets back until after midnight. What's the matter, don't you want to make out?" She nipped his neck.

Usually they would park in the front drive of her house until her father flashed the porch light, telling her it was time to come inside. But Paddy Jack was nervous. Vanessa seemed to know something and she wasn't telling him what it was.

When he didn't answer, she bit his ear.

"Jesus, Harris!" The car swerved, left the road, bounced over the ruts left by the rains, and stopped. Startled, they both sat quiet for a few minutes. Then Paddy Jack gunned the engine. "Okay, Harris, now you're going to get it!" He swung the Chevy, not back onto the road but into the stand of pine trees that lined the length of the fairway, and from there raced the car toward the golf course. He had always wanted to drive across the country club.

"Paddy!" Van braced herself against the dashboard. She was frightened now. "Don't!" she shouted as the car bumped over the fairway. "You're scaring me."

The car shot out onto the course and he spun it left, then felt the

Chevy slip out of control. Vanessa screamed as they spun out on the long wet grass. It had not rained that night, but Paddy realized the greenkeepers must have watered the fairways.

He wheeled the car around and got it under control. Vanessa caught her breath and leaned back. "Why did you do that?"

"I don't know." He shrugged.

"Yes, you do."

"Maybe I just wanted to impress you."

"By getting us killed?"

"Are you kidding? There's no way I would wreck this Chevy."

"Take me home, please. When you get this way, I don't want to be with you." She slid away and leaned against the car door. He was still driving without lights, but it was a bright night and she could see his profile.

He was all angles and hard edges, she thought, watching him. Tough looking. Cocky. That was why her father, her friends, were put off by him. He looked like a hood, they said. That was true. He looked that way now in the dark car, the way his mouth knotted and drew the skin tight over his high cheekbones. They way he hitched his shoulders. He never masked his feelings for the sake of others, nor would he be nice just to get along. He had none of the social graces she had learned from her father. It wasn't his fault. His father, she knew, had deserted the family, gone back to Ireland, and died. And Paddy Jack's mother wasn't nice. Vanessa had seen her working as a maid at Country Club Road parties. Who could blame Paddy Jack for going crazy at times? It was lucky he was normal at all, Vanessa thought.

In the moonlight she could see that he had brought her home the back way, circling around the tenth green, and then driven through the farm fields behind her house. The night-lights were still on at her house, as well as the front-porch light. That meant her father was still at the point, and she was sorry now that she had told Paddy Jack to take her home.

She also secretly wished that he would be more forceful with her, more demanding. But that wasn't his way. He wouldn't even fight for a kiss. "I don't beg," he had told her once, when she put up a little show of not letting him kiss her the first time. "If you want to make out, okay, but if you're going to play hard to get, forget it."

He stopped the Chevy but did not turn off the engine. She knew what that meant. She had hurt his feelings, and now he was going to make her pay. He wouldn't kiss her good night, and at the club to-morrow he would avoid her. For all his tough ways, she thought, he couldn't stand to be hurt.

"You can come in and have a Coke or something," she offered.

"No, I better be getting home. It's going to be a long day tomorrow; I've got players teeing off starting at seven A.M." He had his hands braced against the steering wheel and his chin tucked between his stiff forearms. He didn't look at her.

"Come on, Paddy, don't be a jerk," she whispered. "I'm sorry if I hurt your feelings. I didn't mean anything. My God, you're touchy!"

"I'm not touchy. It's just that I've got this tough day tomorrow."

"Fine," said Vanessa. "You go home to your mom, then, Paddy Jack. But I've got one thing to say. You like to go around with this chip on your shoulder, feeling superior to everyone, thinking everyone is a jerk, and you're a hotshot because no one can beat you. But you haven't played anyone but members and a few local pros; none of them are any good in the first place. You're full of all this great talk about going on the tour, being a PGA pro, and until then you just look down on us as if we're a bunch of jokers and get furious when anyone says anything the least bit critical of you, especially people who are trying to help you make it." She began to cry, and for a moment she could not speak and kept choking as she tried to go on.

Paddy Jack slipped her into his arms and let her cry against his shoulder. He kissed her hair, still warm from the summer sun, kissed the softness of her neck, kissed her damp cheek, kissed her until she began to respond to him. Turning in the dark front seat, she pulled him into an embrace.

Her hands curled into his thick black hair, and she held his face in her palms, opening her lips to his mouth. He had never kissed her that way before; she wasn't sure he had ever kissed anyone that way.

Vanessa knew Paddy Jack was a virgin, but she didn't mind. She liked knowing she was more experienced, more sexual. It was a gift she meant Paddy to share.

"Paddy . . ." She drew his hands across her breasts, steered his fingers to the buttons of her blouse, and when he touched her, she shivered with delight.

She lay back in the seat, forgetting everything in her surrender— that the truck was parked in front of her father's house, that she had so recently been angry at this boy she now passionately loved, all of it was lost in the warm touch of his hands.

"Paddy," she whispered, knowing that he would make love to her then if she wanted him to. In those few moments she had somehow stripped off her white cotton blouse, leaving her breasts bare.

"I'm sorry they're so small," she said when he pulled back, gazing at them.

"They're beautiful," he whispered, transfixed by the sight of the creamy mounds, white against the dark of her summer tan.

"Here," she whispered, "they want you to kiss them." She drew his face down to her breasts and carefully, gently, fed him each of the pink nipples, watched as he licked the perspiration off her soft cones. Sex was so wonderful, she thought. So incredibly wonderful, especially with Paddy Jack.

She could taste her desire for him at the back of her throat. She wanted to slide her hand across the muscles of his stomach, slip her fingers beneath his belt, run her hands lightly across the tightness of his buttocks. She was dizzy with anticipation. But they had to get away from her house.

"Come on." She slipped away from him and pulled her blouse back on. "Let's go onto the course."

Paddy nodded, fumbled with the car door, hurrying. His hands were trembling and he was out of breath. "Would you . . . ?" He stopped and blushed. "I have a blanket I can bring—all right?"

"Good!" Vanessa smiled to herself. She had been sneaking off into the dark golf course since she was in junior high, going with boys from Gatesburg Day School to neck in the bunkers beyond the eleventh tee.

It was on her father's golf course that she had lost her virginity. Given it to Drew Brennan after her sixteenth-birthday party. He was the captain of the day school's lacrosse team, the president of his senior class. When she made love to him, she thought she would be in love for life, but that fall when Drew went off to college in St. Louis he hadn't even driven to the club to say good-bye. It was Christmas before she got over him. And that spring, when she started to hang out around the clubhouse, she noticed Paddy Jack, and fell in love again.

The grass of the rough was coarse between her toes, but the fairway, when they reached it, was smooth. She ran downhill into the hollow of the dogleg, to the cluster of oaks at the bend of the fairway. She wanted Paddy Jack to spread the blanket there, so they would be out under the stars yet as hidden as if in a tree house, close enough to the creek to hear water rushing under the wooden bridge.

"Van! Vanessa, where are you?" Paddy Jack whispered her name in the darkness, afraid his voice might be heard in the houses along the drive.

She spun around on tiptoe in the dark, did cartwheels in the open fairway, danced before him as he came to her. He ran down the slope of rough to where she stood, poised like a ballerina in white, standing still and gleaming in the darkness.

She waited until he was close enough to touch, then darted off, wanting him to chase her, to seize her, to catch her like a prize. And he did, sweeping her into his arms, letting her bury her face in the warmth of his neck.

"Here," she said, when he ran by the oaks. She jumped from his arms and quickly opened the car blanket.

"Here?" He peered into the dark. The green was below them. He could see even the white flagstaff, and to the right of the green were members' homes. He could see lights on the second floor of the Embreys'.

"No one is going to see us." She took hold of his hand and tugged him onto the blanket. "I promise," she whispered, slipping her fingers beneath his shirt.

"Wait!" he asked.

"Shh!" She bent over his body and kissed him quickly. "I know what I'm doing." She reached for his jeans and he held her, tumbled her down on the blanket beside him, and quickly found her mouth. She struggled against him to give herself more pleasure and with her free hand unsnapped her skirt and pulled it off, leaving him to slip off her white panties.

He groaned at first sight of the pale blond triangle of her sex. "You're so beautiful!"

"Kiss me?" she asked, arching toward him.

His lips touched her carefully, and she thought again how all this was so new to him, and how wonderful it was, that it was her body he was loving.

For a moment, they sat still, waiting, watching each other. He looked so serious she thought, apprehensive, and she leaned over to kiss him on the lips, to inhale his smell, and that provoked him, as she knew it would, and he came at her, eager and out of control.

"Wait," she said, but she realized he couldn't, and to save herself from being hurt, she helped him inside, holding her breath at the pain. Then she could not do anything, not even speak, and she moaned as he hunched up and drove against her. Once, twice. Soon he would come, she knew, and she seized him with both hands, tugged his hair. He kept riding her, driving farther, then farther, until finally all she could focus on was her own body. She rocked against him, drew her nails across his skin, wanting, she realized, to mark him, and then he came, and she came, and she couldn't get her breath at all, and she looped her legs around his waist, hooked her body to his and kept whispering to him that it was all right, all right, until he finished, and sank against her, sweating and exhausted.

"Have you ever done this before?" he asked, when he spoke.

She shook her head.

"But you know everything," he said.

"A girl just knows." She smiled at him, remembering how the day after she had sex with Drew Brennan on that same slope of fairway, she could not walk at all, and had stayed in bed all day, telling her father it was because of her period. If her mother had been alive, she would never have gotten away with it. But her father was dumb when it came to knowing about girls.

"Well, what do you think?" she asked, laughing. "Is it better than hitting a golf ball dead solid perfect?"

"Yes, I think it is . . . almost."

He was ready again. He had never pulled out of her, and now she could feel him hardening. It would be even better this time, she knew, lying back on the blanket to let him do what he wanted with her.

Then she heard voices. She wasn't sure at first, but she felt Paddy Jack react and quickly raise himself off her body. He grabbed for his clothes.

"Shh. They won't see us. Be still," Vanessa ordered. She looked over her shoulder. The voices grew louder, approaching from across the creek. They would cross at the bridge, she realized, and if they kept coming up the slope, they would pass within a half-dozen yards of where she had spread the blanket.

"The trees," Paddy Jack whispered, and grabbed Vanessa by the arm, half pulled her into the middle of the dogwoods. They crouched against the trunks and she began giggling at the silliness of them, naked and hiding on the dark golf course. Paddy Jack covered her mouth, swore under his breath for her to shut up. There were footsteps on the wooden bridge and a man laughed. The couple were within a dozen yards of them.

"But it's early," a man's voice said, and Vanessa caught her breath.

She didn't hear the murmured answer. Looking around the corner of the dogwood, she could see the bridge and, at her odd angle, saw them embrace, two dark figures silhouetted in the moonlight.

"I'm going," Vanessa said, and without waiting, turned and ran, pausing only to scoop her clothes off the blanket. She ran naked across the open fairway.

Paddy Jack caught her in the elm trees that lined the country-club road. She had stopped to dress before crossing to her house. His car was still parked in the driveway of her house. There were still no lights on inside. Her father was not home, as she had half hoped he might be, though she knew better. She began to cry.

"Why did you run?" Paddy Jack said, pulling on his own jeans.

"I felt like it."

"Wasn't that Mr. Cutler? It sounded like him laughing. Jesus, you scared me when you started running. I thought they had spotted us or something." He was grinning, feeling safe again with his clothes on.

"I don't know. I don't care." She walked out of the trees and across the road, up to her house.

"Van, don't. Your father's not home." He tagged after her, stuffing his cotton shirt into his jeans. "You said you could stay out."

"That was my father on the bridge," she announced, "with some woman! Goddamn him!"

She ran from Paddy Jack. She ran into the house, ran upstairs to her room, banging the doors behind her. He couldn't do this to her, she swore, throwing herself on her bed. Her father couldn't be having an affair with *that* woman, and she buried her face in her pillow, knowing, as she tried to deny what she had glimpsed on the dark golf course, that it was all true.

# · CHAPTER 30 ·

## GATESBURG: 1961

"YOU'RE NOT GOING OUT with that Harris girl tonight, are you, Paddy?" Caitlin demanded. She put a plate of fried chicken on the table, then turned back to the stove. "We haven't seen you at all this summer. If it wasn't that you show up for meals, I'd think you forgot you had a family now that you're hanging out with the likes of her."

"Hey, Mom! I couldn't ever forget you or your meals," Paddy Jack said, smiling after his mother as he reached across the table and grabbed a piece of chicken off the plate.

"You eat like a pig," Catty volunteered.

Paddy Jack gave her the finger.

"Mommy, Paddy is doing a dirty thing!" Maggie shouted, hoping to catch her mother's attention.

Paddy Jack reached out to swat her, but Maggie ducked away, scooting off her chair.

"Don't you hit my sister!" Emmett squeezed out of his chair and punched the back of his older brother's head.

"Hey! What are you doing?" Instinctively, Paddy Jack slapped back at his kid brother.

"You leave him alone!" Maggie cried. Rallying to her twin's defense, she came back to the table and grabbed Paddy Jack around the neck, pulling at his thick black hair. Emmett faded back into the corner.

"Jesus!" Paddy swore. "She's a maniac."

"Padraic, don't be using that caddyshack language around here," Caitlin ordered. She slammed a bowl of steaming beans on the table. "I'm not sending you to Catholic school so you can come home swearing like some kind of bum."

"Then get the two of them off me! They're like animals, these goddamn brats!"

"All of you are like animals," Catty observed. She pushed her food away and stood.

"And where do you think you're going?" Caitlin asked.

"I can't eat with these creeps! I can't even read when they're around." Catty had brought a book to read to the table, and she picked it up to leave.

"Sit down before I give you the back of my hand. You haven't touched your food, and here I've been cooking for the last two hours."

"I'll eat later, by myself!"

"You will not, girl. I won't have you dragging food out of the fridge all evening, leaving a mess of dishes. I want everyone to eat together, like a family should."

"Then why isn't Mike here? You gave him supper an hour ago!" Catty slipped into her chair and slammed her book down beside her plate. The other children were silent around the kitchen table.

"Your brother has a novena tonight at Saint Pat's. He's getting dressed. Paddy, I want you to drop him off at the rectory. I have to take the truck." His mother glanced at the clock. "I'm due at the Cutlers' within the hour. Catty, did you do my uniform?"

"Yes, I ironed your dumb dress." Catty sighed as she played with her plate of food. "I hate chicken," she said, pushing away her plate. "Why can't we have something good? Last night it was liver, the day before . . ." She went on, and Paddy Jack spoke over her complaining, "You're not working the Cutlers' party, are you?"

"I am. Mrs. Cutler rang me up this afternoon. The colored girl who helps has a child down with the flu."

"But I'm going to the Cutlers', with Van! She asked me today."

"Aye?" Caitlin had sat down herself at the long table and she looked over at him. "Will you be ashamed with me working in the kitchen and you with all those high-up people? Is that what's troubling you? Do you think your rich girlfriend is going to be embarrassed? Well, it's too bad for you. How else am I going to keep food on the table and all of you in clothes, I'd like to know? It's not for myself I'll be working tonight." She forked a boiled potato onto her plate. A high color had risen in her cheeks. "Your father left us penniless. If I didn't take these jobs for pay, you'd all be in foster homes —which is where some of you belong!"

She glanced around the kitchen table. Her outburst had silenced them again.

"Mom, I do what I'm told," Catty whined. It was getting worse every day, she thought. She couldn't wait until school started.

"Some days I wish to God I didn't have the lot of you," Caitlin went on. "Michael is the only one who appreciates what I've done for you. Paddy Jack, and yes, you, too, Catty, you don't do a lick around here that I can see." She kept talking, but she could feel the rage building in Catty.

"Well, I wish I hadn't been born!" Catty burst out. "I'm sick and tired of you picking on me all the time. All you ever do . . . oh, I hate it. I hate it!" She pushed the chair away from the table, and crying, ran from the kitchen and out of the house, letting the doors bang behind her.

No one was eating but Caitlin. Cutting into a hot potato, she glanced at the twins and said, "Eat up, you two." Her voice was firm and flat but she smiled at her youngest children.

The front door banged open and they could hear Catty coming, running back into the house and up the stairs to her attic room. They followed the sound of the footsteps on the bare staircase, and when Catty's bedroom door slammed shut, Maggie spoke up.

"Me and Emmett, Mom, we'll do the dishes," she whispered.

"Don't worry, kids. I can handle them," Paddy Jack said.

"And who will take Michael down to church, I ask you?"

"He can have my car, Mom. Then he won't have to worry about getting home tonight," Paddy Jack said, tired of all the arguing.

"And what about you and your rich girlfriend?"

"Hey, Mom, lay off, okay?" He tried to soften his tone. That was all they seemed to do, fight at the table. His mother was never happy anymore. It was only when Michael was eating with them that she didn't go into some kind of rage at Catty or himself. They were the ones she picked on, not Michael or the twins. "I'll call Van; we can use her car."

"I saw that car of hers. It has no top."

"It's a convertible, Mom. It's not supposed to have a top!"

"And do you think I don't know what a convertible is?" She was about to say more, when Michael came rushing down the stairs and into the kitchen.

"What's the matter with the Cat?" Michael went to the sink to pour himself a glass of water. He had just shaved and showered and was wearing a newly ironed white shirt with his black seminary trousers. "She's up there crying."

"Her nose is out of joint, that's all," Caitlin answered, finishing her meal. "The girl's too sensitive for her own good. She'll be fine fast enough if Kathey Handley telephones wanting to go into town for the movies." Caitlin pushed herself away from the table and stood, moving slowly. She still had the evening's work ahead, another four hours on her feet.

"How you doing, Mom?" Michael asked, watching his mother. When he had come home from the seminary earlier that summer he had been surprised by the way his mother looked. She had lost weight and dyed her hair. For the first time in years, she looked younger, happier. She did not look forty, he thought, and knew it was the outside work that helped keep her fit. It was good she was getting out and mixing with people at the country club, and not being trapped on the farm day in and day out.

"Oh, I've got my same aches and pains." She smiled at Michael and her face softened. "Will you be late, dear?"

"I might be, Mom. Monsignor Donohoe is down from Chicago and he has slides of his trip to the Vatican. I won't get away until I see them, that's for sure. Father Dermot doesn't know how to operate the school's projector."

"I'll wait up." She went past him, carrying her dishes to the sink.

"Leave the dishes, Mom!" he ordered. "The others can clean up the kitchen. Mag, quit playing with your food and help your mother."

"We'll clean up, Mom," Maggie said.

"Go ahead, Mom, and get dressed," Michael added. He turned to Paddy Jack. "Can you run me into town?"

"He's getting his rich girl to pick him up in her fancy car," Caitlin spoke up. "He hasn't a worry about getting places, not with the likes of her around."

"Okay, Mom," Michael said quickly, trying to slip past without a fight. All summer, it seemed, she and Paddy Jack had been at each other's throats. At times Michael wished the summer were over and he was back in the peace and calm of the seminary. "Did you play the exhibition match against Oliver?" Michael asked Paddy Jack to change the subject.

Paddy nodded. "I finished six under."

"Six under! Against a pro! All right, Paddy!" He came around the kitchen and slapped Paddy Jack on the back. "What did Oliver have?"

"Seventy-one. I beat him by four shots." Paddy Jack glanced up, grinning. "I birdied the five and had an eagle on sixteen. Holed a short wedge from off the green. I thought Oliver would shit when that wedge dropped. I must have been outdriving him by twenty yards on the par fours."

"Hey, Mom!" Michael turned around to catch his mother's attention. She was drying her hands at the sink. "Paddy Jack beat the Illinois PGA champ, Tom Oliver!"

"Was there any money in it?" Caitlin asked, pausing in the kitchen doorway.

"No. It was a golf exhibition. The pro got paid by the club to come put on an exhibition. Mr. Harris asked me to play because I'm the best golfer at the course."

"If you beat him, they should have given you money."

"It doesn't work like that, Mom," Michael explained. "Paddy just works at the club." He turned back to his younger brother. "What did old man Harris say?"

Paddy Jack shrugged, then replied between bites. "Nothing. 'Nice game.' You know what he's like."

"Paddy's the best golfer in all of Illinois," Maggie said, nodding her head emphatically.

"And who said so, Miss Sports Information?" Michael came up behind his little sister and, kissing her cheek, embraced her.

"Be careful, Michael, you'll only be getting food on your clean shirt," Caitlin said. "Maggie, clear the table, you and Emmett, and I'll send Catty down to wash the dishes."

"You take the car," Paddy told Michael. "Van can pick me up."

"What are you guys doing tonight? Coming to devotions?"

"Sure." Paddy grinned at his brother. "I don't know what we'll do. Maybe go over to the highway and play miniature golf. Van likes miniature golf; she can beat me."

"What about the Cutlers' party?"

Paddy Jack glanced at the door. Their mother had gone upstairs to change into her black uniform. He shook his head, not looking at Michael. "We're supposed to, but I ain't going, not with Mom there. It would make me feel funny. Her too. It's not worth it."

Michael nodded. All summer they had avoided talking about Paddy Jack and Vanessa, about what Paddy Jack was going to do now that he was out of high school. Michael knew they had to talk about his future, the farm, and everyone else in the family—before it was time for him to return to the seminary.

"Walk me to the car," Michael suggested. Then he kissed Maggie on top of her head as he released her.

"You're going to talk secrets, aren't you?" Maggie asked.

"Yes, we're going to talk about putting you two in reform school," Michael teased, and then saw the sudden look of shock cross Emmett's face. "Hey, Emmett, don't worry. You have to stay here and take care of Mom. Okay?" He smiled down at the twins, thinking that before he returned to the seminary, he would have to take Emmett into Gatesburg to get the kid a real haircut. Their mother had been cutting Emmett's hair all summer, and now he looked like a concentration-camp survivor, with his black hair shaved high about his ears.

Paddy Jack followed Michael out the kitchen door and over to the barn, where he had parked his Chevy in the shade of the trees.

"Are you going to take the pro job?" Michael asked, once they were out of the house. Walking beside Paddy Jack, he dwarfed his brother. At six-four, Michael was six inches taller than Paddy Jack and broader across the shoulders. He made his brother seem much more than three years younger. They did not look like brothers, except that they both had their mother's dark blue eyes and her thick black hair. Otherwise, Paddy Jack had his father's slight, wiry build, his sharp features, and hawkish nose.

"Harris hasn't said anything to me."

"Yeah, but you have the job, don't you?"

Paddy Jack shrugged. "Van thinks so."

They reached the car and Paddy Jack dug into his jeans to pull out the keys. "It needs gas," he said.

Michael grinned. "It always needs gas when I borrow it."

"Well, it does. I'm just asking you to get gas, not pay." He pulled out a money clip thick with bills.

"Where did you get all that?" Michael was startled; no one in his family had ever had that much cash.

"Side bets on the match today." Paddy Jack was smiling. Spending the summer in the sun had left him with a deep tan and it made his eyes sparkle.

"You mean you bet on yourself?"

"Sure, why not? I knew I could beat him. Oliver has never played the course. I had him by three shots by the end of nine." Paddy Jack peeled off a twenty. "This is for the gas. Do you need any money?" He looked up, aware that the money had given him a new edge in his relationship with his older brother.

Michael shook his head. "The seminary gives me what I need. It's a job, too, you know. Look, Pat!" Michael nodded toward the house. "Give it to Mom; she can use it."

"I give her my salary, Mike. What I make on the side, I'm saving." He slipped the money clip back into his tight jeans.

"Saving for what, to marry Vanessa Harris?" Michael studied his brother, searched for a sign of some sort. When they were smaller, there wasn't anything that Michael didn't know about his kid brother, but as Paddy Jack got older and spent all his time at the country club, they had less in common. At times, Michael felt Paddy Jack wasn't much more than a stranger to him, a stranger driving by in Vanessa Harris's baby-blue convertible.

"I'm trying to get a couple thousand together and send Mom and the kids to Ireland. It would give them a chance to see Dad's grave, you know." Paddy Jack was leaning against the top of the Chevy, his arms folded under his chin. He looked away as he spoke, as if what he was saying was embarrassing. "It would be good for Mom, you know, if she could see his grave, the relatives at home." His voice faded away as he stared ahead, looking past the barns to the yellow August sunset.

"Mom isn't going back to Ireland, Pat," Michael answered.

"But I've got the money!"

"It doesn't matter. She'll never go."

"How do you know?" Paddy Jack asked angrily. "You think you know everything."

The kitchen door banged open and Michael saw his mother crossing the backyard to where the truck was parked. She was wearing her black starched uniform with the white lacy collar and trim and had combed her hair into a tight knot at the back of her head. He remembered when he was a little boy her hair had been long, and after she had washed her hair in the kitchen sink and dried it in the summer sun, she would carefully braid it into lengths and pin it on top of her head. She would lean over to where he sat on the linoleum kitchen floor and pick him up, kissing his face and neck until he burst into giggles, and then she'd spin around, dancing with him, as if they were all alone together in some faraway world. He still remembered, with pungent intensity, the warmth of her body, the scent of her shampoo.

"She must hate Dad for going off to Ireland and getting himself killed," Paddy Jack said. He, too, was watching their mother climb into the pickup and race the engine. Both boys winced as she ground the gears shifting into first. "And for not teaching her how to drive a stick."

Michael smiled sadly. "She doesn't hate Dad. I think she misses him."

"Then why in the hell won't she go back home and at least visit his grave? I have the money. She can take the twins."

Michael shook his head and moved around the Chevy. It was getting late.

"Well, why not?"

"She told me—when Dad went back to Ireland—she would never go home again. I remember I started to cry and I asked her why we didn't go with him. Here, I was fourteen, and Dad was leaving us. I was going crazy." He shuddered, remembering the day his father left him on the cold train platform in Gatesburg. "I begged Mom to let us all go to Ireland, and she said to me in this incredibly sad voice—and you know Mom, she never cries, but she was crying that day, right on the station platform. Anyway, she said she couldn't go back to Ireland, ever. I didn't understand what she meant and I kept carrying on like a kid until her patience just snapped. She hit me so hard I could feel my teeth rattling. And she said, 'Hush, Michael, do you want to see your mother in jail?' "

Michael mimicked his mother's voice perfectly and Paddy Jack could almost see the scene on the deserted platform.

"I had to know what she meant, so I kept at her and one day she told me her secret. Not even Dad knew this, I guess, but years ago, during the Second World War, when Mom was working in Dublin, she got involved with the IRA and is still wanted by the Irish police."

"Mom? Did she say what she did?"

Michael shook his head and opened the car door. "She said she'd tell me someday. When I was older."

The kitchen door banged open again and Maggie came running through the apple orchard. She was shouting to Paddy Jack, telling him that Vanessa Harris was on the telephone.

"It's just like Mom, isn't it, keeping secrets. She doesn't think her own family can be trusted with the truth." Angrily, Paddy Jack ran off to meet Maggie, who had stopped to jump for a high-hanging apple bough.

"That's right, family secrets," Michael answered softly, and glanced away, looking directly into the sunset, so it didn't seem odd that he was squinting, hiding a sudden flash of tears and his own secret from his brother.

"That's the finest round of golf I've seen played here at the country club," Caitlin overheard Tom Harris saying. She was behind the owner of the country club, holding a tray of hors d'oeuvres for the guests crowded onto the terrace of the Cutler home. "The boy's got a bright future, don't you think, Tom?"

"A helluva player. The kid could be on the tour now. He reminds me a lot of Gary Player, don't you think?" another man replied, nodding at the crowd of men who clustered around him.

Caitlin looked to see who was talking. She knew the man's face, had seen his photo somewhere, she thought, on one of Paddy Jack's golf magazines. She wondered if it was her Paddy Jack they were talking about.

"He's built like Gary; looks like him; even strikes the ball from left to right the way Player does. I'll tell you all, the last eighteen-year-old that beat me in a golf exhibition was a fella by the name of Nicklaus."

The men laughed and Harris said quickly, "Well, we're trying to keep him here at the club. He's finished with school, and I'm thinking of sending him to take a PGA course for club professionals. He's going to be the club professional next season."

Aye, it was Paddy they were talking about, Caitlin realized.

"I don't know," the pro said. "If several of you fellas got together and formed a syndicate, paid for him to go on the tour, you might make yourself a nice bit of change. The way he strikes the ball, the kid should be playing tournament golf for a living."

"Wait, now!" said Harris, laughing nervously. "Don't be giving these guys ideas. I need Paddy Jack in the pro shop. Besides, he's been seeing my daughter this summer, and, well, if he's going to be part of the family, I'd rather have him working for me than following the tour."

Caitlin kept moving with her tray of tiny slices of cheese, small triangle sandwiches. But she was thinking of what Tom Harris had said: not that Paddy was a great golfer, but that he and Vanessa Harris might get married. It frightened her, realizing Paddy Jack could marry that easily and be gone from her. Gone, not in the sense of being away on the tour, where he might make a name for himself, but gone off to become Tom Harris's son-in-law.

She pushed her way through the swinging door into the kitchen. Well, she hadn't left Ireland to have her son become the lackey of high-up people in America. If Paddy Jack was as good as that other fella said, she decided, picking up a fresh tray of canapes, then she'd get him his chance on the golf tour. She'd not have him settling for second best in Gatesburg, beholden to the likes of Tom Harris.

She went back through the kitchen door into the dining room. It was empty, except for Tom Harris, who was standing with Mr. Cutler. Caitlin walked over to the two men, and said to the host, "Excuse me, sir, but I believe your wife is looking for you. She's back in the kitchen."

When the host turned and walked off to the kitchen, Caitlin said quickly to Tom Harris, "I have to speak with you."

He paused and lifted a canape off the tray. "What is it?" he whispered.

"It's this talk of Paddy Jack joining the club. I won't have it."

"He'll have a good job, Caitlin. Don't worry."

"No!" She shook her head, not looking up at him, but staying close and whispering. "Paddy Jack can do better on the tour."

"He'll do well enough with me," Tom Harris answered. "And Van will be happy if he works here. There are a lot of kids who don't make it on the tour, Caitlin. Be realistic. Regardless of what Oliver says, Paddy Jack is no Jack Nicklaus."

For the first time, Caitlin looked up at the man. And how would you be knowing that? she thought. Because he's Irish? Because he's a poor man's son? But she said none of that. Tom Harris would only deny it. Instead she said the one thing guaranteed to send her son on the tour and free him from a wife who would always be his boss. She looked straight at Tom Harris, and answered him back.

"If you don't send Paddy Jack on the tour, I'll tell your daughter who you've been sleeping with. Do you think she'd want to marry

Paddy Jack if she knew her father was having his way with me?" As Harris stood speechless, Caitlin touched her lace cap for emphasis, then lifted her tray of canapes and went to mingle with the guests on the terrace.

# · CHAPTER 31 ·

## GATESBURG: 1982

MAGGIE POURED OUT THE last of the white wine, dividing it between herself and Vanessa Harris. She never drank at noon and the wine and Vanessa's story had left her slightly dizzy and very sad.

"I remember when Paddy left home," Maggie said. "It was in the fall; we were just going back to school. Emmett and I were only kids at the time, and Paddy Jack came home late one night and told Emmett he didn't want him caddying at the country club anymore."

Maggie leaned forward and pushed the luncheon plate away, making room for her elbows on the kitchen table. As she went on talking, she picked up an orange and dug her fingernails into it. The juice hissed as she broke the thick skin and she thought of Addis and the juicy Jaffa orange Kelemwork sliced for her every morning at breakfast.

"The boys shared a bedroom and it was very late when Paddy Jack got home. Anyway, he was talking to Emmett, whispering really, and packing his clothes. I got up and ran into their room like I always did when Paddy Jack came home late from the club. But this night was different. Paddy was very angry, angrier than I'd ever seen him. He scared me that night.

" 'I don't want you caddying at the country club,' he was telling Emmett. 'I don't want you to have anything to do with them.'

" 'That's my school money. Mom ain't going to let me quit caddying.'

" 'Never mind Mom. I'll send money home to you for school.'

"Emmett was silent for a moment. I crawled in next to him and we both curled up under the covers in his bed. He had been caddying all that summer for the first time, getting up every morning at six o'clock, feeding the chickens and doing his chores, then riding his bike over to the country club. He liked to caddy, liked the money he made, and liked being able to give it all to Mom. Then he asked Paddy Jack, 'How come you don't want me working at the country club? Did I do something wrong? Am I in trouble or something?' There were tears on his cheeks.

" 'Yeah, you did something wrong,' Paddy Jack said to him. 'You're a mick. Shanty Irish. A mackerel smacker.' Paddy took a cigarette out and lit it. He never smoked in the house, but I knew he smoked. Emmett had showed me where Paddy hid his cigarettes.

"Emmett wasn't like me. When I was young, I never wanted to know the truth of something. If I went to bed and thought there was a monster in the closet, fine! I never wanted to climb out of bed and go investigate. Not Emmett. He needed to know the last detail. So he asked Paddy if he was going to quit the country club, too.

" 'Yeah, I'm done with that place. And another thing?' He had stretched out in his bed. 'I don't want you mentioning Vanessa Harris's name to me again. I don't want to hear you talking about her, or her old man, or anything to do with them. They don't like us. They're too good for us, they think. Well, we don't need them! Any of them! We've got a list and they're on it. Got it?' Paddy Jack would always say that: 'Got it?' when he was telling us what to do.

"That night he scared me in a profound sort of way. I never forgot what he said, and I think because of it I grew up with my fist up and ready to take on the world. I did what Paddy Jack wanted. I kept your name on my list, all these years." She smiled sadly at Vanessa Harris.

"Anyway, he left that next morning, on a train for Texas. I remember standing at the station crying my eyes out when he boarded the Illinois Central, carrying his clubs, a small suitcase, and a half dozen of his golf shoes." Maggie paused a moment, noticed that it had become darker, and saw through the kitchen window that it had begun to snow again, heavy, wet flakes. "It was a cold October day, I remember. I wouldn't leave the platform, not until the train disappeared under the bridge. Then I just cried and cried, thinking I'd never see my brother again in my life."

"I'm sorry. Really. I had no idea."

"Of course you didn't. None of this is your fault. I was very young, a very impressionable child, and I loved Paddy Jack. My father had already left the family and so had Father Mike. So I missed Paddy Jack very much. I had no idea what had happened between you. I never felt I could ask Paddy about it and I never mentioned your name. You were *persona non grata* in this family."

"It's so sad," Vanessa said softly, "so terribly sad. But it wasn't my father who sent Paddy away. God knows, he's done his share of the dirty, but he wanted Paddy to take the pro job. It was your mother who insisted."

Maggie stared at Vanessa, uncomprehending.

"Your mother was the one who arranged it. My father told me he was giving the pro job to Paddy—but then your mother came up to him at some party and told him no. She said she wanted Paddy on the tour."

"I never heard that story before in my life."

"It's true. At least, I think it's true. I do know Paddy wanted the job, and I don't think my father would have lied."

"Paddy Jack never said anything about Mom."

Vanessa paused to sip her wine, then leaning back against the wooden chair, said, "I'm not sure he knows. Knowing my father, I'll bet he wouldn't have told Paddy Jack that your mother interfered."

Maggie felt suddenly light-headed, and she wondered if it were just the warm kitchen or if it was the wine. "I was angry when I saw you at the wake," Maggie said. "I was furious you had come, and then I thought, no, let's forget it. Enough is enough. And, besides, Paddy Jack seemed so happy to have found you again."

She looked directly at Vanessa, who replied, "I never forgot him. I don't think one ever gets over their first love."

"Or their first marriage," Maggie answered, laughing.

"Was Jack McGraff your first love?"

"And my first marriage. Yes."

"If you were like me, you refused to listen to your parents and got married to prove your independence."

"No, Mom wanted me to marry. She was married at eighteen herself, but of course that was the way it was done in Ireland. Mom liked Jack—what mother wouldn't? He was good-looking, a congressman, and Irish." Maggie shrugged. "It was all very exciting, being married to someone so important. And the fact that Mother liked him was important to me. I was that kind of girl; I always wanted to please Mom."

"Did you? I never really knew your mother well. I wish I had." Vanessa glanced around the room, added, "This is such a lovely country kitchen; she must've known how to make a home."

Maggie looked at the glass window cabinets, the pine hutch, the milk separator, lacy white window curtains, and the old oak table covered with an African cotton print. "Yes, didn't she? This room was always so warm and friendly."

She did not tell Vanessa that she had spent a week working on the kitchen after she got home from Ireland, giving it this spruced-up country look, painting the walls and scrubbing down the old furniture, which the wood stove, over the winter months, had begrimed with thick soot. Maggie planned to work on her mother's room next, and refurnish it for herself. She wanted to be able to sleep in her mother's room again, as she had done once, when she was a little girl.

"And what about you?" she asked Vanessa. "How does it feel being back in your father's home?"

"Well, I really have no choice. I have two kids in private schools and an ex-husband whose greatest talent is concealing income. I can't get enough child support from Brad, so it's got to come from Gatesburg. Unfortunately, I came back with my tail between my legs only to find that Dad wasn't handling his business affairs much better than I'd handled my marriage. He'd lost interest, or his mind, or something! So I've had to step in.

"One thing I'll give Brad—he never tried to shelter me from business. In fact he insisted that I keep all the books for the family. So maybe I can get things in order at the club."

Vanessa sipped her wine and leaned back.

"I'm sorry. I didn't come to unload all my troubles." She looked across at Maggie. "I just feel a little guilty taking Jack away from you right now. Since he's been back, I've been leaning on him a good deal. He knows about golf courses, of course, and the whole business of running a club. And he's also very wise in ways that surprise me. I need that."

Maggie reached over and took her hand. Vanessa's fingers were cold and trembling slightly. "I'm glad he's been helpful. Don't worry, he's not abandoning me. He'll help me with the farm. We'll make it."

"What are your plans for the farm? Have you thought what you'll do, I mean, after Emmett . . . ?"

Maggie shook her head. "No, not really. I'm sort of taking it a day at a time. I don't want to sell the place out from under Emmett, but I'm not sure it's a going proposition. We don't produce enough milk to support Emmett, let alone pay property taxes. And I just found out from O'Hara that there's a huge mortgage on the property. That's another problem that has to be dealt with." She sighed. "At least the *Post* is good about holding open my job. And since I got home, I've been talking to my literary agent in New York. She thinks I might be able to do a book about being a correspondent in the Middle East." Maggie paused a moment, then added, "And *People* magazine has been in touch. They want me to do a first-person piece for them— 'My Brother Is Innocent,' something like that."

"Oh, no!"

"Well, if I can't raise Emmett's bail any other way, I just might have to do it." As Maggie carried the two lunch plates to the sink, she heard the phone ringing from down the hall. "Excuse me, Vanessa, let me get that." Maggie pushed through the kitchen door and went into the hall.

"Hello?" Maggie said quickly, lifting the receiver on the third ring.

"Maggie?"

"Catty! Hi! Are you all right?" She was immediately alarmed at her sister's tone.

"Yes, I think so. It's Wendy . . . Is she with you?"

"Wendy? No . . . what happened?" Maggie sat down on the second step of the staircase.

"Oh, shit!"

"Catty?"

"She's run away. To you, I'd hoped. I got home from the shrink five minutes ago and found this goddamn note!"

"What happened? Did you two have a fight?"

"More than a fight."

Maggie could hear her sister sighing and catching her breath. "Wendy's in trouble?"

"Yes."

"Pregnant?"

"Yes."

"Oh, no!"

"Oh, yes! She missed her last period. The best I can tell she's still in the first trimester."

"Who's the boy?"

"Jeff Golden, of course. She told us last night. She's scared, Mag, otherwise she would have just gone off and had an abortion. Most girls her age do that all the time. Wendy's different. Regardless of her attitude at times, she's really a very little girl. Maggie, I just can't believe it. And I tell you: I've talked to Wendy about sex and birth control."

"Cat, I understand. It's not your fault."

"Yes, it is. Joe blames me. I blame me! I've been too lenient, and this is what it's gotten me. But I was so afraid of alienating her, so afraid she would hate me the way I hated Mom." Catty was crying into the phone, choking on her tears.

Maggie stood up, tried to pace in the front hallway, but there was no extension cord. She was trapped by the stairs. From the kitchen she could hear the sound of running water; Vanessa was cleaning up the dishes. "Maybe Jeff and Wendy have run off to get married," she said hopefully.

"No, I just phoned the Goldens. Jeff was there. He doesn't even know Wendy is pregnant. They had a fight, he told me, two weeks ago. He hasn't spoken to her since."

"Oh, shit!"

"You're right: oh, shit! Listen!" Catty went on, pulling herself together, "I'm sure she's on her way to see you."

"How do you know?"

"Because she borrowed all of Clare's savings and told Clare she needed the money for a train ticket. Where else would she go? Talk to her, Maggie."

"What the hell can I tell her?"

"Not to have an abortion."

"Catty!" Maggie sat down again on the step and pulled at her long hair, twisting it nervously. "I'm only her aunt. She's your child." Maggie was angry at her sister for putting her in such a position. "Besides," she went on, "I'm not sure how I feel about her keeping the child."

"Well, I do. I wouldn't let Wendy have an abortion!"

"Catty, you have to accept that this is Wendy's decision."

"I will not let my daughter suffer the way I did. I won't let it happen all over again to my family."

"What are you talking about?"

"I got pregnant on my honeymoon night with Sal Marino. You didn't realize it at the time. Mom didn't tell anyone, naturally. And O'Connor arranged for me to be sent off to Iowa. The Franciscan nuns ran a home in Dubuque for wayward girls and unwed mothers."

"But you finished at Wisdom. You never left home!" Maggie protested.

"Only because I lost the baby. I miscarried in the third month. Not surprising, what with all the tension I was under and living there on the farm with Mother and all her hysteria. I'm surprised I didn't commit suicide. But it was all I had of Sal—his child—and I lost it. I'll never forget that night. When Mother found out, she said, 'Thank God!' as if it was a miracle."

"Cat, I had no idea."

"Well, you do now. And I'm not going to let Wendy suffer the way I did, Maggie. She can give it up for adoption later, but she's not going to kill that baby. She'll only spend the rest of her life regretting it." Catty was silent for a moment, then she said, "Look, I'll drive down to Gatesburg as soon as this snowstorm blows through. Keep her with you. Okay?"

"Yes, of course," Maggie whispered, slowly comprehending everything that her older sister was telling her.

"Bye, now, and thank you, Mag."

For a long moment, Maggie sat on the stairs with the receiver cradled on her shoulder. And then she remembered Vanessa waiting in the kitchen, and she said out loud, but to no one in particular, "Welcome into the family, Van."

# · CHAPTER 32 ·

## GATESBURG: 1964

"WHERE'S YOUR SISTER, MAGGIE?" Caitlin asked as the twins ran across the school yard and up to the truck.

"I have her books," Maggie said, dropping them onto the seat of the cab and sliding in beside her mother. "Sister Ann Marie said I would be in the May Day procession, Mommy. I'm going to wear a white dress and follow the May Queen. She picked five girls from our class and five from the seventh grade. Mary Ellen will walk with me because we're the same height."

"And how am I to buy Catty's shoes if she's not here?" Caitlin looked out the cab window to see if she could spot Catty in a group of other high school seniors at the side door to the gym. No, not Catty. She couldn't act like the other girls. Her oldest daughter was like herself, Caitlin sadly realized. It was only Maggie—and Michael, of course—who made her life a pleasure.

Emmett did not follow Maggie into the cab; instead he jumped into the back and made a seat for himself on his book bag.

"Catty knows well enough that I'm buying you all shoes this afternoon. I don't have time to be running into town to shop whenever it pleases herself." Caitlin pulled the truck away from the curb, made a U-turn on the side street, and started down into town.

Paddy had sent her a hundred dollars in his last letter home. She would take that money and stop at Grill's, buy Emmett a pair of brown corduroys. If she got them long in the leg now, she thought, he could wear them turned up, and they'd still be good enough next fall for school.

"Did she drive off with that Italian?" Caitlin asked Maggie. As she turned onto Illinois Avenue, she saw that a freight train was crossing the track and the traffic was backed up for three blocks. Maybe Catty was in one of those cars, she thought, and impulsively she pulled into the empty left lane and drove ahead, searching for the boy's little black car and her daughter.

"Mother!" Maggie cried. "We'll get killed."

"Be quiet! There's no traffic at all." She saw the boy's car then, his little black Ford, and Cathleen. Catty was draped against Sal Marino and running her fingers through his long hair.

Caitlin edged her truck behind Sal's car and blasted the horn.

"Oh, God, they're kissing!" Maggie shrieked, embarrassed.

"She's nothing but a slut, that one," Caitlin said.

"What's a slut?"

"Never you mind!"

Up ahead the train's caboose crossed the street, and the gates went up.

Caitlin saw Sal pull away from Catty to look through the side mirror.

Turning around, Catty spotted the pickup and quickly slid away from Sal. She rolled down the side window and, leaning out, shouted at her mother, "Leave me alone! Goddamnit, leave me alone."

Sal took off, spinning his car into the left lane, though traffic was now crossing the tracks in both directions. He slammed down on the accelerator and the car lurched ahead, burning rubber as it tore the asphalt. They took a corner on two wheels and sped into a side street as an approaching car squealed to a halt.

"Oh, God, he'll kill her," Caitlin shouted, as Sal's car turned into Louisville Avenue. Then, immediately, she began following them down the side street through town.

"Stop, Mom! Stop!" Maggie yelled, watching as Sal's car just missed a truck and then wildly whipped around two more cars and raced downhill toward Front Street and the river.

"Oh, dear Mother of God!" Caitlin whispered. She touched the brakes and slowed. "He'll kill her, he will."

"Let them go! Let them go!" Maggie begged, still shaking at the way Sal's black car had skidded and whipped its way out of town.

"He shouldn't be let drive, that boy. I'll have his license taken from him, I will."

"Mom, let them go. He'll only go faster if we follow." Maggie slumped in the seat, afraid to look through the front window. She could feel the pickup slow, and then her mother stopped at a corner and turned off Union Street.

"Would you know where they're going, Maggie?" Caitlin asked, her voice suddenly calm.

Maggie kept her face tucked between her knees. "No," she said tonelessly.

Maggie wrote Emmett a note the next afternoon, sitting in the kitchen while her mother finished baking. She sat in the corner so her mother couldn't read over her shoulder and leaned on the looseleaf binder she had braced against her knees. When she was finished, she would hide the note in their secret hiding place, and Emmett would find it later.

"Has the cat got your tongue, Maggie dear?" Caitlin asked, glancing at her youngest daughter. Sitting in the late afternoon light, Maggie looked like a painting, Caitlin thought. The soft light glowed on Maggie's navy-blue school jumper and white cotton blouse. It made her cheeks look pink.

"You're a quiet one today. I haven't heard a peep from you since you came home from school." Caitlin wondered again what her daughter might know about Catty, who hadn't come home the night before. After midnight Caitlin had telephoned Father O'Connor and then the police, telling them her daughter had run off with Sal Marino.

"Sister Maura gave us tons of fractions to do, and she never told us once how to do them, and if I don't get them right, I know she's going to flunk me and then I'll never get out of grammar school. I'm going to keeping flunking and flunking until I'm just too old to go to high school."

Caitlin sat down across from Maggie and asked softly, "What was it that Catty said to you? Did she mention what she'd be doing after school?"

Maggie shook her head. "She always goes to the Sweet Shoppe. Her and Sal and all those guys."

Caitlin glanced at the clock. She had last seen Catty at four o'clock the day before. She had the same sudden fear that there had been an accident, but the police would have telephoned, she realized. She said to Maggie, "You should be getting the cows. It's after five already. And where's your brother?"

"I don't know. He's never around when I have to get the cows," Maggie complained, but today she didn't mind going out to the back fields. She wanted to be well away from her mother, and questions about Catty.

"And don't be running them, with their full udders."

"I never run the cows, Mother!" She swept her books and binder off the table and into her arms. "It's Emmett that does, not me!"

Caitlin sat at the table listening as Maggie ran into the living room, paused, and then ran upstairs to her room, where she would change out of her school clothes before setting off to get the cows.

When Caitlin heard Maggie's door bang open upstairs, she pushed herself up from the oak table. She was tired. Her legs hurt from standing most of the day at the sink cleaning fryers. She had delivered fifty chickens to Hagenbuch's Restaurant before picking up the twins at school. She had kept working, afraid to give herself time to worry about Catty. Still she had spent the day listening, waiting for the phone to ring and tell her that Catty had been killed on the highway.

She walked quietly down the hallway to the living room, walked over to the fireplace, and reaching up, pulled a loose cornerstone from the fireplace. There was Maggie's note, carefully tucked away, as she knew it would be. Caitlin set the stone on the wooden mantel and unfolded the note.

> Emmett, what should I do? Should I tell Mom what we know??? About Catty??? She's been calling everybuddy. Sal's Mom! Father O'Connor! Catty is going to come home and then Mom is going to find out we knew, and then, boy, we're going to get killed. I think we should tell her what the kids said. Okay? It's not like telling a secret, because Catty never told us anything. You just heard Kathey Handley. I can't stand keeping a secret from Mom. Leave me a note. PLEASE!!!
> P.S. Ask me if I finished my English homework, then I'll know you left a note, okay.
> ME

Caitlin folded away the note and replaced the cornerstone. She could hear Maggie upstairs, banging doors open and shut as she ran back and forth between her bedroom and the bathroom. The little gypsy, she thought. Siding with her sister against her mother.

She got back into the kitchen just as Emmett came barging in. He dropped his books on the table and pulled at his school tie, then headed straight for the soda bread and butter on the table.

"Emmett, where did Catty go?" his mother asked at once. "I know she ran off with that Italian. Tell me where."

"I dunno," Emmett mumbled, cutting into the bread. "Maybe you should ask—"

Caitlin grabbed him by the shoulder and spun him around before he could finish the sentence. "Where is your sister Cathleen, Emmett?"

"I don't know!"

"Yes you do!" She slapped him across the face.

Emmett pulled free. "Catty doesn't tell me nothing! She thinks I'm a jerk or something. Me and Maggie."

Caitlin grabbed his arm again, digging in with her fingers, and shouted, "Did she run off and marry that Italian?"

"I don't know! I don't know!" he shouted. The plate of soda bread crashed to the floor and in a fury Emmett flung the knife across the room.

He didn't see Maggie. She had come running back into the kitchen, tucking an old golf shirt of Paddy Jack's into her jeans as she pushed open the hallway door. In that split second—as the knife flipped in space, and time stood still—Emmett thought he had killed his sister. Maggie didn't move. She stood staring dumbly as the flying blade caught her in the chest, cut through the red cotton shirt and dug four inches into the flesh between her tiny breasts.

Then she screamed. Stumbling as she fought to pull the long blade from her chest. Caitlin reached her daughter before she hit the floor and lifted Maggie into her arms. As she rushed for the back door, she called over her shoulder, "Telephone the club. Ask for Mr. Harris. Tell him who you are and that Maggie's been hurt. Don't say how, but tell him I said for him to meet me at the County Hospital."

Caitlin spoke calmly, though she could see the blood pumping from her child's chest. "Do you understand, Emmett?" she asked, never raising her voice. In the moment of panic she had become quiet and controlled. When she saw Emmett nod, she said only, "Stay here"; then she ran for the truck.

For a long while Emmett stood perfectly still, disbelieving and too frightened to cry. He could see there was blood on the floor, Maggie's blood, a trail of it leading to the back door.

When he finally did move, it was not to call Mr. Harris. He crossed the kitchen to where his mother kept the mop and pail. He cleaned the kitchen floor, wiping his sister's blood off the linoleum by hand. He continued to scrub, eventually washing the entire kitchen floor, working backward, as he had seen his mother do, until he was out of the kitchen and into the hall. Emmett stopped then, exhausted from the effort, from his fear, and sank into the hallway corner and cried again. Cried because Maggie was dead and he had killed her. Cried because he would go to jail and, he knew, to hell for all eternity.

Later, he telephoned Mr. Harris, then went to sit on the porch with Mac, their golden retriever. Emmett sat quietly for a while, but then began to cry once more, sobbing into the warmth of the dog's long golden hair. Mac draped one heavy paw over Emmett's leg and sat patiently, his pink tongue drooping from his panting mouth.

He would run away from home, Emmett decided. He could ride his bike into town and hop a freight heading south. Paddy Jack was in San Antonio, playing in the Texas Open; Emmett knew that from the PGA tour schedule he had tacked to his bedroom door. Once he was in Texas he would get a job caddying, maybe for Paddy Jack. He'd make money and never come back to Illinois.

Suddenly, Mac jumped up, lifted his front paw, and stared across the front lawn. Looking up, Emmett spotted the white sheriff's car as it turned into the farm road. He ran then, through the house and out the kitchen door, ran without looking around, ran through the orchard to the barn. Ran out the cow door and across the fields, toward the train tracks beyond the pasture. He ran with Mac barking at his heels.

So there was no one in the house when the sheriff's car halted at the back door, and Catty, helped by the policeman, limped up the walk to the kitchen. No one was home when Catty came back from French Lick, Indiana, and the fatal accident at Skelton's Crossing that had killed her young husband.

# · CHAPTER 33 ·

## GATESBURG: 1982

"WENDY, IT'S OKAY. I know why you're here."

"Mom called?"

"Your mother and I have talked a couple times today."

"Shit. She hates me, Aunt Maggie!"

"She doesn't hate you," Maggie answered, backing the pickup out of the parking lot in front of the train station.

"Well, I'm going to have an abortion; you can't stop me," Wendy said all at once, as if staking out a position.

"We can talk about it later." Maggie sighed, wishing she hadn't been drawn into the middle of all this, and then she felt guilty. "Don't worry, honey. You can stay here at the farm. Jeff, too, if you want."

"And I'm not marrying Jeff. That shit!"

"Wendy! Is that the only word you know?" Maggie turned and took a good look at her niece. Wendy's long black hair was swooped up under a man's soft felt hat, and her slim body was engulfed in a heavy, ankle-length fur coat, bought secondhand, Maggie guessed, from a Chicago antique shop. Under all that, she was wearing Calvin Klein jeans, plaid Norma Kamali knee socks, and Perry Ellis lace-up shoes. And jewelry. Big coral earrings, a Navajo necklace of heavy silver, the Cartier tank watch Catty had given her on her sixteenth birthday, and the elephant-hair bracelet Maggie had sent her from Kenya. She was a walking boutique, Maggie thought, half laughing, half envious.

"You sound just like Mom," Wendy complained. "Why don't you give me a break?"

"No one is picking on you, Wendy Ann Duffy. So quit feeling sorry for yourself." Nervously Maggie shifted gear and let out the clutch. Front Street was a sheet of ice and snow, and the pickup was hard to manage. It had been years since she had actually driven on snow.

"Why shouldn't I feel sorry for myself—I'm pregnant!" Wendy exclaimed, and then abruptly, surprisingly, began to sob into her gloves.

Maggie reached over and slid her arm around Wendy's shoulders, tugging her niece closer. She could feel the child trembling beneath the massive old seal coat.

"Wendy, I'm going to see your uncle Emmett," she said softly. "Visiting hours aren't long enough for me to take you out to the farm and come back, not in this weather. Do you want to see him, too?"

Wendy shook her head. "I don't want to talk to him. He's weird. Besides, he killed Grandmother."

"He did not! Who told you that?"

Wendy shrugged, looking away. "I don't know. I heard Mom and Dad talking, and they said, you know, the evidence and everything . . ."

"Wendy, your uncle didn't kill your grandmother."

"Well, if he didn't, how did she die?" Wendy turned to Maggie, prepared to defend her parents' opinion.

"In an accident, that's how!" Maggie was mad now, at Catty and Joe for talking in front of the children, and at Wendy for believing them.

"I don't care," Wendy said next, moving into the far corner of the front seat. "He's weird and I'm not going to talk to him."

"It's not necessary," Maggie said. "In fact, it's probably better if I see him alone." She was about to say more, then took her own advice about not discussing the matter with the children. She slowed the pickup and turned into the parking lot behind the courthouse and jail. The visitors' lot had been plowed, but on that snowy afternoon was virtually empty. There weren't many criminals in the county, Maggie guessed.

"I can't wait here!" Wendy complained at once as Maggie shut off the engine. "I'll freeze."

Maggie took a deep breath and looked away until she had collected herself. "Okay," she said, thinking out loud, "there's a lobby and reception area in the jail."

"I don't want to go in there. Those places are full of bag ladies and creeps. I'll stay here." She pulled the thick fur collar up around her face and peeped out at Maggie. Her eyes were shiny with tears.

"No, you won't. I won't be responsible for your catching pneumonia. Or whatever. Look!" She pointed out the front window. "See that house across the street? The Victorian behind the church? That's the rectory for Saint Pat's. Father O'Connor is home, I know; he's expecting me after I visit Emmett. Go there and tell him who you are. He'll let you wait in the rectory."

"I know Father O'Connor!" Her voice brightened. "From the funeral. He's cute."

Maggie laughed. "Don't tell your mother you said so." She climbed out of the car and met Wendy on the sidewalk. "Tell Father O'Connor I'll be there in about an hour, okay?"

"Okay. But Aunt Maggie? Why does Mom hate him so much? He's really nice, I think."

"You'll have to ask your mother."

"She never tells us anything about Gatesburg. It was only when we were on our way here for the funeral that she told me about her husband. Her first husband, I mean. Not Daddy."

"She told you about Sal?"

"Like it was a terrible secret or something."

"It was a terrible secret," Maggie said. "Did she tell you anything else?"

"Yes, that her boyfriend—husband, I mean—got killed. It was a really horrible story—but why was it such a secret?"

"It's a family trait, I think," Maggie said. "Or maybe all big families have special little secrets. Remember, none of us even knew about your aunt Nora."

"It's crazy, isn't it? Like we were a Mafia family or something."

Maggie looked up as, above them, the courthouse clock chimed three. Emmett would be waiting for her. She said quickly, "You have to remember that secrets were part of their time, part of being immigrants in America. Mom and Dad—your grandparents—came out of a very secretive society. People didn't talk about their feelings and failures, not like they do today. Any sort of vulnerability was considered a weakness.

"You did your work, hard work, for the most part, like ditchdigging or working on a farm. And you took care of yourself. But you never aired dirty laundry in public. No one was told about the family, and nothing was said to the kids. Growing up, we learned things by osmosis or not at all. And the attitude sort of wore off on us."

"But you're not like Mom! I mean, I can talk to you!"

"I'm not your mother, Wendy Ann, that's why you can talk to me." Maggie embraced her niece, then said, "Go ahead to the rectory."

"Aunt Maggie," Wendy said softly, pulling away and looking at her directly. "I love you."

"And I love you, too. When we get back to the farm, I'll get us dinner, and we'll build a fire in the living room and talk. How does that sound?"

Wendy nodded, unable to answer through her tears, and then she blurted out, "I'm going to be all right, aren't I? I mean, I'm not going to die or something?"

Maggie held her by the shoulders to make sure Wendy heard her.

"No, you're not going to die, Wendy. You're going to be okay. We're all going to be all right, the whole family." She kissed the girl's cold cheek, then turned her around and gave her a small shove. "Go ahead. We'll both freeze, standing out in this weather."

Maggie turned and hurried up the courthouse steps. In the sudden warmth of the lobby, her thoughts jumped to her own problems, and she wondered if she could make it through another Illinois winter, the loss of her mother, and Emmett's trial. And do it alone, she thought ruefully, without Jack or Kenneth, without even Father Mike. And she was afraid.

Had Michael arranged for Emmett's bail to be set so high? she asked herself as she followed the corridor signs back to the jail. Another family mystery there, she guessed, another secret that Michael, Father O'Connor, and Lord knows who else were keeping from her. Well, she'd find out. She would use every connection and scrap of influence in her power to find out, because of all her brothers and sisters, it was Emmett that she loved the most.

# · CHAPTER 34 ·

## GATESBURG: 1969

MAGGIE STOOD ON THE back porch calling for Emmett. There were thick leaves and new autumn apples in the orchard obscuring the view, but Maggie could see enough of the barns to tell that Emmett had finished the afternoon milking and turned out the cows. He could come inside and change clothes now. Maggie knew how he was when it came to getting dressed and going anywhere, but she was determined not to let him skip her going-away party.

Walking through the open barn doors, Maggie called for her brother. It was cool inside the barn, out of the hot September sun. She could smell the baled hay and the pigs, smell all the years of animals that had lived in the huge red barn. She thought how only a few years before she had spent most of her time there, feeding the chickens and turkeys every afternoon after school, riding the baler in August, and helping with cornhusking in the fall. Now weeks passed and she never went down to the barns or helped with the livestock. Farming was part of her childhood; all she could think of was college, and leaving home for the first time.

"Emmett!" Maggie called again.

"Yeah?"

Her brother was behind the hayrack and stanchions, shoveling out cow manure.

"We have to leave in an hour, Emmett. Father Mike said we're to meet him by seven." Maggie spoke softly. She knew how Emmett would react if he thought she were bossing him around.

"I got work to do," he said, continuing to shovel.

"Emmett, it's my going-away dinner! You have to come."

"I don't have to do anything."

"Yes, you do. I won't let you skip it. Not when Paddy Jack is flying home especially. Mom says we're going across the river to a new restaurant that Father O'Connor knows in Shelbyville. And, you know, we're celebrating our next birthday, too, because I won't be here in October. Besides, Father Mike is here." She wondered then why she always called her brother "Father Mike" when she was trying to bully people. It was as if his religious title was a threat.

"I don't care. I'm my own boss. I'm out of school, remember?" He pushed the last of the cow manure through the side door, pitching it into the pile that had built up over the summer.

Maggie held her breath a moment as the steaming manure hit the pile, then she said, "If you don't go, it's going to look strange."

"I look strange anyway." Emmett came out from behind the stanchions. He was wearing boots and had pulled a pair of their father's old overalls over his jeans and T-shirt.

"Don't talk like that!" Maggie told him. "Where do you get this idea that you're strange? I told you, Mary Murphy thinks you're the cutest boy in our class."

"Yeah, then how come she went with Fuegner to the prom?" He kept busy, hurrying as if he were late for something, his boots stomping on the barn's wooden floors.

"Because, you jerk, Rich Fuegner asked her. I told you to call. I told you she'd go with Rich if you didn't call."

"I was busy, is all."

"You were afraid to call, is all!" Maggie followed him into the pigsty. "So why didn't you?"

"Because I can't dance."

"Mary would teach you," she said quickly.

"You told Murphy I couldn't dance?" He stopped shoveling corncobs into the sty.

"I sort of told her you needed some practice."

"That's what Rich Fuegner says about you."

"You creep!" Maggie grabbed an ear of corn and threw it at him so hard it skipped off his head and hit the barn wall with a bang.

Emmett began to laugh.

Maggie stamped her foot, then she laughed, too. He was so good-looking, she thought, when he wasn't walking around with a chip on his shoulder, waiting to be offended. She had seen a photo of their father when he was a young man, and Emmett looked like him. It was an old black-and-white photo of her parents she had found among some photographs that her mother had tucked away in the top drawer of her bedroom dresser.

Emmett had their father's thin face, the thick black hair, and beautiful sad blue eyes. Maggie envied his blue eyes and thought it wasn't fair that hers were brown.

"Emmett, please," she begged, "come to the dinner for me. It will be fun, all of us, the family."

Emmett threw back his head, as if that were a joke. "What family?" He slammed the long-handled shovel back into the corncobs. Then, pushing his shoulder against the back door, he trundled a bag of feed across the yard to the chicken coop.

Maggie ran after him, being careful where she walked. The cows had just crossed behind the barns heading for pasture, and fresh, steaming dun pies dotted the yard.

"Our family! Michael, Paddy Jack, you and me. And Mom."

"Some family we've got! Paddy Jack . . . He never writes. Calls Mom maybe once or twice a year to say hello. Sees us only if a golf tournament happens to be in Illinois. And Mike! He comes back to Gatesburg, but does he stay with us? No, he's too goddamn important now that he's monsignor. Big shot in Washington. And when he does come out for dinner, Mom just goes crazy, like he was a movie star or something, while you and me, well, we could just be shit. Hell, he can hardly say hello to me when he's here, not that I give a flying fuck."

"Maybe if you tried, Emmett, instead of cutting out of the house the minute he walks in, as if he had the plague or something. It's as much your fault as his."

"Oh, shut up. You sound just like Mom, the two of you are always on my ass, as if I didn't have enough to do around here: going to school, keeping the farm going, planting crops." He pulled the wedge of wood from the door latch and walked into the chicken coop, scattering the hens as he went.

Taking a deep breath, Maggie followed him. Of all the barn odors, she hated most the smell of chickens. They were dirty birds, and mean. She remembered how the hens had gone for her legs when she was a little girl. But Emmett wasn't going to escape her that easily.

"I don't see you moving your ass to help me," he said. "No, you're too good for that. Now you're going off to college."

"You didn't want to go to college, Emmett," Maggie said quietly, then realized he couldn't hear her over the squawking of the chickens, and she raised her voice. "You've always wanted to work the farm."

Emmett pulled off the tops of the tin feeders and poured in the chicken mix. "What else am I supposed to do? I can't leave the farm. Who's going to work it—Mom?"

"Well, why don't you go to MacMurray? They offered you a football scholarship. Or night school in Vandalia?" She had not really thought about what her leaving must mean to Emmett. They had never been apart. It wasn't missing out on college that bothered Emmett, Maggie realized, but losing her.

"Forget it, okay?" He replaced the feeder lids and came back to the door. He wouldn't look at her. He never looked at any of them. But when Maggie pointed this out to her mother, Caitlin had said, "The boy's shy. His father was the same."

Maggie grabbed Emmett by his shoulders. "Listen to me!"

"What?" He pulled back, hands on his hips, and stood there, staring off.

"Look at me, damn it!" She grabbed her brother again, digging her nails into his arms, wanting to hurt him because of the way he hurt her, hurt all the family, as if he really didn't care about them. "I didn't ask for this scholarship to Georgetown. It was Father Mike who arranged it—blame him!"

"Okay, go to college. What do I care?" He pushed by and went out into the barnyard.

"What's the matter with you?"

He stopped abruptly in the yard and turned on her. She had a moment of panic, as she always did, when his mood changed and his face flashed in that way it had, full of anger and something else.

"You don't see Mike doing anything for me, do you? You don't hear him say, 'Okay, Emmett, it's your turn; you can go to college with Maggie. I'll hire someone to help Mom with the farm.' You don't hear anything like that, do you? Not from Mike or even Paddy Jack. Or what's-her-name Catty. Shit, as far as she knows, we could be dead down here."

"She writes me; we're in touch," Maggie said quickly.

"You are?" He was momentarily thrown off balance.

Maggie nodded. "She writes me care of the Handleys. Kathey gives me her letters." Maggie shrugged. "It's because of Mom, you know." Then she went on, saying calmly, "But you're wrong about Paddy Jack. He helps us."

"Yeah, sure. A couple hundred bucks now and then when he wins. That's chickenshit. I'm the only one in the family that's keeping this farm together."

They walked back the drive toward the house. On the highway, they saw the mailman pull his car up to their box and so they continued along the drive to get their mail. Maggie slipped her arm into his and whispered, "I'm going to miss you."

Emmett didn't answer. It was always hard for him to express himself, Maggie knew, but he did slide his arm around her shoulder and embrace her briefly. Maggie hugged him back, thinking to herself that of all of them it was Emmett no one understood. And because of that, it was Emmett she would have to take care of in the future, whatever else happened to her in life.

When they reached the highway, Maggie pulled down the mailbox lid, took out a bundle of mail and the county daily. She leafed through the letters quickly.

"Mary Ellen said she would write as soon as she got to Kalamazoo, and it's been two weeks. Here, this is for you." She pulled the white envelope from the others, paused only to glance at the return address. "It's from the government. Who do you know in the government?" She gave him the envelope, then spotted the letter she was looking for. "Finally!" And turning toward the house, she tore open the envelope to read Mary Ellen's letter as she walked.

"She's met a boy! Oh, God, I can't believe it. Met him in a class registration line. He's from Illinois, too. From Tinley Park. Where's Tinley Park, Emmett?" She glanced up and saw that he was staring dumbly at his letter. His mouth was open and his face, even after the long summer was working in the sun, was white. "Emmett? What's the matter?" She grabbed his letter and scanned the two thick paragraphs. "Oh, no! Not you!"

"Drafted," he said slowly. "They told me I wouldn't be . . . the farm. Oh, shit, they're gonna send me to Vietnam."

Maggie grabbed his arm. "You're not going to Vietnam, Emmett. I won't let them take you. None of us will, Father Mike, or Paddy Jack. We can talk to Father O'Connor. He can talk to the draft people. You're needed on the farm, right? You just said so yourself. Father Mike is in Washington. He knows people. Who drafts you? Who's on our draft board?" She was crying, suddenly realizing she didn't know the first thing about the draft or how to beat it.

"People from town. Mayor Walker. Bill Vicars' old man. Doc Hebert . . ."

"Father O'Connor knows these people. He can talk to them," she answered quickly, seizing on that information.

Emmett kept shaking his head. "It won't work, Mag."

"Can't you be deferred? You just said they told you . . ."

Emmett shook his head.

"Who makes the decision? Who's in charge for Gatesburg? Father O'Connor can talk to him."

"That's the problem, Mag. In Gatesburg, Father O'Connor is head of the draft board. If I've been drafted, it's because O'Connor wants me to go in the army."

# · CHAPTER 35 ·

## GATESBURG: 1982

FATHER O'CONNOR CAME TO the rectory door himself. With a fisherman's sweater pulled over his black shirt, he looked like someone's Irish grandfather. Maggie watched him shuffle through the foyer of the rectory, peering out over his glasses to see who was at the door.

" 'Tis you, Margaret Mary. The girl said you were seeing Emmett." The old priest pushed open the storm door and stepped back to let Maggie inside.

"I was trying," she said in the hallway. "But they wouldn't let me." As she stepped in from the cold, her eyes began to water, and she reached for some tissues in the deep pockets of her down coat.

"Don't you be fretting, Margaret Mary," Father O'Connor said, touching her arm. "The boy won't talk to me either. Here now, get out of that heavy coat. I'm just having a cup of tea with the girl." He stepped closer and lowered his voice. "Is there trouble with this one?" he asked, jerking his head toward the living room.

Maggie shook her head as O'Connor helped her slip out of her coat. She had bought the down coat in China nearly eight years before, on a congressional tour with Jack. He had bought one, too, at the same friendship store, and she wondered if wearing it reminded him of the morning they kept the Chinese delegation waiting in the hotel lobby when they went back to bed after breakfast and made love for the second time.

"Emmett," the priest prodded. "What's troubling him today?"

"According to the police, he thinks he's some sort of political prisoner and he's gone on a hunger strike. The police chief told me Emmett hasn't eaten all day. And this morning, the guards also found him stripped naked, refusing to wear the prison uniform."

"He's on the blanket, then," said O'Connor, raising his eyebrows.

"That's right, Father, like one of those IRA prisoners in Northern Ireland," Maggie answered, letting her anger show. "The police won't let him have visitors unless he puts on the uniform, and he won't, not even for me." She bent down and tugged at one of her wet boots, jerking it off.

Instead of helping, the priest stood perfectly still, as if lost in thought. Then he said, " 'Tisn't a political prisoner he thinks he is. He's thinking of something else, Margaret Mary, not the IRA or the Sinn Fein."

Maggie stopped wrestling with her boots and waited for the old man to explain.

"It's the Brehon Laws, that's what," the priest said. "Before Saint Patrick got to Ireland, men had a way of dealing with those that had wronged them. An Irishman would stand outside his enemy's house naked and starving until he brought shame to the man for the wrong he'd done. That's what Emmett is doing, Maggie. Now I wondered where he learned of a thing like that? It must have been your mother telling him."

"I don't understand! Who's he trying to shame?"

"The family. He's gone on the blanket to bring shame on his brothers and sisters."

"That's nonsense. I don't believe a word of it!" She pulled off her second boot and then asked quickly, to change the subject, "Where's Wendy?"

"She went to the little girl's room," the old priest said, returning to his leather chair by the fireplace. "Would you like something to warm you up, Margaret Mary? I had Mrs. O'Brien make the girl tea, but if you'd be liking something stronger . . ." He settled himself in the high-backed leather chair, pulling a white blanket over his legs and lap.

Her mother had made the lap blanket for Father O'Connor's sixty-fifth birthday. Maggie remembered her knitting it on the first Thanksgiving that she had brought Jack McGraff home. O'Connor was to have retired then, but the priest had no money of his own and no family to take him in. She remembered that Father Mike had gotten the Diocese to bend its rules and leave the old priest at Saint Pat's.

Maggie suddenly felt sorry for Father O'Connor as she thought of him sitting there in front of the fireplace, night after night, without anyone to share his life. No wonder he had spent so much time with the DeLaceys. It wasn't her mother that had drawn him out to the farm, but all the children, the family he had never had.

"Let me tell you why I came by, Father," she said. If they were his family, let him help her now. "I have to get Emmett out on bail, and I'm having trouble every way I turn. I spoke to John Keenan at the bank about this mortgage on the farm. Mom always told me we owned the place free and clear. Well, it turns out that that's no longer true."

She paused to watch the priest. "Keenan says the farm is mortgaged for a quarter of a million dollars. Did you know about that?"

Maggie heard the toilet flush from the back of the house. Wendy would be returning to the living room, so she went on quickly, "Why was a mortgage taken out without any of us knowing? What was Mother thinking? And what happened to the money? There's no money in her bank accounts, and there's certainly no sign it was spent on the property. The house wasn't even heated when Catty first arrived."

Father O'Connor stared up at Maggie, his pale face caught in the wide circle of the floor lamp's light. He looked ill. "Your mother paid off the bank note in the fifties, Margaret Mary. She never said a word to me about a new mortgage."

Maggie stared back at him. She wondered if it was a sin to call a priest a liar.

"Oh, hi!" Wendy said, coming into the living room. "How's weird Emmett?" No one said a word and Wendy glanced back and forth between them, suddenly aware of the tension in the room. She looked worried; her face was so clear, Maggie could read her thoughts easily.

"No, Wendy," Maggie said tightly, "we're not talking about you. We're discussing the family. Come and finish your tea so we can leave. It's going to be a terrible night, and I need to stop for groceries before we go out to the farm. We might be snowbound for a few days."

"Really?" Wendy's eyes brightened.

"Yes, really." Wendy was still a child, Maggie thought, cheered up by a sudden diversion. Just another pregnant child. Then Maggie turned back to the priest. "Do you have any idea why Emmett's bail is so outrageous? I mean, a half-million dollars!"

"It was Judge Boyer who set the bail." The pastor did not look away from the fire.

"Detective O'Hara says there's a rumor in town that Father Mike arranged it, that he wanted Emmett kept in jail."

"Jesus, Mary, and Joseph, what nonsense!" He thrashed the air with his thin hand. "That Larry O'Hara hasn't the good sense God gave him. Why in God's name would Michael want to do a thing like that?" He stared back at Maggie, his blue eyes watery with age. She would not get the truth from him, she realized. Father O'Connor knew all their secrets, but he would keep them to himself.

"Margaret Mary," the priest went on softly, now speaking in his confessional tone, "the boy isn't right. I'm sorry to say that about your own twin, but look at the way he's behaving over there. They should force the lad to dress and not let him embarrass us by going about naked to the world."

"He's doing what?" Wendy asked.

"I'll explain later, Wendy," Maggie said. "Hurry with your tea, please. We don't want to keep Father O'Connor from his supper."

"It's only five o'clock!"

"Everyone eats early in the country, Wendy." She picked the girl's coat up off the chair and handed it to her. "Don't bother getting up, Father," Maggie said. "After all these years, I'm sure I can find my own way out."

"Thank you, Margaret. This chair is a trap to me these days."

Maggie saw that he had everything within reach. His missals and Bible, a small bell to call the housekeeper, and the remote control for the television set. He was like her mother had been, she thought, trapped by age and arthritis. She remembered the summer he had taught them how to ride Tinker Bell, how he had made her trot in the barnyard and had run alongside the pony, holding Maggie securely in the tiny saddle. Now he could barely walk to the front door of the rectory. He would not be with them for much longer, she realized.

"Father, I must ask you something else about Emmett. It is something I should have asked you years ago."

He glanced again at her, and this time looked afraid.

"Why did you let Emmett go into the army? You were the head of the local draft board; you had influence."

The priest kept nodding before he answered, and then said clearly, as if he were proud of what he had done, "The truth is I could have gotten Emmett deferred. Your mother was angry at me at the time for sending Emmett off to the army. But I wanted the boy to have his chance, to make something of himself. He needed that, you know, after living in the shadows of you all."

"But he was captured, put in a POW camp! He might have been killed!"

The priest raised his hand to stop her outcry.

"Michael and I arranged for Emmett to go to Europe, to be assigned to some safe place like NATO, but the boy wouldn't have it. Your brother volunteered for Vietnam, Margaret Mary. We didn't send the boy to Asia. That was his doing."

"I didn't know," Maggie whispered, feeling ashamed that she had yelled at the priest.

"Margaret Mary, I never wanted anything but the best for all of you children. Do you remember how I'd come out to the farm when you were all no bigger than Catty's littlest one?" the priest suddenly asked, smiling again. "I'd come out after Mass and bake soda bread. You had a pony, Maggie. Do you remember, child?"

The old man reached out and took Maggie's fingers, held them gently in his fragile hand.

"Yes, I remember," she whispered.

"I taught you to ride, didn't I, darling? And we'd go fishing—you and Emmett and myself. I can remember coming home late on Sunday afternoons, you carrying the bass, Emmett running ahead to tell your mother. And Mac! Do you remember the dog?"

Maggie smiled sadly.

"Mac running after Emmett," the priest whispered, staring into the flames as if he were looking into the past. "God, how I loved you all. You were mine, my children; I raised you. Michael, you, and Emmett."

"I know, Father. I remember," Maggie said quickly. She had to get out of the warm rectory before she broke down in tears.

"Father, come out for supper this weekend. Can you do that?" She touched his arm and felt his thin wrist beneath her fingers.

"Thank you, dear, but I don't drive much in this weather."

"I'll come get you, Father, don't worry about driving. Could you come on Saturday or are you busy?"

"Aye, Saturday would be fine, Margaret, God love you. I don't go out much nowadays. 'Tisn't like it was in the old days."

Suddenly, stirred by his memories, he reached up and seized Maggie's arm, pulled her closer. "Your mother was a great woman, Margaret Mary, now don't you forget. Her dying was an accident, child. Don't you be listening to the likes of that O'Hara lad." He let go of her hands, but Maggie did not move. There were tears in her eyes and tears running freely down her face. She could feel the warmth of them on her cheek, and nodding to the priest, she whispered, "Yes, Father, I know."

"People having nothing better to do with their time than start stories. Rumors, you know, nothing but rumors, lies, out-and-out lies, they are."

She could see his face turning red in the light of the floor lamp. Maggie clasped his hands in hers to comfort the man, to reassure him. "I understand, Father. I know what people say about the DeLaceys. It doesn't matter." She nodded as she spoke. "We have each other, don't we?"

"There's not a family in Gatesburg that has done as much as yours —you, Michael, Paddy Jack. Catty, too, in her way!"

"We know it was Mom who made it possible. We won't forget," she said, and then stood. "If Father Mike telephones you tonight, ask him to call me, would you please, Father?"

"Indeed! Indeed, I will." He struggled to get out of the chair.

"We'll let ourselves out, Father. Please, stay by the warm fire," Maggie said, quickly, hurrying.

"Thank you, dear. I'll say a prayer for you, for the both of you."

The pastor sat quietly watching the fire. He waited until the two women had put their boots on, wrapped themselves up against the cold, and gone out into the night. A sudden strong draft of cold wind whipped around him as they left, stirring the blaze. He waited, making sure they were gone, then lifted the telephone and slowly, carefully, dialed long distance. It was Michael himself who picked up the phone in Washington.

"Michael, son? Is that you?"

"Yes, Dermot! What is it?" He sounded brusque.

"He's gone on the blanket, son. Emmett has gone on the blanket. He's trying to show you up, I know, like they did in the old days at the time of the Brehon Laws. Margaret Mary came in here just a few minutes ago to tell me. And worse, she's on to the mortgage. She wants to know what happened to the money."

Michael was silent for a moment, then he said firmly, "Keep him in jail, Dermot. Speak to Boyer again and make sure of it."

"Margaret Mary has got her mind set, son." The old priest sounded worried.

"Don't worry, Dermot. Let me deal with my little sister; you just speak to Judge Boyer. We have nothing to worry about, not unless Maggie finds out what happened to the mortgage money."

"She won't tell a soul about that, would she?" The old priest was alarmed again.

"I can't say, Dermot. We both know how Maggie is when it comes to protecting Emmett."

# · CHAPTER 36 ·

## GATESBURG: 1973

JACK MCGRAFF FLEW HIS single-engine Mooney across Wolf Creek State Park and then followed the Kaskaskia River south into Fayette County. Maggie leaned forward in the copilot seat and looked for Gatesburg in the bright May morning.

They were running late on this trip into Illinois because Nixon had delayed them. Only two days ago they had awakened to find John Dean dismissed; later that day both Haldeman and Ehrlichman resigned. "It's all over," Jack had told her, smiling with delight as he read that morning's *Washington Post*. "We've got that bastard. Even the rats are agreeing to testify."

But they were in Illinois at last, and soon she would see Emmett again for the first time in three years. Maggie had wanted to be the one to meet him in California, when the army flew all the returning POWs home, but she had to present her senior paper to the honor's class faculty. So Jack had arranged for her mother to go. He had paid for workers to tend the stock while Caitlin was gone, sent a local Democrat to escort her from Gatesburg to O'Hare Airport; at San Francisco she was met by another aide with a car and taken to the air-force base where the POWs were arriving. Maggie and Jack had heard from the aide that Emmett had been rather strange when he first arrived, refusing to ride in the congressional car, insisting that he and his mother would make the trip back to Gatesburg alone, without the nurse Jack had arranged. And when Maggie had called that night to welcome him home and introduce him to Jack, Emmett had spoken to her for only a few moments before putting his mother back on the line.

But the several weeks on the farm, Maggie was sure, had done him a world of good.

She spotted Gatesburg on the horizon, at the bend in the river, the cluster of Johnson's corn silos, the old brewery buildings. As Jack banked the small plane, she saw the town's streets, like shiny ribbons in the morning sun running down the slope to the water's edge.

"Jack," she shouted over the engine, "fly over the farm, okay? I've never seen it from the air."

He nodded. She could not see his blue eyes behind the old air-force sunglasses he wore, but he smiled and pulled back on the wheel, turning away from the river and toward the flat farmlands that framed the town on three sides.

Maggie was disoriented for a moment, then she located the country club, the wide patch of new green grass fairways among clusters of trees, and as they came closer and the Mooney dropped in altitude, she saw home: the white farmhouse and red barns, and the fields, all newly plowed for spring planting.

Grinning, she had tapped Jack on the shoulder and motioned to him that she wanted him to drop lower, to fly over the farmhouse itself. While she peered out the side window, Jack tipped the right wing to give her a better view. As the farm came up to meet her, growing larger as the plane dropped, she realized how wonderfully happy she was. She was home; she would see her mother and Emmett; and she had Jack with her for the long weekend. After only a few months as a congressman's wife, she had learned that she could only have her husband for bits and pieces of time. That was the real reason she loved flying; it gave her and Jack time to be alone together.

Maggie saw half a dozen white sheets flapping in the morning breeze. Her mother emerged from the basement carrying a basket of laundry, and when she heard the small plane, she stopped and looked, shading her eyes in the sunlight to track the Mooney as it roared by, tilting and turning over the golf course. Caitlin waved at them, and Jack turned the plane back again, flying lower, less than a thousand feet above the farmhouse and barns.

The milk cows in the barnyard bolted against the wooden fence as they ran before the roaring plane. Suddenly Emmett came out of the barn, running in a crouch, ducking the plane like a boy at play. Maggie didn't realize that anything was wrong until she saw Caitlin drop her clean linen in the yard and rush for him.

Oh, dear God, what had they done! She shouted to Jack over the roar of the plane, "Let's get out of here!" He couldn't hear and smiled back. "Go!" she screamed. "Go!"

Later that day, when they returned to the farm by car, they ate a silent meal alone with Caitlin. As their plane had roared off, Caitlin told them, Emmett followed it, shaking his fist at the sky and screaming obscenities. She had run after him until she was exhausted, then had returned to the farm and waited, sure that Emmett wouldn't miss a chance to see Maggie and would return eventually. He loved Maggie, she told Jack solemnly; even his years in a POW camp hadn't changed that.

Yet Emmett hadn't reappeared to meet them when they arrived, hadn't even joined them at supper. The first sign Jack and Maggie had of his presence was that night, after they had gone to bed, when they woke to the sound of his screaming.

Jack jerked awake, jumped out of bed to stand, and Maggie caught his arm to hold him.

"It's okay, darling," she whispered, pulling her husband down beside her.

"Jesus Christ! God, he sounds frightened to death!" He lay still beside her.

They waited, listening for more screams from the top dormer room where Emmett now slept. They were in his old room, across the hall from Caitlin.

"Mommy warned me," she whispered. "It's like that every night."

"In Vietnam we were the same way," Jack said, rolling over to take her into his arms.

"Well, Emmett still is." She could feel tears on her cheeks and realized she was crying.

"Are you okay, love?"

She nodded against his chest, tried to bury her face in the warmth of his body. He touched her left breast.

"No," she said.

"Sweetheart, please. I need you."

"No, darling." She pulled her head back so she could look at him, but in the dark bedroom, she saw only the shape of his head. She did not want to admit it, but she couldn't make love to him, not in her house, with her mother asleep across the hall.

Emmett screamed again.

"Oh, God!" She sat up, wondered then if she should go and wake him up. The hallway light went on. She saw an edge of it under the bedroom door, then heard her mother on the stairway, going up to see about her son. Emmett would be all right, she thought. He had their mother taking care of him, and she lay back in her new husband's arms and whispered, "Hold me, Jack." Then she turned herself to him, pressing her whole body against the length of his, as if he were suddenly the only safe place in her world, and preparing herself for the morning, when she knew she had to find out what was wrong with Emmett.

When she came down at eight o'clock the next morning, her mother was at the counter mixing pancake batter.

"I'll have breakfast in a few minutes," she said. "And when would Jack McGraff be getting up, that playboy of yours?"

Maggie laughed. "Let's let him sleep as long as he wants. He'll be up soon enough, as it is. I can't get him to rest much. But don't make the pancakes yet. I want to go talk to Emmett. Is he out in the barn?"

"He's well enough, he is," her mother said immediately.

"No, he isn't, Mother. He needs to see a doctor."

"There's nothing wrong with the boy," her mother said again, as if she regretted what she'd told Maggie the day before. "He doesn't need to be fooled with by doctors. They do more harm than good."

"The army will pay for it, Mom. He's entitled to help because of everything he's gone through."

"They took him away from me once, the government did, when I needed him," Caitlin said, suddenly angry. "I asked Michael to call his friends, you know, those people in Washington. All those high-up people, but Michael said it would be good for Emmett, his getting away from the place, learning a trade in the army. But look what happened to him.

"All they taught him was how to shoot a gun, and he wasn't there but six months when those yellow devils captured him. I never thought I'd see him alive again, not after two years, and when he got off the plane, I thought he'd come back from the dead. Half starved to death. I didn't know the boy. I've been feeding him four and five times a day just to get a little meat back on his bones. Now, go down to the barns and get him. It's time he had some breakfast. He's been up since before dawn." Caitlin began pouring pancakes into the skillet, her hands trembling as she did.

Maggie watched her mother. Each time she came home, Maggie saw another sign of her mother's aging. She had never thought of her mother growing old, of changing, of being anything but always there in the kitchen, making breakfast, cooking dinner, constantly working from morning to night. Always there, taking care of her and Emmett, taking care of all of them, year after year. As if this was all she was meant to be in life. It had been a tough life, Maggie knew, but she had never heard her mother complain about anything she had done for them, for any of them. Even Catty.

"Please, Mom!" Maggie said softly, controlling her voice. "Don't start making the pancakes. I want to talk to Emmett."

She walked to the back door and took down her old vest, slid it over her white turtleneck. She was wearing jeans from her high school days that her mother had cleaned and pressed, then folded away in her dresser, saving them for when she would be home again.

"Maggie, not now!"

"I'm not going to mention the war, Mom. Promise. It's just that yesterday, when he wouldn't be here to meet Jack—I want to find out what that's all about." She went through the back door before her mother could say more. She knew how her mother was—"Never go looking for trouble," she'd say, and then place a cap on her true feelings.

But her mother wouldn't be silenced this time. She followed after Maggie. "He's always been shy with people, you know that yourself. Give him time and he'll come around."

"I won't be here long enough to wait for that," Maggie said, turning around but continuing to walk backward, across the orchard. "I want to ask him to be nicer to Jack, that's all."

"Leave him be, Maggie. Leave the boy be," Caitlin whispered, trying not to be overheard by Emmett, who had come to the barn doorway and was watching Maggie cross the orchard.

Maggie smiled, waved her mother's concerns away, and then ran, awkward in the big black boots, to Emmett. It was a chilly May morning, and Emmett looked cold. He stood waiting with his hands deep in his pockets and his shoulders hunched, as if against a wind that only he felt coming.

Maggie had written Emmett while he was a POW to tell him that she was getting married. Her fiancé, she said, had been in Vietnam, too, as a helicopter pilot, and now he was running for Congress. "He sees a big Democratic sweep in the next election," she wrote, "and it's time for him to try, even though he's only twenty-six."

She had sent him a photograph of Jack, one taken in Vietnam in front of his Huey. But when Emmett wrote her back, all he said was, "Ask McGraff if he ever heard of Lamson."

They were on the small back porch of their house in Georgetown when she asked Jack about Lamson. It was shortly after their honeymoon, and Jack was trying to catch up on his work. He had set up her portable typewriter on the glass breakfast table and spread papers and books across the floor. She had retreated to the wicker couch and was stretched out there with an armload of schoolbooks when the mail arrived, bringing Emmett's letter from Hanoi, forwarded by the Peace Committee.

At the mention of Lamson, Jack looked up surprised and then said slowly, carefully, "Lamson was the last mission I flew. It was called Lamson seven-nineteen, and it was the final push of the war. It began in February. I don't remember exactly. The ARVN was supposed to be doing the real fighting; we were only involved with air support. Their mission was to wipe out the Ho Chi Minh Trail in the Laotian panhandle before the Cong moved south again. Congress had just passed the amendment forbidding American troops to enter Cambodia and Laos, so the ARVN had to do most of the work. It was a secret that Americans were involved at all. Why do you ask?"

Maggie shrugged, waved the airletter. "Emmett asks if you knew anything about Lamson."

"I had nothing to do with it," he said quickly, shuffling his papers as he spoke. "I flew brass up to the front on a look-see, but not into Laos, since we weren't permitted over the border."

"What does Lamson mean?"

"Oh, it's an ancient Vietnamese triumph over China. But this Vietnamization was a massive blunder."

"Were you doing any fighting?"

Jack shook his head. "All of us chopper pilots were used to get out the wounded from the war zone, that's all. There was a mess of wounded, because the South Vietnamese really screwed it up. They were to hit Tchepone, a town twenty miles inside Laos—that was their mission—but the army fell apart, started retreating as soon as they came under heavy fire. It was a bloody mess. Jesus, what a mess.

"I must have been going in for wounded twenty, twenty-five times a day. We were flying low, and I could see thousands of dead men along the road. What was worse were the South Vietnamese soldiers. They'd grab on to the choppers whenever we went down to pick up a litter. I can't blame them. They were just trying to get away from the fighting. But we couldn't fly, not with them hanging from the skids. We had to kick them off just to get the damn Huey into the air. And then those bastards started shooting at us, just like the VC."

"Oh, God, Jack, how terrible!" Maggie could imagine the scene, and felt terrible that her husband was involved.

"The South Vietnamese army knew it was over for them. We knew it. We were all operating on dope then. Drugs were so damn cheap. A vial of pure heroin cost maybe ten bucks. I bought a whole carton of joints soaked in opium for the price of a box of laundry soap. The dope was keeping us from going crazy, but we went crazy anyway. Everyone I knew, the guys in my unit, all of us were strung out. We tried to stay high all the time."

"You used opium?"

"You're damn right! I used whatever dope I could get my hands on. I was half crazy most of the time."

"But how could you fly when you were stoned?"

"It was easier being stoned. I never thought about getting killed. The drugs gave me the feeling that I would live forever."

Jack stopped speaking. Maggie had been listening so hard that when he stopped she was momentarily shocked by the surge of noise from the busy Georgetown traffic. It was the first time Jack had said so much about his last days in Vietnam.

"Some of the officers were being killed by their own men. Guys I knew—kids, first lieutenants just over from Bragg—who pissed off their men, or were cracking down too hard on the dope, would get it at night in their sleep. Someone would drop a hand grenade in the hooch and that was it. Fragging, it was called."

"I never heard that," Maggie whispered, stunned by what her new husband was telling her.

"It's true enough. When I wasn't stoned, I just kept praying I'd get out alive. I was scared all the time I was in Nam. I didn't want to be a goddamn hero. I just wanted to get home alive, and with my arms and legs."

He stood up and began to pace. Recalling the war upset him, Maggie realized.

"I left Saigon on June thirteenth, at thirteen-forty," he went on in the same soft voice. "I'll never forget the moment the plane took off. It was the same day the Pentagon Papers broke in the *New York Times*. When I reached Tachikawa in Japan I saw a wire story about the papers, but it wasn't until I was on my way to the States, all those long hours in the C-one-forty-one, that I understood it meant the end of the war.

"Lamson seven-nineteen was just the final example of how we and the Vietnamese had blundered. We lost a lot of men—not our guys, ARVN soldiers—and I was glad the Cong kicked ass." He paused again and looked across the porch to where she was stretched out on the couch. "Why? Why do you think Emmett asked?"

"I don't know." Maggie looked at the letter again. "Maybe that's where he was captured. Do you think that's possible?"

"If it was, he was there by mistake or on an intelligence mission. Yes, tell him I know about Lamson. I know too damn much about it." He sat down again and looked at his yellow legal pad, as if trying to gather his thoughts about the work ahead.

Maggie went up the ramp to the barn door, smiling as she approached her brother.

"Mom says that breakfast is almost ready, but I told her to hold everything for a while. Do you have time to talk?"

Emmett kept watching her, his face thin and gray. He had lost weight, she saw, and it made him look dangerous, the way a dog might be if left to starve. She was suddenly frightened, then as she came closer, she saw the fear that hovered in his eyes. It made him look helpless, like a child awakened in the middle of the night.

"Oh, Emmett! Don't worry. You're home now and safe." She had always been able to handle his black periods, but at that moment she was not sure she could do it anymore. She wasn't sure she could bring him back whole again from Vietnam.

"I need to go down to the river, check the drainage. Come along if you want," he said.

"Good!" She would make his simple offer into a gift. She smiled up at him.

"Are you going to tell me why you don't like my husband?" she asked. They were crossing the cornfield, walking between the rows of stubble. Maggie was having trouble keeping up with him and she grabbed his arm. The question, she hoped, would slow him down.

"Did you ask him about Lamson?" Emmett did not alter his stride.

"I did. Lamson seven-nineteen. It was the code name for the final attack on the Ho Chi Minh Trail. I wrote and told you, remember?"

"It was where I got caught in seventy-one, on February ninth." He stopped again and Maggie glanced around to see what he might have spotted. They were in a muddy field, with icy water between the rows of corn stubs. A hundred yards away was the river, hidden behind the high bank and a thick growth of trees and brush. She could hear the water. It always ran wild in the spring after the first thaw.

"I had gone into Laos on reconnaissance. It was a secret mission, because Americans weren't supposed to cross the border anymore, but like a goddamn asshole I volunteered. There was lots of fire fighting, even that late in the war, and when this job came along, my squad leader asked me to go with him. He was a real gung-ho sonofabitch.

"It was a MAAG mission, or maybe Special Forces, I don't know. They never told us. They just said they wanted a report on how the South Vietnamese troops were doing. I thought I was some sort of hotshot. They dropped us in late in the day into this rice paddy.

"It was, like, this field, with a river nearby. I could hear it, all night I heard that river, and kept thinking of the Kaskaskia, like it is now, when the snow melts. I was so scared that night I kept praying that in the morning, when I woke up, I'd see our house there, at the edge of the field. But in the morning there was nothing at the edge of the paddy but some brown thatched huts, mud walls, moats.

"I was radioman. They had given me this goddamn PRC/ten radio that wouldn't work, but I had my own tools—I learned that in basic —and I worked on it half the night. It wasn't until oh-five-twenty that I could signal out that we hadn't spotted any action, and no ARVN. They told me at base that it was okay. A Huey was coming to get us out. I was to signal every five minutes.

"The river was high, and we were standing in mud up to our knees, just waiting in the rice field for the Huey to come get us. We weren't but five minutes across the border. We were told the South Vietnamese should be reaching us, pushing on to Tchepone, but we were all alone in this empty field. Me, my squad leader, Leffer, and these two guys. One guy, Miller, was from Iowa. And this other bastard, some guy named Resnick. They never made it out.

"The Huey came in all right. God, it was great seeing it cruise over the jungle. I felt, like, I am saved, you know, it was going to be okay. I would live forever, I thought. There were these two Cobras with it, smaller copters that were, like, riding shotgun. Christ, I was so damn happy to see them. I kept telling myself: I ain't never going to volunteer again.

"One of the Cobras banked and came closer, and it couldn't have been fifty feet above the rice field, as if it was looking for us. They couldn't see us because we were hiding down in the rice beds, hiding from the VC. But they have shark noses, those copters, and this one kept nosing around the field, as if it knew we were there. I was only ten or fifteen yards from it and, hell, I wasn't going to let those bastards fly off and leave me. I jumped up, waving, shouting, and I hear Resnick yelling at me. I glance over and he's standing, aiming his side arm at me. And then he starts shooting, like I was the goddamn VC or something, and I fall on my face into the muck.

"As I was falling, I saw this Cobra tip forward, fixing aim, and I knew I was dead. There was a burst of machine-gun fire, but it wasn't even close. The Cobra had spotted Laotians or VCs or something behind us, in the mud huts at the edge of the field, and it was cutting them up.

"I was in the water—it couldn't have been more than two feet deep —and I was thrashing at it, swinging my arms, screaming. I must have been screaming, I was so scared, but I couldn't hear the sound of my voice over the chop's engine. I remember seeing those miserable brown huts just explode in flame. People were running from them, naked kids, women, everyone I guess, running across the bare compound. I saw these silly-ass chickens—they looked like Rhode Island reds—all scattering.

"Anyway, I turn around and Resnick he's coming at me, stumping through the muddy water. He's got his side arm back in his holster and he's saying something but I can't hear him over the machine-gun fire. And then he kinda staggers, looks sick; I didn't even know then what the fuck was going on. I'm still screaming. But I can't hear myself screaming. I can't move. I see Leffer, and he's maybe twenty yards away, but I'm thinking he's like from here to maybe the barn, and I'm never going to get to him. I don't know what to do.

"He waves, signals that we should go across the paddy field, away from the village, and I want to do that. I know I want to do that. I try to run in the water, but shit you can't run through that mud. It's like this shit. I fall down and lose my M-one, but I don't care. I'm going to die, I know. I'm going to die in that muck.

"But I keep thinking: I'll reach the other side. I can see sort of a patch of dry land. A little island, like, and I'm thinking the Huey can set down, pick us up. I glance over at Leffer. He's not there anymore. He was as close as that bank and then he's not there anymore. I can't see anything in the water because of the reeds, and now he's been shot. But I can't see any VC, so I can't figure out who shot him. The Cobra, it makes another pass overhead. It's so close I see the green goggles the pilot is wearing, and then the copter sweeps over me, and the machine gun starts firing.

"They're waiting for me to reach dry ground, I keep telling myself. They can't save me unless I reach this little shit island in the middle of the paddy field. And I'm still waving. And shouting. The Huey itself comes down. It's settling onto the island. I can see a gunner in the doorway. He's carrying an M-sixty, a machine gun, and he's watching me run, crawl, stagger, you know, toward them. I'm still shouting; I'm waving. I'm so goddamn afraid that they are going to fly away and leave me.

"I know there's fighting going on all around me. The VC are firing at the choppers from the woods, and I hear this tremendous crash, and without looking, I know a Cobra has been hit, gone down in the rice paddy. And then I feel a wave of heat as it explodes. At this point I couldn't have been but ten feet from the Huey on the island. I was so close and slowly I see the copter pulling up and off. It's leaving me, I realize. I can't believe it's leaving me, and here I can see the gunner in the doorway. He's leaving me to die there in this fucking paddy.

"I ran for that mother. I was running as fast as I could, soaked down like I was with water. Water in my boots. My feet felt like pilings. But I ran. Jesus Christ did I run. And I grabbed the copter skid.

"The Huey pulls up. It hovers there. Stalling, like. And I hear this firing, see the flashing of bullets, and all I can think about is for them to get this fucker up, out of the rice fields. Here I am hanging there, ready to be sliced in half with machine-gun fire, and then someone stepped on my arm.

"I grab my other hand around the skid, and he kicks again. I start screaming at him that I'm an American. I'm screaming, swearing, but he can't hear me. The chopper is too noisy. I look up, thinking he'll see my face, then he'll know.

"I see him. I get a good look. He's a gunner. Another Spec Four. I can see his name tag: Cowan. I think he's grinning at me, but he's not. He's just pissed that I won't let go. I think he's going to kill me next, pull out his side arm and blow me off the skid.

"But he steps down on my fingers and breaks two. These two. And I scream. I got no strength left in my hand. I make another grab at the skid with my right arm. This is it, I know, but if I can get inside the chopper, make him see who it is—a goddamn American! Not another fucking VC.

"I give it another try, swing my legs up to grab the skid. I was good at this in basic. I got it, too! Then this bastard clubbed my good arm. It broke in two places. Some VC medic set it over there. I'm lucky I didn't lose the damn thing.

"With my arm broken, I couldn't hold on. I was screaming, I know, when I fell back into the water of that stinking rice-paddy hole. Then he started to shoot at me with his side arm, but the Huey pulled up too fast; he missed. And he's gone. The Huey just kept lifting off, flew over the trees and back to Saigon. I caught the helicopter's number, and I spotted the pilot as he banked it. I saw that sucker, and I promised myself: that bastard will pay for leaving me, because, by God, I wasn't going to die in that jungle. No way."

"Please, Emmett, don't tell me any more," Maggie whispered, and felt her legs weaken, felt herself trembling.

"When I was captured by the VC, they force-marched us north to Hanoi. That was when I found out there were others like us, reconnaissance missions sent into Laos. We had been sent in there to be killed by the VC or our own guys. That's why Resnick v. as shooting at me. He didn't want me giving away our position to the choppers. He was on his third tour, and he was smarter than I was about figuring out we'd been set up. My radio wasn't supposed to work. We weren't supposed to be able to get a signal out, and when I got that piece of shit to work, well, they sent the copters in to get us."

"Why?" Maggie asked, through her tears.

Emmett shook his head. "The best we could figure—those of us that stayed alive—was that Nixon and Kissinger needed an excuse to override the congressional rule about troops in Cambodia and Laos. We were going to be the excuse. Nixon could go on television and tell the American people our boys were being captured in Vietnam and taken across the border, therefore, we had to use U.S. troops to go get them. They didn't want us saying we had been captured while on reconnaissance; they wanted us dead."

He gestured awkwardly to the house, fumbling as he spoke. "When you sent the photo, I wasn't sure. I kept telling myself it couldn't be. I could make out only a couple of serial numbers on the airframe in the photo, but they were the right ones. When you drove up here yesterday, I was in the barn loft. I saw him stepping out of the car. Then I knew. I knew for goddamn sure he was the pilot of that chopper."

Emmett turned away from her and shoved his hands into his overalls pockets, trudging back across the muddy cornfield, stepping carelessly through the icy puddles. He walked toward the farmhouse, his thin shoulders hunched up. He looked sick and weak, not dangerous at all.

Maggie couldn't watch him, couldn't look toward the house where her new husband slept in the boy's old bedroom. She spun away, crying, and exposed her face to the raw wind off the river. Jack McGraff had left Emmett to die in a godforsaken rice field, and her brother would never forget, never forgive, nor, she realized, would his sister.

# · CHAPTER 37 ·

GATESBURG: 1982

MAGGIE OPENED ANOTHER BOTTLE of white wine. She felt as if she had been doing nothing but drinking since she had returned home.

That was how women became alcoholics, she thought: slowly and over time. It frightened her just thinking about it; she had seen too many newspaper people end up that way.

Well, this drink she deserved, she decided. She recorked the bottle, picked up her glass, a tumbler of orange juice for Wendy, and went back to the living room, where Wendy was standing in front of the fire.

"Oh, Aunt Mag, can't I have wine? I drink at home. Mom knows."

"You're pregnant, honey, and drinking is bad for the baby."

"Oh, shit."

"Wendy!" Maggie's tone was sharp. "You may or may not want this child, but it's alive."

"You don't have to play mother with me, Aunt Maggie," Wendy snapped.

"Honey! We're not going to spend this evening, or any evening trashing your mother." Maggie sat down and tried to start over. "Let's keep our relationship free of the rest of the family, okay?" She smiled and softened her voice. Wendy didn't need another judgmental adult in her young life.

Wendy nodded. "It's kind of strange, you know, being here." She indicated the house and then shrugged. "The only thing Mom told us about this place is how really terrible it was. You know, how she had to work all day long, never got to play or go out or anything, like she was in prison or something." She shrugged again. "But I love the house!" Her brown eyes widened in pleasure. "Can I sleep in Mom's old bedroom?"

"You can sleep wherever you want, honey," Maggie answered. "And I want you to fix up the room if you like. I'll help you." She hoped that Wendy had come to stay, that this wasn't just her first stop on a long flight away from Chicago. She smiled at her niece and sipped the wine. At that moment Maggie felt parental, and she liked it. It was what she missed in her own life, and for a moment she put off worrying how she could stay on the farm and still make a living. She would write a book on the Middle East, she thought; that was something she could do in Gatesburg. The idea suddenly sounded very tempting.

"You think I should have this kid?" Wendy cocked her head, a DeLacey trait, and looked suddenly afraid.

"Oh, sweetheart, I really don't know what to tell you. I'm so sorry you got yourself in such a fix. What about Jeff? Have you thought about marrying him?"

"No way!" Wendy pulled her legs up and wrapped her arms around her knees. She lay staring at the blaze as she went on. "I can't stand him. He's a jerk."

"He's the father of your child, isn't he? Or is it someone else? Is that it?"

"Aunt Maggie! I know what all you people think, but I'm not one of those girls."

"I don't think that. I simply asked if you were sure he was the father. If so, then he has certain legal rights, and also, legal responsibilities."

"Well, I'm not going to have it. I don't care what you say." Wendy sat up again, as if it were all decided.

Maggie did not respond. She couldn't tell the girl what to do and would not get into arguments about what was right. Maggie looked at the burning logs. The maple was dry and sparks kept flying into the screen. When they were young, they had seldom used the front-room fireplace but had spent most of their evenings in the kitchen, clustered around the old wood stove.

"It's what my mother wants anyway," Wendy said, crying. "She doesn't care what happens to me. None of them care!"

"Oh, darling, you're so wrong." Maggie went to her niece, took the teenager into her arms. "Your mother and father care so much about you. They love you."

"They could have killed me when I told them I was knocked up."

"They don't want you to be hurt, that's all. If you have an abortion, it will hurt you, and if you don't, well, there are many other problems."

"They're ashamed of me. They don't know what they're going to tell their friends at the Glen Ellyn Country Club. They'd like me to just go away and get out of their life. Go die somewhere, that's all."

Wendy began to sob then, deep, helpless sobs. Maggie, tightening her embrace, pulled the child into her lap and let Wendy cry out all her pain. She thought of herself at Wendy's age, and wondered how she might have dealt with pregnancy.

But she hadn't gotten pregnant, not that time, nor ever, even when she was married. It wasn't until she filed for divorce that Jack admitted he couldn't have children. A missing ingredient in the gene system, he joked, and Father Mike had used that bit of information to have her marriage annulled.

The telephone rang while she was holding Wendy and she let it ring. Finally, Wendy squirmed out of her arms to run for the phone. Maggie stopped her, saying, "No, I'd better. It's probably your mother and she'll want to talk."

"Don't tell her I'm being a jerk."

"You're not being a jerk." Maggie bent down and kissed Wendy on the forehead, and then hurried into the hallway and picked up the receiver. She closed the front-room door behind her.

"Mag, it's me." He sounded as if he were telephoning from town.

"Michael?"

"Yes. How are you?"

"Fine. I guess. You've talked with Father O'Connor?"

He paused a moment, as if to phrase his reply, and then said casually, "We just got off the phone."

"Then you know all about the mortgage. Michael, what in the world has happened here? Why did Mother need such a huge amount of money? Do you have any idea?" She sat down on the bottom steps of the dark stairway.

"Yes, I know about it," he went on, again carefully measuring out his words. "Mag, could you fly to Washington? I can't get away at the moment, and we need to talk."

"I can't . . . Wendy is here."

"Wendy Duffy? Is Cat there, too?"

"No, just Wendy. She's . . . visiting." Maggie did not tell Michael about the pregnancy; that was news Catty could break to their brother.

He was silent a moment, and then he said more forcefully, "Maggie, it's important that we talk in person, about this mortgage, and about this nonsense with Emmett over in the jail."

"I'm calling Catty later this evening, and I'll see what can be arranged. But I'm not going to go off and leave Wendy by herself. Besides, there's the livestock; they need to be looked after."

"What about Paddy Jack? He's still hanging out with Vanessa Harris, isn't he?"

"Yes, Paddy's here." Michael might be in Washington, D.C., she throught wryly, but he still knew what was happening in Gatesburg. "I'll speak to him and get back to you. I'll try to come to Washington before the end of the week. I need to stop by the *Post* as well and clear up a few things."

"Good! Call me in the morning." He sounded pleased, as he always did when he got his way, and then relaxing, he said good-bye, explaining that a California call was waiting. "My love to Wendy," he added, hanging up.

Maggie chewed her lip thoughtfully as she replaced the receiver. Lately, she realized, her conversations with Michael hadn't been at all to her liking. He made her feel like furniture, an item he could move around easily in his busy life.

Headlights swatted across the hallway wall as a car turned off the highway and came around the side of the house. Maggie heard the car drive past the house, its heavy wheels crunching the frozen snow.

Probably Paddy Jack, she thought, back from Chicago.

She opened the front-room door and said to Wendy, "I think your uncle Paddy Jack is here. I'm going to let him through the kitchen. Stay here, honey. I'll be right back."

As she walked down the hall to the kitchen she felt the chill. The front-room fireplace was still blazing, but there was little warmth just yards away in the hallway. Emmett was right, she thought: it was impossible to heat the house, not on a night like this when the temperature dropped below zero. She remembered how as a child she would often wake freezing at night and go into her mother's room to sleep with her in the warmth and safety of the big double bed. And in the morning she would stay under the covers until her mother had gotten the fire started in the kitchen's wood stove.

As Maggie reached the kitchen, the bright moon caught that corner of the house and filled the kitchen with pale, ghostly light. She crossed to the windows and peered out.

The car door opened and she saw in the moonlight that it wasn't Paddy Jack at all, but a woman bundled in a heavy coat. Vanessa? No, the car wasn't a Mercedes. Going to the back door, she unlocked it quickly and went out onto the freezing back porch. Before she opened the storm door, she saw who it was, and she called into the night, "Catty! Here, the back door."

Her sister was carrying luggage and it threw her off balance as she tripped through the snow and up the back steps. Then she clomped into the kitchen, dripping with wet snow, her teeth chattering.

"Did Wendy arrive?"

"Yes—she got in about three."

"Good. Maggie, Joe sent me down to get her."

"She's not in a mood to go home just yet, Cat," Maggie said, speaking softly.

"Joe wants to get her back to Chicago for an abortion," Catty went on, speaking fast. "He's blaming me for what happened."

"Oh, Cat. Please, try not to get upset," Maggie said quickly, watching her sister. "An abortion is what Wendy says she wants, so I guess it'll be all right. She'll be willing to go home if those are the conditions. Joe can have his way."

"No." Catty shook her head. "I didn't come here to bring her home. I left Joe."

"Cat!"

Catty moved away from Maggie and paced the kitchen as she went on explaining, "Mother tried to run my life when I was Wendy's age. I told you. She was going to send me away to have the baby, then give it up. I won't do that to my daughter. Wendy can do whatever she wants. And I'm going to support her whatever that decision. I won't do to Wendy what Mom did to me."

# · CHAPTER 38 ·

## WASHINGTON: 1982

"STOP HERE!" MAGGIE TOLD the cabdriver. They had reached
Scott Circle at Massachusetts Avenue, and Michael's office was only
half a block away. She would walk from the circle, she thought; she
needed a few minutes to stretch her legs and decide what to say to
Michael. She had never confronted her oldest brother, she realized,
and she wasn't enjoying the prospect. But she had to go through with
it. Michael was up to something, she knew, although she didn't know
what. Of one thing she was sure—Emmett's welfare came first. No
matter what reason Mike gave for stalling, Emmett's bail had to be
paid, and soon.

Although she dreaded her talk with Michael, it was good to be away
from the farm for a few days. It would give Catty and Wendy a chance
to talk, and Catty needed time to decide if she had really left her
husband or, like her daughter, had only run away from home. Maggie
knew, though, that these practical reasons didn't account for her sense
of relief at being away.

She had only been home from Africa three weeks, but the farmhouse and town were preying on her. She had first put it down to the
weather, and to the flatness of the Illinois landscape. But that wasn't
all, Maggie realized. She couldn't go back to live on the farm. There
was nothing there for her anymore. It wasn't that the town had
changed, or that her mother was gone, but that she had grown beyond
the midwest, knew more of the world. She was another farm girl who
couldn't go home again.

Maggie looked up ahead. The Blue and Whites had their headquarters in a brownstone a few doors down the street. She wasn't certain
that Michael would be there on a Saturday morning, but she knew his
routine. He celebrated early Mass at Saint Matthew's, played hand-
ball at the new YMCA, and then stopped by the office to check his
messages and mail.

She was across the street from his office when the front door of the
Blue and Whites' brownstone opened and Michael appeared. He was

wearing a black turtleneck, sweat pants, and silver Nike jogging shoes. He stepped briefly into the sunlight to let someone out, then turned back inside and closed the door. Maggie paused. The man on the steps was coatless and wearing a suit. As he walked up the street to a waiting limousine, he tucked his tie into his suit coat. It was a gesture Maggie knew. The man leaving her brother's office was Jack McGraff.

An aide opened the limo's door and McGraff slipped into the rear seat. There was a woman waiting there, and Maggie wondered who she was. These days he always seemed to travel in a crowd of press aides, advisers, and women. She did not think of crossing the street to catch his attention, and in moments his car was gone, down Sixteenth toward the White House. What kept Maggie standing in the street a few minutes more was a question she couldn't begin to answer: what was Jack McGraff doing visiting her brother?

Michael's desk stood just beneath the office windows and the bright winter light left him in shadows. Maggie could not see his eyes. He might have been her confessor hidden behind a screen. She stood up and walked over to the windows for a better view. He did not turn to face her, and she was able to watch her brother, as she might a handsome stranger on a plane.

Michael's face caught the light like hewn wood. Great blunt chisel marks shaped his features as if a craftsman had let the profile go unfinished. The strength of his face was tempered by blue eyes that suggested warmth and unexpected kindness. Women, she knew, were always disarmed by the softness of his eyes.

His thick hair, still wet from his morning shower, needed to be cut. It curled around his ears and caught at the collar of his turtleneck,. There was a new grayness at his temples, and gray streaks like fine silk threaded throughout his black hair. He was aging, she realized, and the thought surprised her. She never imagined Michael growing old.

Still, she was pleased that age had made him a better-looking man, handsome in a Hollywood sort of way. He took care of himself and stayed in shape. And she was secretly pleased that other women found him desirable. She wondered then, and not for the first time, if ever in his long celibate life he had had an affair.

"Where are you staying?" he asked. It seemed an odd first question.

"At the Talbart Inn."

"I'll walk you there."

"Michael, I just came! We need to talk."

"We can talk on the way. It's a lovely day. Besides I want the exercise." He was on his feet, reaching for his Lacoste jacket.

Maggie stared at him. There was something wrong. Why was he rushing her from his office?

On the street, he took her arm and said quietly, "We can talk now, Maggie."

Maggie knew at once what he meant. "Your office is bugged?"

"We believe so." He did not seem upset. It was to be expected when one lived in the nation's capital.

"You're sure?"

"Yes. One of our members was in army intelligence. He's found bugs on all our phones and three listening devices in my office."

She felt a sudden chill. "Who?"

"He thinks it might be the British, because he's not familiar with that type of tap. The FBI, he says, prefer one kind, the CIA another. Neither of those is being used in our headquarters."

"Why the British?"

"Because Margaret Thatcher thinks anyone who supports a united Ireland is a terrorist. That bitch!"

Maggie had never heard her brother talk like that, but it was his rage, not his words, that stunned her. Of all the family, he was the gentlest. She had always felt that she had to protect him from the ways of the world. Now she wasn't sure. She realized that she didn't know Michael at all.

"Emmett!" he announced, pressing forward.

"Yes, Emmett."

"Dermot has filled me in about his being on the blanket, all that foolishness." They had reached the corner of N and Seventeenth, and Maggie turned down the block toward her hotel, but Michael stopped, as if this were as far as he was willing to go.

"Maggie, you're wrong about Emmett. I want you to stop trying to get him out of jail."

The tone of his voice stunned Maggie. She was used to being cajoled by her brother. Now she forced herself to answer.

"You're the one causing the problem, Michael. It's all over Gatesburg that you set the amount of bail, you and Father O'Connor. And when was the farm mortgaged to its rafters? O'Hara told me yesterday morning about this two-hundred-and-fifty-thousand-dollar mortgage. Do you know anything about that?"

"Emmett took it out," the bishop said gently. "He did it in the fall."

"That's not possible, Mom would have told me."

"Maggie, you must have noticed in September that Mom's mind was going. She was forgetting everything! Besides, I'm sure she didn't even know. When Emmett came home from Vietnam, we— Father O'Connor, myself, and Mother, too—thought it would be best to put the property in two names in case anything happened to her. I couldn't be an owner because of my vow of poverty, and, well, you were off in the Middle East at the time. That left Emmett. I thought it would do him good to have some legal responsibility. That has proved to be a mistake."

His voice was lower and he was looking away from her, down Seventeenth. The bright winter sun was blinding as it glanced off the new glass office buildings that marked the street. Maggie saw there were tears in Michael's eyes. "Michael, what do you mean?" She moved closer to her brother, suddenly feeling she needed his protection.

"John Keenan telephoned me from the bank the morning of the funeral. He told me Emmett had taken out the loan. Somehow he had gotten Mother to sign the note."

"And the money?"

"No one knows. Gambling maybe. Drugs. The money is gone."

"Oh, dear God."

"That's why the bail is so high. We have to keep Emmett in jail. If he gets out, he might skip Illinois with whatever money is left, and we'd lose the farm for sure."

She knew what Michael was thinking next, and then he said it. "That's the motive, Maggie. Mother found out about the mortgage. Maybe the bank called during one of her lucid moments, and she realized the bank had new paper on the property. The two of them alone there . . . who knows? He got mad, they fought, and . . . I don't know." The priest shrugged.

Michael had stepped a few feet away from her, and now he looked back, cocking his head. He had his hands in his pockets, protecting them against the cold, and in his black trousers and tan jacket he looked like an Irish club fighter.

"Look, Mag," he said, his voice suddenly thick with brogue, "leave the boy on his own. You can't be fighting Emmett's fights forever. You have a life of your own."

"Emmett hasn't said anything about taking the money, not to me, or O'Hara. Larry O'Hara would have told me."

"Maggie, forget about the mortgage." The bishop's voice turned hard again. "At the moment, I think we can get Emmett off on temporary insanity. All this malarkey of going on the blanket helps. It doesn't do any good to raise new problems for Emmett, not when he's looking at a first-degree-murder sentence." Michael sounded bitter.

"Vanessa Harris has suggested a lawyer friend of hers who she said is quite good. She's going to speak to Paddy Jack—"

"Forget Vanessa Harris and her suggestions," the bishop cut in.

"Joe Werth will handle the trial. I've spoken to him and a hearing date has been set for the end of next week. We don't want an outside lawyer coming into Gatesburg and pushing everyone around."

"His name is Foster, and he's from Gatesburg. The point."

"Nor do we need to draw attention to the family's success by hiring a rich man's lawyer. Where did he do his law, Harvard? And now he works in Chicago, right?" Michael's voice was full of contempt. "Joe Werth has been practicing all his life in Gatesburg. It was his father's practice. He knows everyone in town by their first name. People trust him. You know that, Maggie. So if Joe is defending Emmett, well, then we have an edge with the jury. Use your head, Maggie. We have a public-relations job to do in Gatesburg. We have to get sympathy for the family. If not, they'll crucify us."

"Emmett did not kill Mother, Michael, and I am telling you I will not stand by and have you arrange for him to be declared insane!"

"Would you rather have him go to jail for life? That's what he's facing in Illinois for murder. He'd be better off in an institution where he can get some help. Though to tell you the truth, I think Emmett is beyond us all now—especially you, Maggie!"

"What do you mean?"

"Emmett has never forgiven you for marrying Jack McGraff. It's all twisted up in his mind, his war experience, your marriage, his feeling that the one he loved abandoned him. You must have learned at least that much about the human psyche at college."

"No," she answered. "There is nothing unhealthy about Emmett's feelings toward me. He loves me. I love him. I'm not going to have anyone in this family saying that it was Emmett's latent incestuous feelings toward me that brought about Mother's death. I refuse to believe he killed her. In an accident, maybe. That's all!

"And I'm going to get a first-class legal mind, not Joe Werth or any of those country lawyers who hang out with the cops at the Towne's Diner, to defend him. I'm going to get Emmett out of jail whether or not you or anyone else in the family supports me. And I'm going to prove he's innocent—not insane; innocent. He is not going to live the rest of his life in Gatesburg with people thinking he's a crazy killer!"

"Maggie, you'll hurt him in the end," Michael snapped back. "He'll never get out of jail. I've been in touch with O'Hara—"

"That jerk!"

"He's going to be the next sheriff of Gatesburg."

"Yes, on the strength of convicting Emmett."

"Maggie, you're blind-siding yourself on this one." Michael stepped closer. "This is small-town politics. You can complain about the lawyers and the police hanging out at the same diner, but that's where the deals are made. 'You take care of me; I'll take care of you.' Don't tamper with those people and the way that they get things done. If you bring a lawyer down from Chicago, you'll only hurt Emmett. It would do Emmett a lot more good if you left Gatesburg and kept up the image of a sister confident of his innocence, instead of hanging around town and fighting everyone."

Michael was right, she had to admit. She had learned at least that much about politics as a reporter in Washington: how things looked were at least as important as how they really were, if not more so. She was a little surprised that Michael had become so politically deft. Still, she didn't want to let go, to turn Emmett's fate over to people she did not trust.

"I don't know." She sighed, giving up. "Is this Joe Werth up to the case?"

"What does it matter if Emmett is innocent?" Michael countered. "If Emmett didn't harm Mother, then none of us has anything to fear."

Maggie glanced up at Michael, but did not respond. She didn't like all this rush to justice. "I'm afraid no one will protect Emmett, that he'll suffer the consequences because no one, not even his own family, gives a damn."

Michael smiled. "Maggie, you're going to just have to trust me on this one. I'll make sure nothing happens to Emmett." And then he kissed her lightly on the cheek, waved good-bye, and jogged down Rhode Island Avenue toward Saint Matthew's Cathedral, leaving her standing on the street corner thinking again how she never got her way with Michael, that now, just as always, he was still in control, still making the decisions in her life. But not this time, she told herself. For now, and for the first time in her life, she didn't trust Father Mike.

The Talbart Inn on N Street reminded Maggie of a country hotel in Great Britain, especially during the winter months, when they kept a fire going in the lounge, and there was always a crowd of young people and academics filling the hotel. Instead of the bureaucratic gray of most government workers, the men wore tweeds with leather elbow patches, and sober brown wool knit ties. The women were always in jeans, with baggy tops, or knitted suits and flat heels.

She used to meet Jack there when they were first dating. It was always cozy in the lounge, and she would order a Black Russian— that was her drink when she was in college—and she would sit with a schoolbook open on her lap and listen to the professors and their students as they went on about paganism and Christianity in the fourth century, or Wallace Stevens and the contemporary sensibility.

It all seemed so refined and distant, and she wondered if any of them worried about the war in Vietnam or had brothers like hers who were POWs somewhere in Southeast Asia.

For those professors and students, the war was already over. The Paris peace talks had started. The bombing had stopped. And no one was being drafted out of school. She was the only one worried, although she refused to believe that Emmett might not come home to her.

And she had been right. But this time, she was afraid, the DeLaceys might not be so lucky. Her life, which had always seemed so safe, had begun to slowly unravel. Now, as she walked into the hotel, she tried to decide when, at what moment, everything had begun to go wrong.

It had started when Emmett came home from Hanoi, she thought. Vietnam had touched her more than she would admit.

She walked up to the desk and gave the clerk her name, saying she had a reservation for the weekend. Her room was not ready so she signed the register form and then walked into the lounge, where she ordered a Bloody Mary and sat down in one of the high-back wing chairs set close to the fireplace. She was cold again, a deep trembling chill, but it wasn't from the weather. Michael's news of how Emmett had stolen from their mother had chilled her. She wondered if all deaths were like this, if someone's death always released a flood of secrets from the past. She leaned her head back in the wing chair and closed her eyes. The lounge was empty, the hotel quiet in the late morning, and she wished she would fall off to sleep.

"Maggie? Is that you, Margaret?" a woman asked.

Maggie opened her eyes and saw Ann Merrill standing above her. She had been the consul in Addis Ababa while Maggie was there.

"It *is* you! Of all people!" Ann sat down immediately, smiling with pleasure, and squeezed Maggie's hand. "It's so good to see you! What in the world are you doing in Washington?"

"I could ask you the same question," Maggie retorted, sitting up.

"I'm home for reassignment. When did we last talk? Was it the marine ball at the Addis Hilton?" Ann Merrill kept talking, answering her own questions as she slipped out of her down vest. "I was on leave in Paris for a month, and now I'm holding down the Ethiopian desk job at State until I'm reassigned. Oh, gosh, it's so good to see a familiar face in this city. Can we have lunch? How long are you in D.C.?" The questions kept tumbling out.

"I ran into Clayton Rule the other day in Lafayette Square. He said you were back from Addis, because of your mother. I'm terribly sorry, Mag; it must be just ghastly about your brother and all."

"Thank you. Everything will be fine." Maggie forced a smile to silence the woman.

"Have you seen Kenneth?" Ann asked next.

Virginia Graves was right, Maggie realized. Everyone in Addis did know of the affair. Why did she think they were being so clever, she wondered.

"No, I have no plans to see Kenneth." She thought again of his telegram, and his offer to help.

"He's out of Ethiopia for good," Ann went on, whispering now.

"He is?"

"Because of Virginia." The woman's eyes were sparkling. "You wouldn't believe the cable traffic when I took over the Ethiopia desk. Virginia tried to kill herself a week ago. Kenneth was here in Washington working on famine relief money, and one night in Addis, Virginia ran naked and screaming drunk out of the residence, right past the Marine Guard at the embassy gate, and threw herself in front of a lorry coming down Entoto Street. She was damn lucky she wasn't killed; you know how those lorry drivers never brake."

"Oh, my God!" Maggie closed her eyes against the picture.

"The woman's a terrible lush."

Maggie started to reply, but Ann Merrill rushed on with more details. "She's in a sanitarium in Rockville, drying out. Kenneth has gone on medical leave. And, this I hear second hand, he's already filing for divorce."

Maggie wouldn't look over at Ann Merrill. She kept staring at the fire, thinking of how Virginia Graves had threatened her.

"Maggie, I'm not going to play games with you," Ann said softly, leaning closer. "I know about you and Kenneth. We all knew. I mean, you two weren't very careful, really. It's okay." She reached out and squeezed Maggie's hand. "What she did in Addis isn't your fault. There are stories all over Foggy Bottom about that woman, how she behaved when they were posted in Kenya, in the Far East, everywhere!"

"I'm not blaming Virginia Graves," Maggie said, silencing the other woman. "I realize Kenneth had 'girls' like me in his overseas posts."

"If you want to break it off, fine, but don't kid yourself, Maggie! Kenneth Graves is no womanizer. That kind of thing can't be kept secret in the foreign service. After all, you know that now." Ann Merrill laughed.

"He womanized with me."

"You were an exception. Maggie, you should have heard Billy Klinger on the subject of Mrs. Graves. Billy was in Kenya when he was the ambassador, and she claims Virginia's behavior was so erratic they actually assigned a consulate secretary to keep tabs on her in Nairobi. Everyone felt so sorry for Kenneth, they tried not to gossip much about it. But . . . I always assumed he told all of this to you."

"Only a little," Maggie said slowly. "And only at the very end." How like Kenneth, she thought. He would never build a new relationship by betraying secrets.

"Well," said Ann philosophically, "she's in the loony bin, so the secret is out. The least you can do is see him, be supportive."

"I don't think so. I don't even know where he is."

"In Virginia. At his family farm. I saw the ambassador this week, actually. He came up to State for some briefings. Maggie, you would have thought the man hadn't a week to live, he looked so distraught."

Maggie kept shaking her head. "I broke it off," she said. "It wouldn't be fair, unless I knew I had changed my mind."

"Oh, don't be such a Catholic," Ann answered, exasperated. "You're making a big deal out of a little ride in the country. The farm is just beyond Marshall. Take Route Sixty-Six west and just ask for the Graves farm when you get to the town. It's an old Virginia family; everyone will know where they are."

"What if he doesn't want to see me?" Now she was afraid.

Ann Merrill leaned forward and patted Maggie's knee as she smiled knowingly. "Trust me, Mags. He wants to see you."

# · CHAPTER 39 ·

## LAUREL MILLS: 1982

MAGGIE STEERED HER RENTAL Ford past the fences, long white washed ribbons of planking that laced the gentle, soft Virginia landscape. Beyond the fences, wide meadows rolled to the foothills of the Blue Ridge Mountains. And dotting the fields on the warm winter afternoon were horses, sleek chestnut-brown and bay geldings and mares, hunt ponies, and thoroughbreds on both sides of 66 heading west to Front Royal.

At the town of Marshall she stopped for gas and directions.

"The ambassador's place?" the attendant repeated. He was wearing overalls and a cowboy hat and he propped his foot up on her bumper while he filled the tank.

"You're goin' for the horse trial?" He held the nozzle to the gas tank as he watched her, his eyes never leaving the fork of her jeans.

"Yes, I am," Maggie said.

"You're late then." He replaced the cap on the gas tank and wiped his hands off on a rag as he came around the car. "They done had the show jumping by now, I suppose. It'll be over for nearly an hour. Cross-country run is next. Tell you what to do, ma'am." He shoved up his cowboy hat with his thumb. "Go ahead there till you hit route six-forty-seven, hang a left for Flint Hill. That'd be seven-twenty-nine. You go south a ways and you'll see cars parked on the shoulders. The ambassador's place is close by Laurel Mills, but you won't get near till after the trial. Ask anyone 'bout where to find him. Everyone knows the ambassador. That'll be a ten spot, ma'am, for the gas." He smiled down at Maggie and tipped his hat.

Police were directing traffic, waving cars into the pasture land, before she reached Laurel Mills, and Maggie let herself be directed. She really should have telephoned, she thought as her rental car bounced over the rutted field. It was going to be a job just to find Kenneth.

She parked the car and walked toward the crowd out of the makeshift parking lot. When she reached the end of the field, a young girl handed her a printed program of the day's events. She glanced at it as she continued to walk and noticed at once that Ambassador and Mrs. Virginia Graves were both listed as the sponsors. There was even a formal photograph, showing them in happier times. She shouldn't have come, Maggie thought; it was all a silly damn mistake. She stopped walking and looked around at the crowd.

The field was full of people dressed in tweeds and riding breeches, carrying binoculars, car blankets, and thermal coffee bottles. Anglo-Saxons on parade, she thought. Their conservative gear reminded her of when she and Kenneth had gone riding in Addis Ababa, in the open country behind the French Embassy. She had dressed in jeans and a sweat shirt; he had worn his hunt jacket, boots, and jodhpurs. She had looked out of place that day, and she looked out of place here, in the Virginia hunt country. Well, to hell with them, she thought, building up her courage. She had come to see Kenneth and she wouldn't let a bunch of aging preppies chase her away.

The crowd was heading for a long low stone wall, where they focused their binoculars on the lower horizon. Maggie joined them at the wall and scanned the fields. The landscape was bare.

"They'll come from the river, is that right, Chas?" The blond woman standing beside Maggie raised her glasses and searched the low meadowland. Maggie could smell her perfume.

"Should I open the Chablis?" her husband asked. He rummaged in a tote bag resting on the stone fence.

"Yes, darling, that would be lovely," the woman said, not lowering her glasses. "Didn't you think Becky's bay did splendidly on the reining patterns? She hasn't done this well since the Blue Ridge event."

"It's because of that French dressage trainer she's brought over. He's done wonders." The man wrestled with the white wine and silver corkscrew. "Here come the Farnhams. Do you want me to wave them over?"

"Oh, God no! I can't listen to Margo go on anymore about poor Kenneth Graves."

"I certainly wouldn't call Kenneth Graves 'poor.' "

"Oh, you know what I mean." She resumed her watch on the far meadow. "I see them now! Yes, they're reaching the gate. The course looks much longer than three miles, don't you think?"

All along the length of the stone wall, Maggie could hear the crowd exclaim. And now she saw the horses emerge in the low meadow. A tight knot of them jumped a white gate and raced up the slope. They were tearing up the turf in their chase for the next jump, a stack of straw bales less than a hundred yards from where she stood. It was this jump that the crowd was positioned to see, she realized.

"I can see the ambassador. He's in the lead!" The woman rose up on her toes, stretching to see.

"Where's Becky?" the man asked. He, too, had trained his binoculars on the racers.

"She's on the inside, behind him."

"He's coming wide! He's taking the gelding from the side." The man had to shout over the roar of the crowd, the galloping horses.

Kenneth looked enormous on the jumper, all legs and arms, as he raced past where she was standing and took the bales. The horse moved smoothly over the straw with its neck and head stretched forward, but as it hit the turf with its forefeet, its right front leg gave way. Kenneth was tossed forward in the saddle and flung up over the horse's head. His hit the ground with a sickening sound, and Maggie lost sight of him as the other horses caught up and thundered by.

"Oh, God! Kenneth!" she cried. She jumped up on the wall to go for him, but the man beside her grabbed her arm.

"You'll only get hurt," he shouted, "and frighten the horses."

Maggie tried to pull loose, but when he wouldn't let go, she spun around and hit him flat on the nose with the heel of her right palm. She could see the blood start as he let go, swearing after her. Maggie jumped clear of the rock wall and ran into the racecourse.

As the dust cleared, Maggie saw, out of the corner of her eyes, others running for the fallen ambassador. She reached him first and, kneeling down, gently touched his face. There was blood on his face, but she could feel his breath on her hand.

"Kenneth?" she whispered, leaning over him.

He looked up, hearing her voice, and whispered her name as she helped him sit up. "How did you find me?" he asked, gaining his breath.

"By chance." She smiled, thankful that he was all right and amused by his puzzlement. "I'll explain it all later. What's important is you. Are you okay?"

"Of course! It was just a silly fall." He was suddenly embarrassed. "The gelding hasn't been properly trained," he went on, justifying his lack of horsemanship, as he stood up.

"Ambassador, the jumpers are at the white gate," one of the men interrupted, and now they all turned to see that the lead horses had cleared the first jump and were again racing up the rise toward where they stood.

"Come!" the ambassador said, taking Maggie's arm and leading her away from the bales of straw. "Are you alone?" he asked, holding her fast with his eyes as if he still wasn't sure she really had suddenly materialized there on the Virginia countryside.

Maggie nodded. "I came down from Washington to see you."

"Let's go to the house then. That's it, there," he said, gesturing across the valley. "It's called Monadnock, the house on a rock."

Beyond the river Maggie could see the sloping black slate roof of the red-brick mansion. The main section was several stories high, with other sections, built in later years, she guessed, extending the house in graceful additions until the mansion seemed to stretch the length of a football field. Beyond it, there were more buildings, garages, and barns. Behind the house a carnival tent had been erected, its bright canvas stripes making it look as if a huge balloon had settled in the middle of the lawn.

"It's enormous!"

"Yes, I am afraid it is," Kenneth said. "We don't use half of the main part and I rent out both of the coach houses. All the plowable land is leased. The barn is used by a local riding instructor for dressage classes. Events like this horse trial generate some income, and there's a family trust fund to help with the upkeep, but still it's a tough go, keeping it up, especially living overseas. I'm lucky. Zake Ehele, my caretaker, is first-rate."

Maggie was aware then that Kenneth had not let go of her. His hand had only slipped down her arm and taken hold of her fingers.

"You've heard about Virginia?" he asked, not breaking step.

"Yes. I ran into Ann Merrill this morning. I'm terribly sorry, Kenneth."

"Well, she's being cared for now. I should have had her committed years ago—I mean, Virginia's been ill for years—but I didn't think it was fair to the children to have their mother put away."

"Why didn't you tell me this in Addis?"

"Because I was afraid. I didn't want you to think less of me, Margaret."

"We all have family problems, Kenneth," she said, thinking of her own.

They had reached the marshy bottom of the hill, and walking through the thick brown winter grass was as difficult as walking through deep snow. Maggie stumbled, and Kenneth laced his fingers into hers and helped her through as a crowd of guests near the house watched every step. She thought then how open he was being; this kind of display had been missing in their affair, and she wondered if it was wise now to be so attentive in front of witnesses, probably many friends of Virginia. Nevertheless she kept her hand in his. She was tired of hiding her feelings for this man. If they were to be lovers, then she wanted the whole world to know. There would be no more backstairs involvements for her.

"We're serving brunch in the tent after the trials. You'll stay, won't you?"

He was being careful with her, she realized, not presuming anything.

"Yes, of course. I've come to see you."

Maggie recognized a dozen of the brunch guests from the pages of the *Washington Post*. There were several European ambassadors and half a dozen Georgetown socialites who had farms in rural Virginia. There were also sons and daughters of wealthy Washington families that she had been introduced to at parties when she was still married to Jack.

Maids swept by her, carrying trays of food to the center buffet table. They were whispering to each other, giving instructions, and Maggie caught the lilt of their Irish brogues. Turning away from the scene, she walked out from under the tent flap. She had to leave. Who was she kidding? How could she possibly marry Kenneth Graves when she had more in common with his hired help than with his friends?

Kenneth caught up to her on the horseshoe drive.

"Margaret, what are you doing? Why are you leaving?"

"Kenneth, I don't belong here."

He had to seize her arm to stop her. "Enough! Enough of that nonsense. You're as good . . . Goddamnit, you're better than any of this crowd. Some of those people in there have never held a real job in their lives. Maggie, it's not like you to put yourself down. What has brought this on, anyway?"

Maggie sighed. "I don't know. Being home, I guess, back in Illinois. And seeing my family, realizing where I come from."

"Margaret, you have your own life to live."

"You sound like my brother, the bishop."

"He's right!" The ambassador let go of her hand and stepped back, feeling foolish arguing with her in the drive. "Margaret, I have the award ceremony."

"All right, go ahead," she flared.

"Get your car," he asked. "Everyone will be leaving around four, and then we'll take a good look at this family of yours and decide who belongs where."

Maggie shook her head and turned away.

"Margaret!"

"I'm not some sort of minor inconvenience you can delegate away, Kenneth. I won't let you treat me like . . . like Virginia."

He stepped over to her, held her gaze with the kindness of his gray eyes, and said softly, "Margaret, I need you. I need to care for you. That is what love is, not anything else, nor any romantic nonsense. Our relationship isn't something sordid, or brief, or inconvenient. For me the moments of loving you in Africa have been the happiest times I've had in my life. I'm not going to cut you out of my heart now.

"When I think of my future, when I think of returning to this farm someday and living my life here at Monadnock, I think of you being at my side. Don't disappoint me, darling. Don't leave me."

Maggie reached out to touch him.

"I'll speak to Mrs. Hopewell, the housekeeper, and she'll show you to the Roanoke, that's one of the guest suites. You can get some rest, and I'll see you after this crowd leaves. Now go get your car and come back to me."

The Roanoke was a suite of rooms on the second floor of the main house. Opening the door, Mrs. Hopewell said to Maggie, "The ambassador asked me to lay out a robe and slippers, in case you wanted to bathe." The tall, unsmiling black woman stepped back to let Maggie walk ahead of her into the suite. The sitting room was lit with the gold of a winter sunset and the bright flame of a wood fire. "The only ladies' clothes we have in the house belong to Mrs. Graves," she continued. "And you won't want to wear those, will you?"

Maggie met Mrs. Hopewell's eyes. She wondered how long her family had worked for Virginia's. In that part of the country, they might have been master and servant since before the Civil War.

"No, Mrs. Hopewell," she answered. "I don't need to borrow anything from Mrs. Graves."

Alone, Maggie walked to the windows and pushed aside the lace curtain to glance out. The guest rooms overlooked the creek and the farm pond. The pasture land beyond, bare and brown ground, stretched to the low foothills of the Blue Ridge Mountains.

It was a pale, neutral time of day, a pleasant moment, Maggie thought, without the sun or the first rush of cold night air. The last light framed the level land, silhouetted the stone walls, the miles of white fences. Small birds flew in swift, silent patterns, nervous in the short time before darkness.

As she watched, shallow valleys and hollows were smoothed over as the darkness slipped down from the mountains like a gloved hand smothering the land. Overwhelmed with sudden exhaustion, Maggie lay down and quickly fell into a deep sleep.

It was dark when she woke. There were no more lingering golden rays of sunset, and the fire had gone out. At the door to the bedroom she heard steady breathing, barely audible. Carefully, she moved her head on the pillow. She saw the dark shadow of Kenneth paused there, watching her.

"Hello," she whispered from her warm cavity beneath the sheets.

"Did I wake you?"

"Not really. Have your guests gone?"

"Yes, thank God! We're alone."

"All alone?"

"All alone. I gave the house staff the evening off." He came across the room and sat down on the bed. "Mrs. Hopewell prepared something for us to eat and I'll fix it later. It will be rather simple; I hope you don't mind."

"Of course not." She slipped her arm from beneath the quilt and touched him. "Your housekeeper makes me feel like the second Mrs. Rochester."

"Oh, don't be silly."

"I'm sorry, but she does."

"Then I'll get rid of her." He leaned forward and kissed her lightly on the eyelids.

Maggie could smell the outdoors on him, and the tang of brandy. He rarely drank; when he did, it always made him much more reckless and demanding in their lovemaking.

"You smell wonderful, you know," he said.

"How do I smell?"

He smiled down at her, joking. "Oh, I should think your scent was that special smell of a childhood trunk, in which all your things, those forgotten pleasures and joys, have been stored away. And when you open the lid, what comes flowing back to memory is all that happiness."

"I do make you happy, don't I?"

"Very. I'm really only happy when I'm with you." He reached out and slowly traced her profile, his eyes never leaving her face.

"Touch me," she said.

Gently he played his hand down her throat, slipped it between the folds of her blouse, and touched the soft whiteness of her breast, carefully etching the nipple with his fingertips. He moved her slightly in the bed and undid the buttons, freeing both her breasts in the shadowy glow of the fireplace embers. He ran his hand down the length of her back, then pulled away the soft fabric of her blouse, as one would with tenderness lift a light blanket off a sleeping child.

The luminous pallor of her skin shone in the folds of the flowered sheets and the browns and orange of the country quilt. She could remain still forever if he would only keep gazing down at her naked body, as if the sight was all he had ever wanted in life, all that he had ever wanted.

"I love you," he said.

A chill swept into the room and the last glowing log broke in the hearth with a flurry of dying sparks, but when he got up and reached to cover her with the quilt, Maggie shrugged free, letting her long dark hair tumble loose over her bare shoulders. She closed her eyes and waited for him.

Kenneth crossed to the fireplace and fed logs to the embers. She could hear the fire snap and sizzle as the flame bit into the dry wood and then she felt a wave of warmth, as if her body was turned toward a tropic sun. Kenneth was behind her in the room, moving softly in his bare feet, closing doors, undressing. She heard the scratch of wool as he pulled off his heavy turtleneck, and then the intimate sound of him emptying pockets of keys and change. She smiled to herself. He would not come to her until everything was in order. It was what made his love special and strong. Yet when he slipped down beside her, his manner and mood would change. He would be reckless and wild in his abandonment.

She slipped out of her clothes and waited with anticipation, her heart pounding against her taut breasts. She heard him behind her. Then, with one hand he gripped the quilt and sheet, tearing them from the bed.

Maggie felt his lips on her flesh, his kisses beginning at her ankle and slowly mounting the length of her leg and thigh. He turned her then, so that he might kiss the soft, warm interior of her upper thigh and finally the dark expectant webbing of her sex.

Convulsively she arched her body and held her breath, moved to offer her breasts to his approaching lips. Then he took her shoulders and turned her facedown into the wide bed, tossing away the goose-feather pillows under her head. In the glowing light of the fire he seized her by the waist, pulled her against him and slipped inside, making love to her the way she had come to enjoy the most.

She braced herself against his strength and their bodies found a dynamic rhythm. She felt him shiver as he lunged against her, then heave against her again and again, and she fought to keep up with him until they both came in a final rush.

For a moment, as always, she thought he had torn her apart with the force of his coming. She lay still, his wet lips against her ear. She listened to his heart race, then steadily he relaxed, gained his breath, and without moving, he asked if she was all right. She murmured yes and waited for him to slip out of her. He reached down for the discarded sheets and quilt, covered them both, and drew her gently into his arms, held her as he might a child, until they both, warmed by each other and exhausted, fell off to a brief and deep sleep.

When she woke, it was much darker. She could see nothing through the bedroom windows, but the fire still blazed and she realized they couldn't have been asleep for long. She lay perfectly still, content to rest in Kenneth's arms and feel his chest rise and fall, but something woke him, and without speaking, he wanted her again.

She shifted on her back, naked and vulnerable and ready for her pleasure. He knew what she wanted, what she needed from him. She guided him onto her body and held his face between her breasts, then tested the weight and force of his body against hers. "Langano," he whispered, and she welcomed him into her arms.

Lake Langano was the only place they had ever spent a weekend alone in Africa.

Maggie had driven down first to set up a weekend home for them at the water's edge. She made a campfire with driftwood and set a table for dinner, using her own silverware and dishes brought down from Addis Ababa. She cooled white wine in a shallow pool and picked the wild flowers that blossomed after the long rains. Then, in the mounting gloom, she lit the Coleman lantern before slipping out of her clothes and running naked and barefoot to the water's edge.

There was no lingering sunset in the middle of the Rift Valley. The night came quickly, and with it sounds from the bush, as antelope and small gazelle came down to the water. As she swam out in the lake, Maggie looked back at the campsite, the small fire, and tent strung between the low wide branches of the acasca trees. It all seemed so perfect, but she thought how alone she was in the dark and for a moment she feared that Kenneth wouldn't come.

Then she heard the Land Rover and saw headlights sweeping the shoreline. She swam in, stepping out onto the rough sand and picking up her towel as he parked beside her small VW.

She began rubbing herself dry, briskly warming herself in the sudden chill of the evening. Before Kenneth could approach she wrapped herself in the bath towel and stepped up the beach to meet him. He didn't say a word, simply met her in the Ethiopian night and stripped the towel from her body. She stood naked and exposed before him and then he swept her into his arms, lifted her effortlessly off the sandy shore, and carried her into the tent where they made love without speaking until he said her name when he came.

She came now, imagining the banks of Lake Langano as Kenneth moved within her. She felt his strength, but it was gentle this time and succoring. She caught hold of her mounting orgasm and rode with it, faster and faster, concentrating on herself until she was suddenly flooded in a rush of warmth, and she grabbed at Kenneth, found his mouth with hers, and pulled him deeper into her until she tipped over the edge and let go.

They slept again, and this time when she woke, the fire was out. Kenneth woke, too. She could hear the subtle shift of his breathing, but she waited for him to speak. He asked if she was hungry, and she nodded, her head buried against his chest. She hadn't realized she was until he asked.

"What time is it?" she asked.

"Oh, seven or eight."

"It feels as if I've been with you in this bed forever, all our lives."

"I was thinking it would be lovely if we could go away for a few days. Fly down to Palm Beach."

She shook her head. "I wish I could. But I have to get back to D.C. There's family trouble."

"What is it, Margaret?"

"I can't bother you."

"Don't be silly. Is it money? Emmett? I want to help, Margaret. Did you get my telegram?"

Maggie nodded. "I don't think it's fair, dragging you into my problems when you have so many of your own."

"Margaret, I love you. That's all you need to know. Now, how about letting me in on the secret?"

Maggie lay back on the bed and stared up at the dark ceiling. "If only I knew. Every day I uncover something else. It seems my family's past is honeycombed with secrets."

"That's what families are all about, Margaret. Blood doesn't hold families together; secrets do."

Maggie nodded. It was true. She told him everything that had happened since she'd returned from Africa. For a few moments after she finished, he lay quiet. Maggie did not rush him. She knew how Kenneth's mind worked, how he would think through the problem. Finally he spoke. "Do you remember Deep Throat?"

"From Watergate?" she said, startled. "Yes, of course."

"Well, I have the same advice for you as Deep Throat had for Robert Redford: follow the money. It took Woodward to Nixon; it'll take you to your mother's murderer."

# · CHAPTER 40 ·

## GATESBURG: 1982

MAGGIE FLEW BACK TO Gatesburg with a fresh legal pad on her lap. Using her thick black reporter's pencil, she began making notes.

ONE. On what evidence were the police accusing Emmett of murder? A.) The statements of a few drinking buddies. Damning, but only circumstantial. B.) The shotgun that had killed their mother was Emmett's. Yet he said he hadn't used it on Friday morning because the firing mechanism was broken.

Maggie paused. The gun was much more serious, she realized. The gun was prima facie evidence of a sort.

TWO. Motive. The only reason Emmett might have had for killing their mother was the mortgage. That was damaging. Still only the family knew about that, at least so far.

THREE. What had happened to the mortgage money?

She had to begin at number three. She had to go back to the Farmer's First National Bank and see John Keenan. She had to start with the bank note. As Kenneth had told her, she had to follow the money.

As Maggie entered the old, high-vaulted lobby of the Farmer's First National she felt a wave of déjà vu. She was a little girl again, watching while her mother made a payment on the mortgage. All the tellers had children in Maggie's class at grammar school, or else they were parishioners at Saint Pat's, but Caitlin DeLacey never spoke to them. She and Maggie would stand silently on line until they reached a window, and even then her mother wouldn't greet the teller as she slipped money under the iron bars.

"Banks are for the rich," Caitlin told Maggie when she asked her why she never talked to anyone. "All they want from us is our hard-earned money."

Now Maggie was back at Farmer's First, and it seemed to her that while the town itself had been modernized, nothing within the bank had changed. She could smell the same wax, the stuffiness of the overheated building, hear the same clicking of heels on the old marble floor. There was no bulletproof glass, no hidden cameras, no security guard. People still waited patiently in line, and the women tellers knew everyone by name. Nothing really had changed in Gatesburg, she thought, with some satisfaction.

She walked straight to the directors' offices in the rear.

"Miss DeLacey. It's a pleasure." John Keenan came to his office doorway. "And how can we help you today?" He was a tall, thin man, well dressed, Maggie noticed, by Gatesburg standards.

"I'm just back from Washington, where I spoke to the bishop about the mortgage on my mother's farm. Father Mike said you'd show me the papers and fill me in on the details."

"Of course! Of course! No problem at all." The banker pulled open the file drawer of his desk. "As a matter of fact, I've just been reviewing it. Bill Turner from the OID called about it. In fact, as I mentioned to your poor mother the morning of—"

"Bill Turner?" Maggie interrupted.

"He wanted to know what the fair market value was. Meaning the highest price the property would bring in an open market. We supply that on all mortgage notes."

"Yes, but who is Bill Turner?" Maggie asked.

"Bill? He's the director of the state's Office of Industrial Development. The bishop must have mentioned him to you." The banker paused and looked across the desk. "Regarding the sale?"

"Yes. I'm sorry. The name slipped by me."

"Here it is," Keenan said, extracting the note and mortgage from the thick file. "You know, with the state and federal government all getting involved with our lives, none of this is easy anymore. What is it you'd like to see, Miss DeLacey?"

"The mortgage note, please."

"It's our standard form," Keenan explained, handing it across the table. "As you can see, the amount was two hundred and fifty thousand at fourteen percent. The principal balance with interest was all due on or before June thirtieth, 1988. Of course, with all the attention now on that part of town, I shouldn't think . . ."

Maggie had stopped listening. She flipped through the document, searching for signatures.

There they were, the notary's dated signature and stamp, Keenan's own old-maidish copperplate, and Emmett's familiar scrawl. And the names of the witnesses. When Maggie saw them, she felt a grim certainty that she was overlooking something vital.

"Are you all right, Miss DeLacey?" The banker sounded far away.

"Of course." And suddenly Maggie was all right. She had her answer.

"Was this document signed here, Mr. Keenan?" Maggie asked casually, still looking at the signatures.

"Well, in fact it wasn't. Your brother, Emmett—as the bishop explained—wouldn't come to the bank. So the bishop asked if they could go out to the farm. It was easier that way, all around. I signed it here, and had the papers notarized."

"Yes, of course," Maggie said softly. "Now what was that you just mentioned about the new appraisal of the land?"

"Well, because of the interest of the computer outfit that Bill Turner sent down, we asked the appraiser to evaluate it as an industrial site. I just telephoned Bill to report those figures."

"And?" Maggie kept smiling, adding, "With Mother's funeral and all, we never had a chance to talk about it. What is the property's value as an industrial site?"

"In the neighborhood of one point five."

"One point five?"

"That's right. One and a half million."

"I had no idea," Maggie whispered.

"Of course you didn't. Why would you? No one in town would have thought that bottomland of yours could be worth more than a few thousand an acre. But for industrial purposes, you have the only major parcel of land on the river."

Maggie nodded. She hadn't thought of that, but Michael had. And she knew something more as well, something John Keenan certainly wasn't aware of: that the family wasn't for sale, not as long as she was alive.

Maggie told Gatesburg's only taxi driver to drop her off at the country club. There were two other cars in the drive, Vanessa's Mercedes and a green Ford with government plates. The colonial clubhouse looked deserted, but Maggie went inside anyway. She paused at the front desk.

"I'm Maggie DeLacey. Is my brother here? Or Vanessa—Mrs. Adair?"

"Oh, hello, Miss DeLacey. I'm Pat Tranchese, Mrs. Adair's secretary." She pointed toward the clubhouse bar. "They're all having lunch in the Garden Room." Maggie hesitated, and the secretary nodded toward a pair of paneled doors. "Go left through the lounge, and past the nineteenth hole. It's the small dining room at the end of the hallway, beyond the library. You'll see them." She smiled.

Maggie had never really explored the clubhouse, not even when her mother had worked special dinner parties. The building was old, and much of the furniture showed its age: worn upholstery, bare spots in the rugs, spike marks in the hardwood floors. Yet it had the elegant look of a sportsman's club. There were touches of quality and attention in the furnishings, in the carefully chosen prints, and in the way the public rooms were all arranged so they faced the large windows and French doors that looked out over the golf course. Photographs of former members were set on tables and trophy cases of polished silver crowded the hallways.

She hesitated at the door to the library. The room was empty and silent, but a welcoming log fire was burning. Maggie smiled wistfully at the rich walnut walls, covered with beautifully bound books on shelves, and the old leather chairs. It stood for a life she had never known. A small bronze plaque was mounted in the archway, and Maggie stopped to read its inscription.

> Let it be recorded that here at the Gatesburg Country Club on July 5, 1911, James W. Harris shot a course record of 67 while suffering the anguish and agony of a 4th of July hangover. Erected by the Sunday Morning "Foursome." December, 1911.

Maggie remembered then that the country club had actually been founded by Vanessa's great grandfather and was the oldest golf course in southern Illinois. Before the turn of the century, the club had had its own railway depot, and private trains would bring members and their families from St. Louis to spend the summer far from the heat and malaria of the Mississippi.

When she heard Paddy Jack's laugh, Maggie followed the sound down the paneled hallway into the bright Garden Room, where she saw him sitting with Vanessa and a tall black man. They were the only ones in the winter dining room that faced the gardens and the tennis courts, now all blanketed with snow.

"Why, what a lovely surprise!" Vanessa said, coming to Maggie and kissing her lightly on the cheek. "I just spoke with Cathleen, but she wasn't sure when you'd be returning to the farm." Vanessa linked arms with Maggie and together they walked back to the table where the men were already standing.

"Would you care for lunch, Maggie?" Vanessa asked. "We're just having our coffee."

"Oh, no thanks," Maggie said, smiling. "Actually I've come by to see if I could steal my big brother away from you all."

"Who, me?" Paddy slipped his arm around Maggie's shoulder. "Come join us for a moment, Meg. Bill, here, has been telling us about his plans for Gatesburg."

"Not my plans, actually. The state's." The black man took Maggie's offered hand. "Bill Turner, Office of Industrial Development. I've been trying to convince Paddy Jack here to sell us your farm. We have a company looking for a site near Gatesburg, and your place fits his requirements to a tee."

"The farm isn't for sale."

"Really? That's not what your brother suggested."

"Paddy!" Maggie turned to him. "You've never even discussed this with us."

"I'm sorry," Turner interrupted. "I didn't mean Paddy—no, your brother, Bishop DeLacey. He telephoned me last December and said your family was thinking of selling the property. The bishop thought it might make an industrial site, so he invited our cooperation."

Maggie looked to Paddy Jack for confirmation.

Paddy shrugged and seemed embarrassed. "As you can see, Bill, it's news to us. But then, Maggie was off in Africa, and I can be hard to reach when I'm on the tour. Mike was in touch with Mother—and of course, he comes home to Gatesburg a good deal."

Bill Turner was nodding understandingly. "Yes, and I'm sure the bishop knows what's best. He has everyone's interests at heart."

"I'm sure he does," Maggie agreed. "And this is a very interesting proposition, which I promise you we'll think about. Now, Paddy Jack, can you break away and give me a lift home? Or am I interrupting further business?"

"Of course not, Maggie." Vanessa was by her side. "We're finished here. You can certainly steal Paddy Jack away, as long as you return him before nightfall."

"It's been a pleasure meeting you, Miss DeLacey," Turner said. "And I hope we can help out this developer. It would be a tremendous economic boon for this part of the state. And, I might add, your farm could make the whole family quite wealthy."

"It already has, Mr. Turner. We were raised on that farm and it was the best of all possible childhoods. We could destroy that memory by selling off the home our mother loved, but I'm sure you understand that we'll have to think twice about it."

"Now what's the matter, Maggie?" Paddy Jack asked as soon as they were alone in Vanessa's Mercedes. "Why did you get your back up with Turner?"

"He's trying to steal our farm."

"He's not, Mag! Michael called him in. And when you hear the price, you won't call it stealing." Paddy turned the engine over and waited a moment for the car to warm up.

Magie ignored the lure. "Doesn't anyone care about Emmett? It's his home. He stayed behind when we all left. He worked the land. Took care of Mom. He's the one who should decide about selling, not you and Michael."

Paddy Jack maneuvered the car out of the drive and onto the club road.

"Maggie, we're talking big bucks here. In excess of one million, Turner says."

"I don't care if it's ten million. It's not right! Mom worked hard all those years to keep it going, and then Emmett came home from Vietnam and—"

"Mag, there's no need to get romantic about it. There's no point, and besides, whatever you choose to tell the people like Turner, you and I know it wasn't one great picnic growing up there."

"Maybe not," she said angrily, "but I'm glad I grew up on the farm, with Mom, instead of at the country club with all those well-heeled, well-pickled WASPs you're suddenly buddying up to. Which reminds me: if you and Turner were discussing the farm, why was Vanessa in on it? Since when is our business her business?"

Paddy kept his eyes on the road. "I'm sure it's no surprise that we've been talking about getting married," he said. "And if we do, I'd want her to know what was going on."

"There's more to it than that, I'll bet. Vanessa wants you to buy the club and put it back in financial shape—and selling the farm would make it possible for you to do that."

"Vanessa isn't pushing me to sell," he answered quickly. "But what harm would there be if she were? Let's face it, Maggie, Emmett shouldn't be worrying about where he's going to live. He'll probably be in jail for life."

"Paddy, don't you start."

"I've talked to Mike; he told me how Emmett mortgaged the place. It's damn lucky we haven't lost the whole farm."

"Emmett didn't take that money, Paddy."

"Maggie—" he began, but she broke in.

"It's not his signature. I've just come from the bank. I saw the mortgage papers with my own eyes."

"How can you forge bank papers? There are witnesses. Bank officers. The notary."

"The bank wasn't at the signing. Michael arranged for the mortgage note not to be signed at First National. The notary stamp was signed later."

"But there were witnesses," Paddy Jack insisted. "There had to be."

"Of course," Maggie agreed. "Two witnesses: Michael DeLacey and Dermot O'Connor."

They had reached an intersection. Paddy Jack stopped the car and turned to his sister. "Michael told me Emmett had gone behind everyone's back, that he kept the mortgage secret from the whole family."

"Yes, Michael told me the same thing." She stared back at Paddy Jack.

"Jesus Christ!" Paddy started the car up again. "I've got to call Mike."

"No," said Maggie. "You've got to take me into town, to the jail. I need to talk to Emmett."

"Why?"

"To confirm what you and I both suspect: that he doesn't know anything about the mortgage. I want to hear him tell me before I confront Michael."

"Do you think Mike took the money?"

"Someone took it, Paddy. And whoever it was, it was someone we love."

"This is real irregular," the sheriff reminded Maggie as he opened the double set of cell doors. "If a prisoner doesn't want visitors, he's entitled not to have them. But me and Paddy Jack, we go back to our caddy days, and well, I always like to help out Paddy."

"We all thank you, Sheriff."

"If that little twerp O'Hara gets word, it could cost me. He's looking all the time for irregularities. You know, on account of the election."

"I do appreciate your help, Sheriff," Maggie said again. "Perhaps I can help all of us by getting Emmett to stop his hunger strike."

"He's no problem. I have more trouble with weekend drunks than I've had from him. He's just in there doing nothing—staring at the wall, like he's meditating or something."

"He was a POW in Vietnam, Sheriff. He's used to confinement."

"The guards on the late shift, they say he has nightmares. Yells things, you know, in his sleep."

"The war was a terrible experience. He was nearly killed."

"It isn't combat he's screaming about."

"What do you mean? What does he say?"

"Well, ma'am, he keeps screaming out, 'No, Mom. No, Mom,' like a chant or something."

Maggie felt her knees weaken. She was thankful now that Paddy Jack hadn't come back to the cells with her. She didn't know whom she could trust.

"I hope you haven't mentioned this to anyone. The press, I mean."

The big man shook his head.

"Does Detective O'Hara know?"

"No way."

"Thank you."

"But the word's gotten out on the hunger strike. A reporter called this morning, Jim Speier. One of the guards must have let it out. I mean, Jim already had the story, you know; he was just looking for confirmation."

"He sandbagged you!" she said angrily. "I'll bet he didn't know anything but rumors."

"I told Speier to talk to you about it. He said he would check with the bishop," the sheriff answered back, defending himself.

Maggie shook her head. "I'm sorry, Sheriff. You can see all of this has me upset. I'm glad you didn't let anything out."

The sheriff nodded, then asked, "Did you hear the report about the shotgun?"

Maggie waited.

"The fingerprint report came back from the FBI lab in Chicago— we send them everything, you know, when it comes to homicide— and there's something damn odd about the twenty-gauge that killed your mother."

"Yes?" Maggie said quickly, feeling a sudden spring of hope.

"They lifted fingerprints off it, okay, your mom's and Emmett's. But what doesn't figure is that there aren't any prints on the stock or the trigger, just the barrel."

"Meaning?"

The sheriff unlocked the second set of cell doors. "Meaning that whoever shot your mother was sharp enough to wipe off his prints." He stepped back and nodded down the walkway. "Your brother's cell is the last on the right."

There were just six cells, and only two contained prisoners.

Wrapped in a gray blanket, Emmett sat on the cot staring out at the hall. Perhaps he had heard her speaking to the sheriff, but when Maggie stepped up to his cell, he didn't even acknowledge her presence.

A sheetless mattress covered the steel bed in the narrow cell. In one corner a toilet bowl sat, in the other, a metal footlocker. High on the rear wall wire crisscrossed a barred window. A prisoner wanting to look out would have to stand on the chair.

Emmett's back was against the stone wall, and his legs were drawn up beneath him. Except for the institutional blanket, he was naked. He hadn't shaved recently, or combed his long black hair. His eyes were dilated and vacant. He looked wild, Maggie admitted, unwillingly, like a member of the Manson family.

"Emmett," she said.

He did not respond.

"Emmett?" She moved closer to the bars. "You have to speak. You can't just sit there and ignore me."

"Go away."

"I won't go away."

"I don't want to talk to you." He slid down in the bed, pulled up his knees, and tucked himself into a tight ball.

"I can make your bail," she said quickly, thinking of Kenneth's offer. She hadn't wanted to borrow from him, but seeing Emmett had changed her mind.

"I don't want your money."

"Emmett, I can help you."

"I don't want your help."

"Then help me instead," she said, hoping to get his attention. "Tell me what you know about the farm mortgage."

He was silent for a moment, and then asked, "What mortgage?"

"The farm is mortgaged for two hundred and fifty thousand dollars as of last November."

He was silent again, and then, without sitting up, he said, "I don't know about any mortgage."

"You never signed any papers?"

"I said I don't know about it."

Maggie leaned against the cold metal bars. She had known the truth, but hearing it confirmed still shocked her.

"Emmett, please let me bail you out. This hunger strike isn't helping you. People don't know about the Brehon Laws; they just think you're strange."

"What are you talking about?"

"The Brehon Laws. In Ireland. That a man goes naked to humiliate his family for not standing by him."

"I don't know anything about Brehon Laws. But I know about you people. Big shots all over the world, and here I am starving to death in this pissplace."

"You mean you never heard of the Brehon Laws? But Father O'Connor said—"

"That asshole! He thinks I killed her. Mike thinks I killed her."

Maggie kept herself from speaking.

"Do you think I killed her?" Emmett stood up abruptly, startling Maggie so she stepped back from the cell. "Do you?"

"No, I don't think you killed Mom. I think—"

"You think I'm crazy? Crazy like everyone thinks I am."

"You're not crazy, Emmett!"

"You leave me out there all alone with her," Emmett shouted, and then turned to pace the narrow cell, clutching his blanket around him.

"No one cares. None of you, goddamnit; not about Mom, or me, or the farm. I got no money! Nothing! Can't pay the bills. Two of the cows went dry on me in October. She's crazy, I'm telling you. She don't make a bit of sense. She can't remember if she's even gone to the bathroom, for chrissake, and then pisses in her underwear. She smells. We've got no hot water. I can't even wash her clean. I can't heat the house. I can't pay the oil bills. We're starving, I'm telling you. I killed the last sow to put something on the table at Christmas. We don't have anything to eat, except a few eggs and what I canned in September. No one cares. You don't care! They don't care! Everyone gets the hell off the farm and leaves me to take care of her. No one gives a good goddamn."

He was leaning against the cell gate, his head pressed between the bars, sobbing. Then he slid down to the floor in a heap of blankets, scraping his face against the metal.

Maggie knelt down to him, reached her arms between the bars to embrace her brother. "It's okay, Emmett. It's okay," she whispered. "I know you didn't kill her. I know." She, too, was crying as she kept trying to hold him, to comfort her brother as she had done so often when they were children on the farm.

He pulled from her grasp and rolled away, as an animal might, and screamed, "I did!" His eyes were wild in his head. "I did kill her! That's why I want to die in here. I shot her fucking head off!"

# · CHAPTER 41 ·

GATESBURG: 1982

"GETTING EMMETT OUT IS proving more difficult than I expected," Kenneth said as he and Maggie drove out of Gatesburg Airport.

He had caught an early flight out of Washington, transferred at
O'Hare, and arrived in Gatesburg shortly before noon. The night before a snowstorm had swept through southern Illinois, leaving a fresh
five inches, but the roads had been cleared and the February day was
brilliantly bright. Putting on sunglasses to fight the glare, Maggie
stopped Catty's station wagon at the highway exit.

"Were you able to get the bail reduced?"

"No. I got stonewalled on the Justice side, almost from the very
beginning." Kenneth ran his hand nervously through his hair as he
talked.

"Oh, God," Maggie sighed, thinking of Emmett naked in the cold
county cell. "But why did you try the Justice Department anyway?
Emmett's murder charges aren't under federal jurisdiction. I thought
you'd try to get someone who knew Judge Boyer to lower the bail."

"You're right, the case is in the state system, but the feds have a
way of tightening the screws at the local level. You'd be surprised
what can be accomplished from Washington. Except in this case."

Maggie shivered, and she wondered if it was just the drafty station
wagon or if she was frightened already at what would happen to
Emmett. She had not yet told Kenneth, or anyone else, what Emmett
had claimed: that he had killed their mother. It was a confession she
could not allow herself to believe, not now, when there were so many
other secrets in the family. She maneuvered the station wagon onto
the expressway and turned west, toward Gatesburg on the other side
of the river. She could see the downtown streets; they gripped the
cliffs like white fingers. As she pointed out the town to Kenneth, she
said, "I think we should stop for lunch somewhere first; that way we
can talk before joining Catty and Wendy at home."

"Fine, whatever." Kenneth agreed. Then he pressed on with his story. "As I said, I got my friend at Justice to look into the case and he ran into an immediate roadblock. He says it's impossible to get Emmett out on lack of evidence, or even to have his bail reduced. The facts have nothing to do with the case—because as far as he or I can tell, Emmett's being in jail has nothing to do with the murder charge."

Maggie glanced over. "What?"

"The fix is in."

"Fix? What do you mean, *fix*? This isn't Abscam. It's a backwoods murder investigation!"

"First of all, the DeLaceys are hardly a backwoods family. Because of Michael and Paddy Jack, the media have had their eyes on this case from day one. At least, I assumed that's what my friend at Justice was getting at. At first."

"At first?"

"I called half of Washington yesterday. Everyone I know, from circuit judges to old Yale classmates to contacts at the FBI and CIA. I've learned some things you're not going to like, Margaret." He reached over and touched her shoulder.

"Oh, dear God!" Maggie's insides dropped and she forced herself to look ahead, to watch the icy highway.

"The story on the Hill is that Jack McGraff is pulling the strings to keep Emmett in jail."

"That's preposterous!"

"And that he's acting on behalf of your brother Michael."

Maggie slowed the station wagon and tightened her grip on the steering wheel.

"Margaret, there's no question: Jack's involved. His name comes up whenever Emmett's is mentioned. As for the bishop, I'm less sure. I've never met the man and I don't know enough to judge whether he wants his brother in jail. Yet when I asked friends on the Hill whether there was some sort of link between Michael and McGraff, they said yes."

"I don't believe it."

"Margaret," he said softly, "I have proof."

Maggie was moving Catty's car down the exit ramp into Gatesburg.

"Actually, you put me on to it," he said. "When I started hearing that McGraff was helping Michael, I couldn't imagine what the connection might be. Then I remembered your mentioning that Michael claimed his offices were being bugged.

"You said Michael suspected the British, so I telephoned Thurston Clarke, a chap I know at the British Embassy. We were in Nairobi together. He operates in the United States as an economic officer, but he's actually rather senior in their MI-six branch."

At the bottom of the ramp Maggie turned right toward the bridge over the river at Fourth Street. This part of town had not been plowed and the cobbled streets were icy. It was the old Irish section, though blacks had now moved in. This was where Detective O'Hara had been raised. No wonder he was jealous of the DeLaceys, she thought.

"This is very charming," Kenneth said, looking across the bridge at the riverfront stores.

"Yes, like Georgetown, almost."

"But without the street peddlers and Virginia teenagers."

"All of this is new. When we were kids, most of the businesses downtown were boarded up." Maggie pulled into a parking space in front of a coffee shop.

They ordered sandwiches and then Kenneth opened his attaché case and pulled out a small set of files.

"This is what Tony Clarke came up with: MI-six's files on your brother and the Blue and Whites. Half the files are harmless enough. The usual newspaper clips, articles, that sort of documenting of your brother's organization. The top file is the real thing: the results of a covert investigation of your brother and his affairs."

Maggie studied the file tabs as he continued.

"What you have there are records of your brother's trips to Ireland. You're included as well: the trip you took together when your brother went to Belfast in seventy-seven for Pope Paul the Sixth."

Maggie opened the top file. The first page listed the contents.

> BLUE AND WHITE MEMBERSHIP LISTS
> DELACEY IRELAND TRIPS: 1982, '81, '80, '79
> FIRST VISIT TO BELFAST, 1977
> CONNECTIONS WITH KNOWN IRA SUPPORTERS
> TAPED CONVERSATIONS, BELFAST
> MONEY TRANSFER, METHODS AND AMOUNTS, BY YEAR
> NEWSPAPER CLIPS, ETC.

Maggie pulled the Belfast file from the others and opened it.

"The code name of the agent who spied on you is Knight," Kenneth said. "He was born in Northern Ireland and lived most of his life in Belfast. My guess is that he's one of those free-lance informants you find around, working for our side, the Reds, or the Israelis. And getting paid by all of us.

"He was in the Irish Guards—you know, the same ones who are on duty at Buckingham Palace. But this guy didn't have such a cushy assignment. He was on active duty in the Middle East, in Yemen. That's where the MI-six recruited him. They suspected he'd go home to Belfast at some point, and when his service was up he did. Knight was your brother's driver during that 1977 visit. Do you remember him, Margaret?"

"Yes, he called himself Tommy. I don't think I ever heard his last name."

"Harvey. Thomas Harvey."

"He was small and fat with gaps between his upper teeth, so his smile looked like a pitchfork. And he was always cheery, which must be hard in that dreary city. All those gray buildings. Those gray days. The sun never came out when we were in Belfast."

"Why did Michael go there in the first place?"

"It was shortly after he became a bishop. The pope asked him to see what could be done about the Catholic hunger strikers in the Maze prison. This was before Bobby Sands died.

"Michael probably seemed like a good choice for a papal mission. He first came to Washington to teach at Catholic University. When he was at Catholic U. he organized the Blue and Whites. At first it was only a historical and cultural group, something to satisfy the chauvinism of Irish Americans. Michael himself wasn't at all political then. The Blue and Whites came out of the doctoral work he'd done, tracing early Irish Christianity back to Saint Paul. I would describe him then as academically sophisticated and politically innocent. But the campus troubles over Vietnam began while he was at the university, and suddenly he became a Nixon supporter.

"I was in England, where I had gone for the *Post* after my separation from Jack. Michael telephoned that he was flying over to Belfast. He invited me to come because Father O'Connor, our pastor here in Gatesburg, had some family in Belfast and had asked us to visit for him. O'Connor's sister was a nun who supervised a small hospital there."

Maggie glanced down at the open file and read one brief entry. It was a statement by Knight concerning their first meeting in Belfast.

> I went around to the Hotel Europa to pick up the bishop and his sister, Margaret DeLacey. I was working at that time for the papal nuncio to Ulster, as his driver and handyman, and he sent me to drive the bishop and his sister around Belfast. He didn't want them to get hurt. I knew well enough who the bishop was. His picture had been in the newspapers. It was all over Belfast that an American bishop was coming to talk with Maze prisoners.

Tommy had picked them up early in the day, Maggie remembered, and begun their tour by taking them straight into the slums. She remembered the street graffiti vividly. Threats covered every wall, written by one side or the other. One painted message read: NO POPE

IN IRELAND. That one had been neatly printed on the long gray wall, but beneath it, in thick, red dripping letters, was a second message: SCREW HIS YANK BISHOP!

"I don't understand, Kenneth," she said, looking up. "Why would British intelligence give you these files?"

"They want to get the word out about the Blue and Whites. They want to build a case that the bishop is connected with the provisional branch of the IRA."

"That's a lie! Michael isn't a terrorist!"

"The British think he is, Margaret, and you can be damn sure that there are copies of these files with the CIA and FBI. Thatcher won't denounce Michael herself; it wouldn't do any good. She wants Reagan to move on him. So she leaked these files. Michael is in trouble, Maggie. Thatcher has very good relations with the Reagan administration, as you know, and she's pushing Reagan to help her destroy the IRA, once and for all, by cutting off its U.S. support."

"What has Michael got to do with that?"

"My guess is that he's been buying arms."

"Can you prove that?"

"As I said: Follow the money. That's what MI-six has done. These files show that the money the bishop collects at Blue and Whites rallies is deposited in New York, at the Bank of Ireland, then transferred to Dublin, into three separate accounts. From Dublin, letters of credit go to Amsterdam. The money is supposedly used to buy clothing, medical supplies, and toys for the poor Catholics in Belfast. It's all documented, all very innocent. There are even copies of invoices from a Dutch wholesaler backing up the story."

"Well, what's wrong with helping the Catholics in Belfast? For God's sake, Michael advertises for those kinds of donations on TV!"

Kenneth motioned Maggie to be silent. "Why Amsterdam, Margaret? Why can't supplies of that kind be purchased in Dublin, or Belfast itself?" He paused a moment while a waitress served them coffee. When she walked off, he went on.

"I talked to another intelligence contact, this one at the CIA. He was briefly on my staff in Addis before you arrived. I showed him what the Brits had dug up and asked what he thought about the wholesaler in Amsterdam. He says the guy is an arms dealer. One of those bastards who sells guns to terrorists and third-world governments so they can kill each other. According to the CIA, the man operates several export companies as cover."

"Kenneth, both of us know that the British don't allow arms to be shipped into Belfast on Dutch freighters."

"Of course not. This arms merchant ships the guns to Africa, to a missionary convent outside of Kinshasa, in Zaire. The arms are off-loaded, then shipped back to the nuns' mother house in Belfast. The bills of lading list the contents as the personal belongings of nuns returning from the African missions. The name of the convent in Belfast is"—Kenneth paused a moment to scan his notes—"the Passion and Crucifixion Convent and Infirmary." He saw Maggie's look of surprise. "Do you know the place?"

"Yes," she whispered. "We were there—Michael and I. The superior, Mother Agnes, is Father O'Connor's sister."

Kenneth said nothing.

"I don't believe it," she burst out. "How do we know Michael's money went anywhere near this Dutchman?"

"My guess is that the arms merchant is also an agent for the CIA. You know how the agency works. The CIA supplies guns to all sides in any conflict so that no matter who wins, they're in a position of influence."

"If it's true about Father Mike, why doesn't Reagan stop him? The president is always talking about stamping out terrorism, but he's left Michael alone. I haven't heard anything about an investigation."

"Why don't you ask Jack, Margaret? Remember, he's chairman of the Senate Subcommittee on International Terrorism. And I'm sure Reagan would prefer that someone else take the heat for attacking a right-winger like Michael. Who better than another Irishman? Ask Jack if he's setting up a hearing on the bishop; I'd be interested to know what he says."

But Maggie wasn't listening. She remembered something else she hadn't told anyone, not even Kenneth: how she had seen Jack leaving Michael's office that Saturday. She felt suddenly cold, even in the thick heated warmth of the diner.

"But how did Michael get so involved in Northern Ireland?" she said aloud. "We never even got into the Maze, you know. The British army wouldn't let us near H-Block or the hunger strikers. All we ever saw was one pathetic old man at the Passion and Crucifixion Infirmary."

"And who was he?"

"He was nobody, just a prisoner. An ex-prisoner, actually. An old IRA soldier from the forties who had just been released from H-Block."

"Do you remember his name?"

"No, why? Is it important?"

"Yes," he said softly as he reached over and took her hand. "Was his name Adrian Steele?"

# · CHAPTER 42 ·

BELFAST: 1977

TOMMY STOPPED HIS TAXI at the top of the barricaded street and looked straight at the bishop.

"I'd best wait here, if you don't mind. The entrance to the Catholic section is just down the block, on the left. You'll see a marker, I'm sure, or ask any of the lads that're about. I'll park me cab across the road and be in Cunningham's Pub."

From the backseat, Maggie looked out. They were at the top of a cobblestone avenue and could see something of a panorama of Belfast. She thought again how ugly the city was, with its tawdry old nineteenth-century houses, its ominous skies, and everywhere wire, coiled wire, barbed razor wire. Belfast was a cage, she thought, not a city.

"The RUC, that's the Royal Ulster Constabulary, will pat you down at the entrance, but once beyond the gate you'll be safe enough on the Catholic side." He grinned again, showing off his bad teeth.

"You can't enter that section, is that right?" Michael asked. "I'll have a word with the soldiers if you want."

" 'Tisn't that I can't, you see, but being a Prod—a Protestant—I'd be putting myself in a bit of danger, you know, waiting in my taxi. This is a Catholic neighborhood; Taig, as we say. You never know when one of those lads might lob a petrol bomb through the windshield. Don't worry though—you'll be all right, what with your black suit and all."

"A petrol bomb?" Michael repeated.

"Ah, they're all for making them now, Bishop. They fill a milk bottle with petrol and diesel fuel. The diesel fuel makes it hard to extinguish, you see, and then they put a bit of sugar and detergent in the bottle as well so the petrol will stick on the target. It can do a bit of damage, it can."

"A Molotov cocktail," Maggie said.

"That's right! Those Russians, they've never done the world a bit of good."

"I think we should take Tommy's advice, Michael." It was time they moved on, Maggie realized. Parked on the peace line between the neighborhoods, they were an easy target for either side. Without waiting, she opened the taxi door and stepped into the soft rain.

Michael followed her, opening his black umbrella to give them some shelter. As soon as the car door slammed shut, Tommy drove away, spinning the car wheels on the wet cobblestones.

"Perhaps I should have asked for a Catholic driver," Michael said, opening his overcoat so his white collar was visible.

"And then we couldn't have gone into the Shankill Road area, or any of the Protestant neighborhoods. It's okay, Bishop, your baby sister will take care of you." She smiled up at her brother.

They walked down the slope to where the British army had a checkpoint and joined a queue of people going into the Catholic neighborhood. The Catholics moved forward obediently, opening their bundles, purses, and coats, allowing themselves to be searched by the British soldiers and the Ulster police.

When Maggie reached the gate, she opened her coat as the others had done. It was a young soldier and he glanced away, embarrassed as he patted her body.

"American?" he asked, when he finished.

"Yes." Maggie smiled. "How did you know?"

"You're one of those goodwillers."

Maggie shook her head, not understanding.

"With the bishop there." He nodded toward Michael.

"Yes, his sister." News travels fast, she thought: everyone in Belfast, from graffiti artists to soldiers, knew that Father Mike had come from America to help the poor Catholics.

"Well, in you go there, luv. You're safe among the Taigs." He motioned her forward and body-searched the next Catholic entering the ghetto.

The nuns were waiting for them on the front steps of the convent, looking like a flock of black birds in their traditional religious habits. One of the slum children had obviously seen Michael and her and had run ahead to alert the nuns. The soldier was right, Maggie thought. They were safe in the heart of the Taig slum.

"Is it yourself, Bishop?" one nun said, stepping out from under the group's umbrellas. "I'm Mother Agnes, Father O'Connor's sister. Indeed, it is you! I have a picture of the two of you together, Dermot and yourself."

"Hello, Mother Agnes," Michael said, engulfing the small nun's hand in his and glancing around at the other nuns. "Well, now, with all of you out in the rain to meet me, you'd be thinking I was Pope Paul himself."

The sisters laughed.

Maggie smiled. Her brother had slipped easily into his bogus Irish brogue as he charmed the group. She had seen him do this before. He was his most seductive when he was with clergy, his own kind. She felt suddenly distanced from him, as if she were being excluded from a secret rite. Then he turned to her, saying, "And this is my own little sister, Margaret Mary. Our mother sent her along, you know, to keep me out of trouble here in Belfast."

The nuns laughed again, and their high voices rang clear on the gray day like a chorus of song.

"Come in now out of the rain," Mother Agnes said. "It would be a dear shame if you were to go home with the death of cold." She had not let go of the bishop's hand, and she slipped her arm into Maggie's, saying to them both, softly, confidentially, "You've come in the nick of time, I'm afraid. Dermot telephoned yesterday and said you'd been barred from the Maze. Could I arrange for you to see a Maze prisoner, he asked. Well, we have just the one. He was let out of H-Block on Friday last, but I'm afraid the poor man will be in God's hands soon."

Maggie tried to hang back, but Mother Agnes had a tight hold of her arm. Maggie was afraid of hospitals, ever since the time Emmett had almost killed her with the kitchen knife. Whenever she was exhausted from lack of sleep, she still had nightmares of waking in a strange room with her body strapped to a bed, an oxygen mask taped to her face.

Inside the convent infirmary, she saw that the nuns had tried to give the cold brick building the feeling of a home. Only the sight of old men and women in wheelchairs and using walkers reminded her that these were the poorest of Belfast's poor, and the Passion and Crucifixion Infirmary was their final home.

Mother Agnes paused at the door and said quietly, "I'll go with you and make you acquainted. It was a hard time he had in the Maze. And naturally, he's afraid of strangers. The poor man—he has no family in Ireland, north or south." She smiled sadly and whispered, "God willing, he won't be in pain much longer."

It was a small room, painted white, with a narrow iron bed in the far corner and away from the window. Religious pictures and a crucifix hung on the white wall, white curtains on the windows. It was only outside the window, where a garden of bright flowers bloomed in the courtyard, that one caught a flash of color. Maggie saw several nuns outside saying their morning Office. They walked alone, pacing by each other, their heads bowed in prayer. Maggie studied them, the flowers, the crucifix—anything, rather than approach the bed.

But Michael had moved forward, and she had to follow him. Looking squarely at the dying old man for the first time, she thought immediately of the huge street mural they had seen earlier that day.

She and Michael had gone for a walk after his early Mass and spotted the mural painted on a brick wall. It was over fifteen feet long and twelve feet high.

"It's the portrait of a hunger striker, isn't it?" Michael had said. "They've made him look like a suffering Jesus."

Maggie had been silent, stunned by the drawing. The man in the mural was naked but for a blanket; his rosary beads were raised to his lips. Behind him was a huge white *H* enclosed in gray walls. On the left side of the mural the figure of the Blessed Virgin was painted in white and blue, her head wreathed by a gray halo. She was approaching the blanket man to give him her blessing.

The man in the infirmary bed was also suffering. But he clutched no rosary in his thin fingers, nor was there a blissful look on his frightened and fragile face. His hair and beard had both turned white, and his eyes were wild as he glanced about the room. Maggie smelled death as she drew closer. Not the death she had smelled in Beirut, all gunshot and gunpowder, but stale death. Death from age and weather, death from waste and hunger. She remembered a trip she had taken to Bombay, where from her train she had seen people dying in the sun, starving in a land of plenty. It was the same here. The landscape beyond Belfast was green and lush. There was the sea south of the city, and the beautiful Mourne Mountains of County Down. It was a charming country, but in the bare room of the convent infirmary, she felt only the dampness of dying.

Mother Agnes took the man's hand in hers and leaned forward and whispered to him. Then she motioned Michael and Maggie closer.

The old man opened his mouth to speak, and from where she stood at the end of the narrow bed, Maggie saw he had no teeth, that his gums were white and sore. Scurvy, she realized. In this day and age, the man had scurvy.

"Who are you?" he asked Maggie, his voice hollow in his thin throat.

"She's my sister," Michael answered, speaking up. "My sister, Margaret Mary DeLacey."

"Hello," Maggie whispered, and fought to keep back her tears.

The dying man kept staring at her, as if his white, milky eyes were finding it difficult to focus. Then he said, still whispering, with the words coming slowly in his reedy voice, "You're the image of herself, aren't you, girl?"

Maggie glanced over at Michael. She didn't understand but she nodded yes, wanting to ease the man's mind.

"I'll leave you now," Mother Agnes said. "Maggie dear, why don't you pull that chair around beside the bed for yourself." Then to Michael she whispered, "I'll leave you to have a few words with the man."

"Thank you, Mother," Michael answered, keeping his eyes on the old man. He moved closer to the head of the bed as the mother superior left, the beads of her long rosary clicking softly as she walked from the room.

"Can you understand us, sir?" Michael asked. "Despite the Yank accent?" He smiled down at the old man.

The man turned his head on the thin pillow and studied Michael a moment. "Can you understand an old Irishman like myself?" he managed to say. "Are you both wondering who I am and why you're here?"

"You're one of the 'forties men," Maggie spoke up.

A thin smile worked its way to his lips. "Do you know what the 'forties men are?"

Maggie did; Father O'Connor had told her all about it when she was a child. "The old IRA. The men who fought in the nineteen-forties against the British. Men like Liam McMillen, Billy McKee, and yourself."

"Not myself. I was in prison in the forties, during the emergency. That's what we called World War Two in Ireland. Do you understand me, child?" He spoke to Maggie but did not take his eyes off Michael.

"Yes, I understand." Maggie glanced across at Michael, and then asked, "Would you like to tell us about your life, sir?"

"I'm not Catholic, you know. I'm not one of your own. But I'm an Irishman. Not a Prod who sells his land to the British."

"Easy, sir." Michael reached over and touched the man's arm. "We're all for getting rid of the English here." Then he said softly, "Now please tell us something about yourself."

The old man stared up at Michael. He seemed to grow a bit stronger, Maggie noticed, watching him, and his eyes cleared, focusing on Michael, and then he said, as a way of beginning, "I was born in the south, in Dublin, and raised in the Church of Ireland. On my mother's side my family goes back to the time of Jonathan Swift himself. We were against the English domination then; we are against it today. I had an aunt who lost her life fighting the Black and Tan; another stood with Parnell from the first. And great uncles of mine, on my father's side, were executed in the Wicklow uprising of ninety-eight—hanged in the town square.

"We're not Catholics, son, but we have given our lives for this country, and Ireland is as much ours as it was your mother's."

As he kept talking, his voice grew stronger. Maggie couldn't help noticing that he had an educated, upper-class accent. Yet the life he described was not one of any privilege. Imprisoned during the Second World War, he later emigrated to South Africa. "I was given a passport and forty-eight hours to leave Ireland. It was that bastard De Valera. He wanted no more of the Sinn Fein, and here it was the likes of myself who put him in power!"

In South Africa, he told them, he worked in the diamond mines, "did a bit of organizing for the blacks until those Afrikaners kicked me out of Joburg. I worked my way from one country to the next in Africa, doing what I could. It was during those years that I tried to immigrate to America, but your government would have nothing to do with me.

"I came home to Dublin in 1967. I knew the Irish high commissioner out there in Kenya, and he put in a good word for me at the home office. Well, being home was quite a change. To tell you the truth, people in Dublin saw me as a bit of hero, what I had done, you know, during the war, and since then in Africa. They wrote me up in the newspapers, with photos from my days in Mountjoy prison. I was given a pension, thanks to Erskine Childers. He's president, you know, the first Protestant president of the republic.

"Well, I rather liked being a hero, so I came up here to Belfast in sixty-nine to help out. Nothing active, you understand. Just an old bog fossil sent up to draw attention to what the Brits were doing. The truth was, I wasn't up to doing much. But one day, we were having a march, a peaceful one, to protest the civil rights of the Protestants and Catholics, when the police attacked.

"They arrested me right off; I stopped one of those RUC coppers from bashing in a lad. Hit the policeman with my blackthorn, and they took me out to Hollywood barracks. They were going to make an example of me. To show no one was above the law. Well, they had me in the Maze seven years."

The old man stopped speaking to catch his breath. Talking had worn him out.

"Can you tell us more about what happened there?" Maggie asked, leaning closer. She realized then she might write about this ex-IRA prisoner for the *Post*. A human-interest story.

" 'Twasn't pretty what they did to me." He spoke to Michael.

"We'd like to know," Michael answered. "We could tell others in America who support a free Ireland."

"They kept me awake for weeks," the old man began. "I'd be placed a few inches from a wall, my fingers just touching it, and left to stand there naked. When I fell down from exhaustion they grabbed me by my genitals and pulled me to my feet. I was starved. Not to the point of death, but they'd lace glass into the stew and piss on it, then make me eat the filth."

"Jesus, Mary, and Joseph," Michael whispered.

Maggie had written about police brutality in Northern Ireland for the *Post* when the European Human Rights Commission conducted hearings on the interrogation methods. She knew about the English police methods.

"That's right, lad. I don't know how many days they had me at the army barracks. I had a bad stomach from my days in Africa, and I asked to see a doctor.

"This fella in a white coat and stethoscope came into my cubicle. He asked me about my stomach and then poured me a glass of medicine and told me to drink it all down quickly since it would taste dreadful.

"The moment I'd drunk it I started retching, then vomiting on the floor. He wasn't a doctor, after all, just a soldier, and he hadn't given me medicine, but disinfectant. Those bastards stood there laughing as the poison tore up my insides."

"Were you given a trial? Any sort of hearing?" Michael asked.

"They took me before this fellow—I don't know if he was a judge or not."

"What was your sentence?" Maggie asked.

"They gave me life." He said it offhandedly, as if it didn't matter. A life sentence for hitting a policeman with my walking stick."

"Dear God!"

The dying man turned his white head toward her. "I can hear your mother in your voice."

Maggie smiled, wondering what woman from his past he was imagining her mother to be.

"Were you ever in the Maze itself, sir?" Michael interrupted. "Can you tell me something about that?"

"The Maze." The old man closed his eyes and almost smiled. "It sounds like a great fortress, doesn't it? The Bastille, the Tower of London, the Maze. Well, 'tisn't anything more than a prison camp, with sheet-metal quonset huts, wire gauge fences, guard dogs.

"It wasn't so bad at first, living in these huts. We wore clothes, went outside. We thought of ourselves—and right we were!—as prisoners of war. Even the British listed us as Special Category. Then in 1976, it was, the Labor party changed all that. No more Special Category! They said we were nothing more than common criminals."

"And that's when you stripped off your clothes, went on the blanket."

"Ah, that was it. Still they won't let us be. They'd get us up every day and take us outside for a search. Looking for contraband, they said.

"We'd be lined up naked against the fence with our legs spread. They'd stick their fingers up our back passage to see whether we were carrying contraband, and then stick the same filthy fingers in our mouths.

"It got so cold in winter that our hands froze to the wire fence. That made great fun for them: they'd pull us away from the fence and our skin would rip off our palms."

"Why did they finally let you go?" Maggie asked, after a pause.

The old man turned away from her and stared for a moment at Michael before replying, "I'm dying, and they don't want another martyr."

"Sir, you've spent your life in prison and in exile because of what you believe about Ireland," Maggie said. "Was it worth your struggle? The English are still here, and this city doesn't belong to any of the Irish, whether they're Catholic or Protestant."

"I had no choice."

"You did. You could have quit Ireland for good."

He was shaking his head before she finished. "I cast my lot for Ireland when I was a lad. I could never call myself an Irishman, never feel proud, unless I was fighting to make Ireland free. If you have Irish in your blood, you fight for Ireland against the English."

Maggie stood. They were all alike, she thought, all these "freedom fighters." She had talked to a PLO teenager in southern Lebanon who only wanted to kill Israelis. This old man was the same. She wondered how many people he had killed for the sake of a unified Ireland. Now she felt angry at him for what he represented: terrorism. He no longer looked Christlike to her, dying in the white convent room.

Across the bed, Michael also stood, and said to the old man, "We'll leave you now, sir, so you can get some rest. Thank you for telling us your story."

With a ferocity that shocked Maggie, the man reached out and grabbed Michael's hand. He tried to pull himself up, to keep Michael from leaving. She was surprised he had that much strength left in him.

"Would you have a minute more for me, Father?" he asked.

"I'll go ahead, Michael," Maggie whispered. "I'll wait for you in the pub, with the driver."

In the hallway, Maggie found the mother superior, who seemed to have been waiting for them.

"He has the common touch, doesn't he?" Mother Agnes said, speaking of Michael. "Dermot wrote how he was good with people.

He'll have his cardinal's cap next, you can be sure." She winked at Maggie.

"God willing," Maggie added automatically, pausing at the infirmary door.

"Your mother must be so proud, having a son chosen by God for such greatness."

"Yes, she is very proud of Michael," Maggie answered, smiling. "Mother Agnes, I'll be going now. My brother will meet me later. This poor man wanted him to stay, I guess because—"

"I know why the man wishes to speak to the bishop," the nun interrupted. She ushered Maggie onto the steps and waved her good-bye with a smile. Maggie walked up a few yards, then turned and looked back. The nun was still on the steps, and Maggie had the oddest feeling that if she returned to the convent she wouldn't be allowed to enter. She waved once more at Mother Agnes, and the nun waved back, still smiling. For some reason, it seemed to Maggie a smile of triumph.

Michael bent closer to the old man to hear his fading voice. Something was troubling him. Michael had often seen dying men ask forgiveness in the last moments of their lives. Had this man committed some terrible wrong in his past, so that he did not want to die without confessing? In the last moments of his life, it probably did not matter whether he was absolved by a Catholic priest or the Church of Ireland.

"Your mother never told you, son?" the man asked.

Michael pulled back from the dying man, as if to look again and see who this poor IRA fighter really was. He felt a moment of panic, thinking: Had Dermot O'Connor sent him to this convent for a special reason?

The old man whispered, "It was the nun who told me you were coming to Belfast. The pope himself was sending you from America. Sister Agnes, she was a great friend of my mother. A long time ago it was, before the war, when we had a home down in Kerry."

"You knew my mother?" Michael asked. He could feel his legs weaken.

"Ah, I knew your mother, son. She told you, did she, who your real father was?"

Michael paused a moment before replying. "Years ago when Dad —when Cormac left us in Illinois and came back here to Ireland— she told me that he wasn't my father. She never gave me a name. She said only that my father was a great figure in Ireland's struggle for independence."

"No, your father, my boy, was a foolish revolutionary who took advantage of the dear woman and then did not have the decency or courage to keep her as my own. My name is Adrian Steele. And your rightful name is Steele. I am your father, Michael."

Adrian Steele slipped back onto the pillow and kept staring at the ceiling as he went on. "Your mother told me once how she heard the jew's harp that night at Glennamain. A silly country superstition, and I paid her no mind. But it was true enough. She heard the jew's harp beyond the lake and famine wall. She said it was God calling. She never told you this?"

Michael shook his head, then added, to agree with him, "It's just a superstition." He could not take his eyes off the old man.

Adrian Steele moved his head and looked to the gray light of the window. "But it's true enough. I heard the jew's harp myself last night, there in the garden."

"The nuns, perhaps, playing music?"

"Ah, the nuns. God's messengers?" Adrian Steele smiled, pleased with that notion. And then still with his eyes to the pale light of the Belfast day, he went on, "We were very young, your mother and I, and we were full with the pleasure of each other. I hadn't a care in the world. Nor a thought. I wanted to save Ireland for her, save Caitlin from a life of servitude. But I loved her, Michael. I loved your mother, I truly did." He kept nodding his head and looking away again, then said wistfully, as if remembering again the long lost night of love, "You were conceived under slate in the servants' quarters of Glennamain."

The old man tightened his grip on Michael's fingers and asked, "Hear my confession, son. Hear my sins, for I have done you a terrible wrong."

Michael slowly, thoughtfully, blessed the man as he whispered, "I forgive you in the name of the Father, the Son, and the Holy Spirit. I forgive you all your sins in the name of Jesus Christ Almighty. Follow my words, Adrian Steele, say after me this act of contrition."

The bishop gave his father a general confession, then sat quietly beside the bed. The old man had slipped into a thin sleep, exhausted by the effort of speaking. Michael thought for a moment that he should summon one of the nuns but realized as he watched him that nothing more could be done for his father.

Adrian Steele blinked his eyes and stared up at Michael as if trying to place the bishop, and then he asked, "Is she alive, Michael? Is your mother alive there in America?"

"Yes, she is well," Michael whispered, surprised by his own tears.

"Tell her, son. Tell her that you met me. Tell her that I always loved her. Tell her I loved you both all my life."

He reached suddenly for Michael's hand and then gasped as he tried to speak. His eyes were wild, yet he held Michael's face in sight and fought to speak his dying breath. "Do you hear it, son? Do you hear the jew's harp beyond the famine wall?"

Maggie stood at the windows of Cunningham's Pub holding a half-pint glass of Guinness in both hands. She was staring out at the peace line, the long corrugated iron wall that the British army had built between the Protestant section of Shankill and the Catholic ghetto of Falls Road. In the middle of the street that led down to the checkpoint, huge blocks of stone had been set down in uneven rows so that a car or lorry would have to slow to a crawl driving by them. The checkpoint, she could see, would never be rammed by a racing vehicle.

"The stone blocks are called dragon's teeth," Tommy said, stepping up beside her with his own glass of Guinness. "Everything here is given a special name, as if we were proud of all this destruction in Belfast." He spoke without anger.

"It reminds me of Beirut, the war zones between the Moslems and the Christians."

"Ah, religion will be the death of us all, I'm afraid. You and your brother had best be careful, miss. The Prods have no fear of killing a bishop. Or his sister. This is war we're having here in Belfast."

"But my brother is on a peace mission. And Mother Agnes, the nun we're visiting, runs a hospital. She's not involved with the political problems of Belfast."

Tommy grinned, then said softly, "It matters not if she is a nun or whatever. If she's behind that iron wall, living in Falls Road, then by God, she's at war with the Prods. They all are, mark my word on that."

Maggie was no longer paying attention. She had spotted Michael coming through the checkpoint, and she set down her drink and went out at once to meet him.

He saw her, nodded, and began to cross the street, looking both ways at the heavy traffic. Then she heard the motorbike and realized, without knowing why, that something was wrong.

The small bike was coming toward them, weaving quickly through the dragon's teeth. The rider was a teenager, she thought first, then immediately realized what was happening.

"Run, Michael! Run!" Her shrill midwestern voice rang out on the cold Belfast day. Pedestrians paused on the sidewalks, staring after her as she raced into the street. She dove for Michael as the bike roared by. The Belfasters saw the milk bottle, saw the hooded biker lob it toward the Americans, and they, too, ducked for cover.

The bomb crashed against a stone square; the flaming gas and diesel fuels splashed the concrete block, the tarmac, and would have caught Michael, too, in its spray, but Maggie, like a downfield tackler, caught her brother at his knees and tumbled him away from the spreading flame.

It was over in moments. The bomb burned harmlessly, its flame licking the wet street, the dragon's teeth. Maggie heard sirens and police whistles as the British soldiers came running to where she and Michael lay sprawled on the peace line.

She sat up and reached for her brother.

"Michael, are you all right?" She touched his shoulder, and when he turned to her, she saw there was some blood on his face and gravel from where he had skinned himself falling. There were also tears in his eyes which surprised her. She had never seen him cry. "Michael!" she whispered.

"He's dead, Maggie. He's dead."

"Who? What do you mean?" She got to her feet, but he remained on his knees.

"Adrian Steele. He's dead now." It was her brother speaking, but he spoke in their mother's rich Irish tones, no longer making a joke of the Irish brogue, his heritage and his blood.

# · CHAPTER 43 ·

GATESBURG: 1982

WHEN KENNETH WENT UPSTAIRS to wash up, Maggie took the phone into the front parlor, closed the door, and started making telephone calls. She got hold of Paddy Jack, at Vanessa's, and told him how she had posted Emmett's bail that morning.

"Once Kenneth's certified check clears the bank, Emmett will be out—by tonight, I'm sure. So I'm calling to ask you to come for dinner tomorrow night, as a welcome-home party for Emmett."

"Sure, I'll come. Vanessa will, too."

Maggie took a deep breath. "Of course! She'll be family soon."

"What about Michael?"

"I've already called him. He agreed to fly in tomorrow morning."

"He's coming to Gatesburg just for a dinner?"

"I told him he had to come. Tomorrow night will be very special, and not just because of Emmett. Starting tomorrow night, there'll be no more family secrets."

"And your friend . . . the ambassador. He'll be there?"

"Yes."

"Well, there's nothing like baptism by fire." Paddy Jack laughed. "What about Catty? What did she say?"

"I'm about to find out. Come at seven, and as Bette Davis once said, 'Fasten your seat belts—it's going to be a bumpy night.' "

"You sound ready to take on the world, Maggie."

"I'm ready to take on the DeLaceys, Paddy. That's enough."

Maggie telephoned Washington next. She told a friend at the Federal Election Commission what she needed, indicating that the information was for a *Post* story, and asked him to call back as soon as possible. As she hung up, she heard Kenneth on the stairs and met him in the hallway.

"Harris says the FEC information is all computerized and contributions are listed weekly, now that the campaign is gearing up. I told him I was only interested in the December contributions totaling two hundred and fifty thousand dollars and originating in Gatesburg."

Kenneth nodded. He had changed from his three-piece suit into the slacks and the cashmere sweater she had just bought him in Washington. "Then we wait for the call. Would you like a drink in the meantime?" he asked.

"I'd love one." She smiled, and moved into his embrace. "Is it okay if we just sit by the fire and neck for a while?"

"Yes"—he laughed—"as long as Wendy doesn't catch us. Go stretch out and I'll be back with your drink."

"No, I'll go," Maggie said. "I need to check with Catty anyway. She's been out there cooking all morning."

In the kitchen, Maggie found her sister measuring flour for the bread she was making.

"Kenneth and I are going to have a drink, Cat. Care to join us?"

"No thanks, Mag. After I finish here, I'm going upstairs to take a nap."

"You and Wendy were up late, weren't you? Anything decided?" Maggie searched through the overhead cabinet for a bottle of gin.

"Yes, I hope so. Wendy wants to keep the baby. If need be, we'll stay here on the farm until she delivers. I called Joe this morning and told him. He's still upset, but he's coming today with the children and we'll talk."

"How does Wendy feel?"

"Scared. Like her mother." Catty smiled wryly, then added, "Who would have thought raising kids would be this tough?"

"Mom," Maggie answered. "By the way, have you seen the dry vermouth?"

"No, but if we have any, it's in the bottom of the hutch. Speaking of kids, did you see my daughter upstairs? I need her to clean up in here. I feel like I've been on my feet since six A.M."

"Now you sound just like Mom!"

"Oh, God, do I remember," Catty replied. "Mom complained all the time about how much work she did."

"But she did work all the time."

"So did her kids."

Maggie triumphantly produced vermouth from a cluster of liquor bottles and started fixing Kenneth a martini. "Well, what do you think of my beau?" she asked.

Catty stopped kneading dough and looked up. "I think he's very nice and very distinguished."

"Yes, isn't he? No matter where you put Kenneth, he manages to fit in, while at the same time being himself. He's just—dignified. In the nicest meaning of that word."

"It's the gray temples," Catty said, smiling.

"No, it's because he's so sure of himself. I mean, he could be in some village in Ethiopia or striding through Dulles Airport, and he always manages to look in total control, as if he's been doing it all his life."

"Well, let's see how he survives dinner with the DeLaceys."

"I'm afraid he'll be stirring things up a bit," Maggie answered. Catty looked puzzled, and Maggie decided to plunge ahead. "He's turned up some pretty damaging stuff about our dear old family."

"Like what?" Catty separated the dough into two bread pans.

For a moment, Maggie didn't know what to tell her sister. She had planned to wait until the whole family was gathered, then confront Michael with Kenneth's information about him and the Blue and Whites. But it wasn't fair not to tell Catty at least part of what she knew.

"I looked at the mortgage papers," Maggie said. "Emmett's signature is forged. And Michael and Father O'Connor are the only witnesses."

Catty stopped kneading. "Who knows this?"

"Paddy Jack and you."

"Michael took the two hundred fifty thou?"

"I think so."

"Then what has he done with the money?"

"I'm not sure. But I hope to know more soon."

The telephone rang down the hallway. Taking a quick gulp of Kenneth's martini, Maggie headed for it. "That, I think, is my answer."

By the time Maggie came into the living room, Catty had joined Kenneth in front of the fireplace. He had explained to her what information they'd been waiting for.

"The campaign contributions have been laundered?" Kenneth asked immediately, seeing the look on Maggie's face.

She nodded.

"You think Michael has given the mortgage money to a political candidate?" Catty asked.

"That's right." Maggie walked over to the sofa and sat down beside Kenneth, curling her long legs under her.

"But who? Who does Michael care about that much? Besides Reagan, of course, and he doesn't need the money."

"Jack McGraff."

"Maggie! Jack and Michael don't speak to each other, not even on the night of Mother's wake. Didn't they get into a huge fight when your marriage was annulled?"

"Yes—yet in the end, of course, Michael got the annulment. In Washington all politicians fight, but they also do business. That's politics." She thought of the night in Rome and realized that when

Jack had made love to her and asked her to marry him again, he was already making a secret deal with her brother. "When I was in Washington last week, I spotted Jack coming out of Michael's office," Maggie went on quickly, to stop herself from thinking about Rome. "Then Kenneth came up with some information linking the two of them. That telephone call I got was from a friend at the Federal Election Commission. I wanted to find out what money had come from Gatesburg. The way the new Federal Campaign Contribution Act works, Catty, is that no individual can contribute more than a thousand dollars to a presidential campaign. And PACS—that is, Political Action Groups—can only give up to five thousand."

"Then Michael couldn't have given Jack McGraff a quarter of a million," Catty protested.

"There are ways of getting around the law. And Michael has gotten around the law." Maggie picked up her yellow pad and glanced at her notes. "Jack McGraff didn't get a political contribution from Michael. He didn't get any contribution at all from Gatesburg. What Jack McGraff got was a loan—a guaranteed loan of two hundred and fifty thousand dollars from the Farmer's First National. The collateral for the loan was provided by Father Dermot O'Connor of Saint Patrick's Roman Catholic Church."

"Is that legal?" Kenneth asked.

"Maybe, maybe not. Several of the presidential candidates have used the same technique to raise a lot of money, so they can double the amount when they apply for federal matching funds. But the FEC questions it and is already investigating this kind of loan."

"But so far," Kenneth pointed out, "it is legal. And the bishop's name never gets dragged in."

"How can O'Connor guarantee a loan of that much money?" Catty objected. "Saint Pat's isn't worth that much."

Maggie nodded. "But it isn't Saint Pat's property that's being held as collateral. I'll bet our mortgage money went into the church's coffers as a donation, and, therefore, makes Saint Pat's a good risk to the bank."

Catty sat back, shocked. "Then how will we get the money back? We can't possibly repay all that mortgage money."

"We sell the property for one-point-five million, as everyone seems to be suggesting." Maggie stood. She crossed to the front windows and looked across the lawn. The winter day was brilliantly bright and cold.

"So we lose the farm no matter what," Catty said disbelievingly.

"Unless we pool our money and come up with a quarter million. Even so, I don't know if we can raise that much. Emmett's bail has already cost Kenneth a great deal." Maggie turned her back to the window and shook her head. "Kenneth, let's go for a walk. I need to get outside and clear my head. We can check the livestock and pick up the mail."

"Wendy will do that," Catty offered.

"What will I do?" Wendy came in from the kitchen, drying her hands on a towel. "Mom, what are you volunteering me for now?"

"To go pick up the mail."

"Mom! I've just spent hours in that kitchen cleaning the mess you made."

"Easy, easy," Maggie said, slipping her arm around her niece. "Kenneth and I will take care of it."

"Thanks, Aunt Maggie. Mom, I promised Jackie Beaven I'd call and it's already two."

"Fine. Go telephone Jackie."

"I can't just 'go call,' " Wendy snapped, staring down at her mother. "I mean, there's only this one jerky phone in the hallway. I need privacy."

"Wendy Ann, I'm not going to have everyone hide away in their rooms so you and Jackie Beaven can gossip. You're being just a little too demanding, young lady, and inconsiderate of others."

"Fine!"

"Wendy," Maggie said calmly. "When we go outside, you can make your call. The phone cord reaches into the front parlor. Go in there and shut the door. No one will hear you."

Catty glanced over at her sister and shook her head as Maggie and Kenneth put on their overcoats.

"When you call your girlfriend, Wendy Ann Duffy," she said, as Maggie and Kenneth went out the front door, "ask if her family is as crazy as ours."

"No way!" Wendy laughed, plopping down on the sofa, her phone call forgotten for the moment. "Are they getting married?" she asked.

"Yes, I hope so. But your aunt hasn't said anything, so don't bring it up."

"That's great." Wendy grinned. "I mean, he's neat. He looks like Remington Steele, you know, just older."

"I'll tell Aunt Maggie that," Catty said, smiling.

"But Jack McGraff is cuter. She should have stayed married to him, cause he'll be president someday. Why did she dump Jack anyway?"

"It's none of our business."

"But I bet anything you know."

"Wendy Ann, you're being a brat. Do you hear me?"

"I hear you," Wendy answered after a moment. Then she asked, "What's going on, anyway? Why is everyone so uptight?"

"It's because of Emmett." Catty stood. "Kenneth has posted Emmett's bond. He'll be home for dinner tonight."

"Oh, great!"

"And you, young lady, will behave yourself. Understand?"

"Don't make me sit next to him."

"I'm going upstairs and take a bath," Catty said, instead of answering. "Have you finished in the kitchen?"

"Yes, Mother!"

"Good. Now you can scatter the fire so we can clean the hearth." Catty glanced out the front windows. Seeing Maggie and Kenneth walking hand in hand to the mailbox, she smiled. In spite of everything else that was happening in the family, Catty felt a warm rush of affection for her sister. It was nice to feel happy for someone.

"Hey, Mom, I think this old fireplace is falling down."

"What, darling?" Catty asked, turning from the window.

"The fireplace. This stone is loose, I think." Wendy put down the poker and went to the mantel. "Look!" She pulled out the cornerstone.

"Wendy, sweetheart, don't pull down the house."

"I'm not hurting anything. See, it goes back." She started fitting the stone into its space, then paused and said, "There's something stuck in here." Reaching in, she pulled out a thick wad of paper. "What's this?" In her hand were the sheets of lined notepaper, rolled up and secured with a rubber band. As Wendy started to undo the packet, Catty took it from her.

"It's your grandmother's handwriting," she said.

"Who's it written to?" Wendy was straining to see.

"Wait just a minute," Catty answered, and slowly began to read. " 'They tell of the time in the west of Connaught, of the woman who lost six sons to the sea . . .' It's a story, I think, honey," Catty said. She moved closer to the light of the window, continuing to read. It was written in pencil, sprawling lines on paper torn from a spiral notebook.

Catty heard Maggie and Kenneth come up the front steps. As they stamped their boots on the wooden porch, she quickly scanned the final pages. When she reached the end, Catty realized what she was holding.

The front door was pushed open and Maggie hurried in from the cold, calling Catty's name.

Catty stepped away from the window saying, "I found it, Maggie!" She held up the handwritten pages. "I found Mother's suicide note."

Maggie stood facing her sister in the open doorway, letting the winter wind whip through the farmhouse. She, too, held a letter in her hand, and she answered, "And I've found out who killed her."

# · CHAPTER 44 ·

## GATESBURG: 1982

"I'D LIKE TO PROPOSE a toast," Maggie said, rising to her feet. The long dining-room table was set with all the fine Irish linen and china she and Catty had discovered in the attic. All their mother's heavy napkins, silverware, pieces of Waterford crystal and Belleek china, pieces they had never seen when they were children, were spread out now, shining in the soft candlelight. Around the room, everyone raised their glasses and looked toward Emmett, who sat beside Maggie.

Yet it wasn't Emmett Maggie addressed. Her eyes were flashing and there was now anger in her voice. "I'd like to propose a toast to Michael." Surprised by the gesture and the tone in Maggie's voice, the bishop tried to force himself to smile. He was wearing a plain black suit, as was Father O'Connor, whom Catty had seated at the foot of the table. "According to Kenneth, whom you've all met tonight, it is secrets that hold families together. Well, we certainly know that is true in our family. Yet it is also true that money tears families apart —and, Michael, you have let money destroy our family."

The farmhouse dining room was suddenly hushed.

"You forged Emmett's signature on the mortgage," Maggie continued, "and, worst of all, you gave the money to Jack McGraff."

"I did nothing—"

"Michael, please!" Maggie raised her hand. "No more lies, no more shading of the truth, no more manipulating your brothers and sisters. I know the truth. And I want you to tell us why you did it." For a moment she gripped Kenneth's shoulder, as if to find, among her family, one solid place of support. "Why did you take the money and let Father O'Connor—through the bank—lend a quarter of a million dollars to Jack McGraff?"

Everyone at the table turned toward Michael and waited for his reply. "Tell us, Michael," Catty demanded. "Goddamnit! Tell your family."

"Jack McGraff, your ex, was blackmailing me," Michael answered back. "I've been trying to help the Irish Catholics in Ulster, helping them get arms to fight the British. You might not give a damn about the old country, but there are thousands of good Irish Catholics in America who want to help Ireland. They give me money. They come up to me at rallies, wherever I talk, and slip me cash, ten or twenty dollars, and whisper to me to do what I can for those back home." His deep voice boomed across the table and his dark eyes flashed. "Unlike the DeLaceys, these good people haven't forgotten who they are. The Jews in America are allowed to help Israel, yes, but if an Irishman tries to help his own, he's labeled a terrorist."

"We never called you a terrorist, Michael," Maggie replied. "It was your right-wing friends, Nixon and Reagan, who passed the laws you've broken."

"And it is your kneejerk liberal ex-husband who is blackmailing me," Michael shouted.

Maggie shook her head. "You sold out your own family for a bunch of strangers."

Michael studied Maggie for a moment, and then he said slowly, "No, I didn't care about the gunrunning. Or the fact that I might go to jail because of it. I would have appeared in front of McGraff's committee. I could have used it as a platform from which to rally the Irish in America. No, Jack McGraff had something else on the family. Something about Mom. I'm sorry, but I can't tell you."

Paddy Jack looked down at his brother and then spoke up. "You're full of shit, Michael. Don't drag Mom into this. You did it on your own, mortgaged this place. Cut your deal with McGraff and for your own purposes. Maggie's right. You sold out the family."

"Paddy." Michael kept shaking his head. "That isn't true. I . . . can't."

"Is it about Adrian Steele, Bishop?" Kenneth asked. "Is Adrian Steele the reason?"

Michael stared at the ambassador, not responding, and Maggie said softly, "Tell us, Michael. Tell us."

Michael sat back in the chair and stared at Maggie for a moment, and then he asked, "How did you find out?"

"I was the one who found out, Michael," Kenneth spoke again. "Through British intelligence."

Michael nodded, understanding.

"What's this about?" Paddy Jack demanded. "Who's Adrian Steele?"

"He's my father," said Michael. "My natural father. Remember that family Mom worked for in Dublin? Well, Adrian Steele was their son. He got Mom pregnant, and that's why she and Dad left Ireland. I'm a bastard, Paddy. I'm illegitimate. And that's what Jack McGraff had on us. I didn't care about people knowing—except I couldn't let him reveal that about Mom. It wasn't fair, not in the last years of her life.

"So, to mask the payoff, he came up with this bank loan. It was a simple plan: we would sell the farm and pay back the two hundred and fifty thousand. I would assume the loss of my share of the property, and all of you would have been the richer for it."

"But Mother found out, didn't she?" broke in Maggie. "In one of her saner moments she answered the telephone. It was the bank calling about the sale and she learned for the first time that you were selling her farm—the only thing she had left in her life. And you knew she had to be killed."

"Maggie!" Paddy Jack shouted.

Maggie was trembling with fear and, at the same time, trembling with rage as she went on. "Be quiet! Everybody, be quiet! None of you knows what I discovered in the mail yesterday." She picked up the envelope that she had placed next to her and pulled out the contents.

"It's a telephone bill," Paddy Jack said.

"Yes, January's bill. When I looked at it yesterday, I saw that on the Saturday morning of Mother's death, two long-distance calls were made from here. And both were made to your office, Michael. Long distance to Washington, D.C."

"Maggie, please," Michael whispered. He seemed in pain now, but Maggie ignored him and kept talking.

"Emmett thought he had done it—killed Mom when he came running into the kitchen and his gun discharged. Well, his gun did discharge—and it blew out a pane of glass in the kitchen, that's all. Mother was already dead on the kitchen floor, and whoever killed her had carefully wiped the prints from the stock of the gun. But he didn't remove the prints on the barrel, those of Mother and Emmett.

"Emmett said he had handled the gun before he went out hunting. He even tried to pull the trigger, but the trigger was broken."

"What are you driving at?" Catty pleaded.

As much as they had often resented Michael, Maggie saw, the idea that he had killed their mother was destroying them. Still she did not immediately respond. She had rehearsed everything she had to say, and like a courtroom lawyer, she wasn't going to be put off her closing argument.

"You know what I know, Michael. I know that every call into your office is recorded by your secretary. Well, I waited until you boarded the flight this morning, and I telephoned your secretary, Nancy McCaskey. I asked her who called from Gatesburg on the morning of Mother's death.

"Do you remember, Michael?" Maggie waited for him to tell the truth.

"How should I remember?" he shouted back, enraged at what his little sister was doing to him.

"Then I'll remind you," Maggie said coolly. "There were two calls. One from Mother at eight-thirty. A second from Father O'Connor at nine-thirty." Maggie turned her full attention toward the old pastor. "It was you, Father O'Connor—you killed our mother. Then you telephoned Michael and told him you had followed his instructions. It was so simple, wasn't it? You waited for the police to blame Emmett, and then let him starve himself in that damn jail believing all the time that he had done it."

No, the old priest thought, she was all wrong. He stared at Michael, waited for the boy to speak. Maggie had said too many damaging things. He had to tell the family the truth, regardless of what Michael wanted.

"What kind of a man are you anyway?" Maggie said to the family friend. "You sent Emmett off to the army—for his own good, you said—when you could have kept him at home to run the farm. And then when he was given a second chance, you fixed it so he was accused of murder."

Maggie began to cry and she reached again for Kenneth, felt for his support.

"That's enough." Joe Duffy pushed back his chair. "We're frightening the children. Wendy, get the kids out of here!"

"No, Joe," Catty interrupted. "They've heard too much to send them away. It isn't fair. They're family. They're entitled to stay. As Maggie said, as of tonight there are no more secrets in this family. Michael? What do you have to say? Did Father O'Connor call you?"

"No one telephoned me. I was taping a program on that Saturday."

"Michael, I have the telephone bill!" Maggie shouted across the room. She held up the statement.

"It does no good, Michael, son," the pastor said at last, raising his voice so they would hear him. "It was myself who called Michael, and from here. And it was myself who killed your mother."

Vanessa took a quick breath, shocked by the admission.

"You didn't kill Mom," Michael said at once. "As Catty's told us, we have a suicide note," he went on. "The Irish story that Wendy found in the fireplace. It's enough evidence to clear Emmett. I spoke to the sheriff about the note. He's sure charges will be dropped."

Father O'Connor kept shaking his head until Michael finally let him speak. Then he looked around the table and asked, "Do you know that story your mother wrote in her own handwriting? It's an old tale. 'They tell of the time in the west of Connaught, of the woman who lost her sons to the sea . . .' " the priest repeated softly. "It's the story of Eileen Kilmartin, a woman of Ballinakill Bay who drove her husband off with her bad temper and ill moods. Night after night, he would leave the house and go fishing off the islands of Inishark, Inishbofin, and Inishtruk, coming home only when the sun rose over Croagh Patrick mountain and the Twelve Pins and he knew in which direction to turn with the tide.

"But one winter night there was a terrible storm, and no one could see the tip of Croagh Patrick, or the Twelve Pins that rose above the wild moors of Connemara. But this woman fought with her husband, and in the midst of that storm, in the worst of the weather, she drove him out to sea.

"The following morning, as your mother writes, he did not return, nor that afternoon, or night. So with the wind still raging, she sent her oldest son, Enan, out to sea, to find her husband, and she herself went to stand on the high cliffs above Ballinakill Bay.

"No son or husband came home that night, and the next day she sent her second boy into the wild waters. Again no one returned to her. The next day she sent her third son.

"The people of the village came to where she stood and begged her not to lose yet another child to the waves.

"But you see, Eileen Kilmartin thought her husband and sons were not lost in the storm, just hiding from her in the islands. So she called Christy, named after Saint Christopher himself, and told him to bring back the others.

"He was no older than these children and never returned. By morning the day was clear, as blue as glass, but the wind and waves were up, and she called the last of her boys from home.

"The priest came then to beseech the woman, but she'd hear no word of warning and sent away her youngest.

"The day and night passed on the coast of Connaught, the seas calmed, and the wind died. The ocean again was smooth and safe, but no boat came in from the sea.

"The priest left her, the villagers left her, but she never wavered, never turned her eyes from the sea.

"She stood there the whole of that summer day and night and still no husband or son came back to her. At last the priest—for none of the townspeople would care for her—went to the ledge with bread and a pot of pudding, only to find her frozen in the wind, her thin body turned to stone. It was God's will, they all said in the village, for sending her husband and children to an early death.

"And if you go there to the west of Ireland today, and take the coast road north from Tullycrook, you'll see facing the empty sea a stone in the shape of an Irish mother. She is wearing, it seems, the old Irish black shawl, and staring across the waters, still waiting for her husband, still waiting for all her sons, still waiting for their boats to sail from the islands of Inishark, Inishbofin, and Inishtruk."

Father O'Connor stopped reading and looked down the table at each member of the family. " 'Tis but a story, true, but 'tis true enough, I know, though it did not happen in my time, or even my father's time." Then he added, speaking softly, "Your mother, God rest her soul, thought that she, too, had lost her family, sent them away from her." He paused a moment, then stood up, grabbing the back of his chair to steady himself. Joe Duffy, sitting at his right, reached to help the old priest, but Father O'Connor waved his arm away and went on. "I saw Caitlin the morning of her death. I came out to the farm because Michael called me. Your brother Michael did not ask me to kill your mother, Maggie, dear. I did it myself."

"Dermot! Please!" Michael begged.

"I'm too old, Michael, for this carrying around of secrets. Michael had called me early that day. He had heard from Caitlin. As you say, Maggie, the bank had phoned the farm looking for Emmett. They wanted to do another assessment of the property, to figure out its value as an industrial park. John Keenan didn't know Emmett's signature was forged, of course. He told your mother what he wanted, and God rest her soul, she had no idea what was happening in her world.

"Still this was one of her saner moments and she telephoned Michael in Washington. Michael phoned me next and asked me to drive out to this place and have a word with her.

"When I walked into the house, I saw her at the kitchen table. She was loading Michael's old shotgun.

"I said, 'Caitlin, what is it, now?' And she began to cry, saying how even Michael had turned on her, selling off the farm, and she'd have nowhere to go. It was all a misunderstanding, you see. We were going to take care of the poor woman, take care of Emmett, take care of you all." He gestured around the table, beseeching them to understand.

"I went to Caitlin, told her to put down the gun, but she went on how she was going to kill herself, that she had written a note telling you why. I tried to pull the rifle away, but she raised it up, swung it at me. The woman was out of her mind. I reached up, to protect myself, mind you, and seized the stock of it, pulled it free, and the gun went off." He paused a moment, looked down at the floor, then whispered, "Oh, dear God, it was terrible, seeing her there . . . the blast knocked her against the door of the spare room. She fell into a pool of her own blood."

"Stop!" Catty shouted. Timmy had crawled into her arms and begun to cry. "Joe, take the children, please."

The old priest kept talking, oblivious to all of them. "I knelt there in the blood—her blood—and said what I could of the Last Rites. Dear Mother of God, it was so sad. The blood soaked into my trousers." He bent his white head, using both his hands to hold on to the chair.

Michael did not move, did not look up at the others. Maggie felt tears on her face and realized she was crying. No one said anything, but Father O'Connor could not go on.

"Dermot telephoned me," Michael admitted, speaking up to help the old pastor. He spoke calmly, as if now that they knew, it was all behind him and he was free of the secret. "It was an accident. A senseless accident. I told him to leave her, leave the farm, to avoid getting involved. That was a mistake. But it was all I could think of. I didn't want him connected in any way with Mother's death. If there was an investigation, I didn't want some smart-ass reporter to discover the link between him, the church, and the sale of the farm.

"I thought Mom's death would be judged an accident. Half a dozen shotgun accidents just like it happen every hunting season. We all know that. But this cop, this goddamn O'Hara. Who realized that he'd be trying to make a name for himself? And I didn't know that Emmett had gone around telling people in bars that Mom was driving him crazy."

"Yet you were willing to let your brother go to jail," Maggie put in.

"Yes, I was willing, Margaret Mary," Michael answered back. "It wasn't that I loved Emmett less, but that I loved Dermot more. He's been the father I never had, Maggie. Don't you understand? I couldn't turn on him in his old age." He threw down his napkin, as if to stand, then began to say, "Besides—"

"Besides, I told Michael I killed Mom," Emmett interrupted. "I told him on Sunday, when he came out for the wake. I said I killed Mom—I thought I had killed Mom. Things get all messed up in my head sometimes. I was hunting, and then I started to get dizzy, crazy like, and started to think I was back in Nam, and I came running home. When I crashed through the door, I tripped forward, ducking from the gunfire, I thought, and the gun went off and . . ."

He was sobbing and Maggie pulled him into her arms, whispering, "It wasn't you, Emmett. We know now, it wasn't you."

Emmett pulled a napkin off the table and buried his face in his mother's Irish linen.

Over Emmett's head, Maggie looked at Michael, her eyes expressing all the anger and rage she felt for him. "You did this, Michael. You and Father O'Connor knew the truth, and you let him believe he was guilty."

"I would have gotten Emmett out of jail."

"Yes, on insanity. If he didn't starve himself to death first."

"I'm sorry, Maggie."

"Sorry? Michael, you hurt him. You hurt your brother. You hurt all of us. You were going to give away this farm."

"Easy, Maggie," Paddy Jack whispered.

"No, I'm not going to be easy. What gave you the right, Michael? Answer me," she shouted.

"Mom gave me the right, Maggie. When you and Emmett weren't out of diapers, and Dad had left the family. She told me I had to take care of you."

"What about taking care of Mom? You weren't— Nor was I! Or Catty! Or Paddy Jack! It was Emmett who stayed on the farm and took care of Mom." The tears had returned, but Maggie kept talking, kept shouting at Michael, even though Kenneth reached over and took her hand to calm her.

"You were going to sell off the one thing she loved most, sell off this farm, sell off her whole life in America to some industrial park."

"It would mean money for all of you. I was going to make sure that Emmett had a job at the park, as maintenance man or something. It would mean business for Gatesburg. Jobs, new people in town." Michael kept defending himself.

"I don't give a goddamn about Gatesburg. What did this town ever do for Mom? For any of us? All Gatesburg has done is resent our achievements. Talked behind our backs. It's shanty Irish like Larry O'Hara who want to bring us down." Maggie stopped suddenly. She could hear her mother's argument in her voice, and it shocked her. She realized she was out of control. She turned to Kenneth, was about to ask him to take her upstairs, when Father O'Connor spoke up again.

"I was the one, Maggie, who told Michael to get rid of this place." The old priest moved away from his seat, began to come around the table, moving slowly, supporting each step, it appeared, by holding on to the back of the chairs. He kept speaking softly as he walked.

"I saw what was happening out here over the years. Saw the farm run down. I saw Emmett—God love the boy, but he's no farmer. He wasn't like his mother, who could farm better than any man I ever knew. But Caitlin was too old to get up on the back of the tractor, too old to be out in the sun plowing, planting. I tried to speak to the lad; he'll tell you that, but he wouldn't write you, Maggie, or any one of you for help. He thought you'd think less of him. He was tired of failing all his life, tired of being cared for. I remember you at school, Maggie, how you'd be fighting Emmett's battles, keeping him out of trouble."

The priest was standing behind Kenneth, looking at each one of them, and now he let his anger show. "You were a haughty bunch, the lot of you. All you DeLaceys thought you were better than this town, the rest of us. Ah, you got it from your mother, I know that well enough. Caitlin Rush DeLacey, God rest her soul, thought she was better than all the Germans, the Italians, the other Irish in Gatesburg. Better, too, than the likes of your people, Miss Harris." The old man nodded to Vanessa, and then for a moment he was silent, as if he had lost his thought again. Kenneth turned to help him, but the priest went on at once, his voice stronger and more certain of what he had to tell them.

" 'Tis true, you know. Caitlin was better than the likes of us. Better than, God bless him, her husband Cormac. He was no match for that woman, God knows. I've often thought that if Caitlin Rush had not been born in Tourmakeady, in that little village back of the beyond, why, there would have been no stopping her. She never had her chance. Not a proper chance. But she did wonders with what God gave her.

"She took this poor bottomland by the river and made as lovely a farm as you could find anywhere here around. All the farmers knew that, and they were jealous of her for doing it, without a husband, and with just the likes of you to help.

"So when I saw what was happening here, the land going, the house, too—and Emmett, oh, how the lad suffered—I said to Michael, sell the place off, before the land is worthless and you won't get ten cents an acre. And who would have thought the price it would bring —a million and a half dollars. Why, it's a king's fortune, isn't it?"

"Dermot," Michael whispered. "Sit down, Father."

"No, Michael. Let Father O'Connor talk," Maggie said, and then to the pastor, she said, "You were trying to save your church, Father, weren't you? Michael was giving you his share of the sale, wasn't he?" She waited for the old man to nod yes, and then she said, "You could show the cardinal in Springfield then that you had a good parish here in Gatesburg. They wouldn't send you away, would they?"

"He spent a lifetime in this town, Maggie," Michael protested. "He gave his whole life for the Catholics here."

"I don't care," she answered back, staring the bishop down. "What matters to me is Emmett, our family. I would never harm us, and you would."

"There are more important issues in the world than this goddamn family and farm."

"Not to me there isn't, Michael," she said calmly. "There isn't anything more important than one's family, our brothers and sisters. And if you don't believe that, well, then I'm sorry for you. But that's what the priesthood has done to you, and to you, Father O'Connor. The church trained you to live alone, isolated from human contact, from the grace and love of another person. I am sorry for you. You need only to look at Catty and Joe and see their family to realize how little you have in the world, how useless your lives have been.

"It has made you cruel in certain ways. Oh, you talk about family, about love and friendship, but you don't know how to express it. If you did, then you would have never risked the health of Emmett, the life of our mother, nor this farm, with your clever little swindle.

"Your success, Michael, your stature in the world, made you forget who you really are. It made you forget, as Mom would say, 'your own people.' Oh, you talk about helping Ireland, but what about us? What about your own flesh and blood? What happened to you, Michael? When did you forget you had a family?

"I'm sorry for you, Michael. But don't ask me now to forgive you and Father O'Connor from hiding the truth from us. Trying to protect us, you'd say, as if we were all children again in grammar school." She paused a moment, trying to decide if she should say more, and then went on and said everything that was on her mind.

"Yeats wrote once that Ireland was a priest-ridden nation. Well, we're not priest-ridden Catholics, Michael. Not us. Not the DeLaceys. We won't let you treat us like ignorant Connemara bogtrotters. You've underestimated your own brothers and sisters.

"Father O'Connor, you said Mom thought we were better than the shanty Irish from the East End. Well, she was right, we are, and we won't let her down by going along with this scheme of yours to save Saint Pat's, your parish, and Michael's career. But don't try and tell us it was Mom's reputation you were saving. I know Jack McGraff. Regardless of what he has on you, Michael, he'd never use your birth as a way of destroying the Blue and Whites. Jack knows I won't let him." She smiled at everyone, realizing what she had to do next, then said, "And now I'm going to deal with Jack. Don't worry, Michael, your secret will be kept. I'll see to it." And then she turned and left the dining-room table, leaving her brother the bishop standing alone at the head of the family table.

# · CHAPTER 45 ·

GATESBURG: 1982

IT BEGAN TO SNOW south of Springfield. Sitting across from her husband, Maggie looked out the train window at the large flakes and said, "We'll have a white Christmas after all!" Impulsively, happy to be going home again and happy to be married, she leaned across the other seat and kissed Kenneth on the cheek.

"Happy, darling?" he asked.

She nodded. "Yes, very." Changing seats, Maggie slipped her arm into his and curled against him. The train was cold and he spread his camel-hair overcoat like a quilt over her lap. Cozy now, she leaned her head against his shoulder and looked out the window at the sudden snow. It was the first she had seen since the terrible storms of the winter before, the winter that death had brought her home to Gatesburg.

"Are we getting close?" Kenneth asked, crossing his legs restlessly. "I'm afraid I'm too impatient for train travel."

"I'm sorry—maybe we should have driven down from Chicago," Maggie said. "But I wanted to arrive home by train." She had decided on the train trip while she and Kenneth were still in Africa. Catty had mentioned in a letter that rail service to Gatesburg would soon be discontinued. "I agree with Amtrak. No one wants to take the long train ride home to Gatesburg." But Catty was wrong: Maggie wanted to go home, at least once more, and by train.

"I know." Kenneth kissed Maggie on the forehead, then followed her gaze out the train window. "Where are we?" he asked.

"Crossing the country club. Did I tell you that Paddy Jack and Vanessa are finally buying it? There's the clubhouse on the ridge. When we were kids, Emmett and I used to call it the White House." For a moment, staring out at the driving snow, Maggie felt the ghost of the girl she once had been, when this rolling land had been all the world she knew, and Addis Ababa, Washington, and Rome had been just names in her schoolbooks, places on a map.

"Good God, what's that?" Kenneth asked, pointing.

"Ugly, isn't it? It's the new housing development."

"I don't remember seeing that when I was here before."

"No, but it was there. When we were kids, all of this was open fields and farmland. Now our farm is the only one left on this side of the river." Maggie pulled out of Kenneth's arms. "There's home. See!"

Through the snow blowing across the open pasture, swirling around outside the window, Maggie could make out the farm. She saw the cluster of barn buildings, the white farmhouse, and in the driveway, a half-dozen cars parked in the circular drive.

"We'll be the last ones there," she said.

"Perhaps we should have called ahead and told them when to expect us."

Maggie shook her head. "No, I didn't want Catty to go to any trouble. She was worried enough about Joe connecting with Dad and Nora at O'Hare in Chicago. Joe was meeting their flight and driving down with them and the younger kids. Catty, I'm sure, has been here for most of the week."

The train passed the farmhouse and back fields and followed the river into the trees beyond the pasture land. They would be in town shortly, and Maggie planned to call Emmett to come pick them up. Meantime, she thought they could wait in the coffee shop where they had stopped for lunch the first time Kenneth was in Gatesburg, but now she realized she didn't want to go back into that diner. It held too many memories. She sighed and said a quick prayer that Christmas wouldn't be like that: full of sad memories, regrets, and silent accusations.

The train was slowing to switch tracks. Maggie stared out the window again and watched the traffic on Illinois Avenue. There were not many cars downtown on the snowy Christmas Eve. In the distance, high over the rooftops, she saw the steeple of Saint Patrick's and realized what she had to do.

"We can get a taxi at the station, can't we?" Kenneth asked as they prepared to get off. He was organizing himself, straightening his tie.

"No, darling, we're going to church first. We're going to Saint Patrick's."

At Saint Pat's rectory, there was a light in the front room, and the porch light was on as well, yet the house seemed empty as Maggie rang the bell. Perhaps he had already gone out to the farm, she thought, but then through the glass she saw him come into the hall. He was wearing a fisherman's sweater that their mother had made for him in the last year of her life.

"Merry Christmas, Michael," Maggie said, and kissed her brother lightly on the cheek. She could smell his after-shave, and the heavy odor of the sweater's wool. "I've come to make peace," she said formally, and then, to soften the moment, added with a laugh, "I brought a diplomat along to help us."

"Hello, Maggie," Michael said, smiling. "Hello, Kenneth. Merry Christmas. Come in! Come in! What a surprise. I'm glad you stopped by. I heard the train, and I guessed you might be on it. Catty said you were arriving this evening."

"It's changed so," Maggie exclaimed, pausing at the doorway to the front room. All of Father O'Connor's old upholstered furniture was gone, replaced by the Italian modern that Michael had had in his Watergate apartment.

"Yes. But the convent in Arizona provides a furnished apartment for its chaplain, so Dermot didn't have to ship his things out there. Actually, I think he was tired of the furnishings. I had the Knights of Columbus take it for their building over on Wabash."

"How is he?" Maggie asked, feeling a moment of guilt. It was her accusations, she knew, that had forced Father O'Connor's transfer and retirement.

"Oh, he's doing just fine. Better than I would have guessed. The nuns are good to him, and the weather is certainly easier on him than our winters. This spring I'm planning to drive out for a visit." He paused for a moment, as if he had something else to say, then went on quickly, "May I offer you something to drink? A celebration at having you both home again? Kenneth, as I remember, is a martini man." He was rubbing his hands together, and Maggie could see that he was nervous, having them both with him in the rectory.

"Yes, and I'd love one. But let me fix them. You two take this chance to talk."

Maggie smiled. "Thank you, Kenneth. I'll have a whiskey, no ice." She looked over at Michael and shrugged. "It's living in Africa among all the Brits—it affects the way you drink. I'm afraid it would make Mom turn over in her grave." She sat down in one of the matching black leather chairs and slipped off her fur coat.

"And for you, Father?" Kenneth asked, taking his coat and setting it down on the back of the leather sofa.

"Thank you, Kenneth, but I've been working away here on a short scotch and I think I'll stay with it a bit longer. I'm sure we'll be having champagne at the farm this evening, what with the celebration and all, and I need to keep myself sober for midnight Mass." He eased himself into his chair and Maggie noticed that, like O'Connor, he had everything within reach. All that was different were their styles. Now there was a white touchtone phone on a glass-and-steel endtable, and a Lucite magazine rack on the other side. The *Sacred Heart Messen-*

*ger* and *Catholic Digest* were gone, Maggie noticed, replaced by the *National Review* and *Commonweal*. On the table were Michael's missal and *RN*, Nixon's memoir.

"You look wonderful, Maggie. Africa must still agree with you."

"Married life agrees with me, Michael. I've never felt better. It's called being in love." She was beaming, showing off her well-being, and as she watched her older brother settle himself in front of the fire, she realized how their relationship had changed. He had aged over the year, but she no longer felt she was the little sister seeking his approval and help.

"And how are you, Michael?" she asked.

"Oh, I'm doing fine. Just fine." The fingers of his left hand nervously tapped the metal arm of the chair. "We're in the middle of a big fund-raising drive," he said, as if that were uppermost on his mind. "I'm hoping to make enough to reopen the high school. We have a growing number of Catholic families, so maybe Our Lady of Wisdom can be revived. Of course, we won't be able to get the nuns back; there aren't enough left in the order. But I've been in touch with a group of Irish brothers looking for a school in America. You know, Ireland produces more religious than they have room for."

"And the Blue and Whites? Who is directing them?"

"A good woman, a greenhorn by the name of Nuala Brett. She was appointed president at the last general conference. As Mom would say, she's as smart as a tack. She's having the Blue and Whites bring orphaned children—Catholic and Protestant—to America next summer. A fine idea, really. And with me being gone . . . well, that has killed off the need to investigate the organization. Which is good."

He kept looking at the fire as he spoke, nodding as if he were agreeing with himself. That happened to people who lived alone, Maggie knew, feeling a wave of pity for her brother. It was a hard penance he had imposed on himself. But she knew, too, that the Catholic hierarchy had forced this decision once they heard about smuggling guns to Ireland. He was lucky to have lost only his organization, and not his bishop's title. Taking Saint Pat's as a parish was a wise move on her brother's part, she realized, even though it meant a loss of all his power and influence. It was here he would spend the rest of his priestly life.

"Do you miss it?" she asked. "Being on television, flying around the world?" She could hear Kenneth, clinking ice cubes in the kitchen.

"No, no, I don't miss it at all." He waved off the notion. "It was more a pain than anything else, being in the public eye. I'm happy here, too, Maggie, living in Gatesburg." He met her gaze, and Maggie could see some peace along with the sadness.

"I love you, Michael," she whispered. "That's what I wanted to stop and tell you before we joined the others."

"Thank you, Maggie. I've made peace with myself, but it was you that I had hoped to hear from. It's no good, the two of us at odds."

"Are you getting on with Emmett?"

"We say hello, stop and talk if we meet in town. He's getting better, I think. His treatment up in Chicago is helping, Catty says. And he has this medication, if he starts feeling pressured. Of course, I haven't gotten him back to Holy Mother Church," he added, smiling.

"Nor me." She laughed.

"Ah, but I pray for both your souls."

"Thank you, Michael. I need the prayer."

"We all do, Maggie."

"Michael, I have a favor to ask . . ."

"Whatever you want, dear."

"While we're home—Kenneth and I—would you bless our marriage? You know we weren't married in the church, because of Kenneth's divorce, but I know the church's rules are loosening. And, after all, you're still a bishop!"

"Maggie, nothing would give me greater joy. I'm saying Mass tonight at the farm. Catty asked if I would, for Cormac and Nora. It was very nice of her to ask. You know, I never said Mass at the farm, not once while Mom was alive, and I'm sorry for that. She would have liked it, I know, but I never thought of it."

"There's a lot we didn't do, Michael, when Mom was alive. But we can't go back, can we, or blame ourselves?"

"You're right enough. The real job is trying to make do with the rest of our lives. I'm trying my best to get this parish back in order. It had gotten away from Dermot, I'm afraid. Not surprising, really—running a parish is more of a job than I would have guessed."

"At least you landed on your feet. That's more than Jack McGraff can say."

Michael glanced at his sister. "The Illinois papers say he'll lose his Senate seat."

"Is Illinois becoming even more conservative?"

"I don't think it's that. But he lost a lot of support when he pulled out of the presidential campaign. I don't think he could have beaten Mondale, let alone Reagan, but once Jack lost his financial support . . ." Michael paused a moment, trying to decide whether to say anything, but before he could ask, Maggie answered his question.

"I told Jack if he didn't return the two hundred and fifty thousand dollars to our family, I would campaign across the country against him. I think just the thought of me telling people not to vote for him was too much for his ego."

"Would you have done it?" Michael asked, suddenly curious.

Maggie smiled. "Oh, you know how I get when I'm pushed."

Michael nodded, and then stared into the flame for a moment before he said, "Dermot is right about you, Maggie. Of all the family, you're the one who inherited Mom's way. Her courage. Not me, certainly. Nor Paddy."

He looked over and then, leaning closer, whispered, as if it were yet another family secret to be shared, "Don't give it away, Maggie DeLacey Graves. Don't throw away your chance to bring honor to her, to all of us." He took his sister's hands in his then, and that was the way Kenneth found them, holding tightly to each other, as he brought in the tray of celebration drinks.

Together they drove out to the farm for Christmas Eve. Emmett had strung lights around the edge of the front porch, framing the big Christmas tree in the living room window. The farm looked like a Christmas card, and Maggie wondered why they had never strung lights when she was a child. But Caitlin had never cared about Christmas once the children were old enough to know there was no Santa Claus.

"Stop here, please," Maggie said, seeing that Michael was about to drive around to the back. "I think my new husband deserves to go in through the front door."

"You two go ahead," Michael said. "I'll park and bring in the bags."

Someone had cleared the narrow flagstone path, and Maggie led the way to the porch. She was not wearing boots, and teetered on the ice in high heels. She caught Kenneth's hand for support.

"You look beautiful," he said, and kissed her wet lips.

"Thank you," she whispered, and then, turning toward the house, looked through the front window to catch a glimpse of the family before they saw her. For a moment she simply took them all in, as a photographer might pause before snapping the picture of a family gathering.

She saw Catty's children first. They were sitting on the floor before the fire, with a jigsaw puzzle spread out on the coffee table. Then Catty, on the sofa with Nora. As Maggie watched, they looked up as Emmett came into view. Maggie sighed with relief. He looked so healthy, much better than he had seemed at her wedding in Virginia. His medical treatment was helping.

Through the glass panes of the front door, she spotted Paddy Jack and Vanessa coming down the hallway from the kitchen. But someone was missing. She scanned the living room a second time, searching for the last piece in the puzzle. She saw her father then, sitting near the fire. He turned to look, too, and he seemed worried, unsure of what was happening. He was frowning, staring up into the light.

He looked fragile and tired. The plane trip and drive to Gatesburg might have been too much, and she wondered if it had been a good idea to bring him back to America. But it was Nora's idea, one she had suggested in her letters to Catty. Nora wanted their father to see Gatesburg again, to see their mother's grave at least once before he died. And Maggie said another quick prayer that her father would have a wonderful Christmas with them, and that he would finally find his place with all his children.

Then Maggie saw why they were all gathered together in the living room. It wasn't to await her arrival, but Wendy's. As Maggie watched, Wendy came down the stairway carrying her baby and walked in to join the others. Her father, Joe, was with her, guiding her across the room.

There were tears in Catty's eyes, Maggie saw, and a look of pride as she watched her daughter lean forward, speak slowly to her grandfather, and then present him with his first great-grandchild.

Maggie slipped her arm into Kenneth's and, smiling through her own tears, whispered, "Come along, darling. It's time to join the family."